CRIMINAL
INJUSTICE

CRIMINAL INJUSTICE

Confronting the Prison Crisis

edited by

ELIHU ROSENBLATT

South End Press — Boston, MA

Library of Congress Cataloging-in-Publication Data

Criminal injustice: confronting the prison crisis/ edited by Elihu Rosenblatt.

    p.   cm.

Includes index.

ISBN 0-89608-539-2 (alk. paper). —ISBN 0-89608-540-6 (alk. cloth)

1. Corrections—United States. 2. Prisons—United States. 3. Prisoners—United States. 4. Criminal justice, Administration of—United States. 5. Criminal statistics—United States.

I. Rosenblatt, Elihu.

HV9471.C73   1996

365'.973—dc20   96-32716

                                    CIP

South End Press, 116 Saint Botolph Street, Boston, MA 02115

02 01 00 99 98 97   2 3 4 5 6 7

*In memory of Jim Lewis, whose spirited
and tireless activism on behalf of
prisoners with AIDS
will continue to inspire us*

*For Martha Zane, Benjamin, Coby,
Sarah, Allison, Gabriel, Malaya, Fenua,
and all our future warriors*

PERMISSIONS

"The Fortress Economy," by Alexander C. Lichtenstein and Michael A. Kroll, was originally published by the American Friends Service Committee, Philadelphia in 1990. Reprinted by permission of the American Friends Service Committee, Philadelphia.

"Gardens of the Law," by Joel Olson, was originally published by *The BLAST!*, August/September, 1994. Reprinted by permission of the author.

"The Criminalization of Poverty," by Sabina Virgo, is extracted from a speech that was delivered at the conference of the International Human Rights Coalition on December 8, 1990. It was originally published by *Crossroads Magazine*, October, 1991. Reprinted by permission of the author.

"The Politics of Super Incarceration," by Mike Davis, was excerpted from "Hell Factories in the Field," originally published in *The Nation*, February 20, 1995. Reprinted by permission of *The Nation* Magazine, ©1995, The Nation Company, L.P.

"The Prison Discipline Study" was originally published by the Prison Discipline Study. Reprinted by permission of the authors.

"Resistance at Lexington," by Laura Whitehorn, was originally published by *Prison News Service*, September/October, 1992. Reprinted by permission of the author.

"Building Bridges," by Lin Elliot, was originally published by *Breakthrough Magazine*, 1993. Reprinted by permission of the author.

"Prisoners Respond to AIDS," by Judy Greenspan, was originally published in the newsletter of the Resist Foundation, December 1993. Reprinted by permission of the author.

"Medical Treatment at Chowchilla," by Joann Walker, was informally published in *Writings from Women Prisoners at Chowchilla* by the Coalition for Women Prisoners at Chowchilla (now the California Coalition for Women Prisoners), 1993. Reprinted by permission of the California Coalition for Women Prisoners.

"Behind the Walls," by Nancy Kurshan, was originally published as "Women and Imprisonment in the U.S.—History and Current Reality," in *Cages of Steel*, Ward Churchill *et al.*, eds., (Washington, DC: Maisonneuve Press), 1992. Reprinted by permission of the author.

"Politics of Confinement and Resistance," by Karlene Faith, was excerpted from *Unruly Women: the Politics of Confinement and Resistance*, (Vancouver: Press Gang Publishers), 1993. Reprinted by permission of the author.

"Sisters Inside," by the staff of *Kinesis*, was originally published in *Kinesis*, June 1987, by the Vancouver Commission on the Status of Women. Reprinted by permission of the authors.

"Women's Control Unit," by Silvia Baraldini, Marilyn Buck, Susan Rosenberg, and Laura Whitehorn, was originally published as a pamphlet, printed by Out of Control: Lesbian Committee to Support Women Political Prisoners, and distributed to prison activists nationwide in the fall of 1992. Reprinted by permission of the authors.

TABLE OF CONTENTS

ACKNOWLEDGMENTS

A big shout goes out to Jim and the Bulldozer folks at *Prison News Service* for their dynamic, relentless work over many years, putting out an amazing paper that sustains and inspires me and many others.

For their inspiration and encouragement over the last few years this project has spanned: Leona Benten, Travis Loller, Jess Alexander, Robert Paton, Cheryl Ibabao, Laurie Adams, Stanya Kahn, Mom and Dad, Margaret and Ewald, Lisa S-F, Heidi Lieberman, Nancy Galvin, Lysa Samuel, Peter Brownell, and AnnaLisa Couturier.

For compañeras/os whose example and whose personal and political support have spurred me on: Riva Enteen, Pam Fadem, Doug Spalding, Barbara Duhl, Kitty Costello, Tim Smith, Linda Evans, Judy Talogan, Dorsey Nunn, Robin Templeton, Pat Clark, B♀(rita d. brown), Eddie Hatcher, Sue Kuyper, Anne King, Little Rock Reed, Lisa Roth, Lisa Rudman, Judy Greenspan, and Judy Appel.

Special thanks to the Vanguard Foundation, the Milarepa Foundation, and the Tides Center, whose financial and organizational support has been invaluable to PARC's development and the creation of this book.

For their critical role in helping build and sustain the work of the Prison Activist Resource Center, out of which this book was born: McKay, Henrietta Shannon, Peter Jacques, Julie Browne, Hannah Tashjian, Emanuel Sferios, Chris Burnett, and Katie Friedman.

For the invaluable assistance, guidance, and criticism they have given for this book and for our larger political project: Corey Weinstein, Luis Talamentez, John Bilorusky, Pam and Ramona Africa, Terry Lunsford, George Gundrey, Michael Stein, John Anner, Noelle Hanrahan, Jennifer Beach, Tony Platt, Muhjah Shakir, Luke and Marti Hiken, Sharon Martinas, Angela Davis, Michael Novick, and Lorenzo Kombo'a Ervin.

To Asha and the whole South End Press collective for having the vision to get this book out to a wider audience, and all their work to improve and refine it.

To the many political prisoners for their inspiring example, their encouragement, their strength and clarity. I can only hope this book and PARC's other work can give back to our movements half of what you have given us over the years. And to all those not mentioned here, thank you!

PREFACE

The hope of liberty and of opportunity is the only incentive to life, especially the prisoner's life. Society has sinned so long against him—it ought at least to leave him that. I am not very sanguine that it will, or that any real change in that direction can take place until the conditions that breed both the prisoner and the jailer will be forever abolished.

—Emma Goldman from "Prisons: a Social Crime and Failure," 1911

The book you are holding is a tool for exposing a giant hidden monster in the political landscape of life in the United States. *Criminal Injustice* was designed as a primer for people who are working to raise consciousness in their communities, their schools, their workplaces, and inside prisons and the prison system.

Why produce a book such as this? The ideology of domination has enjoyed significant gains in recent years. Its priority remains creating a culture constantly policing and constantly policed. At this moment in history, there is significant activism aimed at fostering social justice, ending racism, and fighting poverty. Yet somehow, the project of dismantling the prison system is hardly on the progressive agenda. The reality is that we are not on the verge of any large-scale restructuring—much less abolition—of the repressive apparatus that imprisons, tortures, and breaks the spirits of such huge numbers of people. This apparatus is not limited to maximum-security prisons, but rather is made up of a vast conglomeration of institutions including federal, state, and local courts, police forces of all kinds, district attorneys and attorneys general, all part of what is called "the criminal justice system." Language is powerful, and often serves to perpetuate the lies and distortion of domination. These days I try to use the term "criminal prosecution system." It would be more accurate to call it "criminally unjust."

The necessary changes in the U.S. system of imprisonment (and indeed, its eventual abolition) will not come from the benevolent initiative of government officials. The changes will be forced upon the system by prisoners organizing and by the collective action of an angry, educated populace. This book is one building block in the overall work of raising consciousness, of sparking fires. As a political tool, it seeks to accomplish a dual task. First, it should raise questions for those whose assumptions regarding prisons tacitly or actively support the mainstream justification—"we need this punitive system to deal with all those 'sub-humans.'" Second, it should give facts and perspectives to fuel and focus the arguments and criticisms of those who already believe that "justice for all" is a lie.

This book should be a useful resource for prisoner support and prison reform/abolition activists. However, it is meant to reach beyond activists and educators already familiar with prison issues. Whether you are active around environmental issues, abortion rights, AIDS, housing and homelessness, open government, or domestic violence, the information presented here will help you to raise awareness of prison issues in clear, graphic ways. Whether you teach social science in a university or history to high school students, whether you're organizing a discussion group for friends, or workshops for a three-day conference, the resources in this book will help you to inform, inspire, and provide direction for further education, and indeed action!

A Hidden Monster

For most folks in the United States today, prisons are seen as an unfortunate necessity. How can progressive movements best respond to this characterization? Prisons do not occupy the same political space in the mind of "the Left" today as they did 10 or 20 years ago. Prisoner support and prison reform and abolition activism have largely been eclipsed by other concerns, such as homelessness, the environment, and reproductive rights. I believe that progressive and radical activists can and should increasingly make the prison crisis a central focus of our work, since the political, economic, and social dynamics at work in many of today's pressing issues are dynamics that are especially visible as they relate to prisons:

- The AIDS and public health crisis is exposed most dramatically as it occurs in the context of prisons.

- The most graphic and brutal expression of racism in the United States can be found when looking at the nature of, and the statistics regarding, the prison system.

- The clearest and most exaggerated violations of due process and judicial procedure in U.S. history have been executed in the thousands of cases of political prisoners and prisoners of war.

This is not to suggest in any way that people working on any of the myriad issues facing us today should drop that work and devote all their energy to prison-related activism. It is to suggest that *prisons are a key indicator, a crucial leverage point with which to expose the true nature of our culture and political economy.* In a sense, prisons can be seen as a barometer for all that is ill at the core of our society, described most succinctly by bell hooks as "white supremacist capitalist patriarchy."

Prisons and the Larger Undercurrent of Repression

I wish to be clear as to the scope this book will cover. Its focus, though quite wide, is on merely the tip of a massive iceberg. *Criminal Injustice* deals for the most part with prisons, institutions where the federal or state governments confine people they have deemed "felons." But prisons are the extreme on a long continuum of repression, a continuum consisting of county and municipal jails, work camps, juvenile halls, detention centers, psychiatric wards, and other institutions increasingly driven by a law-and-order agenda. Indeed, throughout the United States, courts, police departments, and local and state governments muster growing forces to execute a strategy of permanent repression—most evident in the literal occupation of urban neighborhoods such as South Central Los Angeles.[1]

The same type of hegemony at work in the realm of economics exists with the criminal prosecution system. Just as every major newspaper has whole sections devoted to "Business" and almost nothing for "Labor," virtually all reports of crime and imprisonment are told from the perspective of the cops and the courts. While government and mass media have recently ushered in an enormous wave of fear about violent crime, the real nature of the criminal prosecution system is carefully hidden away from public view by those same individuals and institutions in big business and government who "manufacture consent" and engineer mass culture. Criminal defense attorneys and neighborhood organizers are rarely featured on mainstream TV. Rather, a staggering number of shows are dedicated to depicting DAs and the police as some band of mythical crusaders for justice and truth. Nothing could be more misleading. Addicted television viewers are fed racist and scapegoating programs such as *Cops*, where shaky and sensational video operators accompany aggressive foot-soldiers on the front lines in the Reagan/Bush/Clinton drug war,[2] traversing urban and suburban ghettoes, glorifying the ideology of domination while rarely showing the brutality and harassment that are a daily reality for the nation's poor people and people of color.

If we are to effectively confront the ever-increasing dehumanization and militarization of our society, activism around prisons must be enlivened now more than ever. The task ahead is to bring the issues explored in this book to the widest possible array of communities, thus raising not only our consciousness, but the political stakes as well.

How This Book Can Be Used Effectively

This book has been divided into six sections, each containing an introduction followed by several readings. The first section is an overview that helps to set the larger context of the prison system, both currently and historically in the United States. Each of the remaining sections focuses on a major aspect of the overall crisis. The authors included here come from varying bacgrounds. There are attorneys, academics, activists, and prisoners; they represent a wide political spectrum from reformers to unequivocal abolitionists. While some of the contributors come out of the activism of the 1960s and 1970s, others were politicized during the Reagan/Bush years.

This range of perspectives should be a breeding ground for debate and critical analysis. Part of the point of a book like this is to examine ideas from different parts of our movements, and work towards synthesis, building strategy that can win radical changes in this extremely repressive time.

My vision is that *Criminal Injustice* can be used as an integral part of classes, forums, discussion groups, or even an argument with one's brother-in-law. Having clear, readable, graphic resources should enable the user to draw people into discussion, to have a springboard for critical analysis, and perhaps to break through the prevailing resignation that we so often hear: "Okay, so conditions may be bad, but what else can we do? Violence is human nature and there is just no other way to deal with criminals!"

In advocating the ultimate abolition of prisons, I understand that there are some highly disturbed and ostensibly unrehabilitatable individuals who—because of the likelihood that they will wantonly kill or otherwise violate other people (without government sanction)—have justifiably been somehow isolated in society. However, the repression and depravation that are the cornerstones of modern imprisonment do not *begin* to address the roots of such a person's violence. While highlighted by the media, serial killings are actually quite a poor indicator of the level of violence in our society. Criminologist Philip Jenkins has estimated that serial killings make up only two percent of all murders in the United States.[3]

Through a complex matrix of extremely negative influences on human behavior (television, war, shopping malls, poverty), the society we have created is profoundly abusive to the human psyche. It is thus an effective teacher that violent acts such as rape, murder, executions, and the torture that is prison are just.

The facts and analysis presented here (and elsewhere, in studies that reveal the increasing rates of violent attack)[4] underscore how our society, while hailed as "civilized," is in fact extremely violent. The existence of serial killers is evidence of the nature of this society—not of "human nature." At the hands of the state and of people in their communities, millions are daily terrorized—by physical, sexual and ritual abuse, by rape, psychological torture, poverty, racism, and neglect. This is not some obscure social problem to be sorted out by psychiatrists and academics. Our culture is increasingly driven by hate and fear, and it is this culture that fosters and perpetuates a chronic climate of violence.

The priorities of those in power are clearly twisted when more punitive law-and-order policies and institutions take precedence over housing, health care, and education. Until we radically alter the fundamental economic and political constructs on which we currently operate, the conditions of violence that are used to justify the building of bigger, stronger, higher-tech, and more numerous penal institutions will only increase.

I believe the political project at hand has many prongs. One is to confront, dissect, and counter crime hype by exposing and educating against the real dangers people face, such as poverty, police abuse, environmental hazards, dwindling health care and education, and the assault on our bodies by the tobacco, alcohol, and food industries. Another prong is to foster the active refusal of the paradigm in which punishment, revenge, and the commodification of all existence are primary and in which rehabilitation, growth, trust, and respect are meaningless. Many believe that the answer to our problems lies in warehousing people, as opposed to rehabilitating them, and as opposed to committing our resources to just and equal social systems.

Others of us are striving for a society where prisons would not be needed and could not be justified. To counter the individuals and institutions that devalue and destroy the human spirit, we must organize and agitate on every level in every arena. We *can* replace the society that these chapters describe.

We may feel that the problems outlined here are too vast for us to have any impact on what seems an intractable situation. Yet we should take courage and inspiration from the many stories of resistance coming from both sides of the prison walls. There is a plethora of resources for anyone wishing to learn more and take action. There are many different types of work that need to be done in building an effective prison movement. There are many ways of supporting individual prisoners, of educating, and of organizing campaigns and actions.

This book can be a catalyst for change. It is not, of course, a definitive document. There are so many areas of the crisis and so many inextricably linked issues that I could not cover here in greater depth (or for some, at all). Some of these include: prison abolition literature and movements; prison uprisings; mandatory minimum sentences; gang violence and truces; "Three Strikes You're Out"; families of prisoners; grand juries as a tool for repression; police abuse and community control of the police; psychiatric abuse of prisoners and conditions on psychiatric wards; the criminalization of the homeless, youth, and immigrants; the racist movement for bio-medical intervention; conditions and struggles in other countries; war and military resisters and military prisons; rape in prisons; medical neglect; and jailhouse lawyers.

Yet, this book *should* be an evolving tool. To this end, the Prison Activist Resource Center (PARC) has created a companion volume— which will be updated on a continual basis—for educators and activists. This *Organizers' Guide* includes extensive resources, many of which address the above issues.[5] I also encourage readers to contact us with suggestions, comments, or questions. Together, we can build stronger networks to effectively confront this growing crisis.

NOTES

1. See Damu Smith, "The Upsurge of Police Repression: An Analysis," *The Black Scholar*, January/February 1981; Institute for the Study of Labor and Economic Crisis, *The Iron Fist and the Velvet Glove: An Analysis of the U.S. Police*, (Berkeley: Center for Research on Criminal Justice), 1975; Ken Lawrence, *The New State Repression*, (Chicago: International

Network Against New State Repression), 1985; Mike Davis, *L.A. Was Just the Beginning—Urban Revolt in the United States: A Thousand Points of Light*, Open Magazine Pamphlet Series #20, (Westfield, NJ: Open Media), 1992; Mike Davis, *Beyond Blade Runner: Urban Control—The Ecology of Fear*, Open Magazine Pamphlet Series #23, (Westfield, NJ: Open Media), 1992; Elihu Rosenblatt, "Repression and Resistance: A Chronological Evaluation and Resource Guide," unpublished paper for Western Institute for Social Research, November, 1991.

2. For related background information, see Jonathan Kozol, *Savage Inequalities: Children in America's Schools*, (New York: Crown), 1991; and Clarence Lusane, *Pipe Dream Blues: Racism and the War on Drugs*, (Boston: South End Press), 1991.

3. Phillip Jenkins, *Using Murder: The Social Construction of Serial Homicide*, (New York: Aldine de Gruyter), 1994.

4. Elliot Currie, *Confronting Crime: An American Challenge*, (New York: Pantheon), 1985; also see the periodic reports, U.S. Bureau of the Census, *Statistical Abstract of the United States*, and U.S. Bureau of Justice Statistics, *Criminal Victimization in the United States* (Washington, DC: GPO).

5. The *Organizers' Guide* is a free manual that includes a directory of groups, a bibliography, a selection of leaflets and brochures, and examples of recent activism. The *Guide* is available through PARC (see the order form on the last page of this book).

SECTION ONE

OVERVIEW

Of the approximately 34 million serious felonies [committed in the United States] in 1990, 31 million never entered the criminal justice system, because they were either unreported or unsolved. This means that 90 percent of serious crime remains outside the purview of police, courts and prison officials. The remaining 10 percent is further eroded as a result of screening by prosecutors and dismissals or acquittals. In California, 65 percent of adults arrested for felonies are convicted, and of these, 20 percent are sent to state institutions.

—Joan Petersilia of the conservative think tank,
the RAND Corporation[1]

These chapters give a broad outline of the economic and political forces that make our current imprisonment system the cruel joke that it is. The authors provide a clear picture of the overarching issues, and lay bare, with statistics and critical analyses, the true nature of life behind bars, and the myth that the situation is anything less than a crisis. These selections show how racism and the criminalization of poverty are central to the maintenance of prisons as a system of social control. While the practice of incarceration may have been initiated by the benevolent ideas of Quaker reformers, it is quite clear that today's prison system has instead advanced the vision of the slave-owners, business tycoons, and imperialists who founded this country.

This section does not address the day-to-day conditions in prisons—the situations that make them outrageous, and that make prisoners revolt. Yet to understand the crisis in prisons, it is vital to look at just what occurs in the specific institutions, to have at least a thumbnail sketch of the ongoing crimes against humanity that make up the material reality of incarceration in the land of the not so free. Therefore, the following section includes a compilation of excerpts that illustrate the conditions for so many of our caged fellow human beings.

Who is in prison and why? Why does the system seek ways to imprison as many people as possible in as harsh a manner as possible, having given up on even the pretense of rehabilitation? How do prisons act as an extension of the segregation and oppression that were the core of slavery and Jim Crow? Why are low-income defendants far more likely to be imprisoned when the loss to society from "white collar" crimes "far exceeds the economic impact of all burglaries, robberies, larcenies, and auto thefts combined?"[2]

Since so many people see prisons as an adequate and unavoidable solution to crime, or misunderstand the criminal prosecution system, uncovering the myths and giving a detailed analysis of the situation are crucial. The pieces in this Overview help reveal the economic and political role that the prison system plays in the larger society. They also explore racism and the criminalization of poverty as foundations of the prison system.

·   In "The Fortress Economy," Alexander Lichtenstein and Michael Kroll explain the place that prisons occupy in our economy (and indeed our culture). They argue effectively that while law-and-order policies have traditionally been conceived of as ensuring public safety, a broad range of evidence exists to show that social justice (e.g., the protection of civil rights and abolition of institutional racism) is an absolute requirement for true public safety. The authors also address issues such as drugs, the social bias against ex-offenders, and the recent debates regarding prison labor and the privatization of prisons.

Marc Mauer and the Sentencing Project in Washington, DC have done considerable work to help us see exactly who is, and just how many people are, locked up. Included here are tables from the most recent version of their important study, *Americans Behind Bars: The International Use of Incarceration, 1992-1993*.[3]

The piece by Joel Olson of *The BLAST!* is an overview of the repressive role prisons play in our society. In his very readable rantings, the author smashes the myth that the purpose of penal institutions is to deter crime, arguing that imprisonment is, instead, about social control.

In an inspiring piece written as the keynote address for an International Human Rights Coalition meeting in December 1990, Sabina Virgo critically examines propaganda and socially constructed notions of crime, revealing how our ideas of what is criminal and deserving of punishment can, and indeed must, change. She goes beyond the statistics to analyze in depth just what they mean, and what they say about the society we have made. She reminds us that decisions to cut school funding, cut health programs, build prisons, or imprison people are political decisions, not removable from their context of wealth and power. She asserts that it is struggling individuals and communities who can and must "build a powerful, caring movement for change."

Giving an historical viewpoint on prison labor and exploitation, Julie Browne's piece "The Labor of Doing Time," is an excellent explanation of how slavery still exists and is being re-institutionalized in the United States today. And finally, we have "The Politics of Super Incarceration." The author, scholar-activist Mike Davis, is well known for his cogent analysis of culture and politics in Southern California, and has researched and written extensively about the new "law-and-order" agenda grinding its way through the "Golden State." Here, Davis paints a vivid portrait of the culture and economy that support the massive growth in prison construction. The piece also serves as an excellent introduction to the political forces at work in the business of punishment, a business where California leads the nation on every count.

NOTES

1. *L.A. Times,* October 4, 1992.
2. Alexander C. Lichtenstein and Michael A. Kroll, *The Fortress Economy: The Economic Role of the U.S. Prison System,* (Philadelphia: American Friends Service Committee), 1990.
3. For other sources of statistics, readers should see several recent reports: Mark Koetting and Vincent Schiraldi, *Singapore West: The Incarceration of 200,000 Californians,* Center on Juvenile & Criminal Justice (American Civil Liberties Union [ACLU] 415.621.5661), July 1994; Nkechi Taifa, ACLU Legislative Counsel, public memo of June 25, 1993 (updated March 14, 1994), re: Unwarranted Disparity in Sentencing Between "Crack" and Powder Cocaine, (ACLU 202.544.1681); Nkechi Taifa, ACLU Legislative Counsel, public memo of February 9, 1994, re: Racial Bias in the Criminal Justice System (ACLU 202.544.1681).

1

THE FORTRESS ECONOMY

The Economic Role of the U.S. Prison System

Alexander C. Lichtenstein and Michael A. Kroll

Few topics are more volatile than crime and the problem of how society should respond to it. The fear of street crime leaves countless people trapped in their homes. Illegal drugs and the violence they engender are widely considered our society's most serious problem. For politicians, nothing spells ruin so quickly as being perceived as "soft on crime." In this atmosphere, a chorus of voices is demanding that the criminal justice system "get tough" with offenders. More prisons, longer jail terms, fewer restraints on the actions of police and the courts: these are the measures that are proposed to make our streets safe and curb the violence in our daily lives.

It is unfashionable in the extreme to question whether such policies will actually work. Those who do are often dismissed as fools, "bleeding hearts" who care more for criminals than for their victims. Yet the question demands to be asked. Taxpayers are called upon to spend billions of dollars every year to build bigger prisons and lock up more and more of our fellow citizens. Is this money well spent? Whose pockets is it going into? Will it bring justice to offenders or security to the law-abiding? These questions about money are far from trivial. As a way of protecting the public or stopping crime, the U.S. prison system can only be seen as a monumental mistake—an insane juggernaut whose only rule is to keep growing. But when prisons are analyzed as economic institutions—in terms of both their own structure and their function within the larger society—they begin to make a grim kind of sense. This essay explores some of the economic aspects of the prison system. It examines who goes to prison and why—and how this relates to larger trends within the U.S. economy. It also takes a look at the economics of the prison industry itself. This approach can teach us a lot about what is wrong with our prisons. Most important, it can suggest some directions for more just—and more effective—solutions to the problems of crime and violence.

"Convincing Case of Failure"

Imprisonment is usually justified by appeals to one of two philosophies: protecting the public or rehabilitating the prisoner. By either standard, however, the evidence that prisons do not work is overwhelming. Those states that have the highest budget for law enforcement—including courts, prisons, probation, and parole— also have the highest levels of crime. If there is any empirically established relationship between crime and imprisonment, it is that prisons foster crime.

Table 1	
States with Highest Criminal Justice System Expenditures*	**States with Highest Crime Rate** (per 100,000)**
CA: $160,244,802,000	CA: 6,173.8
NY: $123,946,002,000	TX: 5,070.6
TX: $64,926,359,000	NY: 5,872.4

*Bureau of Justice Statistics, *Sourcebook of Criminal Justice Statistics*, (Washington, DC: GPO), 1994.
**U.S. Dept. of Justice, "Crime in the U.S. 1994," *Uniform Crime Reports*, (Washington, DC: GPO), 1994.

This is not to say that prisons function mainly as "schools for crime," although it is partly true that people in prison do learn new criminal skills. Far more important is that prisons are violent institutions that breed violent individuals. As psychiatrist Seymour Halleck says, "If one had systematically and diabolically tried to create mental illness, [one] could probably have constructed no better system than the American prison system." —→ Mental illness
Even the most staunch advocates of repressive "law-and-order" policies have hardly a good word for prisons. The former chief justice of the U.S. Supreme Court, Warren Burger, once asked rhetorically, "What business enterprise could conceivably continue with the rate of 'recall' of its 'products' that we see with respect to... our prisons?" The answer is obvious: none. Likewise, former U.S. President Richard Nixon, known in his day for his extremely conservative views, once termed prisons "a convincing case of failure."
At present, the United States has the highest rate of incarceration in the world. Nonetheless, crime continues to plague our society to a

degree unknown in other countries—countries that do not come close to our rate of imprisonment. (See Tables 3, p. 19 and 4, p. 20.)

In this context, the image of the "bleeding heart liberal"—that universal object of scorn—is one that deserves particular scrutiny. Implicit in this characterization is an assumption that public safety and social justice are somehow at odds—that policies that protect the civil rights of prisoners or challenge racism in the prison system cannot really be effective in stopping crime.

A far more compelling case can be made that social justice is a requirement for public safety. Racism and economic bias are structural features of the U.S. prison system. Understanding this relationship can yield important insights into why that system functions so poorly to protect the public. *Social justice = public safety*

Who Goes to Prison and Who Does Not?

Studies have shown that more than 90 percent of the adult population has committed offenses that are punishable by imprisonment. Few, however, actually go to prison. Contrary to popular belief, the seriousness of a crime is not the most crucial element in predicting

Table 2					
CHANGES IN VICTIMIZATION RATES 1980 - 1991					
Offense Category	**Victimization Rates per 1,000 Population**				
	1980	**1986**	**Change**	**1986**	**1991**	**Change**
Burglary	84.300	61.500	-27%	61.500	53.900	-12%
Violent Crimes:						
Murder*	0.102	0.086	-16%	0.086	0.098	+14%
Rape	0.900	0.700	-22%	0.700	0.900	+29%
Robbery	6.600	5.100	-23%	5.100	5.900	+16%
Assault	25.800	22.300	-15%	22.300	25.500	+14%
Total Violent Crime:	33.400	28.200	-16%	28.200	32.400	+15%

*Murder rates, reported by the FBI per 100,000, are shown to three decimal places in order to observe trends.
Source: Marc Mauer et al., *Americans Behind Bars: The International Use of Incarceration, 1992-1993*, (Washington DC: The Sentencing Project), 1994.

Table 3
INTERNATIONAL RATES OF INCARCERATION, 1992-93

Nation	# of Inmates	Incarc. Rate*	Nation	# of Inmates	Incarc. Rate*
Australia	15,895	91	Luxembourg	352	921
Austria	6,913	88	Macau	600	158
Bangladesh	39,539	37	Malaysia	22,473	122
Belgium	7,116	71	Mexico	86,334	97
Brazil	124,000	84	Netherlands	7,935	49
Brunei	186	70	New Zealand	4,694	135
Bulgaria	8,688	102	Northern Ireland	1,901	126
Canada	30,659	116	Peru (est.)	20,000	91
Cyprus	193	32	Philippines	16,122	30
Czech Republic	368	158	Poland	62,139	160
Denmark	3,406	66	Portugal	9,183	93
Egypt	35,392	62	Republic of Ireland	2,155	62
England/Wales	53,518	93	Romania	44,011	193
Fiji	731	96	Russia	829,000	558
Finland	3,295	65	Singapore	6,420	229
France	51,457	84	Slovak Republic	6,517	123
Germany	64,029	80	Solomon Islands	179	56
Greece	6,252	60	South Africa	114,047	368
Hong Kong	10,576	179	Spain	35,246	90
Iceland	101	39	Sri Lanka	10,470	60
India	196,221	23	Swaziland	760	88
Indonesia	41,121	22	Sweden	5,668	69
Italy	46,152	80	Switzerland	5,751	85
Japan	45,183	36	Thailand	90,864	159
Kiribati	81	112	United States	1,339,695	519
Korea (South)	62,711	144	Western Samoa	197	122

*Rate per 100,000 population

Source: Marc Mauer et al., Americans Behind Bars: The International Use of Incarceration, 1992-1993, (Washington DC: The Sentencing Project), 1994.

who goes to prison and who does not. Society's losses from "white-collar crime" far exceed the economic impact of all burglaries, robberies, larcenies, and auto thefts combined. Nonetheless the former class of criminals are far less likely to go to jail than the latter. One study found, for example, that 53 percent of low-income defendants received prison sentences, compared to only 26 percent of high-income defendants. The violence of a crime is another way of measuring its seriousness. Are prisons mainly reserved for the dangerously violent? The answer is again no. Well over half of all prisoners were convicted of crimes that did not include violence, such as burglary, larceny, drug possession, or disturbing the peace. Violence ≠ Prison

What does determine who goes to prison? A large part of the answer is certainly race. Today, for example, African-American males *Why* are 6 percent of the U.S. population, yet nearly 50 percent of prison inmates. The California Youth Authority imprisons more than 9,000 youngsters, more than any other jurisdiction in the country. Some 75 percent are young people of color.[1] (See Tables 4 and 5, below.)

Detailed breakdowns for different communities of color are difficult to determine, in part because of the way government statistics are gathered. A listing of the total state and federal prison population for 1987 gave no separate figures for Latinos; that same year, Latinos

Table 4		
INCARCERATION OF BLACK MALES		
Nation	# of Black Male Inmates	Rate of Incarceration (per 100,000)
United States	583,024	3822
South Africa	106,107	851

Source: Marc Mauer et al., *Americans Behind Bars: The International Use of Incarceration, 1992-1993,* (Washington DC: The Sentencing Project), 1994.

Table 5		
U.S. INCARCERATION RATES BY RACE (MALE AND FEMALE)		
Race	# of Inmates	Rate of Incarceration (per 100,000)
Black	626,207	1947
White	658,233	306

Source: Marc Mauer et al., *Americans Behind Bars: The International Use of Incarceration, 1992-1993,* (Washington DC: The Sentencing Project), 1994.

were listed as 14 percent of the inmates of county jails, a number roughly double their proportion in the population.[2] Native Americans are generally listed as 1 percent or less of the prison population, but they too are imprisoned at a vastly disproportionate rate, and prisons have a crippling impact on Native-American communities.

Nationwide, the rate of imprisonment for African Americans is nine times that for Euro-Americans. In 10 states, all in the North, the incarceration rate for African Americans is more than 15 times that for whites.

Another striking indicator of institutional racism is the lengths of prison terms. When time served is compared for similar offenses—including first-time offenders—African Americans serve far longer sentences than whites. In the federal prison system, sentences for African Americans are 20 percent longer for similar crimes. If time served by African Americans were reduced to parity with whites, the federal system would require 3,000 fewer prison cells—enough to empty six of their newest 500-bed prisons.

While 3 percent of adult white males are under some type of correctional control (incarceration, probation, or parole), for adult African-American males the figure rises to 33 percent. Black males have an 18 percent chance of serving time in a juvenile or adult prison at some time in their lives; white males have a 3 percent chance.[3]

Women make up only about 7.4 percent of the total U.S. prison and jail population. In the past few decades, however, the rates of imprisonment for women have grown even faster than for men—paralleling the disproportionate growth of the numbers of women living in poverty. And their numbers are even more heavily drawn from communities of color. More than 60 percent of incarcerated women are African-American or Latina. Most female prisoners were convicted of shoplifting, prostitution, or other economic crimes.[4]

Such institutionalized racism has been a feature of the U.S. prison system since its inception. In 1796, the New York legislature voted on the same day to free all slaves residing in the state and to authorize the state's first prison. In 1833, French writer Alexis de Tocqueville reported that African Americans accounted for 25 percent of U.S. prison inmates, although their percentage of the total population was far smaller than it is today.

In this context, it is significant that the 13th Amendment to the U.S. Constitution, which abolished slavery, carved out one exception, permitting involuntary labor "as punishment for crime." In the South, after the Civil War, the chain gang and convict lease quickly became the dominant forms of punishment. Prisoners were sold to the highest bidder and worked in coal mines, brick yards, or turpentine camps. Others were used by the states to work on badly needed improvements to roads and other public works. Over 90 percent of these Southern convicts were African-American.

Nonetheless, while racism is clearly an important force in the construction of the U.S. prison population, it is obviously not the only one. Even though people of color are imprisoned at a disproportionate rate, a majority of prison inmates are still whites. To fully appreciate the functioning of the prison system, we must also understand the impact of class.

Jailing the Unemployed

Across all racial groups, prisoners are drawn from the poorest sectors of society. A large percentage are unemployed at the time of their arrest or have only sporadic employment. Of those with jobs, many have incomes near or below the poverty level. Seventy-two percent of prison inmates and 60 percent of jail inmates have not completed high school; many are illiterate.[5]

The social policies of the 1980s caused an unprecedented increase in the number of people living in poverty in the United States, as well as a widening gap between the incomes and living standards of the rich and poor. Throughout this entire period, prison populations grew rapidly. With budgets slashed for every type of social service, prisons now stand out as the country's principal government program for the poor.

Most of the people behind bars have committed economic crimes. A sampling of prison admissions in 1983 revealed that close to 49 percent of all convictions were for property offenses like burglary, larceny, or auto theft. Another 14 percent were for robbery— which, though classified as a violent crime because it involves taking property from a person, is nevertheless economically motivated.

The statistical link between unemployment or underemployment and imprisonment is borne out in the demographic characteristics of prison populations. In 1990, 58.2 percent of all those jailed (about 561,700 people) were unemployed at the time of their arrest. Roughly 68 percent earned less than $15,000 a year.[6] State prison populations reveal a similar link. In Florida, for example, of nearly 30,000 people imprisoned in 1986, barely half (52 percent) were employed full-time at the time of their arrest. Nearly half earned less than $500 a month.[7]

In 1976, the Joint Economic Committee of Congress heard testimony that there was "wide agreement that unemployment creates economic and psychological stress that frequently is manifested in criminal behavior." The committee also heard figures showing that each 1 percent increase in unemployment sustained over a six-year period could be associated with an increase of more than 3,000 new state prison admissions.[8] From this perspective, prisons may be seen as warehouses for people who have no place in the economic order.

Prison inmates are mostly part of what is known as the "secondary labor market." Such people tend to work intermittently at low-paying jobs and see little hope for change in their future. The slightest misfortune may drive entire families into desperate poverty. The contemporary U.S. economy relies on the presence of a large pool of such temporary, underpaid workers to fill the dead-end service jobs that are increasingly coming to dominate the labor market. As fewer manufacturing jobs are available, the possibilities for stable, secure employment and economic advancement are shrinking for all working people.

In such an economy, high unemployment rates benefit employers who offer minimum-wage jobs, by ensuring the presence of a flexible pool of less-skilled workers. Those who move in and out of such jobs are often the same people who fill the jails and prisons. As poor people become ever more marginalized in the economy, their numbers in prison grow accordingly.

Ironically, prisons have been touted as a solution to economic decline, especially in rural areas. Prisons, filled with unemployed people of color from the inner cities, are being sold to economically depressed rural communities as a source of jobs for their growing numbers of unemployed—who are usually whites. "A new corrections center can be a real economic boost to a rural community, especially if the community lacks a major local industry," says William Choquette, a senior vice-president of Gilbane Building Company, an architectural firm specializing in prison construction. *Brings jobs for whites*

The Federal Bureau of Prisons published a brochure on the value of prisons to rural communities. "With local economies ailing in many parts of the country," the bureau states, "local leaders often see a potential federal prison as a recession-proof economic base."[9] In fact, prisons are more than "recession-proof"—they are the one industry that benefits from recession. In 1983, a year of deep economic recession, the Bureau of Labor Statistics ranked "corrections" as the twelfth fastest growing occupation in the United States.

Corrections 12th fastest occupation

The apparent economic boost offered by prisons is deceptive, however, because it is artificial and nonproductive. In this respect, prisons are similar to military bases. Prison jobs are hazardous and low paying; according to the *Corrections Yearbook*, in 1993 the average entry level salary for a prison guard was roughly $19,000. Rural communities quickly become dependent on the prison, which will ✱never produce revenue or expand a community's economic base.✱

Prisons and the Social Fabric

The discussion above is not intended to minimize the seriousness of crime, whether violent or not. The point is rather that swelling the prison population has failed to reduce crime. The racial and economic bias built into the prison system also works against crime victims. Poor people and people of color are also the most frequent victims of crime, and they stand to suffer the most from repressive policies that fail to stop, and in many ways instead fuel, criminal activities.

Prisons illustrate how racial and economic discrimination reinforce one another. As noted above, prison inmates are drawn from the ranks of the economically marginalized of all races. As an institution, however, prisons have a far greater impact on communities of color because of their disproportionate representation in prison populations.

In California, for example, 39 percent of African-American males aged 20 to 29 were either in prison, jail, probation, parole, or under California Youth Authority in 1994. This high percentage of African-American men under governmental control is strikingly disproportionate, since African Americans only make up seven percent of the general population.[10]

These high incarceration rates parallel the harsher impact of economic dislocation on communities of color. The official unemployment rate for African Americans and Latinos is roughly twice that of Euro-Americans. Median income for African-American families is 56 percent that of white families. Thirty percent of Black households have no assets, surviving on what they earn week by week. Further, official unemployment rates significantly underestimate the real rate of unemployment. U.S. Department of Labor statistics for 1996 indicate, for example, that at any given time 50.5 percent of African-American men are without jobs.[11]

All of these forces have a profoundly negative effect on a community's ability to sustain family life. Women are increasingly left

Cycle of poverty + crime

alone to face the responsibilities of economic survival and child-rearing. They, too, have little access to stable employment, while at the same time social services have been cut almost to nothing. Of those women who fall under the control of the prison system, a large proportion are single mothers. Thus another effect of prisons is the placing of countless children into foster homes or juvenile detention centers. The economic costs of maintaining so many children and youth under state control are very high. The human costs, stretching on into future generations, are incalculable. More than with any other group in society, the cycle of impoverishment and imprisonment has a devastating impact on young people of color. In 1993, more than 45 percent of African-American children lived below the poverty level. While the overall incarceration rate for juveniles was 221 per 100,000, the rate for Latino youth was seven times higher, at 481 per 100,000; for Black youth, a staggering 810 per 100,000.[12]

The economics of the ghetto mean that for survival, parallel illegal economies have sprung up, further reinforcing the patterns of crime and imprisonment. "Kids sell drugs to get money," asserts San Francisco Sheriff Mike Hennessey. "It's that simple." He recommends an economic recovery plan along the lines of the New Deal's Civilian Conservation Corps and other government jobs programs as the only way to redevelop the inner cities. "We need to take the millions of dollars slated for construction and operation of prisons and at least match it with job training and placement programs," says the sheriff. "If we, as a nation, tried as hard to create job opportunities for unemployed youth as the drug sellers try to sell drugs, the battle would be more than half won."

Instead, many young people give up early on a fruitless search for meaningful employment and economic advancement. They drop out of an alienating school environment, and look to crime as their only path to economic gain. Under these circumstances, jails, juvenile homes, and prisons often play a more powerful socializing role for thousands of young people than school, family, or work.

In U.S. society today, alienation and drugs are a critical problem for all youth, not just young people of color. A major new study of 350,000 young people found that drug and alcohol use by white students actually exceeded that by African-American youth, in some cases by a very wide margin. "In no school studied so far, whether fed by low-income housing projects or affluent suburbs, [was] alcohol and drug use as high among Black students as among white," says Marsha

Keith Schuchard, research director for the Parents' Resource Institute for Drug Education (PRIDE), that conducted the study.[13]

This finding exposes the racism of media images that depict drugs as mainly an inner-city problem. These false images help build support among whites for expansion of the prison system. As a result, the social fabric is damaged for white communities as well—because public resources are directed toward incarcerating the most marginalized members of society, rather than developing real solutions to the myriad problems posed by alcohol and drug abuse.

While substance abuse may be a universal problem, it is still true that the violence engendered by the illegal drug trade falls most heavily on communities of color. Prisons, meanwhile, are simply an added force for violence, despair, and community destruction.

Dilemmas of Ex-Offenders

At San Quentin state prison in California, when prisoners complete their sentences, they are taken, handcuffed, to the gate, given $200, then uncuffed and sent alone into the world, presumably to begin a new life as law-abiding citizens. Yet ex-prisoners face tremendous obstacles when they try to become productive members of society.

Prison does little to provide a prisoner with skills or resources to find a job outside. Prisoners must adapt by learning survival skills that are often diametrically opposed to those that promote survival in the outside world. Prison punishes independent thinking and action. It promotes the violent resolution of personal conflicts and breaks apart the bonds of friends and family. Prison fosters dependency, idleness, violence, and the deterioration of human relationships—all of which make reintegration into freedom much more difficult.

"A person coming out of prison has four choices, " notes a 1982 study by the New York-based Vera Institute of Justice. "He can get a job, which will be difficult; he can go on welfare, which is demeaning and difficult;... he can commit crimes; or he can die... If jobs are not accessible, more will opt for crime."

Tragically, the statistics bear out this conclusion. An estimated 34.8 percent of prisoners released in 1991 nationwide were rearrested for a felony or serious misdemeanor within three years of discharge.[14]

Most people who end up in prison come from environments where unemployment and underemployment are endemic, and adding the stigma of "ex-con" does not enhance their job-finding potential. A criminal record may serve as a legal barrier to many occupations and sectors of the economy. When work is available, it is often low-paying and sporadic.

For those ex-prisoners who do find work, their median income is 50 percent lower than for the rest of the labor force.[15] Looking for work without any economic cushion promotes panic and a sense of degradation that can trap ex-offenders in a downward spiral. Often they return to economically depressed neighborhoods and must rely on impoverished family members for support. Ex-prisoners are inevitably suspects in the eyes of the local police and are therefore detained, questioned, jailed, and held at high bail whenever suspects are needed for unsolved crimes—all further disrupting potential employment.

Some programs, many of them founded during the heyday of rehabilitation in the 1960s, attempt to break the cycle by providing ex-prisoners with wage subsidies, steering them into training programs, helping them find and keep jobs, and otherwise trying to ease their transition back into the free world. But during the 1980s, services to ex-prisoners, like so many other social programs, were gutted by federal and state budget cuts. When the Comprehensive Employment and Training Act (CETA) was restructured by Congress in 1982, ex-inmates were dropped altogether as a target group.[16] The cutbacks took place during an era of severe economic recession. As a result, increased numbers of destitute and unskilled prisoners were dumped into the already glutted secondary labor market. Scarce low-paying jobs were their only alternative to the temptations of drug dealing and other crimes.

An Expensive Way to Fight Crime

With the nation's inmate population increasing at a rate of more than 1,227 prisoners per week,[17] prison construction is booming. The Federal Bureau of Prisons is now engaged in what it terms "the largest prison expansion program in history." Nearly 200 prisons are currently under construction—at a cost of more than $4.3 billion.[18] Worse, according to the Clark Foundation, construction costs, which alone can strain a state's budget, make up only 6 percent of the total cost of planning, building, financing, operating, and maintaining a new prison over 30 years.

Table 6		
AFRICAN-AMERICAN MALE TRENDS IN		
INCARCERATION AND HIGHER EDUCATION		
Year	**Number Incarcerated**	**Enrolled in Higher Education**
1990	499,000	484,000
1992	583,000*	537,000

*Figure represents jail inmates for 1992 and prison inmates for 1993.
Source: Marc Mauer et al., Americans Behind Bars: The International Use of Incarceration, 1992-1993,
(Washington, DC: The Sentencing Project), 1994.

Prisons have an economic down side that is seldom addressed. Corrections budgets deplete state coffers. For example, individual towns may gain some jobs from the $400 million Connecticut intends to spend on 4,600 new prison cells. At the same time, however, almost every city in the state is having to slash its school expenditures due to statewide cutbacks. Priorities

"Prisons are taking everything there is," a Michigan state senator recently complained. "It's the biggest growth industry in the entire state." In California, where the prison population has soared 250 percent since 1980, "the choice is almost upon us," writes corrections consultant Paul de Muro, "between education and health care on the one side and prisons on the other." [Note that at the time of publishing, the incarceration budget has surpassed the higher education budget in California.—E.R.]

In the 1980s, the U.S. imprisonment rate nearly doubled—even though the overall crime rate increased by only about 7 percent. Meanwhile, the costs of imprisonment are also rising quickly. Ten years ago, *per capita* expenditures for state and local criminal justice systems (the amount each woman, man, and child in the country pays each year to fund these systems) stood at $95. Today, the comparable figure is $211 per year, for a total of $51.4 billion nationwide. It is hard to argue that these burdensome costs have bought public protection.[19] How?

We pay

Who Profits from Prisons?

While the benefits of prisons may be questionable for the public, they are undeniable for a variety of private corporate interests. To the $84 billion spent for state and local criminal justice systems, we can add the amount spent for federal criminal justice agencies (more than $17 billion in 1992)[20] and private security systems ($11.2 billion in 1993).[21] The annual total thus lies in the neighborhood of $112.2 billion.

By contrast, the amount of direct losses to individuals, households, banks, and other businesses due to crime is approximately $10 billion per year. In other words, for every dollar directly lost by victims of crime, we spend about $8 to apprehend and punish the perpetrators.[22]

Prisons take on another face if one views them as generators of profit. Some of those who profit from the business of imprisonment are easy to identify, like architects. According to the chair of the American Institute of Architecture's criminal justice committee, there are now over 100 firms specializing in prison architecture. One Michigan entrepreneur, who is marketing what he describes as "do-it-yourself, easy-to-assemble portable jails," comments that "once this thing goes, we're talking about scads and scads of money."

Architects are far from the only people with a vested interest in the proliferation of prisons. The corporate world is extensively involved with prisons. San Quentin offers more than 250 products for prisoners to purchase, from cupcakes and fried pies to perm-cream relaxers and pinup calendars. The wares annually exhibited for sale to corrections professionals at their convention include institutional hardware like Aerko International's Mister Clear-Out ("The state-of-the-art in Tear Gas Hand Grenades, especially designed for indoor use") and the wares of the Peerless Handcuff Company ("A Major Breakthrough in Cuff Design!"). More prosaic products include the Muffin Monster from Disposable Waste Systems, Inc. ("It will grind up into small pieces all the things inmates put down toilets"); the food distribution company Servomation ("Justice Is Served"); and the Coca-Cola Company ("Time Goes Better with Coke!").

Rich Sikes, a former inmate at Leavenworth Federal Penitentiary, comments that "prisons are the number one industry in America, after war." Actually, in many cases the two industries overlap. The American Security Fence Corporation of Phoenix, Arizona, manufactures the double-edged, coiled razor blade that graces most prison fences (Razor Ribbon, "The Mean Stuff!"). According to the company's promotional literature, their top-of-the-line product, Bayonet Barb, which "combines awesome strength... and vicious effectiveness" is "manufactured in strict accordance with Military Specifications." Likewise, GTE Security Systems of Mountain View, California, sells an electrified fence called Hot Wire. Tested on the field of battle, the product is advertised as being "so hot that NATO chose it for high-risk installations; so hot that thousands have found their place in military installations ranging from sub-zero Alaskan winters to sizzling Southeast Asian summers."

From architects to academics (who study prisoners and the prison system), from food service vendors to health care firms, from corrections bureaucrats to psychologists and social workers, there is a lot of money being made from the proliferation of prisons.

Prisoners as Cheap Labor *Save govnt money/profa*

The terrible idleness of prison life can in itself become a coercive mechanism. Many prisoners are anxious to work, whatever the job or pay, because it is better than doing nothing, and small amounts of cash or savings are better than none at all.

In 1995, UNICOR, the federal prison industries, earned a profit of more than $46 million on $459 million in sales. This profit rate was made possible by the low level of prisoner wages, between $0.23 and $1.15 an hour. Moreover, the inexpensively produced road signs, missile components, military blankets and supplies, mailbags, and executive furniture for government officials subsidized other divisions of the federal government.[23]

Prisoners in Delaware, meanwhile, helped save the state $25 million by working for 15 cents an hour constructing a new prison. Many states run prison industries along similar lines, usually deducting about 80 percent of prisoners' earnings—already minimal—for taxes, room and board, family support, and victim compensation. Some prisoners are paid for their work with "good time" credits, enabling them to buy back their freedom over time—as in the pre-Civil War system of indentured servitude. Four states do not pay prisoners anything for production work.

Increasingly, private industry is also taking advantage of this captive labor force. Private firms are attracted to the prison labor pool because prisoners are legally denied rights that free workers enjoy.

Table 7					
CHANGES IN IMPRISONMENT 1980 - 1991					
	1980	**1986**	**Change**	**1986**	**1991**	**Change**
Prisoners:	329,821	545,378	+65%	545,378	824,133	+51%

Source: Marc Mauer et al., *Americans Behind Bars: The International Use of Incarceration, 1992-1993,* (Washington DC: The Sentencing Project), 1994.

No voice to rights

They cannot unionize. They do not have to be covered by Workers' Compensation, and their health care is subsidized by the state. They are not covered by the Fair Labor Standards Act. They do not voice grievances, except at the risk of incurring the arbitrary discipline of prison authorities. They can be hired and fired at will, and they do not have to be paid minimum wage.

Prison labor is perfect for employers with seasonal labor needs and late-night or weekend shifts. The same is true for industries with short-term manufacturing cycles who want to keep labor costs and benefits low, and hire and fire quickly and easily. For example, TWA and Best Western use prisoners to take overflow reservation calls. According to the *Wall Street Journal* (November 12, 1985), Best Western started a prison labor program "after having trouble hiring people to work only when needed for the overflow."

Prison labor is now emerging as a complement to the international movement of jobs. For decades, U.S.-based corporations have been moving abroad to avoid high domestic wage rates as well as labor and environmental regulations. Now, "such factors as the increasing costs of overseas labor, the expense of relocation, and the shipping expenses involved have caused some manufacturers to recognize that American prisons, with their abundant supply of labor, are an attractive alternative to foreign-based production."[24]

Private prison industries are ostensibly nonprofit, but philanthropy is hardly their motive. Businesses can receive tax breaks for running prison industries, which also permit them to increase inventories at a low cost. Rehabilitation through prison labor is also problematic. Expanded prison labor can decrease private-sector work release or ex-offender programs, since companies have more to gain from keeping a trained prisoner in the prison labor force, where he or she has no rights.

Private prison industry can actually contradict the goals of rehabilitation. To make prison work profitable, prison officials are asked to "minimize programming interruptions" by suspending treatment, educational, and vocational activities to accommodate industry's desire for an eight-hour workday.[25]

No programs for ⊕

The Private Prison

In recent years, some corporate promoters have begun looking beyond the secondary economic benefits of the prison industry. They are now maneuvering to have the system itself turned over to the private sector.

Private industry is being touted as the solution to the prison problem, the salvation of a system that is clearly failing. "It is time to get government out of the prison business," says Peter Greenwood, director of the Criminal Justice Program for the Rand Corporation, a private think tank in California. "When you're looking for innovation, you don't look to government, you look to business."

The president of the National Corrections Corporation of Santa Fe, New Mexico, makes the case for private prisons in his company's promotional literature. "Let's say it's a 150-bed jail. At 100 inmates, charged at a rate per inmate per day, you break even. At over 100 beds, you make a [modest] profit... If you can get up to 95 percent capacity, it is possible to make a [good] profit, like a motel, which is usually only about 68 percent full."

Introduced with great fanfare in the mid-'80s, the privatization drive was far less visible by the decade's end—in part because of the host of legal problems posed by the concept. The National Sheriff's Association, the National Coalition for Jail Reform, the American Bar Association, and various state legislatures have all gone on record either opposing the idea or raising serious questions about its propriety.

Nonetheless, 103 local jails in 18 states are now privately run.[26] The Immigration and Naturalization Service (INS) has also quietly contracted with private firms to run at least five detention centers for undocumented immigrants.

A leading advocate of private prisons is Jack Massey, founder of the Corrections Corporation of America (CCA). Massey was previously a founder of the Hospital Corporation of America, a for-profit hospital chain. His CCA, based in Nashville, Tennessee, is the nation's largest private prison firm.

In 1986, the Prison Officers Association (POA), a professional guards' union from Britain, toured the CCA's showcase facility, a 360-bed state prison in Chattanooga, Tennessee. The POA was appalled to find that inmates were "cruelly treated" and disruptive prisoners "gagged with sticky tape." In the female unit, the visitors said they were "not amused or impressed" by the warden's "licentious remarks" or by his descriptions of strip-shows performed by female inmates for male guards. Ultimately, CCA's attempts to take over the Tennessee state prison system were ruled unconstitutional in federal court.[27]

A widely publicized 1984 case illustrates some of the problems posed by private prisons. In this case, 16 inmates of a privately run INS detention camp sued both the INS and the private operator. The 16 Colombians, who had sought to enter the country as stowaways, had been confined in a windowless 12- by 20-foot cell designed to hold six people. A private security guard, who had no training in the use of firearms, killed one of the Colombians and seriously injured another because his shotgun went off accidentally while he was using it as a cattle prod. The INS sought to evade the suit by arguing that the abuses in question were the sole responsibility of the private firm operating the camp. This argument was rejected, however, by a federal district court, which affirmed that government bodies cannot contract out their legal accountability for what happens to people they imprison.[28]

In addition to these human rights issues, critics have pointed out a host of economic pitfalls associated with private prisons. For example, when prisons are public property, taxpayers must approve the issuance of bonds to finance their construction. Private financing, however, requires no public approval—even though the public will ultimately pay, nonetheless. In Jefferson County, Colorado, voters twice rejected a bond issue for a county jail. Construction of the facility was then turned over to private interests and the $30 million construction bond was underwritten by E. F. Hutton.

✶Privatization not only sidesteps government fiscal accountability, it actually raises costs in at least three distinct ways. First, borrowing money is more expensive for private concerns than for government bodies, because the government presumably cannot go bankrupt. Thus privatization means prison fees will reflect higher interest rates on construction bonds. Second, building prisons would qualify private firms for a variety of tax breaks, thus adding the hidden cost of depleted state revenues. Third, critics warn, if the privatization idea ever caught on, there would be little to prevent private corporations from gaining a monopoly over a state's prison facilities and then substantially raising its rates.

In 1985, a private firm sought to build a 750-bed prison on a toxic waste dump in Pennsylvania—land it had purchased for $1. According to a spokesperson for the state's Department of Corrections, "If it were a state facility, we would certainly be concerned about the grounds where the facility is located. [As for a private prison, there] is nothing in our legislation which gives anyone authority on what to do." The plan was abandoned when it prompted the Pennsylvania legislature to call for a moratorium on construction of private prisons.

Privatization poses the threat of profound conflicts of interest, because private prison operators would profit from keeping people in prison, not from finding ways to return them to their communities. Overcrowding and reduced services would spell higher profits. And private employees would inevitably provide biased information to parole and disciplinary authorities—assuming these functions were left in the hands of the state.

Labor rights are another area of concern. Public employee unions have opposed privatization because they see it as a move to undercut or even eliminate union representation for prison employees. Again, with privatization the economic incentives would all work to reduce training and pay levels for prison guards and other staff, with the potential to seriously worsen abuses of every description.

The most chilling possibility would be a combination of privately operated prisons with private prison industries. With reduced public accountability and state oversight, the potential for abuses of an imprisoned labor force is almost beyond imagination.

For the present, the move to turn the prison system over to private hands appears to be stalled, although not entirely stopped. Yet in the current atmosphere of cost-cutting, deficits, and government fiscal crisis, such proposals seem likely to re-emerge with renewed vigor. Private prisons may very well become the most serious threat to human rights, public accountability, and responsible economic policies in the entire history of the U.S. prison system.

Alternatives to Expansion of the Prison System

There is no denying that the U.S. prison system is in crisis. The debate is rather about the proper direction for a solution: expanding the failed system or moving in another direction entirely. As the final section of this essay argues, the fundamental answers to the problems of crime lie entirely outside the criminal justice system, in an end to social and economic inequality. In the short run, however, far greater reliance should be placed on alternatives to incarceration.

Some longstanding alternatives have problems of their own, yet are still far cheaper and at least as effective as imprisonment. While imprisonment costs the public more than $52 per day per prisoner, the average cost of probation in 1994 was only $2.30 per day per probationer. Parole cost between $2.96 and $10.95 per day per parolee.[29]

Other forms of custody that do not involve imprisonment are halfway houses, third-party custody, and house arrest. According to the Congressional Budget Office, it costs less than half as much to confine a person in a halfway house as in a prison. Yet, when the Federal Bureau of Prisons had to cut its budget during the early 1980s (a budget that has since begun to soar once again), it responded by closing the halfway houses—and asking for more prisons.

Monetary fines can be effective where amounts are based both on the seriousness of the crime and on ability to pay. These proportional fines, or day-fines as they are called in the countries that rely on them (mainly in Scandinavia and West Germany), entail no expense to the public, no burden on the prison system, and no social dislocation. They have proven successful for a wide range of offenses, including some violent crimes. The sliding scale ensures that the impact of the fine will be felt equally by rich, middle class, and poor.

In a growing number of states and localities, restitution and community service are becoming more routine. Restitution works best when the offender has the financial resources to pay for it, but it can also be part of a community service sentence. In such arrangements the offender may work directly for the victim or for a community agency that deducts restitution payments from the offender's wages.

Every proposed alternative to incarceration, of course, should be examined on its own merits. Some so-called alternatives merely have the effect of widening the net of the criminal justice system, bringing people under correctional control who formerly would have been left alone. In other cases, community-based alternatives have mainly benefitted white, middle-class offenders, leaving prisons to be filled by an ever-increasing percentage of poor people and people of color.

Human rights activists and civil libertarians are particularly concerned with the growing popularity among corrections professionals of electronic monitoring "bracelets" and "boot camps," also known as "shock incarceration." Electronic bracelets, which contain small transmitters, allow an offender to remain at home or at work while his or her movements are tracked electronically by local authorities. Critics have noted that this technology has the potential for extension beyond its current uses into government surveillance of political activists and others.

Shock incarceration programs operate on the assumption that offenders need training in discipline in order to lead lawful lives. These programs rely on harsh physical conditions, severe treatment, public humiliation, and militaristic group organization to coerce participants to change their behavior. Both the "boot camps" and electronic monitoring programs virtually ignore the needs of most offenders for literacy training, substance abuse treatment, job skills development, housing, and job placement. Both are coercive, offering offenders a shorter sentence in exchange for participation.

A thorough examination of all of these possibilities is beyond the scope of this essay. The main point here is that in order for alternatives to work, prison expansion must cease. History has shown us repeatedly that as long as prisons are built, they will be filled. Sanctions for criminal behavior that do not depend on warehousing hundreds of thousands of people will prevail only when warehousing is no longer available as an option.

Table 8
INCREASE IN NEW COURT COMMITMENTS
TO STATE PRISON BY CRIME TYPE, 1980-92

Offense	Court Commitments 1980	Court Commitments 1992	Increase 1980-92	% of Total Increase
Total	131,215	334,301	203,086	100%
Violent	63,200	95,300	32,100	16%
Property	53,900	104,300	50,400	25%
Drug	8,900	102,000	93,100	4%
Public order	5,200	29,400	24,200	12%

Note: Columns do not add up to 100 percent due to rounding and a small number of "other" offenses.
Source: Marc Mauer et al., Americans Behind Bars: The International Use of Incarceration, 1992-1993, (Washington, DC: The Sentencing Project), 1994. Data calculated from Darrell K. Gilliard and Allen J. Beck, Prisoners in 1993, (Washington, DC: Bureau of Justice Statistics), 1994.

Turning Away from Justice

It is a bitter irony that the high cost of prisons cuts into the health, education, and welfare services needed by the very people who, lacking such supports, often end up in prison. The ultimate victims of these punitive policies are the same poor communities that have the most to fear from crime.

Critics of the prison system argue that prisons breed more violence, not less, when prisoners are returned to the outside world. Dr. Terry Kupers, a psychiatrist who has studied the effects of confinement, testified at a recent hearing challenging conditions at San Quentin. People who are "denied human needs," he said, "such as adequate contact with loved ones, a decent private space to live in, some control over their own environment, some productive outlet, and a chance to learn and grow become increasingly resentful. Fear, hostility, and confusion well up inside them."

Kupers' views are echoed in the words of Larry Smith, a long-time prisoner in California, who has said, "Prison teaches you that violence not only works, but works quickly. People are manufactured into explosive machines and released without decompression. The explosion will come, but not necessarily here. [Prisoners] will explode—but individually, when they're out in the community."[30]

If one views the U.S. prison system as a reasonable response to lawbreaking, then crime, violence, and drugs seem like problems that can never be solved. To gain a deeper understanding of the purpose of prisons, it is far more helpful to analyze them as a response to major transformations of the U.S. economy: capital flight, the shift to a service-sector economy, the de-population of the inner cities, an increasingly segmented labor force, the economic marginalization of communities of color, the rise in youth unemployment, and the de-funding of social services of every description.

Crime could be fought by increasing the participation of poor communities in education, social, and economic institutions. The money poured into maintaining the prison system could be used to create jobs, improve education and training, and stimulate economic opportunities. This was the conclusion of the National Urban League in its 1978 study, "Strategies for Controlling Crime," which stated that "the top priority of the federal government's agenda to deal with the crime problem should be a national policy of full employment."

Instead, the social policies of the past decade have reflected a consistent choice to abandon poor communities, especially communities of color, to increasing economic dislocation and the inevitable growth of criminal activity. As a result, our society is polarized further and further—not only into the haves and the have-nots, but also into the incarcerators and the incarcerated.

Meanwhile, African Americans and other people of color are stigmatized as criminals and drug addicts, through media images that subtly (and not-so-subtly) mask the equal participation of whites in the culture of addiction, crime, and violence. The deepening polarization of society thus becomes a self-perpetuating cycle—in which the image of the criminal "underclass" is used to garner support for the very policies that contribute to the destruction of poor urban communities.

Prisons do not protect society from crime. Instead, they avoid the far more challenging solution of economic justice by reinforcing patterns of economic and social inequality. It is only by discouraging reliance on incarceration that we can seek humane and democratic ways to make our communities healthy, productive, and, most of all, safe places to live.

NOTES

1. *San Jose Mercury News*, February 19, 1989.
2. Bureau of Justice Statistics, *Sourcebook of Criminal Justice Statistics*, (Washington, DC: GPO), 1988.
3. Bureau of Justice Statistics, *Report to the Nation on Crime and Justice*, (Washington, DC: GPO), 1987; Marc Mauer, *Americans Behind Bars*, (Washington, DC: The Sentencing Project), 1994.
4. U.S. Courts Probation and Pretrial Services Division, *Federal Probation*, (Washington, DC: GPO), March 1986.
5. *Report to the Nation on Crime and Justice*, 1987.
6. *Comparing State and Federal Inmates*, (Rockville, MD: National Criminal Justice Reference Service), 1991.
7. *Annual Report*, Florida Department of Corrections, 1986.
8. M. Harvey Brenner, "Estimating the Social Costs of National Economic Policy," Joint Economic Committee of Congress, 1976.
9. Federal Bureau of Prisons, "Acquiring New Prison Sites: The Federal Experience."
10. V. Schiraldi, Sue Kuyper, and S. Hewitt, *Young African-Americans and the Criminal Justice System in California: Five Years Later*, (Washington, DC: Center on Juvenile and Criminal Justice), 1996, p. 3.
11. U.S. Dept. of Labor, *Bureau of Labor Statistics*, (Washington, DC: GPO), March 1996.
12. *Sourcebook of Criminal Justice Statistics*, 1988; U.S. Census Bureau, *Current Population Survey*, (Washington, DC: GPO), 1994.
13. *Philadelphia Inquirer*, December 19, 1989.
14. Camille and Henry Camp, *Corrections Yearbook*, (South Salem, NY: Criminal Justice Institute), 1994.
15. Peter H. Rossi, Richard A. Berk, and Kenneth J. Lenihan, eds. *Money, Work, and Crime: Experimental Evidence*, (New York: Academic Press), 1980.
16. "Can Ex-Offender Job Programs Survive Reaganomics?," *Corrections Magazine*, June 1982.
17. *Sourcebook of Criminal Justice Statistics*, 1994, p. 540.
18. *Corrections Compendium*, (: Sega Publishers), January/February 1996.
19. National Council on Crime and Delinquency, *Focus*, July 1989.
20. *Justice System Directory and Intergovernmental Expenditures*, (Washington, DC: GPO), 1992.
21. *Security Distributing and Marketing*, January 1994, p. 20.
22. Note that $10 billion is the authors' estimate based on *actual direct* losses. Current figures available from the National Institute for Justice (NIJ) are inflated to account for every conceivable related cost to victims, including potential wages lost, mental health expenditures, and "quality of life" losses. The National Institute for Justice puts the total figure at $450 billion. NIJ, *Victim Costs and Consequences: A New Look*, (Chicago: American Bar Association), February 1996.

23. "Washington Business," *Washington Post*, January 21, 1985.

24. Gordon Hawkins, "Prison Labor and Prison Industries," *Crime and Justice: An Annual Review*, 1983.

25. See also Phil Smith, "Private Prisons: Profits of Crime," *CovertAction Quarterly* no. 44.

26. Private jails are in operation in Arizona, California, Colorado, Florida, Kansas, Kentucky, Louisiana, Maine, Mississippi, New Mexico, Oklahoma, Pennsylvania, Rhode Island, Tennessee, Texas, Utah, Virginia, Washington, and Puerto Rico. (Charles W. Thomas and Diane Bollinger, *Private Adult Correctional Facilities Census*, 9th ed., March 15, 1996.) In addition, there are 80 private correctional facilities (other than jails), in the United States. (*Sourcebook of Criminal Justice Statistics*, 1994.)

27. Russ Immarigeon, "Prison Bailout, " *Dollars and Sense*, July/August 1987.

28. 589 F. Supp. 1028 [S.D. Tex. 1984], cited in Ira Robbins, "Privatization of Corrections: Defining the Issues," *Federal Probation*, 1986.

29. *Corrections Yearbook*, 1994.

30. "Inside America's Prisons," *Pacific News Service*, March 1984.

2

GARDENS OF THE LAW

The Role of Prisons in Capitalist Society

Joel Olson

Prison isn't a place to keep the "bad apples" from spoiling the rest of society. It is for the social control of the entire population—good and bad apples alike. Capitalism requires a politically obedient population that can be put to work making profits for the wealthy. Prisons ensure this politically docile and economically useful population. Prisons are useful for the powers that be; they are only a problem for those locked inside them, their loved ones, and those who want a free society.

Prison Myths

Prisons are not about decreasing crime. In 1976 the Panel on Research on Deterrent and Incapacitative Effects examined the role of prisons in deterring crime. Their report concluded that states like California and Massachusetts, for example, would have to increase their prison populations 150 percent and 310 percent (from mid-'70s levels) to achieve a 10 percent reduction in crime. Minnesota's Assistant Commissioner of Corrections admits, "There is no evidence of a relationship between the incarceration rate and violent crime. We're in the business of tricking people into thinking that spending hundreds of millions [of dollars] for new prisons will make them safe."[1]

Prisons are not about rehabilitation. In 1981 New York State Correction Commissioner Thomas Coughlin confessed, "The department is no longer engaged in rehabilitative and programming efforts, but is rather forced to warehouse people and concentrate on finding the next cell." Packing in more and more bodies inside their walls is what prisons do; rehabilitating lost souls in order to return them to society is not.

Perhaps most shocking of all to our common sensibilities, prisons are not about punishing people for crimes they commit. Of course, this is one of the things they do (as well as punish people for crimes they did not commit), but it is not the primary function of prisons. Prisons are first and foremost about social control, about suppressing dissent, about creating a more politically obedient and economically useful population. Sure, they isolate and warehouse "criminals" to keep them from the rest of us, but prisons are about controlling "the rest of us" as much as they are about controlling criminals.

How Prisons Achieve Social Control

In a capitalist society, when most people think of crime, they do not think of the acts themselves so much as they do an imaginary "criminal class" that commits them. It's always these few "delinquents" that commit violent crimes and that have to be brought under control, so the story goes. The criminal in capitalism is defined not so much by their specific unlawful acts, but by the lifestyle s/he leads: gangsta, hoodlum, dope fiend, dealer, thug, whore. The criminal exists before the crime is even committed; a criminal's prison record is merely a badge that recognizes him or her for doing what is expected. This is one reason why rich white people rarely go to jail: the rich and the white are not defined as "criminals" in this society, therefore when they break the law it's easier to have sympathy for them for "making a mistake" and to give them a lesser punishment, or no punishment at all.

Prisons are not just the storehouses of this criminal class—they produce criminality by concentrating otherwise decent people into a cramped, crowded, and oppressive environment. In prison, an individual is subject to isolation, confinement in a control unit, violence, torture, gang activity, guard brutality, organized white supremacy, and a life of boredom and useless toil. When and if a prisoner is released, s/he is often condemned to a life of poverty and run-ins with the law. Prisoners have a difficult time getting a job because they are required to notify all potential employers of their felon status on job applications. College scholarship funds for former prisoners have been slashed or eliminated. By sticking people in prison, the prison system condemns them to poverty and stigmatizes them as lifetime members of the criminal class.

The criminal class is the scapegoat for America's social ills and the justification for spending millions of dollars on building more

PRISONS AND BLACK GENOCIDE

The United States imprisons over 1.3 million people, a larger number than any other country in the world. Depending on geographic location, between 65 and 85 percent of those we imprison are people of color—those of Afrikan descent, Latinos and the original people, Native Americans. On any given day, one out of four Black males is under some form of social control, which is a higher rate than in the once openly white supremacist country of South Africa. In other words, apartheid in America is even worse.

If you are a young male of Afrikan descent in this country, and if you are poor, should you get arrested your bail will be set so high you become an economic hostage. For you, the phrase "innocent until proven guilty" has little meaning. You will sit in a cell for up to two years without having been found guilty of anything. You will certainly not get a trial by a jury of your peers. You will be defended by a public defender who has a caseload so vast you cannot possibly be treated as a priority, and finally you will serve a sentence that is 30 percent longer than a Caucasian would receive for the same crime. If you have seen this same thing happen to your father, your uncles, your cousins, if you look around at the broader picture of what is happening to men, women, youth and children of your nationality, it is not hard to conclude that there is genocide being committed.

The definition of genocide, according to the United Nations, is: a) the killing of members of a racial or religious group, b) the causing of serious bodily harm to members of a particular group, c) deliberately inflicting on a group conditions of life calculated to bring about its physical destruction in whole or in part, d) imposing measures intended to prevent births within the group, and e) forcibly transferring children of that group to another group.[1]

If we use this definition, it is not hard to see how the mass imprisonment that is occurring fits that definition. Coupled with data on high infant mortality, early death of the elderly of color, lack of the same medical treatment, opportunities and education that is afforded to whites, and the realization becomes more compelling.

—*Bonnie Kerness*

1. United Nations, *Convention on the Prevention and Punishment of the Crime of Genocide*, Article 2, Paris, 1948.

prisons, hiring more cops, and for drafting tough new "anti-crime" laws. But by trying to make life tough for criminals, we make life tough for ourselves, because the laws that get passed to control the criminal class apply to everyone. If you, the "good citizen," somehow run up against the law, well, you must be a delinquent, a member of the notorious criminal class. Better shape up, obey the laws and avoid any trouble so you won't be one of those, those... *criminals*!

By distinguishing "criminals" from the rest of society—not for people's actions but for who they are—prisons and the "fight against crime" are used to attack target populations and garner obedience from the general population. This is what led writer Michel Foucault to write, "Let us conceive of places of punishment as a Garden of the Laws that families would visit on Sundays."2 Prisons are places where criminals are punished, but they are also "gardens" that remind citizens of what could happen to them if they were to become a "criminal." In this way, prisons help craft a more obedient population outside the walls, outside the garden. Prisons put the cop inside your head. Prisons control your life even if you've never been inside one.

Black People are America's "Criminal Class"

While prisons control the population on the outside by demonizing "criminals," they control "criminals" through terror.

In the United States the criminal class created by capitalism and the prison system are poor people of color, especially African Americans. Over 33 percent of African Americans lived below the poverty line in 1994,[3] and they make up 48 percent of the U.S. prison population. One out of three Black men aged 20 to 29 is under some form of criminal justice control, which is more Black men than are in college.[4]

This is not because Black people commit more crimes. The total number of crimes committed in America is huge (estimates range between 13 and 49 million annually, for example).[5] Only a tiny fraction of the people who commit them are ever imprisoned.[6] It has been well established that while most of the nation's drug users are white, the vast majority busted for drug crimes are Black.[7] Why are most of those who are caught and convicted Black?

The only possible answer is that African Americans are the specified "criminal class" of America, or are at least its biggest subgroup (Latinos and Chicanos are an increasingly large subgroup as well). Of course, most poor Black people are not criminals, but that's the role they are forced into in the United States. As the author of *The Coming of Black Genocide* argues, "Black men are considered a criminal class, who must be pushed out to keep white people safe. Anything that is done to them, anything at all, is ok. Everyone is told to fear them, they are the threat."[8]

Because Black people are the United States' criminal class, and because in a capitalist society the criminal class must be subdued by terror, obedience from Black people is acquired through terror: police violence, locking up loved ones, etc. Just as the rest of the population doesn't have to actually go to prison to be made more obedient by the prison system, Black folks don't have to actually spend time in prison to be terrorized by it. As Malcolm X said, "Don't be surprised when I say I was in prison. We [African Americans] have all been in prison. That's what America means, prison."

The Role of Control Units

Just as prisons create a docile and useful population outside prisons, control units create obedience and usefulness within prison walls. Prisons put the cop in the citizen's head; control units put the cop in the criminal's head. It's not the "worst of the worst" who get thrown in control units, it's a specific section of the prisoner population, chosen for the perceived threat they pose to order and obedience.

As in the larger society, the vast majority of those locked up in control units are Black. For example, all but a few in the management control unit at New Jersey State Prison are Black. Most are in there because they make trouble for the prisoncrats: they are jailhouse lawyers, political prisoners, activists, and revolutionaries. Especially Black revolutionaries. As Ralph Arons, former warden at Marion admits, "The purpose of the Marion Control Unit is to control revolutionary attitudes in the prison system and in the society at large." The crime itself doesn't matter—George Jackson did 11 years for a $78 robbery—it's the class you belong to that determines whether or not you will go to prison, and once in prison, whether or not you will end up in lockdown in a control unit. And your class is determined by your "revolutionary attitudes," i.e., a refusal to obey those in power.

Prisons and Liberal Democracy: Brothers in Blood

The notion that crime, the "criminal personality," and imprisonment naturally go together is a capitalist myth. We need to separate the issue of imprisonment from the issue of crime; they are not about the same things, and one does not cure the other.

One complaint by liberals of the new incarceration society the United States is building (those few liberals who haven't jumped onto the "get-tough-on-crime" bandwagon, that is) is that it is incredibly expensive. Of course, on the surface they are right; some control unit facilities cost $800,000 per prisoner just to build, and that doesn't include living costs for the prisoner ($30,000-40,000 a year for general population prisoners). However, those who hold power in this society see things a little bit differently, and regard the rising costs of imprisonment as worth the investment. Since prisons control not just the "criminal class" but the entire population, compared with the possibility of a Northern Ireland-style military occupation of American cities, prisons actually obtain social control of the entire society at a relatively low social and economic cost for the rich. For most folks, though, the cost is devastating, which is why prisons must go.

Capitalism and its sidekick liberal democracy give us the vote, constitutional rights, consumer buying power, and a trunkful of goodies. Why aren't we free? Because though some of us have toys, we still don't have power in this society; that privilege is reserved for capitalists and the state. Why does this tiny class of society have all that power, while the majority has so little? Why don't we just take power from the rich and "vote the bastards out"? Because the ruling class have developed other ways to control the population, so that our political power is much weaker than we are led to believe. Prisons are the linchpin to this social control; they guarantee our submission to the powers that be by opposing "citizens" to "criminals."

The way to fight this is for those of us on the outside to align ourselves with those on the inside. Together, we can dispel the popular notion that crime and prison automatically go together. Together, we can expose prisons for their true nature. This can't be done outside the context of fighting capitalism, patriarchy, and a white supremacist society. As capitalism and imprisonment go together, so must they fall together. The gardens must burn.

NOTES

1. Criminal Justice Research Associates telephone interview with Assistant Commissioner Dan O'Brien, May 28, 1996.
2. Michel Foucault, *Discipline and Punish*, (New York: Vintage Books), 1979, p. 111.
3. *Black Americans: A Statistical Sourcebook*, 1994, p. 190.
4. Marc Mauer, *Young Black Men and the Criminal Justice System: Five Years Later*, (Washington, DC: The Sentencing Project), 1995.
5. National Institute of Justice (NIJ), *Victim Costs and Consequences: A New Look*, (Washington, DC: NIJ), January 1996.
6. Annually in the United States, there are more than 11,876,000 arrests, 945,500 convictions, and only about 339,000 people sentenced to state and federal prisons. *Black Americans: A Statistical Sourcebook*, 1994; Bureau of Justice Statistics, *State Court Sentencing of Convicted Felons*, (Washington, DC: GPO), 1994; Bureau of Justice Statistics, *Sourcebook of Criminal Justice Statistics*, (Washington, DC: GPO), 1994;

Henry and Camille Camp, *Felony Sentencing in the United States: 1992*, (South Salem, NY: Criminal Justice Institute), 1992.

7. Mauer.

8. Mary Barfoot, *The Coming of Black Genocide and Other Essays*, (New York: Vagabond Press), 1993, p. 28.

3

THE CRIMINALIZATION OF POVERTY

Sabina Virgo

A friend of mine recently showed me a book of quotations she had. As I was looking through it, I found something that was written by an anonymous poet in the 1700s. It was a little old, and a little formal, but I liked it. It goes: "The law will punish man or woman that steals the goose from off the hillside, but lets the greater robber loose, that steals the hillside from the goose."

Talking about "the greater robber" seemed particularly appropriate during the biggest financial rip-off in U.S. history—orchestrated by the richest men in this country. And I thought about the billions of dollars the Savings and Loans criminals stole, and about how most of them will get away with it, and will never even see a court room. And I thought about the complete insanity of how we define crime in our society. "Steal $5, you're a thief; steal $5 million, you're a financier."

Thirty percent of the wealth of this country is controlled by half of one percent of the people. Eighty percent of the wealth is controlled by 10 percent of the people. I think that's a crime. And I remembered another old saying: "Behind every great fortune there is a crime."

I looked up the word "crime" in the dictionary. It was defined as "an act which is against the law," and applies particularly to an act that breaks a law that has been made for the public good. Crime in one country may be entirely overlooked by the law in another country, or may not apply at all in a different historical period.

What that really said was that concepts of "crime" are not eternal. The very nature of crime, the dictionary said, is social, and is defined by time and by place. And by those that have the power to make the definitions. By those who write the dictionaries, so to speak.

The more I thought about that, the more profound it became. The power to define is an awesome power. It is the ability to manipulate our ideas—to limit our agenda, to mold how we see, and to shape what we look at. It is the power to interpret the picture we see when we look at the world. It is the power to place a frame around that picture; to define where it begins and ends—which is the power to create our collective consciousness.

And that is, after all, what pictures, what paintings do—they define what we see. They give us the painter's interpretation of reality. They give us illusion. The difference is that when we look at a painting of an ocean, we know that we are looking at a painting—and we know that there must have been a painter. We don't think we are looking at the ocean itself.

But when we are not looking at a painting, when we are looking at society, we've been convinced that the interpretations of society that we've been taught are not interpretations—we think they are the real deal; that is, the truth.

That kind of social propaganda is not only tremendously powerful, it is also mostly invisible—and we can't fight what we don't see. Most of us accept the images and the definitions that we have been taught as true, neutral, self-evident, and eternal; so the power to paint the picture—to define what is right and wrong, what is lawful and what is criminal—is really the power to win the battle for our minds. And to win it without ever having to fight it.

In the 1830s, the state of England defined poverty as a criminal state. And England created special prisons for these special criminals, and called them debtor prisons. So in England, in the 1800s, being poor—that is, not having enough money to pay to live—was a jailable offense.

But when we look at England during the Industrial Revolution, we see that it was not just Tom and Dick and Jane and some of their close friends who were poor. An entire class of human beings that was created by the Industrial Revolution was both exploited and defined as criminal by the owners of the technology, who had the power to both define crime, and create poverty. If the women, men, and children who were working 16 hours a day were the ones who had the power to write the laws, or to create the conditions of their lives, they would not have defined themselves as the criminals. And they wouldn't have put themselves in prison.

But they didn't write the laws, or build the prisons, or create the social vision of the times. And so people went to jail, not for exploiting, but for being exploited. Then, as now, definitions of legal and illegal are made by those in power—by those who control the economy and the institutions of the country. This truth is reflected in an adaptation of the Golden Rule: "He who has the gold makes the rules." And who goes to prison and who doesn't, who is poor and who is not, is based on our accepting those rules.

Though some of us may question the system's fairness in applying its rules, most of us don't question the basis of the system itself. That is, we don't question the relationship between those who own and those who don't. And though most of us vote every four years on *who governs*, we never vote on, and rarely question *the system that governs*. And because we don't ask that question, we don't challenge the legitimacy of that system. We accept it. We don't step outside of the frame around the picture. We don't disconnect the dots.

As long as we accept certain ideas, like, "you can't change human nature," or "the poor will always be with us" (an idea probably not authored by poor people), as long as those ideas are the "givens" of our everyday lives, then society doesn't need to struggle with us to defend what we already accept.

Aristotle said, "Poverty is the parent of revolution and crime." But when the paintings are all painted by the same school of painters, and when the social system is not even in the picture, then revolution is not a solution, because society is not responsible for poverty. So poverty and crime are made the responsibility of poor people, and criminals are jailed and separated by cages and by definition from the rest of society.

If we question any of this—if we say that prison destroys people, that prisons are overflowing and crime still increases, that the cost of imprisonment is more than the cost of education—if we say that poor people and people of color are over-represented in prison... If we say all that—and if we say that we think something is terribly wrong—we are told, again and again, that our system is inherently just and that it affords each and every one of us pretty close to an equal chance to succeed.

And if we continue to question, well, then they are willing to adjust some parts of the picture, to make sure that we believe that the injustices of society are not part and parcel of the social structure. Because as long as we believe that, they can continue to manipulate us, and tell us that both the system and the injustice just sort of exist—unrelated, side by side—like a force of nature. And if we accept our system as a natural force, like the weather... Well, we all know you can't do anything about the weather.

Bertolt Brecht, a German anti-fascist poet and playwright asked, "Which is the greater crime, the robbing of a bank, or the founding of a bank?" That is not a question that was given to most of us in our homework assignments from school. Bankers were businessmen, we were taught, not criminals. Being a criminal, after all, means being guilty of something—and not being a criminal means being innocent. But if those of us who are homeless and hungry are innocent, then who or what is guilty?

U.S. law says that children are innocent. If they suffer, if they are hungry, or without clothing or shelter, if they are abused or injured, the law does not find the child guilty. Society does not call children "unfit children."

But somehow, we who suffer as adults, we who have neither clothing nor food nor shelter, are found guilty. Because if the system isn't at fault, then the fault must be ours—and those of us who suffer must be victims, not of systemic failures, but of personal deficiencies. Just like we were in England in the 1830s.

If we look at any downtown urban center, if we look at the lines of people waiting for food or for a bed at the missions, if we look at the people living in cardboard boxes on the streets of the cities—we must know that a crime has been committed. When we look at the faces of dispossessed people, we see faces that look like the faces of people who lived here when California was part of Mexico. We see faces of people who came here from Haiti and from Central America. And we see the faces of people whose great-great-grand-parents were abducted and were brought here from Africa. So many faces from Africa.

One half of all African people born in this country live in poverty. That is a 69 percent increase in the last 25 years. One out of two children born to African-American parents is born in poverty. One of every three seniors live in poverty. One of every four men is under the control of the prison system. And the life expectancy for a Black man in Harlem is less than for a man in Bangladesh.

If we know that, we must know that a crime has been committed.

They tell us that we are a rich country. They tell us the system is flourishing, and the stock market is up. We are so productive, they tell us, because business in the United States provides the source of "our prosperity" and "our way of life." And though some of us may have internalized their viewpoint, if we are not of their color or not of their class, their way of life is not ours. And if it turns out that white men are the richest—well, the white men who run the country tell us, it is probably because they are the smartest and work the hardest.

Speaking at Michigan State University in 1963, Malcolm X said, "If I take the wages of everyone here, individually it means nothing, but collectively all of the earning power or wages that you earned in one week would make me wealthy. And if I could collect [them] for a year, I'd be rich beyond dreams. Now, when you see this, and then you stop and consider the wages that were kept back from millions of Black people not for one year, but for 310 years, you'll see how this country got so rich so fast, and what made the economy as strong as it has been. And all of that slave labor that was amassed in unpaid wages, is due someone today."

Jailing Black men is one way to keep the bill unpaid. Criminalizing poor people is another way. And flooding African-American and Latino communities with drugs is still another way. Whoopi Goldberg said, "The government said it is illegal to have Cuban cigars in this country—and it is almost impossible to get a Cuban cigar. The government also said it is illegal to have drugs, and you can get drugs anywhere." That's what Whoopi said.

Drugs, poverty, and prison are used to crush resistance in communities with histories of resistance. Drug sub-economies and subcultures are imposed. And drug money becomes survival money in communities where unemployment for people under 22 runs between 50 and 60 percent.

Some African-American and Latino youth, growing up jobless and poor, and seeing no strong alternate vision, join gangs, and are doing business, not challenging it, and they are being sent to jail for their trouble. The Crips and the 18th Street Gang pose much less of a threat to the power structure than the Panthers or the Brown Berets did. Gangs and drugs don't challenge the rule of corporations.

In fact, the values of corporate America are accepted on the streets, and gangs are mimicking capitalist technique. Police in Colton, California found a business card at a drug bust in Colton's newest crack house. The card said, "If you offer good, high quality, uncut cocaine at a reasonable price, Southern California will beat a path to your door. This is our guiding principle—why not give us a try." The address was proudly printed on the card.

Suspected gang members and dope dealers aren't the only ones being sent to jail. Their parents are being sent there, too. Parents of "suspected gang members" have been arrested for not stopping the "gang affiliations of their children," and laws are being proposed to evict tenants from public housing, if anyone in the family has been convicted of drug use. So that they can all be homeless—and guilty of another crime. I wonder if George and Barbara Bush could be evicted from their "public housing" if their son Neil were convicted of bank fraud?

Isn't it clear that a crime is being committed?

Although we may differ about the degree of government complicity in flooding communities with drugs, the effect of the obvious flood is the destruction of lives. The creation of addicts who are then defined as criminals. But being an addict is not always a crime. It sort of depends on who is addicted and what they are addicted to. Working-class addiction to crack is a crime. But middle- and upper-class addiction to drugs or alcohol is a disease. When Betty Ford said she did pills, we all respected her courage for admitting it, and named a rehab center after her. When Kitty Dukakis drank rubbing alcohol, we all felt bad, and no one put her in a cage.

But if Native-American, African-American or Latino youth do drugs, or sell them, and are caught, they are caged. If they are not caught, they can make $800 to $900 a day selling crack. Or they can make $4.25 per hour at McDonald's. Or they can be unemployed. This is America, and we have the right to choose.

U.S. society is the structure that defines the choices, and decides which of the people that break its laws go to prison. Putting the wives of presidents in jail in not an American tradition; nor is putting presidents there. Judges and lawyers don't choose to send the heads of corporations to prisons too often, so when Michael Milken was found guilty of stealing billions, he was genuinely shocked that the judge gave him 10 years.

Judges don't do that too often to people like him. Mostly, they send poor people to prison, people without jobs. They send unemployed people there at three times the rate that they do employed people. And, more often than not, they send people of color there, who now make up 60 percent of the people in prison. And they choose to execute people of color, particularly Black men, far more often than whites.

Since capital punishment was resumed in 1977, no white man has been convicted and executed for killing an African man or any member of a minority. Statistics show that Black defendants have a three to four times greater chance of being executed—no matter what the crime—than their white counterparts. But, in the double-think and triple-speak of the men who run the country, former Attorney General

Dick Thornburgh doesn't want those numbers considered when Black men are being sentenced to death. Thornburgh said that those statistics, if used, "would create racial bias, and would impose unwanted racial quotas on our death penalty laws."

But the system, having created all of this, is once again absent from the list of those responsible. Because if the victim is at the same time the criminal, then the system is uninvolved—it is not even brought into the equation. So no solutions are found. Poverty, crime, and violence increase. All poor people are suspect. Communities of color are targeted. Human suffering and social disasters are portrayed as natural disasters—as something the system is trying to cope with, instead of something the system created, and is complicit with.

People see no other recourse, and so the enforcement arm of the system comes to be seen as a solution—we see the use of battering rams, and the cordoning off of entire sections of communities. We see street sweeps and round-ups. We see young men defined as "suspected gang members," and arrested. We see seven billion of the nine and a half billion dollar budget for the "war on drugs" being used to hire more prosecutors, and build more jails. And we see civil liberties limited, and the so-called "war" being used to support restrictive laws and infringement of constitutional guarantees.

The former Chief of Police of the city of Los Angeles called the use of drugs "treason." He said that "casual drug users should be shot." He also said that Michael Milken should be sentenced to "community service."

L.A. Times and *Nation* columnist Alexander Cockburn wrote: "Angry people will strike out with such weapons as are available to them, and effective weapons are hard to come by in a country run under one party rule, in the interests of the rich and the corporate." Representing one face of that one party, John Silber, the Democratic nominee for Governor in Massachusetts in 1990, said that he wouldn't take his campaign to the African-American community of Roxbury, because "There is no point in my making a speech on crime control to a group of drug addicts."

Racism, tried, true, and reliable, continues to be used to divide us, and continues to provide an easy, convenient lie—a multipurpose justification for what is wrong in this society. For much of white America, gangs, drugs, and violence define communities of color. And the forces that produce the drugs and define the crime laugh, as they say, all the way to the banks. Which many of them own.

Haven't we figured out that a crime has been committed?

Working-class white people are manipulated by rich white people, and encouraged to feel superior because that keeps them from seeing who their allies and their enemies really are. It keeps their vision inside the picture frame. And the picture they're living in isn't so pretty. Working-class white people are losing their homes and their apartments through redevelopment. They're losing their jobs through plant closings and corporate mergers. Their children go to schools that don't teach, because there is no money for education. They can't pay their medical bills, and there is no national health care. They're angry, confused, and afraid, and don't understand why their lives are getting harder.

But hard as things may be, some white folks know that they're living better than some other people do, better than Black people do—and so, instead of joining with Black people to change the picture, many whites have been convinced that they have a vested interest in keeping things just the way they are.

In a similar way, men—who generally have more power and money in society than women do—many men have been convinced that it is in their interest to support the *status quo*. Controlling and criminalizing women, particularly poor women, and women of color, is one way of keeping the *status quo*. In the last 10 years, along with increasingly violent racism, there has been a concerted attack on women's rights, and there has been an increase of crimes that are defined by gender.

A woman's right to control her own body is close to being defined as criminal. An anti-affirmative action, anti-civil rights Supreme Court—made up of eight men and one upper-class woman, will be passing judgement on the rights of all women. And the irony is that the legal system, which may make abortion a criminal act, can also define giving birth as a crime—that is, if they have defined the mother as a criminal. Addicted mothers, after being denied the right to end their pregnancy, can be arrested for giving birth and endangering the life of their child. But again, it is not wealthy pregnant addicts who end up on the six o'clock news. It is not rich alcoholics who are dragged into court and into jail. It is women who are poor, and it is their poverty that defines their criminality. But it's not mothers who withhold the money for pre-natal care, and for drug rehab programs—it's society.

By making mothers guilty, society shifts the responsibility for endangering the health of children away from billions in health care cuts, and focuses blame on the individual. It's the parents, not the lack of services, that are held responsible. Blaming parents in America for lack of health care is like blaming travelers in the desert for the lack of water. In the desert, people die from lack of water, and in poor communities, children die from lack of health care. Children die when the social service budget is cut. But that, somehow, is not a crime. Children died when the governor of California cut funds for measles inoculations. Children died, and parents suffered—but the governor wasn't indicted. There is a saying that there is a rich man's TB, and a poor man's TB. The rich man recovers and the poor man dies. I guess its the same with the measles.

In China there is another saying: "The beginning of wisdom is calling things by their right names." Cutting social service systems is cutting life support systems. People die. If any one of us went into a hospital and disconnected a life support system, it would be called murder. But when politicians cut the social service budget, it's not called murder, it's called fiscal responsibility.

Don't we know that a crime has been committed?

It is illegal to sell sex for money. But the increased rate of addiction in poor women has increased the rate of prostitution as a way of getting money for drugs. If a woman gets money by selling her body on the street to a trick, she goes to jail. But if she sells her body in a penthouse to Donald Trump, she could be on the cover of *People* magazine. So the act of selling sex is either a crime or not, depending on the class of the seller, or of the buyer.

Because of increased poverty, and because of an expansion in what is defined as criminal, women are being sent to prison at rates increasing by 15 percent a year. That is twice the rate for men. And over one-half of the women in prison are women of color. Most of them are under 30, live in poverty, didn't complete high school, and had sporadic work histories. They are mothers, they were the heads of their households, and they are separated by prison bars from their 250,000 children—most of whom are in foster care. Statistics show that 60 percent of the boys who are in foster care will end up in prison. Or will join the 50,000 people under 21 who are living on the streets of California.

The people in power study those figures, and they discuss those figures. But no one who is in pain now will be in less pain when their studies and discussions are done. And no one who is rich now will not be rich as a result of those studies. And no laws will be changed as a result of those studies. Because the people who commission the studies wrote the laws.

In the United States, when the government sends a check for $525 a month to support a mother and child, that money is called welfare. It is called a subsidy for the poor. But when the government underwrites the debts of Chrysler and Penn Central, that's not called welfare. When it subsidizes agribusiness, or undertaxes corporations, that subsidy doesn't even have a name. It's invisible. It's the canvas the picture is painted on. And if it did have a name, you can bet it wouldn't be called welfare, and it wouldn't be called fraud.

Tax loopholes and regressive taxation are not called subsidies for the rich. They're not called "welfare." When people in power talk about people on "the public dole" they are not talking about the people who steal millions from the public—not talking about Michael Milken, or Leona Helmsley, or Frank Lorenzo. But if income taxes of the rich were put back to their 1966 rates, that would increase revenues by $60 billion a year.

Yet when people talk about welfare criminals, they're not talking about that. And that's because the criminals are defining the language, making the rules. And as they misappropriate millions, and steal billions, they use millions to have us focus our anger and frustration on "welfare cheats"—you know, women and children and $525 a month.

The illusion works in foreign policy as well. U.S. foreign policy has brought a new group of immigrant poor to this country. And to welcome them, the United States provided new facilities called detention centers—or prisons—for the new arrivals. The INS acts as hosts to the guests. In April of 1990, 5,000 Haitian guests felt so welcome in Florida that there was an uprising in Miami at the Krone detention and processing center.

But not all immigrant poor are housed in prison centers. Only some of them are. Anti-Castro Cubans who came here used to be given more money than the welfare grant for a family of four (speaking of welfare). And while Haitian refugees are put in camps in the United States, and while Southeast Asian refugees are put in camps in the Philippines, and while Salvadoran refugees are defined as illegal, Soviet Jews are welcomed, and anti-communist Eastern Europeans are invited by new immigration quotas. So, the crime of immigration, like so many other crimes, seems to be based more on who's doing it than what they're doing.

If we are Haitian or Salvadoran, being here, being identifiable, and being poor, makes our very existence criminal. We are called "illegal aliens." We are illegal, while the United States spends almost $2 million a day to pay for destabilization in Haiti and war in places like El Salvador. While Jonas Savimbi lobbies Washington, while the U.S. government sends hundreds of millions to the Afghan rebels and the Khmer Rouge, we are illegal. Oliver North is free, and La Migra imprisons us.

We are imprisoned and we are denied the right to work by laws and by lack of papers that say we are legal people and we need to work, to eat, and to live. And when we do what some of us did in the lands of our birth—when we become street vendors—we find that is illegal, too. The police sweep the streets, and we are arrested for breaking "The Law." The INS is notified. We are taken to jail. We are criminals.

And so some of us work in illegal sweat shops, for up to 14 hours a day. We make as little as two dollars an hour. We sleep on pads on the floors where we work. They told our story on television, but nothing has changed. We are the underground economy of the illegal and the exploited.

Don't we know—isn't it clear—that a crime is being committed?

In Columbia, U.S. banking penetration and the Columbian debt has created an economy based on coca leaves. Columbian peasants grow the only crop they can, and the United States defines an entire country as criminal—and debates the use of force across the oceans—and battering rams and street sweeps in North America are translated into talk of combat troops and drug sweeps in South America. Poor people in Columbia, and Peru, and Bolivia, are not defined as victims of the international debt, but are rather held responsible for cocaine addiction in the United States. They are both exploited by the international drug trade, and found guilty of it.

In the United States, it is a crime to be poor. And the poorer we are, the more criminal we are. If we are so poor that we have no place to live, and if we live on the pavement, or on a road, or sleep in a car, or in a park, we have committed a crime. It's against the law to sleep on the streets, or in a park. There is a saying that goes: "It is equally forbidden for the rich and the poor to sleep under the bridge." I have looked, and I have not seen Charles Keating lying on a blanket by the L.A. River. I have not seen Michael Deaver hanging out near cardboard alley. Dennis DeConcini is not waiting in line at the mission. Because the rich never really lose everything. But the rest of us can. And we can find ourselves without a job or a place to live because of the crimes of men like Deaver and Keating. We end up in jail and they end up in front of ethics committees.

The political decisions of the government, the investment decisions of the Keatings and Deavers, are decisions about who will be
poor—and corporate decisions made in the late '50s to remove industry from communities of color were decisions about who would be
unemployed. Decisions by developers about redevelopment are decisions about who will be homeless. Those decisions affect each one of
us. But we have no say in them—as we have no say in most social and
economic decisions that affect our lives. Because that, somehow, has
never been part of our "democracy." Because we have no say, creating
homelessness is not criminal—but being homeless is. Runaway
plants, and plant closures are legal—but vagrancy is not, and looking
for work on the street is not. Because we have no say, toxins are
dumped every day, but most whistle-blowers are fired, and the EPA
looks the other way.

The definition of crime is limited, and so the scope of what we
demand redress for is equally limited. In the "victim's bill of rights,"
the victim is someone who has suffered an individual act of violence.
But when the act of violence is not committed by one person against
another person, when it is committed by the government or multinational corporations, and when the victim is not a person, but is "the
people," then not only is there no "victim's bill of rights," there is not
even a trial, because there has been no crime. Because the criminals are
in charge. And they *do* commit crimes. Capital crimes. Every day. Crimes
of racism. Crimes of sexism, of military intervention. Crimes against
children. Crimes against the environment. The result of their crimes is
our suffering. We see our life support systems strangled and choked. We
see latch-key children and drive-by shootings.

The jails are overflowing but that doesn't seem to help, because
the real criminals aren't found in jail. They are found in the board
rooms and in the White House. They are the one-half of one percent
of the men who control 30 percent of the wealth. They are the 10
percent who control 80 percent. And under their misleadership, over
five million of us are homeless, 37 million of us have no health
insurance, 30 million of us are illiterate, 30 million more are function-
ally illiterate, one million of us are in prison, 20 percent of us live in
poverty, and most of us are just a few paychecks away from being
without shelter.

Under their misleadership, we live in a world where the air and
the water are polluted, the earth is toxic, and the chemicals that are
poisoning us keep being produced. Under their misleadership, a war
was waged in the Gulf; a criminal war, fought by poor people, whose

lives were risked for profits and cheap oil. And the lives of African-American and Latino men and women were, once again, jeopardized disproportionately. And under their misleadership, there is a war being waged at home. A war against people of color. A violent war that is daily getting more brutal.

Most of us don't feel safe, or valued. Most of us are afraid—but we don't talk about it. We don't trust each other. We don't feel powerful. For most of us, the world we live in is out of control and threatening. It is not written anywhere that is has to be this way. But if we want it to change, we have to change it. We have waited hundreds of years for the people in power to change it, and they haven't and they won't, because they created it and it serves them.

So the question before us is how to be more than a witness to a crime. The question before us is how to paint a new, beautiful painting. How to build a powerful, caring, movement for change—an independent movement that can challenge power and can win. A movement that, if it won, would have a clear vision, and would know what to do. A movement that would have a concrete plan for transforming society, a plan to re-industrialize and rebuild. A plan for employment and education, for housing, and for the environment. A concrete plan to deal with racism, sexism, addiction, and pollution. So that we would know what tomorrow could look like, and would have an idea of how we would get there, and how we would pay for it.

Before that kind of movement can be born, we need to reach out to each other, and evaluate our work, and learn the lessons it has to teach us. We need to talk to each other, and find out what has kept us apart—and how we can change that.

The time seems right for that. We seem ready to talk about why our movement is fragmented. To talk about why we have many organizations, but little unity, and few victories. Why we have individual leaders, but no collective leadership. The time seems right to see why we are waging a piecemeal attack on a giant. To ask if that's part of why we've been struggling for so long, but are no closer to power and liberation than we were 50 years ago. And time, maybe, to put the idea of winning back in our vocabulary.

We need to take time to talk—so that we can build a movement that is focused enough, and strong enough, to create a humane society. A society where people care for each other, and value each other, where we live with dignity and respect; a society where the water is clean, and we can see through the air. Where racism, and poverty, and sexism, and oppression are words from the past. A society where our differences enrich us, not divide us. A society that loves us, and helps us grow.

The most important work that we can do in our lives is to help bring that world to birth. All of us know that. That's the work we do. That's why we're here.

> Speech delivered at the conference of the International Human Rights Coalition, December 8, 1990

4

THE LABOR OF DOING TIME

Julie Browne

Slavery is being practiced by the system under the color of law...
Slavery 400 years ago, slavery today; it's the same thing, but with
a new name. They're making millions and millions of dollars enslav-
ing blacks, poor whites, and others—people who don't even know
they're being railroaded.

—Political Prisoner Ruchell Magee[1]

Despite a chilling official silence, 1995 was a bombshell in the
"war on crime." In this one year alone, 150 new prisons were built in
the United States and 171 existing prisons were expanded. This was
the year the crime bill was passed, mandating that 100,000 additional
police officers be added to the already enormous law enforcement
establishment. In California, this was the first year that the state
budget allocated more money for prisons than higher education. Most
astonishingly, with one short day of media attention, 1995 was the year
that Alabama's governor Fob James, and other state officials, made
the callous and horrifying decision to reinstate the nationally abolished chain gang.

The return of chain gangs, as well as the return of convict leasing,
in the last decade, comes on the back of extensive state-run prison
industries and convict labor programs. As the prison population has
continued to grow, convict productive labor and employment has
developed into one of the largest growth industries. The significance
of this movement toward mass incarceration must be seen in a historical context. It is crucial to understand that, though incarceration has
been normalized as society's natural response to crime, there was not
always a prison system in this country. Examining how the prison
system was developed and how it operates today, it is clear that this
form of social control has been deeply linked to the institutionalization
of racism, working-class oppression, and labor exploitation.

History

The 13th Amendment to the United States Constitution reads:

"Neither slavery nor involuntary servitude, except as a punishment for crime whereof the party shall have been duly convicted, shall exist within the United States, or any place subject to their jurisdiction."[2]

Before the abolition of slavery there was no real prison system in the United States. Punishment for crime consisted of physical torture referred to as corporal or capital punishment. The first penitentiaries were designed in England and France in response to growing criticism of the extreme use of public violence as the only means of deterring crime. In *Their Sisters' Keepers,* Estelle Freedman explains that the basis of the penitentiary was that the detention itself was the punishment, and the "penitentiary ideal consisted of extreme isolation of criminals from society, extensive supervision over their daily lives, and compulsory productive labor."[3]

One of the first penitentiaries in the United States was opened in Auburn, New York. With a structure combining separated confinement with silent collective work, this penitentiary became the model for most prisons in the United States. A few years after this first prison was opened in Auburn, New York in 1817, a local citizen was given a contract to operate a factory within the prison.[4] In these initial penitentiaries the state used convict labor for government production and contracts were given to certain private businesses to operate within the prisons. Prisoners were also leased out to private bidders to be housed, fed, and worked as slaves, which was referred to as the Convict Leasing System. Initially, inmate labor was purported to assist in the discipline and redemption of criminals; however, the potential net profit from convict labor was the driving force of the popularity of the Auburn system throughout the South.

Historian Fletcher M. Green wrote that by the 1840s, "the development of prosperous prison industries was the most earnest concern of the wardens in all state prisons, and the penitentiary that was the least expensive was considered the most successful."[5]

After the Civil War, the 13th Amendment officially abolished slavery for all people except those convicted of a crime. Legally allowing any such individual to be subjected to slavery and involuntary servitude opened the door for mass criminalization: a social mechanism designed to bar the liberty and equality that was the promise of emancipation from slavery. When African Americans were no longer legally held as slaves or property, there was a tremendous increase in the number of African-American convicts. Before the Civil War, laws called the Slave Codes governed the rights of slaves and all African Americans in the South. When slavery was legally abolished, the Slave Codes were rewritten as the Black Codes, a series of laws criminalizing legal activity for African Americans. Through the enforcement of these laws, acts such as standing in one area of town or walking at night, for example, became the criminal acts of "loitering" or "breaking curfew" for which African Americans were imprisoned. In the late 19th-century South, an extensive prison system was developed in the interest of maintaining the power, race, and economic relationships of slavery.

Convict Leasing

The convict lease system functioned with the Black Codes to reestablish and maintain the race relationships of slavery by returning the control over the lives of these African Americans to white plantation owners. This is illustrated by the fact that in 1878, Georgia leased out 1,239 convicts, 1,124 of whom were African Americans.[6] Through the convict lease system, bidders paid an average $25,000 a year to the state, in exchange for control over the lives of all of the convicts.[7] The system provided revenue for the state and the profit of unwaged, unprotected workers for plantation owners or private industries. Racial and economic motivations were far more central than public safety and rehabilitation.

From the beginning there was criticism of the cruelty and brutality in the convict lease system. Journalists, community members, ministers, dockers, and union organizers worked to draw attention to the experiences of state prisoners. Women, such as Rebecca Felton in Georgia and Julia Tutwiler in Alabama, organized demonstrations and "crusades" targeting specific camps or politicians. Finally in the 1890s, legislative reports were issued describing the brutal daily beatings, often with leather straps studded with wooden shoe pegs, inflicted on the workers in these camps.[8] The rise in prison reform organizing in the 1930s also brought attention to some of the experiences of female convicts.

One investigative committee in Tennessee found that women were being made to work in a hosiery mill, and were often flogged, hung by their wrists, or placed in solitary confinement as punishment for poor productivity at the work site.[9] In the face of these demonstrations and public reports, politicians could no longer ignore the descriptions of African Americans being beaten with whips so heavy that if they survived, their wounds were never able to heal. Mississippi was the first southern state to abolish the convict lease system, with a constitutional amendment enacted in 1894 prohibiting the lease of convicts, "to any persons or corporations, public or private." In Tennessee, years of strikes involving convicts and union workers together forced the government to abolish the lease system. By the 1930s every state had abolished convict leasing.[10]

Chain Gangs

As the southern states began to phase out convict leasing, prisoners were increasingly made to work in the most brutal form of convict forced labor in the United States, the chain gang. The chain gangs originated as a part of the mass organization at the turn of the century to create extensive quality roads. In the 1890s, Good Roads Associations were developed in each of the southern states and they established a statutory labor system, wherein every able-bodied road hand in the state was required to work for four or five days a year on public roads and highways.[11] In North Carolina and Georgia, politicians realized that the use of forced convict labor in road work was more economically efficient than using compulsory free labor, because convicts could be worked harder, for longer hours, and over a more sustained period of time. Georgian politicians and prison officials began releasing male misdemeanor convicts into road work programs. Georgia was the first state to begin to use the chain gang system to work male felony convicts outside of the prison walls. The chains were wrapped around the prisoners' ankles, shackling five prisoners together while they worked, ate, and slept. Chain gangs became very economically and politically popular among most Southern politicians as they witnessed convicts working from sunup to sundown in Georgia.[12]

The fundamental "reform" in abolishing convict leasing and replacing this system with chain gangs was that the state now owned the convicts and their labor. Whereas previously the bureaucracy of the state had been the supplier of convict labor for private industries, they now became the direct exploiters. For over 30 years, African-American, and some white, convicts in the chain gangs were worked at gunpoint under whips and chains in a public spectacle of clear chattel slavery and torture. Eventually, the brutality and violence associated with chain gang labor in the United States gained worldwide attention. As reformists learned about the endless stories of prisoners dying in sweat boxes after being beaten by the guards, and of teenage boys being whipped to death, they began organizing and calling for an end to the use of extreme violence against convicts. Historian and theorist, Walter Wilson, was particularly critical of the ideology behind these movements, since they focused only on the most outward displays of violence. In 1933, Wilson wrote of this reform movement:

> When some of the inhumane tortures that constantly occur on the gangs are forced into the light, reformers and liberal apologists for capitalism are "shocked" and call for an investigation. The investigation usually whitewashes the prison system as a whole by pinning the blame on one or two subordinate guards who are then dismissed. The reformers then go into ecstasy over their "victory."[13]

Cases involving the dismissal of certain guards were hailed as the "abolition of whipping," until the next horrifying story of torture was released. Reformers failed to address the fundamental problem of violent domination, control, and isolation forming the basis of the penitentiary system from which the chain gangs had emerged. They failed to realize that there could be no benevolent form of a chain gang. Consequently this system of overt slavery persisted through all the minor reforms. The chain gang was finally abolished in every state by the 1950s, almost 100 years after the end of the Civil War.[14]

Current Convict Labor Programs

In the 1990s, the California Department of Corrections (CDoC) maintains that convict labor is only a peripheral program within the larger system confinement and punishment of convicts. However, the Prison Industry Authority (PIA) is a multi-million dollar industry that is dependent on the productivity of California prisoners. As inmates are classified for placement in an institution, they are surveyed for almost 50 different work skills, from appliance repair to x-ray technician, to determine which institution they should be placed in.[15] Clearly, the experience and work skills these convicts already have coming into the institution counter the notion that convict labor programs are about job training and education.

The Department of Corrections maintains that work in the institution is voluntary; however, each day worked reduces a prisoner's sentence by one day.[16] Therefore, those who refuse to work will serve twice as long a sentence as the convicts who agree to work. In addition, the "Work/Privilege Group" classification process further punishes prisoners who refuse to work. There are four work/privilege classifications for prisoners: A = full time work, B = half-time work/waiting list, C = refuses to work, D = special segregation unit prisoners. The prisoners who refuse to work, labeled as Group C, are "not entitled to family visits, and are limited to one-fourth of the maximum monthly canteen draw. Telephone calls are permitted only on an emergency basis as determined by the institution's staff. While access to the yard is allowed, no special packages or access to other recreational or entertainment activities are allowed."[17] These extreme coercive tactics contradict the claim that labor is voluntary.

The Prison Industry Authority

In California, prisoners have been manufacturing goods for state agencies since the turn of the century. In 1944, the Prison Reorganization Act created the California Correctional Industries Program to oversee all prison manufacturing programs. In the 1980s this office was transformed into the Prison Industry Authority. Through these industries the inmates have produced all of the work that supports the prison system, such as making the clothes, washing the clothes, and building the cell equipment, day room furniture, lockers, and mess hall tables. Prisoners have made shoes, bedding, clothing, detergents, stationery products, license plates, and furniture for all state agencies. In addition, convict laborers have provided "special services" such as dental lab work, micro graphics, and printing. The women's prison industries have generally been in the areas of reupholstery, fabric production, laundry, and data entry. In men's prisons all of this work is done, as well as metal production, wood production, and the operation of farms, dairies, and slaughterhouses.[18] This enormous, multi-million dollar industry was purportedly created to address the problem of "inmate idleness," according to the CDoC, by helping in rehabilitation, building effective work habits, and providing job training. Yet a prisoner who spends her 10-year sentence processing stationery products on an assembly line or washing laundry has not learned any highly employable skill, nor been mentally and emotionally challenged through this service to the state.

By 1982, when the California Correctional Industry was transformed into the Prison Industry Authority, the issue of inmate rehabilitation wasn't even included in the industry's statement of purpose.

The legislature created the PIA so that the industries run within California prisons would be economically independent and self-supporting, "allowing it to function outside the normal State budgetary process." Given the rising cost of imprisonment and the increasing tax burden, the PIA had been "vested with the powers and responsibilities characteristic of a private corporation," placing profit at the center of the organization of production.[19] The current mission statement of the PIA is:

1. Producing and selling, at a profit, quality goods and services at competitive prices with timely delivery.
2. Maintaining a safe, clean, secure, and efficient environment that promotes work ethic.
3. Expanding markets and developing new products.[20]

There is nothing in this mission statement that indicates any commitment to training or rehabilitation. The PIA mission statement focuses on the profiteering interests of an industry that can rely on a stable, growing, exploitable population of workers who are prohibited from organizing on their own behalf.

Conservation Camps

In addition to the industries operating within California prisons, convicts have worked in that state's fire control and forest conservation in the Conservation Camp system since 1915. The CDoC now operates 33 male Conservation Camps and 3 female conservation camps, providing "the backbone of the state's wild land fire fighting crews." The prisoners work for the Department of Forestry and Fire Protection and the Los Angeles County Fire Department.[21] Since it is low-security imprisonment, the Camps program is considered a privilege by many prisoners, though the work is extremely dangerous and many prisoners are injured in the program. And, of course, the prisoners are still denied the right to organize collectively. The average prisoner working in the conservation camps is paid 25 to 75 cents an hour. The Department of Corrections considers the program a tremendous success, because the Department of Forestry saves over $70 million annually using convict labor.[22]

The Joint Ventures Program

The Joint Venture Program of the California Department of Corrections is the board responsible for contracting out convict labor to "any public entity, nonprofit or for profit entity, organization, or business."[23] This program was created by the passage of Proposition 139, the Inmate Labor Initiative of 1990, which was an initiative to overturn the 1882 abolition of convict leasing in California. A poll conducted by the *San Francisco Chronicle* found that less than 25 percent of the electorate was aware of Proposition 139 less than one month before the election.[24] However, when voters read the ballot description, a majority passed this initiative allowing private business to profit from convict laborers. Work that had been done on the outside is now done by convicts who are paid 20 percent of minimum wage, worked under constant armed supervision, unable to legally unionize, and unprotected by the Fair Labor-Standards Act.

One of the most important aspects of Proposition 139 is its repeal of the principle that labor in prison must be voluntary:

> The people of the state of California find and declare that inmates who are confined in state prison or county jails should work as hard as taxpayers for their upkeep, and that those inmates may be required to perform work and services.[25]

The initiative mandates that prisoners be made to work to pay for their imprisonment, and reintroduces private industry into the prison to benefit from this unprotected labor. By June of 1994, 13 corporations were operating in California prisons, including a computerized telephone message center for Tower Communications in the California Rehabilitation Center in Norco, green waste recycling for Western Waste Industries in the California Institute for Men in Chino, and electronic component manufacturing for Quality Manufacturing Solutions, Inc. in the Central California Women's Facility in Chowchilla.[26]

Within the current processes of economic globalization, the establishment of the Joint Venture Program has opened California prisoners to be used as a new labor supply and to be manipulated within the world economy to meet the interests of transnational corporations. Within the global economy, the United States is becoming an increasingly service-based economy, and many of the manufacturing and textile jobs prisoners are supposedly being trained for don't even exist here anymore. Economic globalization has completely altered the relationship between capital and labor that existed within the economy of this capitalist nation-state, where massive increases in incarceration directed at working-class communities and communities of color would formerly have interfered with the interest of many corporations by diminishing the labor pool. The hypermobility of capital has created an economic setting that allows for mass incarceration, because there is no longer a strong economic need for a large, free, unskilled, unemployed population of workers in this country.[27] Capital can easily expand its supply of labor to include any exploitable population of workers throughout the world, including incarcerated workers.

The New Chain Gang

Since the first chain gangs were sent to work in Alabama in 1995, several other states have responded positively to the idea, and Arizona has already begun modeling the program in their own prisons. The chain gang system in Alabama not only forces prisoners to work to pay for their own imprisonment, but also establishes convict labor as a form of punishment. The 400 medium-security convicts on the chain gang, often convicted of theft or bouncing checks, are assigned to work for a 30-day period. If they receive negative reports during these 30 days, they can be assigned another 30 days. There is no limit to the amount of time a convict can be forced to remain on the chain gang if he is perceived to be disobeying the rules, regulations, or "the orders of the staff."[28] Beyond the terror of working at gunpoint for twelve hours a day, performing hard labor while constantly chained to five other men, the chain gang system in Alabama grants an extremely dangerous excess of power to the guards who can, at their own discretion, extend the duration of the prisoners' punishment.

Several prisoners have voiced protest to the return of this horrific practice. Michael Lamar Powell, a convict in Limestone Correctional Facility in Capshaw, Alabama, has been particularly aggressive in writing public statements to expose the injustices of imprisonment in Alabama and across the United States. This recent essay, "Modern Slavery: American Style," addressed the significance of the return of chain gangs in Alabama and the lack of any real criticism in the international response.

> Alabama is now proving the past is not always past. Alabama has become the first state in the nation to re-institute chain gangs. However, the worst part about chain gangs in Alabama is not the young men chained together in groups of five as they urinate and defecate... not the cuts and bruises that the chains inevitably

defecate... not the cuts and bruises that the chains inevitably leave on the legs and ankles of the young men... the inadequate or total lack of medical treatment... the total lack of access to the courts... nor the dehumanization of these young men in chains and their abrupt return to the slavery of their ancestors. The worst part of the chain gang in Alabama is that the rest of the world rushed to see it.   .

...The rest of the world is jealous. They too want their own slaves. So they wait and watch so that they can do it too, so they can do it with less problems. America, the last country to outlaw slavery, now becomes the country to teach the rest of the world to enslave legally.[29]

On May 4, 1995, the papers were flooded with pictures of prisoners working in chains. The pictures were romanticized and nostalgic in such a compelling way that *Life* magazine followed up this one-day photo opportunity with a photo essay on the chain gangs. The first line read, "The chains are strangely beautiful."[30] As Michael Lamar Powell wrote, the mainstream media response was not criticism and outrage, but rather surprise and interest. [As the result of a class action lawsuit brought by the Southern Poverty Law Center, claiming that chain gangs are cruel and unusual punishment, in June 1996, Alabama abandoned the practice of chaining inmate work crews together.—E.R.]

Resistance

Despite the current unbelievable repression of prisoners rights, many prisoners like Michael Lamar Powell continue to write and voice dissent and resistance to the exploitation of labor in the prison system. When given the opportunity to organize, there have been many prison strikes where prisoners withheld their labor to force the prison officials to meet their demands. In the 1970s, when many nationalist revolutionaries such as the Black Panthers and Young Lords became political prisoners, convicts were able to successfully organize the Folsom State strike and the Attica uprising, which included specific demands to empower convicts as workers, and call attention to the exploitation taking place. Today, prisoners continue to resist, and organize solidarity. Bill Dunne, a political prisoner in Leavenworth, Kansas spent several months in segregation for stamping the receipts for the cabinets he was packaging with "SLAVE LABOR IN THIS PRODUCT." I'm sure that actions similar to those taken by Bill Dunne are taking place throughout the convict labor enterprises.

Conclusion

The exploitation, inhumanity, and injustice in the convict lease system and the chain gangs need to be brought back into public consciousness; however, the movements that emerge in resistance to these systems must not model the same pattern that has unfolded throughout the history of prison reform. We must break out of the notion that we are trapped by some proverbial pendulum, and that lives will simply be sacrificed and oppressed in the necessary conservative turn of our political process. Throughout U.S. history, social movements have abolished different systems of brutality and exploitation only to have them return in a short time. We must admit that gradual changes within a system cannot be effective if the larger system itself is the problem. Chain gangs and convict leasing are not a brutal aberration within a just and humane criminal justice system; they are an extension of the racist and class-biased systematic exploitation of convict labor that has formed the basis of the U.S. prison system since its inception. There will never be a benevolent form of imprisonment. The reform that we have a responsibility to demand is the abolition of the prison itself.

NOTES

1. Ruchell Magee, in an interview with Kiilu Nyasha, "Freedom is a Constant Struggle," KPFA Radio, August 12, 1995.

2. U.S. Constitution, Amendment 13 (ratified December 6, 1865).

3. Estelle B. Freedman, *Their Sisters' Keepers*, (Ann Arbor: University of Michigan Press), 1981, p. 8.

4. Fletcher M. Green, "Some Aspects of the Convict Lease System in the Southern States," *Essays in Southern History, vol. 31*, (Durham: University of North Carolina Press), 1949, p. 112.

5. Green, p. 115.

6. Green, p. 120.

7. Green, pp. 116-118; Walter Wilson, *Forced Labor in the United States*, (New York: AMS Press, Inc.), 1933, p. 63.

8. Green, p. 121.

9. Wilson, p. 62.

10. Green, pp. 121-123.

11. Alexander Lichtenstein, "Good Roads and Chain Gangs in the Progressive South: "The Negro Convict is a Slave," *The Journal of Southern History*, (Athens, GA: Southern Historical Association), 1993, p. 87.

12. Lichtenstein, pp. 88-98.

13. Wilson, *p. 68*.

14. "Free Labor Rebelled Against It," *Solidarity*, United Auto Workers, March 1995.

15. Prison Law Office, *The California State Prisoners Handbook*, Section 3.17, pp. 79-80.

16. *The California State Prisoners Handbook*, Section 3.17, pp. 115-118.

17. *The California State Prisoners Handbook*, Section 3.17, pp. 83-84.

18. Prison Industry Authority, "Inmate Employment in Existing Enterprises," June 30, 1992.

19. Prison Industry Authority, "Over 140 Years of History."

20. Prison Industry Authority, "Mission Statement," Annual Report Fiscal Years 1991-1992.

21. California Department of Corrections, "The Conservation Camps Program," unpublished description of the program.

22. "The Conservation Camps Program."

23. California Department of Corrections, *Joint Venture Program*.

24. David Tuller, "Prop. 139 Raises Debate on Employment of Prisoners," *San Francisco Chronicle*, October 31, 1990.

25. California Department of Corrections, "Proposition 139," *Joint Venture Program*.

26. California Department of Corrections, "Joint Venture Employers," *Joint Venture Program*, June 1994.

27. For further reading on economic globalization and the hypermobility of capital, see David Harvey, *The Condition of Postmodernity*, and the writing of Saskia Sassen.

28. Alabama Department of Corrections, "Chain Gang Orientation," Dormitory 31.

29. Michael Lamar Powell, *Modern Slavery: American Style*, 1995, p. 4.

30. Brad Darrach, "Chain Gangs," *Life*, October 1995, p. 65.

5

THE POLITICS OF SUPER INCARCERATION

Mike Davis

The road from Mecca follows the Southern Pacific tracks past Bombay Beach to Niland, then turns due south through a green maze of marshes and irrigated fields. The bad future of California rises, with little melodrama, in the middle distance between the skeleton of last year's cotton crop and the aerial bombing range in the Chocolate Mountains. From a mile away, the slate-gray structures resemble warehouses or perhaps a factory. An unassuming road sign announces Calipatria State Prison.

California now has the largest penal system in the world. Over the past decade, the state has built Calipatria, located 220 miles southeast of L.A., and 15 other new prisons—at a cost of $10 billion (interest included). An emergent "prison-industrial complex" has become the dominant force in the life of rural California and competes with land developers as the chief seducer of legislators in Sacramento. It has become a monster that threatens to overpower and devour its creators, and its uncontrollable growth ought to rattle a national consciousness now complacent at the thought of a permanent prison class.

Like the rest of the state prison system, Calipatria operates at almost double its designed capacity. In county jails and medium-security facilities, squalid tiers of bunk beds have been crowded into converted auditoriums and day rooms. In "upscale" institutions like Calipatria, however, a second prisoner has been shoehorned into each tiny 6-by-10-foot cell.

When "double-celling" was first introduced into the system a decade ago, it fueled a new wave of inmate violence and suicide. Civil liberties advocates denounced the practice as "cruel and unusual punishment" but a federal judge upheld its constitutionality. Now inmates can routinely expect to spend decades or even whole lifetimes (34 percent of Calipatria's population are lifers) locked in unnatural, and often unbearable, intimacy with another person. The psychological stress is amplified by the drastic shortage of work for prisoners, condemning nearly half the inmate population to serve their sentences idly in their cells watching infinities of television. As behavioral psychologists have testified in court, rats confined in such circumstances invariably go berserk and eat each other.

The prison staff at Calipatria speaks with measured awe of Don Novey, the former Folsom guard who, as president of the California Correctional Peace Officers Association (CCPOA), has made the correctional officers the most powerful union in the state. Under his leadership the CCPOA has been transformed from a small, reactive craft union into the major player shaping criminal justice legislation and thereby the future of the California penal system. Part of the secret of Novey's success has been his willingness to pay the highest price for political allies. In 1990, for example, Novey contributed almost $1 million to Pete Wilson's gubernatorial campaign. The CCPOA now operates the second most-generous PAC in Sacramento.

Novey has also leveraged the union's influence through his sponsorship of the so-called victims' rights movement. Crime Victims United is a satellite PAC, receiving 95 percent of its funds from the CCPOA. Through such high-profile front groups, and in alliance with other law-enforcement lobbies, Novey has been able to keep Sacramento in a permanent state of law-and-order hysteria. Legislators of both parties trample one another in the rush to put their names at the top of tough new "anti-crime" measures, while ignoring their impact on prison capacity.

This cynical bidding war has had staggering consequences. Joan Petersilia, a researcher at the RAND Corporation, found that more than 1,000 bills toughening sentencing under felony and misdemeanor statutes had been enacted by the legislature between 1984 and 1992. In aggregate, they are utterly incoherent as criminal justice policy, but wonderful as a stimulus to the kind of carceral Keynesianism that has tripled both the membership of the CCPOA and the average salary of prison workers since 1980. From the beginning of the prison boom, at the end of Jerry Brown's administration in 1982, a host of critics have tried to wean the legislature away from its reckless gulagism. They have produced study after study showing that super incarceration has had a negligible impact on the overall crime rate (which, in any event, has not significantly increased); and that a majority of new prisoners are either nonviolent drug offenders (including parolees flunking mandatory urinalysis) or the mentally ill (a staggering 28,000 by official estimate). They have also repeatedly warned that a day of reckoning would come when the state would have to trade higher education, literally brick by brick, to continue to build prisons.

That day, indeed, has come. While California's colleges and universities were shedding 8,000 jobs between 1984 and 1994, the Department of Corrections hired 26,000 employees to guard 112,000 new inmates. But instead of hitting the brakes, the legislature went full throttle. Last spring's "three strikes" law doubles sentences for second felonies and mandates 25 years to life for "three-time losers." To make the law constitutionally invulnerable to reform (except by an almost impossible two-thirds majority), it was also presented to voters as Proposition 184 in November. Proponents of the measure—led by the CCPOA and Michael Huffington—outspent opponents (primarily the California Teachers' Association) 48 to 1 ($1.2 million versus $25,000). However, since most Democratic candidates, including Kathleen Brown and Dianne Feinstein, supported the measure or were silent, voters had little opportunity to hear opposing arguments or weigh the epochal consequences of the law. The proposition passed easily.

It's a measure of their complicity that prior to the election the Democrats refused to publicize the damning official estimates about the impact Proposition 184 would have on prison capacity. These were issued last March by the CDoC's Planning and Construction Division. Simply to house the projected 1999 inmate population at the already intolerable 185 percent occupancy level, the state will have to build 23 new prisons (beyond the 12 already authorized). "This would require construction of more than four and one-half prisons per year in each of the next five fiscal years," the planners wrote. Within 10 years, they predict, the penal population will increase 262 percent, to 341,420 inmates (compared with 22,500 in 1980).

Commenting on these projections, a spokesman for Governor Wilson simply shrugged his shoulders: "If these additional costs have to be absorbed, I guess we'll have to reduce other services. We'll have to change our priorities." Which "priorities" were clarified in October, when researchers at RAND published an exhaustive fiscal analysis that concluded: "To support implementation of the law, total spending for higher education and other government services would have to fall by more than 40 percent over the next eight years... If the three strikes law remains in place by 2002, the state government will be spending more money keeping people in prison than putting people through college." As it happens, the scales have already tipped: state spending on operation and construction of prisons and jails (approximately $5.2 billion and rising) outweighs state spending for higher education (approximately $4.7 billion and falling).

It is sobering to recall that the CDoC, with 30 major "campuses" is already more expensive than the University of California system, and that young Black men in Los Angeles or Oakland are twice as likely to end up in a prison as in colleges. Proposition 184, moreover, promises a dramatic escalation in racial disparities. In the first six months of prosecutions under the new law, African Americans (10 percent of the population) made up 57 percent of the "three strikes" filings in L.A. County. This is 17 times the rate for whites, say public defenders here, although other studies have shown that white men commit at least 60 percent of all the rapes, robberies and assaults in the state.

For State Senator Tom Hayden, who vigorously opposed Proposition 184, California is sinking into a "moral quagmire" reminiscent of Vietnam: "State politics has been handcuffed by the law-enforcement lobby. Voters have no real idea of what they are getting into. They have not been told the truth about the trade off between schools and prisons, or the economic disaster that will inevitably result. We dehumanize criminals and the poor in exactly the same way we did with so-called 'gooks' in Vietnam. We just put them in hell and turn up the heat."

At Calipatria, meanwhile, the administration is already tinkering with the thermostat. Daniel Paramo, the prison's "community resources manager," cheerfully acknowledges that, faced with the Proposition 184 population explosion, the CDoC is considering putting a third inmate in each mad-rat cell. "We'll simply pack in as many inmates as the state orders. And, if the courts finally impose a limit, I guess we'll just build some new prisons."

SECTION TWO

CONDITIONS FOR RESISTANCE

Turn on almost any daytime radio talk show and it will be clear: the war against prisoners is on. Reactionary forces in the United States have popularized the false notion that prisoners have "too many rights," that it is unfair for convicted criminals to "have it so easy." Behind these complaints about "glamour slammers" and the supposedly easy lifestyle enjoyed by prisoners is a deep-seated vindictiveness, a nationwide call for increasingly harsh punishments. This conservative agenda is about criminalizing and dehumanizing people, and thus even the most basic of human rights are seen, instead, as "privileges." The ultimate goal is to make people believe that prisoners do not deserve any human rights, and to strip away the few rights prisoners maintain. In no way is this trend illustrated more sharply than by the brutality and the severe medical neglect that is endemic throughout the U.S. prison system.

Prison officials have long shown deliberate indifference to prisoner health issues. Prisoners throughout the United States suffer from health problems ranging from toxic water supplies to psychiatric illness and tuberculosis, but medical care in prisons continues to be inhumane and inaccessible.

The horrifying statistics regarding heart disease, breast cancer, malnutrition, and so many other preventable diseases illustrate that we live in a disposable society. This is enforced by policies of government and the corporate medical establishment that continue to define health care as a profit-oriented venture, treating symptoms with band-aid fixes that fail to address the larger, more complex roots of the health care crisis. The state's health care agenda, as defined by institutions such as the American Medical Association, the Food and Drug Administration, and the insurance industry, demonizes alternative, holistic medicine and ignores the important roles played by a massively polluted environment and the destructive lifestyles thrust upon us all.

Now largely inaccessible and unaffordable to huge numbers of people, health care must ultimately become something we practice as an integral part of community life, instead of something we buy from a corporation. Unfortunately, this is not on the immediate horizon. There is now a large body of literature concerning nutrition, alcoholism, drug addiction, the neglect of mental health, the neglect of children and elders, exercise, respiratory and cardiovascular diseases, work-related injuries, and the severe contamination of our bodies by carcinogenic and neurologically destructive chemical compounds. Even the most cursory look at this literature provides conclusive evidence that our ongoing faith in Medical Progress is foolhardy.

It is in this context of the state's blatant disregard for people's health and well-being overall that we must place the health crisis, especially that faced by prisoners with HIV and AIDS.

AIDS is, as many health issues are, about wealth and political power. It is about race, gender, and economic inequality. It is about greed, education, and a basic lack of democracy. Largely, AIDS has also been about the politics of the everyday lives of lesbian, gay, and bisexual people. It was only a few years after the onset of the AIDS pandemic, however, that it was no longer seen as exclusively affecting homosexual communities. When straight conservative white people, famous people, and children started to test positive for HIV and eventually die from AIDS, a long and historically significant process of perception shifting began. But mind you, these drastic shifts were not due to an aware and caring media acting in the public service. Rather, a mass movement—spearheaded by groups such as the AIDS Coalition to Unleash Power (ACT-UP)—through direct action, education, and grassroots public pressure, changed not only many public policies and municipal and state health care agendas, but the very nature of the language that we use when talking about the issues. There were several elements of this shift: Much of our culture slowly began to see the crisis as not limited to sectors of the population they could marginalize; a heated intellectual and practical debate arose regarding "guilty" and "innocent" victims of the disease; and the mind set of a significant portion of the population began to move from myths to facts and from fear to understanding.

Despite these advances, we have a long way to go. Prisoners with AIDS are precisely the underclass that mainstream culture refuses to look at, refuses to deal with. Prisoners with AIDS often face what amounts to a death sentence. I believe our activism needs to assert loudly that their criminal status is not the issue—prisoners with AIDS have the right to live!

The physical and mental health conditions that exist for prisoners, and especially prisoners with AIDS, are sharp and graphic illustrations of the skewed priorities of the medical and penal establishments. In exposing and denouncing the reality of AIDS and other aspects of the health crisis in prisons, we assert that health care is a human right—not a privilege. Creative and pointed activism that strives for this can lead our society to more seriously address the emergency of how we take care of ourselves and each other.

The chapters that follow are very successful at bringing these issues to the forefront. Cases like that of Vaughn Dortch, ruthlessly scalded by guards at California's Pelican Bay State Prison and left with second and third degree burns over one third of his body, are *not* isolated incidents. "Exposing the Myth of Humane Imprisonment," a 1991 report of the Prison Discipline Study (PDS) in Sacramento, CA, details the legal, physical, and psychological abuses to which prisoners are routinely subjected, and dissects the fiction of "humane" imprisonment. Although it is now five years old, the central findings of the PDS are still relevant: "1) That severe physical and psychological abuse are the norm in maximum-security prisons throughout the county; and 2) That the most frequently disciplined groups of prisoners are jailhouse lawyers, Black prisoners, and prisoners with mental handicaps. There is no significant variation by state or region." (Many of the worst conditions exist in the nation's control unit prisons. See Section Six, "The Nationwide Lockdown.")

In this period of history, when politicians and corporate elites are manipulating language to fit imperialist policy objectives, it is important to realize who the real criminals and terrorists are. It is instructive to remember that the United States is the biggest warmonger of all time. It is important to recall that everything done by Hitler's

Third Reich was preceded by a "legal process" in which the masses of people supposedly had a say.

Despite reactionary fuming about prisoners in the United States having *too many* privileges, in actuality, prisoners are daily being stripped of their basic human rights. C. Stone Brown's piece on the Federal Crime Bill and the Anti-Terrorism and Effective Death Penalty Act gives us a chilling reminder that the protections of our human and civil rights as supposedly guaranteed by the Constitution are extremely elastic. The passage of laws that limit *habeas corpus* and the Bill of Rights, such as those described in Brown's article, indicate that the government is in the process of rolling back fundamental rights for both prisoners and non-prisoners.

Our culture leads us to believe that prisoners are simply either crazy, or passive objects bemoaning their fate. A closer look at prisons shows us thriving pockets of culture; vibrant sub-cultures; loving relationships; family ties; creative expression that is at once graceful, loud, poetic, and angry; significant academic and scholarly achievement; dynamic legal representation; strong organizing efforts; spiritual growth; and, of course, sustained resistance. The resilience of the human spirit portrayed by Laura Whitehorn in "Resistance at Lexington" reminds us that behind the prison walls, dignity and humanity are upheld by the simplest acts. Prisoners struggling against the brutality of the prison system remind us of the connections to be made, and that we are fulfilling our humanity in the fight for *justice*, not the application of *law*.

In "Building Bridges," Lin Elliot begins, "To be queer in prison is to be silenced." Elliot struggled for, and eventually achieved, some recognition of lesbian and gay prisoners by the political lesbian and gay communities outside the prison walls. As he outlines, however, this struggle for visibility continues. Elliot offers a much-needed perspective on how society's oppression of gay/lesbian/bi/transgendered people manifests itself inside prisons, and specifically in the Washington state system. Much of the work of prison activists involves responding to and issuing calls for solidarity. Now, as lesbian/gay/bi/transgendered prisoners and their advocates are organizing in dynamic ways for human and civil rights, our solidarity and unremitting advocacy are invaluable.

Some of these pieces come from a collection of materials prepared by ACT-UP. In 1991, ACT-UP gave its work on prisoners with AIDS new life by joining with prisoners themselves to form the California HIV Activist and Inmate Network. This network, pulling together the efforts of a dedicated and talented array of activists throughout the state, demonstrated and issued demands that clearly articulated the needs of prisoners living (and dying) with HIV/AIDS. Things changed. Direct action got the goods. Statewide, ACT-UP placed sufficient pressure on the California Department of Corrections, the California Medical Facility (CMF) at Vacaville, and the California Institution for Women to bring a major review process and some meaningful gains for the struggles of those behind the prison walls.

As with any long-term struggle, however, battles won do not herald an end to the fight. In the late summer and fall of 1992, health care at CMF-Vacaville deteriorated, and several prisoners went on medication strike and later hunger strike to protest the conditions and the deaths of several prisoners with AIDS.

6

IN CRITICAL CONDITION

Abuse, Neglect, and Poor Health Care in U.S. Prisons

Every so often, we at the Prison Activist Resource Center get e-mail from someone wanting to know why we advocate for prisoner's rights. "Shouldn't we make it harder on criminals?" they ask. Or worse, "Why are you pro-criminal? Don't you care about the rights of victims?" Many people have been led to believe that prisoners fabricate the stories of abuse, medical neglect, and inadequate facilities. Our hope is that this compilation will arm people with facts that can expose prisons for the hell that they are.

One part of the reactionary trend toward stripping prisoners' rights is the effort to paint prisoner lawsuits as "frivolous." Yet in the pages of publications such as *Prison Legal News* and *Prison News Service* there are hundreds of accounts of abuse and neglect. Courts across the country are regularly filled with cases filed by prisoners trying to get relief. While there may be some cases of prisoners filing lawsuits on issues that could instead be resolved administratively, huge numbers of suits are in response to the constant violation of prisoners' basic human and civil rights.

Fighting for those rights is no easy task. Yet politicians are attempting to limit prisoners' access to the courts. In a recent editorial, the Prison Law Project of the National Lawyer's Guild spoke out against limiting access to courts, noting that doing so is likely to create more violent situations.

> Jailhouse lawyers work under incredibly difficult circumstances. Being locked in their cells for up to 23 and one-half hours a day, their access to law library materials is limited. They are often forced to "research" their cases by providing case numbers to "runners" who go to inadequate libraries searching for the single case and bringing it to them for a limited period of allotted time. They are allowed infrequent access, if ever, to the library itself to browse through books. They are limited in their ability to copy

and type. Many are forced to pay fees for filing even though they have been declared indigent. Facing brutal treatment for challenging prison administrations, it is a miracle of the human spirit that those incarcerated continue to seek relief in the American judicial process. Often it is the only remedy available to them.

Access to the courts by the more than 1.5 million people currently incarcerated is a guaranteed right that should never be limited. Were prison administrators responsive to the courts and were the courts to censure the egregious conditions, the number of lawsuits would decrease naturally. The fact is that the courts have a hands-off policy towards prisons: no warden is ever sanctioned, no prison is shut down, and the litany of tortuous conditions goes largely ignored by the courts. Prisons are, in effect, free-fire zones for those who run them.[1]

The next time that someone upbraids you for being soft on crime or asks why you don't care about victims' rights, point them toward these cases and suggest that our notions of "crime" and "victims" must change and expand. Citing cases such as those that follow will help us expose and denounce this brutal system.

Selected Cases

These examples are far from exhaustive. They are merely a few of the reported incidents and conditions, intended to show the scope and range of atrocities committed in U.S. prisons every day. Many instances of poor living conditions, health violations, and guard brutality never get printed in any newspaper or brought to light in court. For each example cited here, however, there are many others that have been brought to public attention, often to no avail.

The nation's prisons are seriously overcrowded, at more than 112.3 percent capacity, on average.[2] This causes and exacerbates a failing of infrastructure in many institutions. Sanitation and heating are also extremely poor in many institutions. For example, Human Rights Watch reported that at the California Institution for Women, showers often broke, bathroom floors flooded, and inmates reported conditions where 32 women had to use one toilet. Inmate to inmate violence, assaults, and sexual abuse is rampant.[3]

On September 22, 1991, an uprising (mostly in protest of living conditions) occurred in the Maximum Custody Unit in the State

Prison at Deer Lodge, Montana. Following are some of the conditions that followed the uprising, according to the American Civil Liberties Union as reported by the International Indian Treaty Council (IITC) and Prison News Service.

1. The prisoners were left for four or five days without clothing or mattresses.

2. They were fed two meals a day, consisting of cold sandwiches—beverages were withheld. Nutrition was so bad that several prisoners developed scurvy.

3. They were denied hygiene items. No towels were distributed for at least four days. Showers were denied for three weeks.

4. Prisoner privileges were revoked and were not reinstated.

5. Access to telephones was denied, visits were prohibited, and correspondence was withheld.

6. Prisoners were denied access to legal materials and were prevented from contacting their attorneys for the entire three weeks that they remained in the Reception Unit (where many prisoners were held after the uprising).

7. Indian prisoners were prevented from practicing their religion.

8. Prisoners were left chained without justification. This even applied to mentally handicapped prisoners.

9. Prisoners were subjected to mace attacks for refusal to talk with investigators from the Attorney General's Office.

10. Arbitrary and severely brutal punishment was inflicted on prisoners in the weeks immediately following the riot. Scott Seelye and five other prisoners were hogtied... This meant being chained in leg irons and handcuffs, with one leg being drawn up to the arms, resulting in their chest coming off the floor. They were left like this naked for two days on the cold concrete floor. Some of the prisoners suffered potentially permanent nerve damage.

11. Indian prisoners were singled out for the most brutal attacks. They were continually called the most racially derogatory terms.

12. Prisoners were denied medical examinations and treatments.

An IITC report detailed the aftermath of the uprising: "Prisoners were instructed to strip and lie face down on the floor where they were handcuffed. Mace was used against them. They were forced to run barefoot through broken glass to reach the front door of the cell block, where they were met by a gauntlet of sixty to seventy armed guards. The guards struck the handcuffed inmates as they ran by, in some cases inflicting injuries requiring medical attention. The prisoners from the maximum security unit were then placed in an adjacent field called 'No Man's Land.' They were forced to lie there naked for many hours, sustaining sunburn on their backs and legs. They were taunted, beaten and kicked by guards. No hygienic measures were allowed, and inmates were forced to urinate or defecate where they lay..."[4]

Many of the poor conditions and much of the mistreatment at the Iowa Correctional Institution for Women were brought to light in a lawsuit filed by 14 prisoners there. Some of the clear violations of these women's civil and human rights follow:

1. Authorities imposed a punishment on prisoners called "four pointing," involving tying naked prisoners by the hands and legs to a bed in a spread-eagle position where they can be viewed by guards and passersby. "Some women have been held in this position for several hours," states the suit.

2. Prisoners were not evacuated during a fire, causing some to suffer smoke inhalation.

3. Prisoners were subject to isolation, physical abuse, sexual harassment, exploitation, and a lack of due process in disciplinary matters.

4. Prison authorities permitted overcrowding and unsafe and unsanitary conditions, and failed to provide medical care.

5. Mail was censored and access to courts was unduly limited.

6. Women in segregation were frequently forbidden to wear clothing, and were forced to shower with their hands cuffed and fastened to their waists while being supervised by male guards.

7. Menstruating women were denied sanitary protection and women were held in cells that had human feces smeared on the walls and broken glass on the floors.

8. Prisoners were served food that had spoiled or had been contaminated with hair or insects.

9. Prisoners who complained or tried to defend themselves were punished.

The Disabled Prisoners Justice Fund was created to protect the rights and meet the legal needs of prisoners with disabilities. The Fund grew out of the pleas made by prisoners who are in grave danger as a result of extreme abuse and deprivation of their constitutional rights, their human rights, and their civil rights as people with disabilities. Some of the chilling abuses the Fund struggles to expose and rectify include:

- prison officials confiscating wheelchairs, rendering prisoners unable to move from their beds;

- denial of catheters and leg bags so that prisoners who lack bowel and bladder control are made to lie in their own waste;

- prison officials authorizing guards to turn off the water in disabled prisoners' cells, so that they are unable to drink water or wash themselves;

- denial of even the most minimal health care, including the treatment of decubitus ulcers (easily preventable but extremely serious cases of tissue breakdown, otherwise known as "pressure sores" or "bed sores");

- psychological abuse such as guards goading and taunting prisoners over loudspeakers so that a whole cell block can hear ("Hey Jones! Need another diaper? Shit in your pants again?").

This type of abuse happens on a daily basis in prisons and jails in every state in the country. Even in relatively progressive states such as New York, disabled prisoners experience incidents of the type Amnesty International legally defines as torture. One can well imagine what happens in the states, such as Texas, that are infamous for their ill treatment of prisoners.

Kenneth Young was an HIV-positive federal prisoner who was transferred to the U.S. Penitentiary at Lewisburg, PA. While in the Transfer Segregation Unit at Lewisburg, Young was sexually assaulted by his cellmates several times. He repeatedly requested protective custody from a number of prison officials who repeatedly ignored his pleas and taunted him for seeking protection. After one prisoner had raped him and ordered him out of the cell, Young, in order to be removed from the cell, flooded the cell by stopping up the toilet. Prison officials placed Young in a "dry cell" with no toilet or running water. Young was allowed to use the toilet once in a three-day period. He was provided with a plastic urinal 29 hours after being in the dry cell. He was not provided with toilet paper or drinking water, nor allowed to wash his hands before meals or to bathe. Young was forced to urinate and defecate on the floor of his cell, which the orderly refused to clean. Young filed a suit against prison officials claiming a violation of his Eighth Amendment rights. The district court dismissed the case for failure to state a claim.[5]

From 1974 through the early 1980s, the Texas Department of Corrections was forced into sweeping reforms, largely due to a class-action suit brought by prisoners' rights groups on behalf of all 15,000 inmates. Landmark decisions in the suit, *Ruiz v. Estelle*, resulted in critical consequences for prison systems nationwide. Among the abuses being fought by the case were practices that Texas prisoners knew to be all-too-frequent. Some of them included legal and verbal harassment, racial discrimination, threats, arbitrary rectal searches, arbitrary and unnecessary use of Mace and tear gas, unjustifiable solitary confinement, confiscation of property, denial of use of law libraries, refusal to deliver mail, and improper censoring of legal correspondence. The suit was organized in several major themes: overcrowded and unsanitary living and working conditions; substandard medical care and deliberate indifference to medical needs; vague rules and illegal procedures regarding summary punishment; violation of prisoners' rights to be free from assault and the threat of assault; and interference with prisoners' access to courts and the legal system.[6]

ACT-UP's Campaign 1991-1995

In 1991 and for almost three years following, ACT-UP San Francisco had a small but thriving Prison Issues Group that was able to galvanize activists across the state to come together and fight for the rights of prisoners. Their call to "Unmask the California Death Camps" was responded to by hundreds, even thousands who demonstrated, organized, rallied, and zapped public officials with phone calls and faxes, demanding that ACT-UP's demands be heeded.

Some of the facts that ACT-UP was responding to, at the time, included:

- At prisons such as California Institution for Women (CIW) and California Medical Facility at Vacaville, prisoners were dying at alarming rates, sometimes unattended in their cells, and in some cases were not removed from their cells for days after dying;

- Peer counseling programs vital to the prevention of unsafe practices that spread infection were either unheard of or under severe fire;

- Food and kitchens in those and other prisons were found to have rodent droppings and roaches;

- Between 1988 and 1989, AIDS cases in state and federal correctional systems tripled, a disproportionate number of these cases represented Blacks and Latinos as compared to the AIDS impact in the general U.S. population;

- From 1985 to 1989, the increase in cumulative AIDS cases rose 72 percent in prisons, as compared to a 50 percent rise in the general U.S. population;

- As of 1989, there had been 1,453 AIDS deaths in the state and federal prisons in the United States;

- Only eight state or federal and one city/county system allowed prisoners access to experimental therapeutic drugs, and none of them were women's prisons;

- No prison systems provided prisoners with bleach for cleaning drug injection and tattoo needles;

- When issued, pre- and post-HIV test counseling was of inadequate length and content, and breaches in confidentiality occurred frequently;

- In 1990, the infirmary at CIW was inspected by the California State Board of Health, and declared inadequate and substandard in these categories: physician and nursing care, pharmacy, dietary kitchen, patient handling, and medical policies and procedures;

- The infirmary at CIW was found to have fire hazards throughout and unsanitary conditions, including unsafe storage of infectious waste;

- HIV-positive prisoners at CIW were being forced into punitive segregation, regardless of whether they were actually ill.

Largely as a result of the direct action campaigns waged by ACT-UP on behalf of prisoners with HIV and AIDS, some changes have been made in parts of the system that have made life somewhat more bearable for some prisoners. By no stretch of the imagination, however, have conditions overall improved in any real sense. In many cases they have gotten worse.

These are some of the current conditions that prisoners with HIV/AIDS in California prisons are faced with:

- It routinely takes two to three weeks for a prisoner at the Central California Women's Facility (Chowchilla) to see a doctor, if she is lucky enough to have a Medical Technical Assistant (a guard with some first aid training) approve a doctor's visit;

- Women at Chowchilla are often not tested for AIDS unless they are showing AIDS symptoms;

- While there are at least 100 women known to have HIV at Chowchilla, there is no HIV/AIDS medical doctor;

- Women who are HIV-positive or who have full-blown AIDS get no routine exams or clinical follow-up;

- There is a waiting time of several months to see a gynecologist at Chowchilla, and women with level-four pap smears are not receiving follow-up care;

- Conditions at the newest women's prison, Valley State Prison for Women (VSP) are even worse. VSP has fewer medical services and its Security Housing Unit has been used to lock down women with full-blown AIDS and other serious illnesses.

NOTES

1. National Lawyers Guild Prison Law Project, letter to the editor, *San Francisco Daily Journal*, November 9, 1995.

2. Camille and Henry Camp, *Corrections Yearbook 1992*, (South Salem, NY: Criminal Justice Institute), January 1, 1994.

3. *Prison Conditions in the United States*, (Washington, DC: Human Rights Watch), 1991, pp. 38-42.

4. For further information regarding this uprising (and prison conditions in general) see *Prison News Service*, especially no. 37, September/October 1992.

5. *Young vs. Quinlan*, 960 F.2d 351 (3rd Cir. 1992).

6. For further details, see Steve J. Martin and Sheldon Ekland-Olson, *Texas Prisons: The Walls Came Tumbling Down*, (Austin: Texas Monthly Press), 1987.

7

THE PRISON DISCIPLINE STUDY

Exposing the Myth of Humane Imprisonment in the United States

In 1990-91, to assess the extent and dimensions of severe discipline in contemporary prison settings, the Prison Discipline Study (PDS) distributed a questionnaire nationally to prison administrators, guards, prisoners, and prisoners' visitors and families. There were 15 multiple choice questions concerning issues related to custody levels, disciplinary housing, severe punishment and demographic information. Additional comments were also encouraged.

For distribution, the PDS relied on channels trusted by prisoners that were completely independent of prison administrations or government. The Study meets standard academic criteria for significance in social research.

In spite of both covert and overt intimidation by prison administrations against those responding, we received 650 responses from 41 states: 31 percent from California, 29 percent from the South, 19 percent from the Midwest, 12 percent from the East, and 9 percent from the Northwest. The typical respondent was a longtime prisoner in a maximum security prison (see Table 1, p. 93).

Findings

The central findings of the PDS are: 1) severe physical and psychological abuse are the norm in maximum security prisons throughout the country; and 2) the most frequently disciplined groups of prisoners are jailhouse lawyers, Black prisoners, and prisoners with mental handicaps. There is no significant variation by state or region. (See Tables 2 through 5, pp. 95, 96.)

Jailhouse lawyers help other prisoners, many of whom are illiterate, to participate in formal grievance and appeal procedures both within the prison and in the courts. Hundreds of respondents commented that the internal justice system in all prisons is arbitrary, biased, and inconsistent, thus generating constant grounds for administrative and legal challenge. Respondents observed that because of this, guards and administrators have a standard practice of "singling out jailhouse lawyers" for discipline in retaliation for challenging the status quo. Individual comments also verified the well-known racist nature of a criminal justice system that sentences disproportionate numbers of Blacks to disproportionately longer and harsher (e.g., death penalty) sentences as well as to more severe discipline within the prison. And because they are inappropriately placed, and don't receive suitable treatment, prisoners with mental handicaps represent management problems for guards, who abuse them as a result. Injury is added to abuse with the frequent practice of housing those who are unstable and disturbed with other prisoners as a method of punishing those prisoners who guards dislike.

Table 1
CHARACTERISTICS OF SAMPLE (605 respondents)

Characteristic	% of sample	Characteristic	% of sample
Status		*Type of Facility Reported On*	
Guard	0.2	Minimum-security	3.3
Administrator	0.5	Medium-security	14.2
Prisoner	93.7	Maximum-security	66.1
Visitor	1.2	Control unit	6.9
Family member	2.0	Psychiatric unit	2.9
Expert observer	0.8	Medical unit	4.7
Lawyer	1.6	County jail	4.7
		Juvenile facility	0.3
Years of Observing Prison Routine			
Less than 1 year	2.8		
1 to 3 years	16.8		
4 to 10 years	50.3		
More than 10 years	30.1		

The data showed that solitary confinement, loss of privileges, and physical beatings constitute a definable "package" of disciplinary activities within the various prisons. Table 2 (p. 95) reveals that these beatings are performed in a combination of ways. That is, multiple methods of corporal punishment are employed. Foremost among these are the use of fists, boots, and clubs (in that order).

About 100 respondents indicated that they have witnessed beatings after a prisoner has been restrained with handcuffs or steel shackles. Another 40 testified that guards performed a "body slam" (i.e., being thrown to the floor or against a wall face first) after prisoners have been cuffed behind the back. Another 30 respondents reported seeing "goon squad" beatings (i.e., a formal or informal group of guards assaulting a single, often handcuffed, prisoner). Methods of severe physical beatings were reported to include the use of mace, tear gas, Tasers, fire hoses, flashlights, riot batons, mop handles, rubber hoses, and wooden bullet guns.

A total of 25 of the female respondents also attested to either being beaten, raped, or restrained to a bed naked and sexually ridiculed by male guards. One female prisoner testified that she lost her baby after guards shot her with a stun gun.

Fifty-seven respondents reported "hidden" physical abuse. Methods used included setting up fights between prisoners by housing known enemies in the same cell or releasing enemies at the same time to a public area (called "dog fights" or "cock fights" by the guards). Also, prisoners are beaten in their cells or assigned to security housing areas for the purpose of administering a beating away from the view of others. Others complained of being forced to do hard labor while sick or infirm.

Table 4 (p. 96) indicates that the frequency of mental discipline is nearly the same as the frequency of physical beatings. Only 10 percent of the sample has never witnessed such discipline. The remaining 90 percent verified that it does occur, mostly on a routine basis. Among the various methods of mental discipline examined in the study, nearly 40 percent of the sample witnessed prisoners receiving involuntary psychiatric treatment or medication. And nearly a third (32 percent) attested to incidents involving verbal abuses and racial slurs, food tampering, frequent unnecessary shakedowns and body searches, false write-ups, and death threats.

Severe psychological abuse is at the very core of incarceration with the purpose being to "beat people down." Most respondents reported that an environment permeated by "mind games" can be the most debilitating part of imprisonment. A longtime prison visitor summarized the common experiences of prisoners by saying:

Physical abuse has a beginning and end, while psychological abuse is all-pervasive. It affects everything done, every decision. Even those who want to stay out of trouble are deeply affected often to immobility over measuring every little detail of an interaction: a glance, a new routine, a letter a day late, a refused appointment, a change in the diet tray, a comment about the mail. Every small encounter may have multiple meanings and serious disciplinary repercussions.

The study reveals that there are multiple behaviors that bring about severe disciplinary action (see Table 6, p. 97). The leading causes are: 1) prisoners being verbally hostile to guards; and 2) prisoners refusing to follow orders. It is important to note that the leading "cause" of severe discipline—being verbally hostile to guards—is considered only a minor security infraction in most correctional institutions throughout the United States (Bureau of Justice Statistics [BJS], 1989). It is also important to note that physical beatings are not a formally sanctioned punishment for rule violations in any U.S. prison system (BJS, 1989). Hence, prisoners are most likely to endure severe punishment—including illicit beatings—for personal, nonviolent (and otherwise petty) verbal responses to prison guards.

Table 2	
FREQUENCY OF PRISONERS RECEIVING BEATINGS BY STAFF (583 respondents)	
Frequency	**% of Sample Observing**
Never	10.7
Rarely (once per year)	14.1
Occasionally (one time per month)	34.5
Routinely (as a matter of common practice)	10.7

Table 3	
METHODS USED IN PHYSICAL BEATINGS OF PRISONERS BY STAFF (467 Respondents)	
Method	**% of Sample Observing**
Fists	86.7
Boots	70.7
Clubs	66.6
Stun Guns (Tasers, etc.)	25.1
Other	35.3

Table 4

FREQUENCY OF PRISONERS RECEIVING MENTAL DISCIPLINE BY STAFF
(533 respondents)

Frequency	% of Sample Observing
Never	10.6
Rarely (once per year)	6.4
Occasionally (one time per month)	11.4
Routinely (as a matter of common practice)	71.6

Table 5

MOST FREQUENTLY DISCIPLINED GROUPS OF PRISONERS
(567 respondents)

Group	% of Sample Observing
Jailhouse lawyers	60.8
Black prisoners	48.5
Prisoners with mental handicaps	37.9
Gang members	31.0
Political prisoners	29.8
Latino/a prisoners	27.0
Gays/Lesbians	26.6
White prisoners	22.6
AIDS patients	19.9
Prisoners with physical handicaps	18.7
Asian prisoners	5.1

A review of the comments from respondents revealed another category of people who are singled out for severe discipline with great frequency. These people can best be described as exhibiting personal integrity: "those with principles or intelligence;" "those with dignity and self-respect;" "authors of truthful articles;" "motivated self-improvers;" "verbally expressing one's opinion;" "wanting to be treated as a human being;" "reporting conditions to people on the outside." Those who respond to their environment based on internal criteria and/or file grievances, lawsuits, or think for themselves, or are different or the wrong color, are singled out for harassment, abuse, and punishment.

Table 6
BEHAVIORS BRINGING ABOUT SEVERE DISCIPLINARY ACTION
(566 respondents)

Behavior	% of Sample Ovserving
Being verbally hostile to guards	68.9
Refusing to follow orders	61.7
Violating prison rules	50.5
Fighting with other prisoners	45.8
Objecting to cell changes	39.0
Possession of contraband	35.5
Refusing to take psychiatric medication	22.8

Table 7
PREVALENCE OF DISCIPLINE (576 respondents)

Type of Discipline	% of Sample Observing
Solitary confinement	72.7
Loss of privileges	71.4
Physical beatings	70.8
Mental discipline	49.7

Table 8
TIME SPENT IN SOLITARY CONFINEMENT

Maximum Time Spent	% of Sample Observing
Hours	0.8
Days	2.8
Weeks	6.7
Months	26.3
Years	63.2

Summary

Over the past 50 years the image of a humane American prison has become the conventional wisdom among academics, government officials, and the public. The central findings of the Prison Discipline Study shatter this myth.

The myth holds that there is a distinct temporal ordering to severe prison discipline: prisoners make unprovoked attacks against guards, who respond with a judicious level of (high-tech) discipline designed only to force rule-compliance and preserve prison security.

There is nothing arbitrary, frequent, or brutal about it. It is all done in a professional manner by alienated prison guards. This is the corner-stone of the myth of humane imprisonment, and rests on the lack of serious investigation into prisoners' actual experiences. The PDS has examined reports from prisoners and found that severe discipline is frequent, and is delivered for petty violations in a discriminatory fashion most often to punish those who are literate, Black, or able to fight back.

Mainstream penology holds that the beating of prisoners by guards is a rare occurrence in modern prison communities. Yet Table 7 (p. 97) shows that more than seven out of ten respondents (70.8 percent) have in fact witnessed such beatings. Notably, Table 7 also shows that almost the same percentage of prisoners have witnessed solitary confinement and loss of privileges as routine forms of prison discipline. Solitary confinement is described in the academic literature as the most individually destructive, psychologically crippling, and socially alienating experience that could conceivably exist within the borders of the country. Researchers have recorded signs of severe psychological pathology among prisoners who are incarcerated in solitary for periods up to a year. The myth of imprisonment holds that 20 days of continuous punitive segregation is the maximum. As our data shows, the maximum amount of time most commonly spent in solitary confinement is not 20 days; rather it is more likely to be periods of months and most commonly years (see Table 8, p. 97).

Today over 40 percent of the U. S. adult prison population are confined to maximum-security institutions (American Correctional Association, 1989). Maximum-security prisons are not intended for rehabilitation; rather, they are intended to be punitive, and are viewed as prisons of last resort. Prisoners are increasingly given long sentences, housed in high-security prisons and even higher security (and more brutal) units within these prisons, and warehoused without rehabilitative opportunities. The excessive physical and mental punishment documented in the PDS completes the present picture of imprisonment in the United States.

The injury suffered by prisoners results in the destruction of the very social behaviors and personality traits required for successful reintegration into society. The consequence is that the communities from which prisoners come and to which almost all will return are adversely affected. These mostly poor and minority communities must receive and cope with ex-prisoners who are often in worse shape than before incarceration. Thus, our prisons damage the very communities in our society that need more support, renewal, and rehabilitation. The brutality documented in our prisons reaches out into every home and workplace in the United States, changing our lives in dramatic and significant ways.

8

LEGISLATING REPRESSION

The Federal Crime Bill and the Anti-Terrorism and Effective Death Penalty Act

C. Stone Brown

Crime, whether real or imagined, serves a variety of interests in U.S. society. Crime is a commodity that gets politicians elected, creates millions of jobs, and yields enormous profits to news media conglomerates, who compete to report the most heinous crimes. Television, especially, is Washington's propaganda dispenser. And to keep the public from rejecting draconian legislation such as the Violent Crime Control and Law Enforcement Act of 1994 and the Anti-Terrorism and Effective Death Penalty Act of 1996, the public was forcefed a dosage of tabloid crimes that would convince them to not only accept but embrace such legislation—even if that meant forfeiting basic constitutional rights.

For many, the Violent Crime Control and Law Enforcement Act of 1994 (known as the Crime Bill) represents one victory in the continuing battle to counter the supposed escalation of crime over the past three decades. This reasoning suits the interests of lawmakers who use crime as an election springboard. However, it contradicts reality. As David Burnham points out in his book *Above the Law*, "during the whole twenty-year period that presidents from Nixon to Clinton were agitating the public about the national crime menace, the best available evidence shows American people were actually experiencing less and less crime."[1] If crime rates have actually been decreasing over the past 30 years, then why is the United States incarcerating more people (1.5 million) than ever before? One answer to that question can be found within the provisions of the Crime Bill legislation.

The Crime Bill

The Crime Bill, one of the most significant pieces of legislation to be passed in this decade, will roll back rights and restrict liberty well into the 21st century. Take, for instance, the Crime Bill initiatives pushed through by House and Senate Republicans. House Bill HR 666, nicknamed "The Beast," handcuffs the Fourth Amendment by allowing evidence seized in an illegal search to be used in criminal proceedings. HR 666 permits the police to search your property without a warrant under protection of a "good faith" rule: if the police think they *could have* obtained a warrant, an exception will be made. Have law enforcement officers exhibited behavior in the past that would reasonably lead the public to believe that they would act in "good faith"? Ironically, the bill itself lacks good faith, since it uses a double standard; this law is enforced in drug cases, but not in cases involving gun trafficking or tax crimes.

The passage of Senate Bill S3 is even more damaging to the Fourth Amendment. Bill S3 severely restricts civil remedies for illegal searches and completely removes the exclusionary rule. If one of the federal law enforcement agencies (such as the Federal Bureau of Investigation; Alcohol, Tobacco, and Firearms; or the Drug Enforcement Administration) steamrolls its way into your home without a warrant, handcuffs you, assaults you and your family, and finds no evidence of criminal activity—tough luck.

The largest single allocation in the Violent Crime Control and Law Enforcement Act of 1994 is for prison construction, which has little to do with crime prevention, revealing the true motives of the bill's sponsors. Apparently the idea of crime prevention is not a viable alternative for the authors of the Crime Bill—even though it would cost society a great deal less. The Grants for Prison Construction Based on Truth-in-Sentencing (Title V) authorizes $10.5 billion to be spent in rising increments over six years ($232 million in 1995, $997.5 million in 1996, $1.3 billion in 1997, $2.5 billion in 1998, $2.7 billion in 1999, and $2.8 billion in 2000). The Crime Bill is intended to increase the growth of prison construction, not decrease crime. Crime Bill statisticians have obviously used computer models to project the growth of crime rates beyond the year 2000, and to ensure that none of the buildings constructed with our $10.5 billion will be vacant, the Crime Bill establishes more stringent laws and longer sentencing. Furthermore, since job training, education, anti-violence counseling, and other rehabilitative services don't promote prison construction, very little of the Crime Bill funds were allocated for these activities.

Three Strikes

Baseball and crime are as American as apple pie, and if used with political skill, both can be expected to yield substantial votes in the political arena. The legislative marriage of crime and baseball was an inevitable union in a nation that leads the world in incarcerating its citizens. For Washington politicians, a Willie Horton-type advertising pitch can garner the same amount of votes as throwing out the first pitch on baseball's opening day.

The "Three Strikes, You're Out" law is yet another legislative gimmick that is supposed to make people feel safer through the questionable means of putting repeat offenders in jail for life, without regard for the seriousness of the crime. In reality, this law clogs state court systems with petty cases and condemns more nonviolent offenders to life sentences.

Unfortunately, the public swallowed the Three Strikes pill before considering what the side effects might be. While Three Strikes advocates claimed that the legislation would take criminals off the streets, with the massive influx of new convicts, thousands of non-felons had to be released instead. In addition, one criminologist noted, "We are finding people willing to die in a gun fight with cops, rather than spend their life in prison."[2] Indeed, this is no game for officers who find that suspects with two strikes are often "three" times as tough to apprehend for the third strike. Since the third strike will put them in jail for life, they have nothing to lose by killing police officers to evade justice. Far from decreasing violent crime, Three Strikes is likely to escalate it.

Another false deference to the need for public safety is the allocation of funds to place 100,000 new police officers on U.S. streets. The thought of having 100,000 new officers on the streets is very comforting to certain segments of the public. Of course, the word "street" is political code language for "urban crime," which is the true target of the Crime Bill and the focus of crime hype—overlooking the crimes of corporate and suburban America. It is in the low-income neighborhoods of U.S. cities that the majority of added police presence will be felt. However, more police officers won't necessarily equal less crime; as far back as the first Kerner Commission Report on Urban Civil Disorders (1968),[3] studies have shown that increased police presence often leads to an escalation in criminal activity, which invariably leads to a cycle of more arrests and more jails. Which brings us back to the motive of the sponsors of Three Strikes laws: prison construction.

Countering Terrorism

The Oklahoma City and World Trade Center bombings—and the media furor that surrounded them—gave birth to U.S. "terrornoia." Suddenly the possibility of large-scale terrorist activity, long since a reality in Europe and other parts of the world, had made its way to America's doorstep. Tragedies in and of themselves, these events also fostered a climate that allowed legislators apparent free rein to create laws that would erode rights provided for under the U.S. Constitution.

At the signing of the Anti-Terrorism Act, President Clinton remarked:

> From now on, we can quickly expel foreigners who dare to come to America and support terrorist activities. From now on, American prosecutors can wield new tools and expanded penalties against those who terrorize Americans at home and abroad. From now on, we can stop terrorists from raising money in the United States to pay for their horrible crimes. From now on, criminals sentenced to death for their vicious crimes will no longer be able to use endless appeals to delay their sentences, and families of victims will no longer have to endure years of anguish and suffering.[4]

The president's comments were obvious allusions to the bombings in Oklahoma and New York, and spoke to his desire to prevent such tragedies from ever happening again (the supposed purpose of his counter-terrorism legislation). The word "counter" was undoubtedly used in the Crime Bill for its presumptive connotation; the label positions the United States as a victim, rather than as an aggressor, its true status. The notion of the United States passing legislation to "counter" terrorism is a cruel political joke for many people and nations around the world.

In *Triumph of the Market*, Edward Herman observes:

> In the mainstream paradigm, the West is the victim of terrorism because of its openness and the envy and hatred of the subversive forces of the world (Saddam Hussein and Iraq, Muammar Qadaffi and Libya, and, in the Evil Empire years and the vision of Ronald Reagan... the Soviet Union).[5]

The sponsors of the Anti-Terrorism Act recognized the power this deceptive phrase has to gain public support. Like the passage of the Crime Bill, signing the Anti-Terrorism and Effective Death Penalty Act of 1996 (once known as the Omnibus Counter-Terrorism Act of 1995) into law was dependent on the effectiveness of the propaganda campaign waged on the public.

In marked contrast to the media hysteria that followed both bombings, the passage of the 1996 Anti-Terrorism Act received suspiciously little media fanfare. This is especially troubling considering the threat this act poses to bedrock principles upon which the First, Fifth, and Sixth Amendments stand. The Anti-Terrorism Act allows the government to activate "alien terrorist removal procedures" without having to give even a nod to due process—a clear violation of the Fifth Amendment. Furthermore, despite the fundamental Sixth Amendment right of the accused to confront their accusers and any evidence presented against them, under this act, non-citizens can be accused, tried, and deported without ever appearing in court. In fact, this law allows the government to avoid even informing the accused that an investigation or "trial" took place.

As if this were not frightening enough, the Anti-Terrorism Act also relaxes electronic surveillance laws, expanding the government's ability to investigate (spy on) groups or organizations the government "suspects" of terrorism. Moreover, the bill grants the president sweeping new powers to selectively target unpopular domestic groups, as well as arbitrarily criminalize activities he or she determines a threat to national security.

In February 1995, approximately 10 weeks after the Oklahoma bombing (and well after it was known that "Islamic fanatics" had nothing to do with the attack), President Clinton issued Executive Order 12947. This order, later attached to the Anti-Terrorism Act, bars all financial transactions with at least 12 Middle East groups officially designated as terrorist organizations, and prohibits U.S. citizens from providing these groups with even humanitarian support. It also provides the Secretary of State with the power to selectively add an unlimited number of other organizations (domestic or international) at his or her discretion, without any formal review.

Executive Order 12947 also permits the Justice Department to request physical searches (under the authorization of the Federal Intelligence Surveillance Act [FISA] Court) without ever obtaining a search warrant in open court. This "secret court" has the power to authorize electronic surveillance within the United States in the name of national security, and while previously any evidence collected by FISA mandate could not be used in criminal court, Clinton's executive order has relaxed this restriction.

How will Executive Order 12947 affect domestic political activism? Presidential executive orders are not up for public review, and consequently are often abused by the administrations that issue them. As recently as 1981, the Reagan administration implemented a series of secret executive orders that made it easier for the government to meet its Central American foreign policy objectives. And these objectives led to the maiming, and slaughter of innocent people. The Reagan administration's repression of the Committee in Solidarity with the People of El Salvador (CISPES) is one example of how the government can abuse power by selectively targeting groups or organizations that oppose its policy objectives. In *Break-ins, Death Threats, and the FBI,* Ross Gelbspan notes:

> The FBI requested and won approval from the Justice Department to launch an investigation into CISPES on grounds that it was representing a hostile power—the Salvadoran FMLN [Farabundo Marti National Liberation Front] rebels—and, as such, had violated the Foreign Agents' Registration Act. That was the beginning of a massive FBI operation which targeted more than one thousand domestic political groups—and hundreds of thousands of citizens—opposed to the president's policies in Central America.[6]

Executive Order 12947, signed into law by Bill Clinton, mirrors such operations from the Reagan-Bush era. It seeks to stamp out any activism that counters the administration's domestic and foreign policy objectives.

The Death Penalty

Under the Crime Bill, 60 new offenses are punishable by death, including terrorist homicides; murder of a federal law enforcement official; and large-scale drug trafficking, drive-by shootings, and carjackings that result in death. The bill also calls for the death penalty for large-scale, continuous drug enterprise offenses, even if no death resulted.

The death penalty provisions of the Crime Bill not only extend capital punishment crimes, but remove basic constitutional due process. They threaten to create "assembly-line" executions by placing strict limitations on *habeas corpus appeals in federal court. Advocates of the death* penalty have argued that capital punishment is ineffective as a deterrent because the time between arrest, conviction, and execution is too long. Supposedly in order to turn the death penalty into an "effective deterrent," the sponsors of the Crime Bill and other repressive legislation have targeted habeas corpus.

The *habeas corpus* remedy has been available to federal prisoners in this country since the Judiciary Act of 1789. *Habeas corpus* commands the government to "bring the body" that is under custody before the court, and establish to a neutral and detached legal tribunal that the prisoner's sentence or incarceration is lawful. For those who oppose the death penalty, and for innocent convicts who await execution, *habeas corpus* is the last line of defense from the executioner. The Crime Bill death penalty provisions mandate that convicted defendants are prevented from having meaningful independent federal court review on claims of wrongful conviction or sentencing. For instance, the new law limits prisoners on Death Row to a single federal appeal, which must be filed within six months after the state appellate process has expired. Furthermore, it prohibits federal judges from granting appeals unless they find that the state court acted "unreasonably." It is conceivable under this legislation that a defendant could be executed without getting even one appeal in federal court. This will certainly increase the chances that an innocent person will be executed.

We are taught that U.S. laws have been written to match the penalty to the crime, and to protect the innocent from prosecution. The appeals process in death penalty cases are in place for this reason; the public and the courts want to be absolutely certain that the state is executing the right person. By reducing the number of appeals and all but destroying *habeas corpus*, the federal Crime Bill virtually eliminates our basic constitutional right to due process.

The Anti-Terrorism and Effective Death Penalty Act attempts to finish the job the Crime Bill started. Under this act, prisoners are prevented from submitting a second or successive petition unless they first receive permission from a three-judge panel of the Court of Appeals. And even the Court of Appeals is bound to specific exceptions to a general rule established by Congress for granting petitions. At the time of this writing, the Supreme Court was set to hear a case that would challenge the constitutionality of the Anti-Terrorism Act's *habeas corpus* provisions. *Felker v. Turpin*, a Georgia death penalty case, will question the circumstances under which a state prisoner will be able to file a second or successive *habeas corpus* petition. It is likely that although certain provisions of the act will stand, making it extremely difficult for prisoners to appeal, other provisions will be stricken as unconstitutional.

Many legal observers and progressive activists are asking what "terrorism" (by definition a federal crime) has to do with the right of *state* prisoners to appeal their convictions. The answer must be—nothing at all. One can only conclude that the *habeas corpus* reform provisions of the Anti-Terrorism Act aren't intended to prevent terrorism, but to prevent state prisoners from exercising their constitutional right to due process.

The public is quick to call for a tougher stance on crime, but slower to understand the consequences of such a stance. Under the Crime Bill and the Anti-Terrorism Act, evidence illegally seized can now be used in court, prison construction is touted as the best approach to reducing crime, and immigrants can be accused of a crime and deported without even knowing a trial took place. These are just a few of the consequences of "getting tough on crime." Is this what the public voted for? Before being so hasty to demand harsher legislative solutions to crime, we should remember Benjamin Franklin's warning: "They that can give up essential liberty to obtain a little temporary safety deserve neither liberty nor freedom."[7]

NOTES

1. Quoted by Bruce Shapiro, "How the War on Crime Imprisons America," *The Nation*, April 22, 1996, p. 20.
2. Christopher Reed, "Three Strikes and You're Out: Anti-Crime Measure Could Cost Millions to Implement," *The Guardian*, October 13, 1995, p. 5.
3. Report of the National Advisory Commission on Civil Disorders, *The Kerner Report*, (New York: Bantam Books), 1968.
4. White House Briefing, April 24, 1996, *Federal News Service*.
5. Edward Herman, *Triumph of the Market*, (Boston: South End Press), 1995, p. 153.
6. Ross Gelbspan, *Break-ins, Death Threats and the FBI*, (Boston: South End Press), 1991, p. 21.
7. Quoted by William M. Kunstler and Phillip Smith, "Mugging the Fourth," *CovertAction Quarterly*, Summer 1995, p. 54.

9

RESISTANCE AT LEXINGTON

Laura Whitehorn

From August 12 to 14, 1992, the first sustained act of resistance in 20 years by women imprisoned in the u.s. federal prison system took place. On Wednesday night, August 12, there was an argument between two prisoners in the central yard area ("Central Park"), at about 8:30 p.m. It was over quickly, and everyone was walking away, towards the housing units, because we have to be inside at 9:00 p.m. A lieutenant came running over to see what had happened. He yelled, "Hey, you! Stop!" When no one stopped, he grabbed the first Black woman he saw, lifted her in the air, and body-slammed her to the ground. Other women yelled at him that she wasn't even involved in the argument, but he kept on attacking her. Then he dragged her to her feet, and another guard took her to the lieutenant's office.

About 100 women witnessed this attack. They were all very upset by it, and gathered to talk to the captain. At 9:00 p.m., all but about 15 returned to their housing units, after being assured that the beaten woman would be released back into general population, and that a thorough investigation would be undertaken.

This was not the first instance of physical brutality at Lexington—nor, certainly, of racism. The male guards have been putting their hands on us more and more—both in frequent pat searches, and whenever they want us to move, or to stop, or whatever. This particular lieutenant had threatened several women with brutality. The normally high level of racism had also recently heightened, following the L.A. verdict and the uprisings there. Several Black women who had complained of prejudice had been put in the hole for "inciting to riot."

But this time, it all struck a nerve. On Thursday, word traveled: don't go in at 4:00 p.m. (the major daily "standing count" throughout the Bureau of Prisons [BOP]). Stay out in Central Park and demand that the women be released from the hole and the lieutenant suspended.

At 3:50 p.m., when the hourly "movement" began, the scene in Central Park was tense and exciting. Usually, it's rush hour—1,900 women, in the largest women's prison in the world [this is now surpassed by California's Chowchilla prisons, which confine more than 5,700 women.—E.R.], rushing to the units to try to get a few things done before the 4:00 p.m. count. On this Thursday, instead, it was like gridlock: everyone moved slowly, if at all, waiting to see what would happen.

At 4:00 p.m., a guard made an announcement ordering us all to go inside for a count. Many did, but 90 of us stayed out, and moved into the center of the Park. We sang Bob Marley's "Stand Up for Your Rights," and chanted "Stop Police Brutality," "We Want Justice," "Let Them Out of Seg," and "Figueroa (the lieutenant) Must Go." Ringed by guards—including a SORT (SWAT) team in full regalia—we demanded to speak to the captain. While we demonstrated, we heard shouts of support from the windows of the housing units, and at least two "all available officers" codes to different units—meaning that the women who had returned to the units for count were doing some kind of support actions, too.

We had to shout the captain down when he finally came to talk to us because he was telling too many lies. Finally, he said that the lieutenant would be back at work on Monday, and we all knew there was no point in any further discussion. We were handcuffed and escorted to segregation—most of us were taken to the old High Security Unit, which has been out of use almost entirely since the BOP was forced to close it in 1988. Seven women to a cell, no blankets, no water—it was payback time.

The next day, 12 of us were chained up and taken out on a bus to Marianna, Florida (the new women's high-security unit). As each of us was taken out of the prison, the whole place was locked down. But it was midday, so there were over 100 women in Central Park on their lunch breaks. As each of us was escorted through the Park, we were cheered—loudly, enthusiastically, joyfully—by everyone there.

I've since learned that while we were in transit to Marianna, a smaller group of women repeated the action in Central Park at 4:00 p.m. on Friday. There were also quite a few small fires set in various housing units during the night. And a number of women were shipped out to FCI-Dublin (California) after we 12 were shipped to Marianna.

For a few bright moments, we felt free. As we moved into Central Park, defying the daily grinding regulations and control of prison life, we were liberated from the fear that holds prisoners in check. We had the power of justice on our side and in our eyes as we looked at one another.

The most common thing you hear people say at Lexington is "If men (prisoners—the place used to be co-ed) were here, the police wouldn't get away with this. Women don't stick together, so the prison can put anything they want on us."

But we proved that's not true. The racism and brutality that go down every day just didn't go down on this day. We'd had enough, and we trusted and respected ourselves and one another enough to stand up together. The demonstration was international—inspired primarily by Jamaican, Haitian, and African-American women, it was joined by Latina women and some white women as well. It was clear, for once, that if the police could continue to attack Black women (as they do every day—for example, at any given time the hole holds more Black women than any other nationality), then no one could be safe.

Anger is a constant reality in prison, and the entire prison system is designed to ensure that anger is turned inward, to destroy one's own self-respect and humanity, instead of being turned outward towards the system and the oppressors. It took courage to resist all that, in the context of the total control, abuse and disrespect of women that constitutes women's prison. We had to trust one another, that we would not be standing out there alone. As we looked around at one another, we knew that our demonstration was a victory, no matter what punishment might follow. A small flame of power, sisterhood, and dignity had been rekindled.

10

BUILDING BRIDGES

Lin Elliot

To be Queer in prison is to be silenced. Incarcerated Lesbians, Gay men, Bisexuals, and other Queer people receive no positive support for our identities. At the very best, we are ignored; more often we are subject to abuse and violence from other inmates and to harassment and discrimination by staff. We are constantly bombarded by the compulsory heterosexuality of television, novels, religious literature, and mainstream "men's magazines" that are readily available inside, while Queer-oriented material (whether erotic zines or community newspapers) is frequently banned as "a threat to the orderly operation of the institution."

Furthermore, we are left with no outlet at all for our sexuality. Even in states such as here in Washington—where there are no laws against homosexuality—consensual sex between prisoners is against prison rules and can result in severe punishment, even loss of "good time," thereby extending a person's sentence. (Indeed, prison officials seem to draw no distinction between consensual acts and sexual assault: I have seen men receive the same punishment for making love in the privacy of their cells that other inmates received for forceful rapes.) And where straight prisoners often have access to conjugal visits, especially if they are married, Queer relationships are given no such recognition. A Lesbian or Gay couple who have been together for many years will be denied the comfort available to any straight "marriage of convenience."

Prisoners as a group are among the least considered and most powerless people in our society, a fact that has become increasingly important as the United States has embarked on an orgy of prison construction that is truly unprecedented. The "land of the free" now imprisons a larger percentage of its population than any other country in the world. And, while accurate figures on the number of incarcerated Queers are not available, my own experience, both as a prisoner and an organizer, suggests we are represented far out of proportion to our percentage of the general population.

By far the most painful aspect of being a Queer prisoner is that we often find ourselves doubly silenced—not just by society at large, but in our own communities as well. Several years ago I was in the county jail awaiting sentencing at the time of the Seattle-area Pride March. I very much wanted to be involved and to express my solidarity with my siblings on our own special day. So I wrote a short message explaining why I couldn't attend and asking the community to remember Queer prisoners when they marched. I sent my piece to the Pride organizers, hoping that it could be used in the Pride program. Apparently not. I never received any response at all.

Soon after that, I started working, along with several dedicated friends "outside," to create The League of Lesbian and Gay Prisoners (LLGP), a network of people concerned with the special problems of incarcerated Queers. Our goal was to make it possible for prisoners to be more involved in, and contribute to, the community, and to build some bridges across the isolation that prisons inevitably create.

Needless to say, it isn't easy. The nature of "correctional" systems works against us. Despite rhetoric about the value of maintaining ties to the community, I have never encountered a prison where the rules governing mail, phone calls, and visitation didn't seem deliberately designed to complicate outside relationships to the point of extinction.

Day-to-day life in prison differs radically from the experience of friends on the street, which can create a sense of disconnection even between people who are in close contact. And incarceration creates such an imbalance of power—financially, psychologically, emotionally—that despite everyone's best intentions, it can be nearly impossible to create and sustain positive across-the-wall connections. Positive action on both sides is necessary to restore the balance.

Following a forum on prison issues that LLGP put on for Queer Nation/Seattle—the presentation was a collaboration between a prisoner, an ex-prisoner, and a non-prisoner—an activist friend gave me some advice. "What you need to do," she suggested, "is offer us some concrete example of what we can do. After all, it's not like you're asking me to recruit voters, which is something that has been done before. For most of us, building bridges between inside and out is a new idea." So, what I would like to do is to briefly sketch what I believe to be the most important areas for collaboration between prisons and the larger Lesbian and Gay community, and try to suggest why I believe this collaboration is not only possible, but urgently necessary.

- *Challenging Discrimination*. It is no accident that the groups most responsible for the recent backlash against Queers on the outside are also very active in prison. Fundamentalist churches, groups like the Aryan Nation, the racist skinheads, and other hate groups are all willing to reach out to prisoners (and quite often to staff as well). It's ironic that the more liberal political and religious groups, which are supposedly founded on inclusive principles, seem for the most part absent from prisons. This represents a tremendous loss for progressive causes. America's prisons are a vast untapped reservoir of talent, commitment, and experience—the waste of human potential that they represent is terrifying. Certainly, in this day and age we can't afford to let ourselves be divided.

   I would like to see groups and coalitions working against hate groups and neo-fascists on the streets make a positive effort to link up with progressive prisoners, to help us resist the brainwashing and recruiting that goes on in the prisons, and that often serves the administration's goal of keeping prisoners separated from each other and preventing organized resistance. Outside groups would benefit from increased knowledge of how hate groups function, and prisoners would gain support and positive connections with the community.

- *AIDS Education/Prevention*. Statistics show that prisoners with AIDS live, on average, half as long as people with AIDS (PWAs) on the streets. In New York State, AIDS is already the leading cause of death among prisoners, and estimates on the percentage of the population that might be HIV-positive are horrifying. The fact that a large proportion of prisoners are, or have been, intravenous drug users is in itself reason for serious concern.

   And yet, prison administrators continue to favor a speak-no-evil/see-no-evil policy (reminiscent of the Catholic church). Since consensual sex, drug use, tattooing, etc. are universally against prison rules, administrators refuse to allow—with some rare exceptions—any open discussion of safe sex, needle exchanges, or other proven methods for controlling the spread of the virus.

   In addition to this, medical care in prisons tends to be very poor, and ignorance and fear among staff often lead to HIV-positive inmates being neglected or abused. Nutrition is substandard, and close living conditions make inmates very susceptible to exposure to opportunistic infections. Very few states have any sort of compassionate release program for terminally-ill inmates.

A number of groups in various areas have come together to support prison AIDS activists. In Toronto, the Prisoner's AIDS/HIV Survival and Activists Network (PASAN) has created a comprehensive program for dealing with AIDS in prison and presented it to the Canadian government. This brief calls for mandatory education for all inmates and staff, condom distribution and needle exchanges, confidential testing and counseling by outside agencies, access to adequate medical care including experimental treatments and clinical drug tests, and compassionate release procedures. Beyond these specific points, however, the PASAN plan is a total strategy of the sort that the government should have initiated years ago. It should be a starting point for all prison AIDS work.

Coalitions like PASAN and ACT-UP also provide a workable model for prisoner/non-prisoner alliances to deal with other issues of mutual concern. As in any work where the goal is the empowerment of an oppressed group, guidance must come from the prisoners themselves—from our knowledge of the reality of life in America's prisons.

Building bridges between prisoners and the community is a necessary process of challenging the exclusivity of our culture, and building a new kind of community based on acceptance—where hopefully, someday, there will be no need for cages or walls.

11

PRISONERS RESPOND TO AIDS

Judy Greenspan

In the 1960s, inspired by the Black Power movement and struggles for independence and self-determination in Vietnam and elsewhere, a fledgling and defiant prisoner-led rights movement emerged behind the walls of jails and prisons throughout this country. The demands of this movement echoed the demonstrations, political upheavals, and rebellions taking place in the streets at the time.

Unfortunately, in the decades since the '60s and '70s, the prisoners' rights movement has waned. Some of its leaders, like George Jackson, were brutally murdered by the racist prison system. Control units emerged as a tool to isolate prisoner leaders from the general prison population. Many of the organizations on the outside that had helped with legal efforts and published prisoners' newsletters no longer exist, or no longer have the staff or finances to support these struggles. As the people's movements on the outside died down, so did the organizing efforts on the inside.

The AIDS activist struggle of the 1980s, however, has given rise to a new movement behind the walls. Led by prisoners with the Human Immunodeficiency Virus (HIV) and Acquired Immune Deficiency Syndrome (AIDS), and by their supporters, prisoners have come together to combat the spread of AIDS and break the barriers of fear that surround the epidemic. The heroes and heroines of this new AIDS movement have faced enormous hurdles: hostile prison administrators; AIDS-phobic guards and medical staff; violence from other prisoners; segregation; punitive transfers; discrimination; parole turndowns; and even death.

Donald Woods, a Wisconsin prisoner with AIDS, sued the governor and the Department of Corrections for violating his confidentiality rights by divulging his HIV status to other prisoners. Two years after the lawsuit, Woods was roughed up and restrained by guards who stuffed a towel in his mouth. Woods, whose HIV status was well-known throughout the prison, died of asphyxiation later that day.

Prisoners with HIV/AIDS, peer educators, and prisoner activists on the inside have a very basic agenda—they are fighting for the right to live. They are asking for the most basic survival tools—decent medical care, compassionate release, and peer education programs. These demands are revolutionary within a prison system dedicated to custody, control, and punishment.

As the former AIDS Information Coordinator of the ACLU National Prison Project, and now a member of ACT-UP/San Francisco's Prison Issues Committee, I have worked for many years with the prisoners who are part of this movement. I have written to and visited with these heroic men and women and, when necessary, I have demonstrated outside the gates of their prisons. I have learned that AIDS activism inside takes many forms. Calling a demonstration behind the walls is extremely hazardous, so prisoners have had to utilize a variety of other tactics to accomplish their goals.

AIDS Organizing Behind the Walls

In October 1993 in San Francisco, I had an opportunity, along with other AIDS activists, to meet and talk with some of the former prisoners who are leaders of this new prisoners' rights movement. The occasion was the first National Roundtable on AIDS in Prison, organized by the Correctional Association of New York. Former prisoners had fought to be included at this conference, and we worked to maximize their voices. Their stories are crucial and need to be told.

Organizing in prison is as dangerous as being an open member of the Communist Party was during the height of the McCarthy era. Your very being is illegal. Prison administrators have only one *modus operandi* for prisoners who associate with other prisoners or with people outside in order to improve prison conditions. These prisoners are treated as subversives and/or as gang members. They are locked down, removed from public view, denied membership in inmate councils, and often transferred to maximum-security prisons or control units far from home.

For example, Brian Carmichael, a prisoner organizer at the California Medical Facility at Vacaville (California's prison hospital for men) who was working closely with ACT-UP/San Francisco, was thrown into the "hole" and charged with being a member of a gang called "ACT-UP." On its face, this incident sounds humorous, but for

Carmichael, who was to be released on parole in two months, the accusation of "gang membership" was extremely serious. Fortunately, the charges were dropped due to public exposure, by ACT-UP and others, of this ridiculous charge.

When Jimmy Magner was a federal prisoner with AIDS, he was a thorn in the side of the Federal Bureau of Prisons. He was openly gay and just as openly outspoken. While inside, Magner founded a newsletter for prisoners with HIV and AIDS called PWA-RAG (People with AIDS, Rights Advocacy Group) which has become a voice for prisoners around the country. With the support of his mother, and the assistance of individuals in such groups as the American Friends Service Committee and the ACLU National Prisoner Project, Magner was able to distribute his newsletter to prisoners and their advocates nationwide.

Due to his efforts, Magner spent a lot of time being transported from one federal prison to another—a tactic known as "diesel therapy," and one reserved for prisoner organizers. But Magner survived even incarceration at the Springfield federal prison hospital, notorious for its miserable living conditions, unlicensed physicians, and poor medical care. Jimmy Magner was released last year and continues to publish PWA-RAG from the outside.

Many prisoners fight the spread of AIDS by learning about the disease and teaching others. Prisoners routinely write away to outside AIDS service organizations for HIV/AIDS education brochures that are passed from hand to hand through the prison. Unfortunately, since the epidemic was first recognized behind the walls, prison administrators have been loath to provide educational materials at all, and what they have distributed has been filled with messages of abstinence and threats about the illegality of sex and drug use in prison, rather than practical information about protecting oneself from HIV.

Despite the recommendations of such organizations as the National Commission on AIDS and the World Health Organization, most prisons and jails do not distribute condoms or bleach, thus making it very difficult for AIDS educators to teach prisoners how to have safer sex and to clean their "works." In one prison in New Jersey, a group of prisoners ordered 1,000 copies of the Surgeon General's report on AIDS. When the brochures arrived, they were seized by hostile prison administrators, who labeled the brochures contraband (illegal) and refused to distribute them.

Prisoners, both HIV-positive and their supporters, have been forced to begin their own peer education programs with or without official sanction from the prison administration. The most successful of these programs is the AIDS Counseling and Education Program (ACE) at Bedford Hills, a women's prison in New York state. ACE was formed in the mid-'80s as a result of organizing by a few HIV-positive women, concerned HIV-negative women, and two seasoned organizers and political prisoners, Judy Clark and Kathy Boudin, both doing time at Bedford Hills. ACE flourished openly at the prison for some time, but when word of the group got to the powers-that-be in the state Department of Correctional Services, it was officially shut down.

With great perseverance and courage, the women inside Bedford Hills quietly kept the program going and did what they could to gain outside support. The Superintendent at the prison seemed to play ACE both ways, sometimes being supportive, and sometimes very controlling, targeting certain women for expulsion from the group as it gained public attention. In order to survive, ACE has had to accept some limitations in its work, but it is nevertheless recognized as a model peer education program.

Many of ACE's graduates have become AIDS educators and prisoner advocates upon release. Maria Hernandez, one of ACE's founders, helped start ACE Out, a support organization for HIV-positive women leaving Bedford Hills. Hernandez travels around the country showing the video, "I'm You, You're Me, Women Surviving Prison, Living with AIDS." Hernandez' goal is to go inside women's prisons to meet with peer educators and support groups and show the video.

Peer Education

Early attempts to set up peer education programs at men's prisons in New York state were largely unsuccessful. Prison administrators seemed to be even more threatened by the idea of men organizing around this issue than they had been by the women at Bedford Hills, in part because there are so many more men in prison than there are women. Also, because of the geographic isolation of the prisons, the activists found it nearly impossible to rally the public awareness and support that is essential for such organizing efforts. Thus, prison administrators easily clamped down on all rumored peer education projects.

Prisoner leaders, such as David Gilbert, Cruz Salgado, Juan Rivera, and Yusuf Shakur, were routinely locked down (placed in isolation) and transferred from Auburn to Attica, to Clinton, and to Eastern (all New York state prisons located hundreds of miles from major metropolitan centers) to sabotage their activities. Under the guise of "security" concerns, prisoners are often transferred to another prison without notice. The tactic can be very effective because prisoner organizers are separated from their personal belongings for weeks and sometimes months. Many of their papers, leaflets, letters, and newspapers are "lost" during these moves.

David Gilbert, now at Great Meadow prison, points out that today, six years after his first attempt, there is still no comprehensive peer education program in any of the maximum-security men's prisons in the state. He also says that support from outside has been sporadic at best. [Since this was written, Great Meadow has instituted a marginal peer education program. Gilbert is still at Great Meadow, training peer educators. Despite this progress, New York State has only eight such programs in a system of thirty-eight prisons, and is infamous for shutting down programs and locking up organizers as soon as they are seen being effective.—E.R.]

Mike Flashner, who did 17 years in Massachusetts prisons, has had more success. When he was first approached by another prisoner, Ed Marchione, about joining a campaign for AIDS education, he was reluctant. He was worried about the stigma involved with fighting the disease. However, after reading some literature and realizing how serious the epidemic was on the inside, he ran over to Marchione's housing unit to enlist in the program. According to Flashner, what other prisoners thought about him wasn't important anymore. "Saving someone from contracting this disease while doing time outweighed that philosophy," he said.

Flashner jumped headfirst into this new movement and helped found the first peer education program at the Massachusetts Correctional Institution at Norfolk. The AIDS Awareness Program eventually spread to Gardner and other men's prisons and has now been accepted by the Department of Corrections.

The program has also become a springboard for other forms of activism. The men organized a compassionate release campaign for several prisoners dying of AIDS-related illnesses. Flashner and other prisoners testified, while still behind bars, at legislative hearings on medical care and compassionate release issues. While in prison, Flashner made plans to attend the AIDS in Prison Roundtable. He was released in September 1993, and with the financial assistance and support of ACT-UP/Boston, he was not only able to attend, but also brought Patricia Stoffere, a former prisoner and leader of the AIDS Education Program for Women at the women's prison in Muncy,

Pennsylvania. Flashner is the founder of a new organization of prisoners and former prisoners, PAIN, Prisoners AIDS Issues Nationwide.

Prisoners On Strike

Some prisoners have been forced to take drastic action to respond to the AIDS crisis. In September 1992, at the California Medical Facility (CMF) at Vacaville, prisoners with HIV/AIDS and their HIV-negative supporters in the Pastoral Care Services Program went on medication strike to protest the death of several prisoners with AIDS. Over 150 HIV-positive prisoners issued a set of demands focused on medical treatment, and refused to take their medications until conditions improved.

The striking men felt that some of the deaths could have been avoided if there had been an HIV/AIDS medical specialist at the prison and if the guards were sensitized to the prisoners' medical situation.

Lawrence Wilson, a former prisoner with AIDS, was at Vacaville when the medical emergency erupted. Although Wilson was released just before the prisoners began their protest, he provided a link between the prisoners inside and AIDS activists outside. This former prisoner brought the prison AIDS crisis outside the walls for the world to see. The combined intervention of the prisoners' actions, ACT-UP demonstrations and media work, and a scathing report by a key state legislator, brought significant changes to Vacaville.

One month after the report was issued, CMF opened a prison hospice and a convalescent unit for terminally-ill prisoners. The prison also began a national search for qualified HIV/AIDS treatment specialists. Buzzers were placed in the rooms of prisoners to alert medical personnel of any emergency situations. Extra blankets were given to prisoners who requested them, and long overdue repairs were made on the walls of the HIV and the hospital units.

Activists on the Inside

Noticeably absent at the Roundtable in October were the voices of the HIV-positive prisoners and peer educators still inside. Many are serving long sentences with little or no chance of parole, and have devoted their prison time to fighting the AIDS epidemic in whatever ways they can.

Linda Evans, a political prisoner at the federal women's prison in Dublin, California (FCI-Dublin), founded a peer education program for women prisoners called PLACE (Pleasanton AIDS Counseling and Education). When Evans got to FCI-Dublin in the beginning of 1991, there was no organized HIV/AIDS education or support. Using the Bedford Hills ACE program as her inspiration, Evans helped to pull together a group of women who began to research AIDS education materials. Soon this group received permission to present HIV/AIDS education to women at their orientation to the prison.

Later, PLACE began to conduct classes in the living units. And this past summer, PLACE opened a new chapter in prison AIDS activism when it was able to bring the AIDS quilt to the prison. Many women worked on quilt panels remembering women prisoners and children who had died of AIDS. These panels were sewn together and added to the International AIDS quilt. A candlelight memorial service was held on Saturday night, August 28, 1993, and on Sunday, the women shared memories over an open microphone of loved ones who had died. According to Evans, at least 700 women prisoners and many staff viewed the quilt. Women at the prison were so moved by the event that they decided to adopt the children's AIDS ward at Children's Hospital in Oakland. Hundreds of women made cards and knit gifts for children at the hospital for the holidays.

At about the same time as PLACE began, a similar project was started at the Shawnee Unit, the high-security federal women's prison in Marianna, Florida. In 1993, women in the Shawnee AIDS Awareness Group sponsored an AIDS Walkathon inside the prison that raised money for an AIDS organization on the outside. According to Silvia Baraldini, a political prisoner and one of the groups' founders, "The walkathon put life into the group and transformed it, because it was activist."

Support from Outside

AIDS activism behind the walls is often carried on boldly by one prisoner who is willing to risk the stigma and threats that come from an AIDS-phobic prison administration. One such prisoner is Fred Beasley, a prisoner with AIDS at Jackson State Prison in Michigan. For the past four years, Beasley has been single-handedly educating and advocating on behalf of other prisoners. He has assisted several terminally-ill prisoners with their medical parole. Unable to find support from anyone in the prison administration, Beasley has increasingly turned to organizations, like ACT-UP, on the outside to assist him in his work. Beasley provides a clear and strong example of a prisoner activist loudly fighting the epidemic in one of the largest state prisons in the country.

Eddie Hatcher is another prisoner leader who has used his organizing experience to benefit prisoners with HIV/AIDS. Hatcher, a Native-American political prisoner, was doing an 18-year sentence for occupying the editorial office of a newspaper in Robeson County, North Carolina, to protest racism and mistreatment of Black and Native peoples. In addition to publishing a prisoners' rights newsletter (with the assistance of his mother), Hatcher filed lawsuits on behalf of HIV-positive prisoners and conducted a national campaign for compassionate release on behalf of a prisoner who was dying. Hatcher was denied parole again at the beginning of November 1993. It seems the parole board was reluctant to release such a dynamic organizer into the community. He was, however, finally released in November 1994, and continues to organize in North Carolina for the rights of all oppressed people.

In many prisons around the country, prisoners with AIDS and peer educators are struggling for simple recognition—for permission to be peer educators. A group of women prisoners at the Central California Women's Facility (CCWF) at Chowchilla submitted a simple two-page proposal for an HIV/AIDS peer education program in March 1993. This group of women has had to fight to receive AIDS education materials from the outside. Packages of literature from AIDS service organizations and resource groups have been routinely marked "Return to Sender" by the prison censors. Only after several weeks of public pressure from the outside were materials finally allowed into the prison. [Since early 1995, a peer education program (though limited by administrative red tape) has been in effect at CCWF. However, participants are not allowed to provide support services for the increasing number of women who are dying in the infirmary.—E.R.]

The fight inside for medical care will be much harder to win. Joann Walker, an outspoken peer educator, wrote from CCWF, "The struggles here are hard and many! For HIV/AIDS incarcerated women, there is an ongoing war for proper medical treatment, high-protein diets, and fairness from staff and inmates."

These prisoners need the advocacy and support of AIDS activists, human rights advocates, and all communities committed to social justice, to make their voices heard. All too often, their pleas for assistance have gone unanswered. While working for the National

Prison Project, I tried to interest outside organizations in supporting prisoner struggles. I remember a series of phone calls to AIDS activists and ACT-UP chapters in Texas. I couldn't get anyone to rally to the defense of Curtis Weeks, a Black prisoner with AIDS who was convicted of attempted capital murder for spitting on a guard. Weeks was sentenced to life in prison for the crime of being HIV-positive.

Later on, the American Civil Liberties Union National Office wrote a brief on his behalf, but no activist organizations responded to his case. On the other hand, one phone call from me rallied the entire ACT-UP/Philadelphia chapter in defense of Gregory Smith, a Black, HIV-positive, gay prisoner charged with attempted murder for biting a prison guard. For several years, ACT-UP put up a valiant political fight on Smith's behalf. I was lucky enough to attend many rallies and marches the group called. Unfortunately, Smith lost his last state appeal and now faces 25 years in New Jersey state prisons, convicted and sentenced based on his HIV status.

More organizations and individuals are needed to support the work of prisoners with HIV and AIDS. Sometimes that support may be as simple as making a phone call or xeroxing an AIDS educational brochure. Activists on the outside can help find speakers for AIDS awareness programs inside, or organize a demonstration to demand that dying prisoners receive compassionate release. By working closely with prisoner AIDS activists and peer educators, we can help give prisoners a voice on the outside and make an important contribution to the struggle for justice and social change in this country.

12

MEDICAL TREATMENT AT CHOWCHILLA

Joann Walker

On September 21, 1993, I was feeling very poorly. I had a very bad cold and my right arm was swollen. My T-cell count was down to 166. I went to the C-yard clinic for help. I was told by the MTA [Medical Technical Assistant, a guard with a little first aid training—*E.R.*] that if I was not running a fever, it's not serious. This did not only happen to me, it also happened to other HIV/AIDS incarcerated women here at the Central California Women's Facility (CCWF) at Chowchilla.

The incarcerated women with HIV/AIDS at CCWF always have great problems with the medical department. No one seems to understand (or doesn't want to understand) that HIV/AIDS cannot be treated like a common cold! I have been told by the medical staff that the medical administration instructs them to treat HIV/AIDS just like a cold.

The system here is set up to oppress, depress, and stress out any incarcerated woman who wishes to fight back with a pen instead of her fist! I write all day long if need be. There must be a change made here. Program Administrator (PA) Gloria Henry, who runs C-yard (where most HIV-positive women are housed), and serves as the HIV/AIDS coordinator, said that I could not take a counseling course or become an HIV/AIDS (peer) counselor while doing time here. This is ridiculous!

The women would rather talk to the four incarcerated educators than to the staff. We (the four peer educators) are well-informed and self-educated! The institution lets us go from yard to yard to educate other incarcerated women. There has been a great response from the population and HIV/AIDS testing requests have gone up tremendously. Needless to say, we are very proud of the work we do.

The four peer educators deal in facts. If we do not have documented proof, we do not talk about it. I am the paper pusher, the information getter, the HIV/AIDS advocate at Chowchilla. I raise pure hell around here, because there is no other way to get things done.

It's sad but true! I often run into trouble all the time because I will speak up and out. I have no problem fighting the system. I want to put a call out around the world:

HELP THE HIV/AIDS INCARCERATED WOMEN AT CCWF!

SECTION THREE

WOMEN IN PRISON

Prisons reflect and amplify the male supremacist dynamics of our society. In fact, because prisons and the criminal prosecution system are so carefully removed from the scrutiny of prisoners' supportive communities and advocates, blatant sexism and victimization often go unchecked. Cops, attorneys, judges, and guards go out of their way to brutally enforce control over the lives and bodies of the women they imprison.

Although the percentage of prisoners who are women is relatively small, women make up the fastest growing subset of the entire prison population. The issues of women in prison cut across each of the other topics to which sections of this book have been devoted and male supremacy and sexist injustice are intimately connected with the overall dehumanization so apparent in other areas of the crisis. Male privilege (and domination), and the protection of that privilege have long been and continue to be central to the criminal prosecution system.

Perhaps most illustrative of the unequal justice that applies to women are the countless cases of battered women in prison, convicted and sentenced for fighting back or killing their abusive partners in defense of their lives and/or the lives of their children.

This section's opening piece sets the context by giving some statistics and analysis of this crucial issue, compiled from reports prepared by groups such as the California Coalition for Battered Women in Prison and the National Clearinghouse in Defense of Battered Women.

For more than 10 years, Nancy Kurshan has been an active member of the Committee to End the Marion Lockdown (CEML). CEML is a Chicago-based prisoners' rights and anti-control unit group she helped to found. In "Behind the Walls: The History and Current Reality of Women's Imprisonment," she highlights the historical process by which the separate penal institution for women was created, and the roots it has in the witch hunts, burnings, and patriarchal power structures of 17th-century Europe and New England. This piece also examines the current material reality of women in prison today, and how women are rebelling against that reality.

Women in prison have always been made invisible by mainstream culture. Throughout this century, even progressives and reformers have been conspicuously unaware of the reality of women's imprisonment. In "The Politics of Confinement and Resistance," Karlene Faith details an inspiring movement for women's liberation—a movement in which giving voice to women inside is central. Faith's many years of experience organizing and teaching on both sides of the prison walls have given her valuable insight into the power dynamics that drive the sexist practice of incarceration, and here she makes crucial connections between the way women are seen and treated in society at large, and the specific indignities and harsh treatment they face in prison. Taking apart the very words we use to describe the problem of women's imprisonment, she brings us to a new understanding of women's experience of violence and repression.

Excerpted largely from her 1993 book, *Unruly Women*, this piece is not only a feminist indictment of the culture of mass imprisonment, but a dynamic story of educators and activists who came together and created the Santa Cruz Women's Prison Project, a ground-breaking community building exercise that challenged and empowered hundreds of women prisoners, educators, activists, artists, and entertainers throughout California in the 1970s. Reading about this revolutionary program is a refreshing reminder of the potential power of a committed group of people with shared vision.

"Prisons and Social Control," a piece from the Vancouver publication *Kinesis*, addresses the issues confronted at the crossroads of 1) the demands for justice by women in a society where there is little or no justice for women and 2) feminist vision of a culture without imprisonment. The article is rich as a springboard for dialogue among feminists, prison reform activists, and radicals of any stripe.

Sylvia Baraldini, Marilyn Buck, Susan Rosenberg, and Laura Whitehorn address the United States' current control unit for women: Marianna, Florida. They point out the subtle yet extremely important differences between the type of control exercised at Marianna and that practiced at Lexington. (Also see Chapter 28, "Lexington Prison High Security Unit.")

One of the most significant ways women are institutionalized in the United States is in psychiatric facilities. While the psychiatric assault on millions of women in the United States is a vital issue, it was outside the scope of this book. More information is available in the *Organizers' Guide* available from PARC (see last page of this book).

13

WOMEN IN SOCIETY

Statistics on the Condition of Women

Crimes Against Women

- The Surgeon General has reported for at least 10 years that battering is the single largest cause of injury to U.S. women.
- Women of all class levels, educational backgrounds, and racial, ethnic, and religious groups are battered.
- In national surveys, approximately 25 percent of U.S. couples report at least one incident of physical aggression between them during the course of their relationship.
- In one survey, 25 percent of wives and 33 percent of husbands interviewed thought that "a couple slapping one another was at least somewhat necessary, normal, and good."
- Over 50 percent of all women will experience physical violence in intimate relationships. For about 25 percent of them, the battering will be regular and ongoing.
- At least every 15 seconds, a woman is beaten by her husband or boyfriend.
- An estimated 10 percent of incidents of domestic violence are reported.
- In about 85 percent of reported spouse assault and homicide cases, police have been called at least once before. In about 50 percent of those cases, police have responded five times to family violence incidents prior to the homicide.
- Children are present in 41 to 44 percent of homes where police intervene in domestic violence.
- At least 53 percent of all battering husbands also batter their children. And 75 percent of women surveyed in some studies report that their children had been physically and/or sexually abused by their batterers.

- Between 25 and 45 percent of all battered women are abused during pregnancy.
- In many U.S. cities, more than 50 percent of women and children seeking shelter are turned away due to lack of space.
- Almost 90 percent of the hostage-taking in the United States is domestic violence. Most hostages are the wives or female partners of hostage takers, although children are frequently taken hostage.
- In some surveys, 90 percent of battered women who reported assault to the police actually did sign complaints, but fewer than 1 percent of the cases were ever prosecuted.
- Abusive husbands and lovers harass 74 percent of employed battered women at work either in person or over the telephone, causing 56 percent to be late for work at least five times per month, 28 percent to leave early at least five days per month, 54 percent to miss at least three full days of work per month and 20 percent to lose their jobs.
- Thirty-three percent of teenage girls report physical violence from their date. Twenty-one to thirty percent of college students report at least one occurrence of physical assault with a dating partner.
- The injuries that battered women receive are at least as serious as injuries suffered in 90 percent of violent felony crimes, yet under state laws, they are almost always classified as misdemeanors.
- Each day in the United States, between five and eleven women are killed by a male intimate partner, between 1,800 and 4,000 per year.
- Women are more likely to be killed by their male intimate partners than all other homicide categories combined.
- Ninety percent of women murdered are killed by men, most often a family member, spouse, or ex-partner.
- Over one-half of all women murdered are killed by a spouse or partner.

Women and Criminal Prosecution

- Studies show that the vast majority of women who kill their abusers do so as a last resort in defense of their own lives and that many have stayed with abusive partners because they have been beaten trying to escape or because they rightly feared an attempt at escape would cause their partner to retaliate with violence.

- Self-defense is involved approximately seven times more frequently when women kill men than when men kill women.

- There are hundreds of women in California prisons and thousands of women in prisons nationwide convicted of killing an abusive partner.

- Recent studies indicate that 41 percent of women in prison and 44 percent of women in jail had either been physically or sexually abused at some point during their lifetime prior to their incarceration.

- An estimated 50 percent of women in prison who reported abuse said they had experienced abuse at the hands of a husband, ex-boyfriend, or boyfriend, compared with 3 percent of male prisoners reporting such abuse by female partners.

- As of December 1994, there were 113,282 women in U.S. prisons and jails, 7.37 percent of the incarcerated population.

- While the male prison population has increased by 160 percent since 1980, the female prison population has increased by approximately 275 percent. In 1980, there were over 13,000 women in federal and state prisons. By the end of 1992, that number had increased to over 50,000.

- Of the 45 women on Death Row nationwide in 1993, almost half (approximately 49 percent) had a history of abuse and are there for the murder of an abusive spouse or lover.

- Battered women who defend themselves are being convicted or are accepting pleas at a estimated rate of 75 to 83 percent nationwide.

- Women in the United States are much less likely to commit homicide than are men. During the years 1980-84, women perpetrated only 14 percent of all homicides committed by those 15 years or older. Men committed 86 percent of all these homicides. While only 14 percent of those homicides committed by men involved victims who were partners, 51 percent of those committed by women were partner homicides. Between 2.1 and 8 million women are abused by their partners annually in the United States.

- Most women imprisoned for killing an abusive partner are first-time offenders.

- The national data on women in state prisons provide further evidence that the increase in incarcerated female populations is not due to increases in more serious criminal behavior. In 1979, women were sent to prison for nonviolent crimes roughly 51 percent of the time, and violent crimes roughly 49 percent of the time. In 1986, women were sent to prison for nonviolent crimes roughly 59 percent of the time and violent crimes roughly 41 percent of the time. In 1991, women were sent to prison for nonviolent crimes roughly 70 percent of the time and violent crimes roughly 30 percent of the time. (See Table 1 below.)

Table 1		
Year	Violent Rate	Nonviolent Rate
1979	49%	51%
1986	41%	59%
1991	30%	70%

- Of the 37,253 women serving time in jails in 1989, 1.8 percent were convicted of murder. This was down from 3.8 percent in 1983.
- In 1991, female defendants comprised 17.1 percent of the defendants in all cases, however, they comprised only 5.9 percent of those who had committed a violent crime.
- Chief among the many reasons for the growth in numbers of incarcerated women is the increase in drug-related convictions and the advent of mandatory sentencing for these offenses. According to the Federal Bureau of Prisons almost 60 percent of the women in their custody are serving sentences for drug charges.
- Of the women in state prisons in 1991: 46 percent were Black; 50 percent were age 25-34; 53 percent were unemployed at the time of arrest; 58 percent were high school graduates, holders of a GED, or had been to college; and 45 percent had never been married.

Criminal Conditions

- Overcrowding is common in women's prisons: At the California Institution for Women (CIW) at Frontera, there are over 2,500 prisoners instead of the 1,011 capacity. In New York's Bedford Hills prison, many prisoners are double-bunked; beds are even placed on the half walls that separate individual cubicles.

- Female prisoners' family demands contrast with their male counterparts: 80 percent of imprisoned women have children and of those women, 70 percent are single mothers. Prior to their imprisonment, 84.7 percent of female prisoners (as compared to 46.6 percent of male prisoners) had custody of their children.

- A conservative estimate is that 250,000 children are separated each year from their mothers by jail and prison walls.

- The American Correctional Association, in a 1987 survey of 200 local jails, found that only 47 percent allowed contact visits between incarcerated women and their children. In California, only 8 out of a total of 56 county jail systems offer a special parent/child extended contact visitation program.

- Mothers in prison are less likely to be visited by their children than are fathers. This occurs primarily for two reasons. There are fewer prisons or jails for women; therefore, women are shipped out to other counties or remote areas of a state more often than men. In addition, children of female defendants are more than twice as likely to be placed in foster care or forced to relocate to live with relatives than are children of male defendants, who most often live with mothers or grandparents.

- A survey conducted in 38 states revealed that 58 percent of the prisons or jails serve exactly the same diet to pregnant prisoners as to others and in most cases do not meet the minimum recommended allowances for pregnancy.

SOURCES

Facts come from the National Criminal Justice Reference Service and Statistics Packets prepared by the National Clearinghouse for the Defense of Battered Women in Philadelphia.

Original sources include:

Bureau of Justice Statistics, *Family Violence*, (Washington, DC: Bureau of Justice Statistics), 1992.

———, Prisoners in 1992, 1992.

———, *Sourcebook of Criminal Justice Statistics*, 1991.

———, *Survey of State Prison Inmates*, 1991.

———, *Women in Prison, Survey of State Prison Inmates*, 1991.

George J. Church, "On Prisoners and Parenting: Preserving the Tie that Binds," *Yale Law Journal*, vol. 87, 1978, p. 1408.

Congressional Testimony to the Senate Judiciary Committee Hearings on Women in Prison, June 29, 1993, by Ellen Barry, Legal Services for Prisoners with Children.

Russell Dobash *et al.*, *The Imprisonment of Women*, (New York: Basil and Blackwell Publishers), 1986.

Beverly Fletcher *et al.*, *Women Prisoners: A Forgotten Population*, (Westport: Praeger), 1993.

Russ Immarigeon and Meda Chesney-Lind, *Women's Prisons: Overcrowded and Overused*, (San Francisco, National Council on Crime and Delinquency), 1992.

National Women's Law Center, *Women in Prison: Growing Numbers, Growing Problems*, (Washington, DC: National Women's Law Center), 1993.

"Pregnant in Prison," *The Progressive*, vol. 52, February 1988, pp. 18-21.

"The View from Behind Bars," *Time Magazine* (special issue), Fall 1990, pp. 20-22.

14

BEHIND THE WALLS

The History and Current Reality of Women's Imprisonment

Nancy Kurshan

They call us bandits, yet every time most Black people pick up our paychecks, we are being robbed. Every time we walk into a store in our neighborhood, we are being held up. And every time we pay our rent, the landlord sticks a gun into our ribs.

—Assata Shakur, 1972

These people in this judicial system, their concern is not for justice, as they claim. That is what they come in disguise of, to strip the people of everything. When I say strip, I mean rob, murder, exploit, intimidate, harass, persecute, everything to destroy the mind and body. They seek to take a person and make a complete vegetable of them.

—Ruchell Magee, 1974

Prisons serve the same purpose for women as they do for men; they are instruments of social control. However, the imprisonment of women, as well as all the other aspects of our lives, takes place against a backdrop of patriarchal relationships. We refer here to Gerda Lerner's definition of patriarchy: "The manifestation and institution-alization of male dominance over women and children in the family and the extension of male dominance over women in society in general. It implies that men hold power in all the important institutions of society and that women are deprived of access to such power."[1] Therefore, the imprisonment of women in the United States has always been a different phenomenon than that for men; the proportion of women in prison has always differed from that of men; women have traditionally been sent to prison for different reasons;

and once in prison, they endure different conditions of incarceration. Women's "crimes" have often had a sexual definition and been rooted in the patriarchal double standard. Furthermore, the nature of women's imprisonment reflects the position of women in society.

In an effort to examine these issues further, this essay explores how prisons have historically served to enforce and reinforce women's traditional roles, to foster dependency and passivity, bearing in mind that it is not just incarcerated women who are affected. Rather, the social stigma and conditions of incarceration serve as a warning to women to stay within the "proper female sphere." Needless to say this warning is not issued equally to women of all nationalities and classes. For this reason, our analysis will also take into account the centrality of race in determining female prison populations, both in the North and the South and pre- and post-Civil War. We believe that white supremacy alters the way that gender impacts on white women and women of color. The final avenue of exploration of this chapter will thus concern the relationship between race and women's imprisonment. We will attempt to show that the history of the imprisonment of women is consistent with Audre Lorde's comment that in "a patriarchal power system where white skin privilege is a major prop, the entrapments used to neutralize Black women and white women are not the same."[2]

As long as there has been crime and punishment, patriarchal and gender-based realities and assumptions have been central determinants of the response of society to female "offenders." In the late Middle Ages, reports reveal differential treatment of men and women. A woman might commonly be able to receive lenient punishment if she were to "plead her belly," that is, a pregnant woman could plead leniency on the basis of her pregnancy.[3] On the other hand, women were burned at the stake for adultery or murdering a spouse, while men would most often not be punished for such actions. Such differential treatment reflected ideological assumptions as well as women's subordinate positions within the family, church, and other aspects of society. Although systematic imprisonment arose with industrialization, for centuries prior to that time unwanted daughters and wives were forced into convents, nunneries, and monasteries. In those cloisters were found political prisoners, illegitimate daughters, the disinherited, the physically deformed, and the mentally "defective."[4]

A more general campaign of violence against women was unleashed in the witch-hunts of 16th- and 17th-century Europe, as society tried to exert control over women by labeling them as witches.

This resulted in the death by execution of at least tens of thousands, and possibly millions of people. Conservative estimates indicate that over 80 percent of all the people killed were women.[5] Here in the United States, the witchcraft trials were a dramatic chapter in the social control of women long before systematic imprisonment. Although the colonies were settled relatively late in the history of European witch-hunts, they proved fertile ground for this misogynist campaign. The context was a new colonial society, changing and wrought with conflicts. There were arguments within the ruling alliance, a costly war with the indigenous people led by King Philip, and land disputes.[6] In the face of social uncertainty, unrest and "uncivilized Indians," the Puritans were determined to recreate the Christian family way of life in the wilderness and reestablish the social patterns of the homeland.[7] The success of their project was an open question at the time, and the molding of the role of women was an essential element in the defense of that project.

Hundreds were accused of witchcraft during the New England witchcraft trials of the late 1600s, and at least 36 were executed. The primary determinant of who was designated a witch was gender; overwhelmingly, it was women who were the objects of witch fear. More women were charged with witchcraft, and women were more likely than men to be convicted and executed. In fact, men who confessed were likely to be scoffed at as liars. But age, too, was an important factor. Women over 40 were most likely to be accused of witchcraft and fared much worse than younger women when they were charged. Women over 60 were especially at high risk. Women who were alone, not attached to men as mothers, sisters, or wives were also represented disproportionately among the witches.[8] Puritan society was very hierarchal, and the family was an essential aspect of that hierarchy. According to Carol Karlsen, the Puritan definition of woman as procreator and "helpmate" of man could not be ensured except through force.[9] Most of the witches had expressed dissatisfaction with their lot, if only indirectly. Some were not sufficiently submissive in that they filed petitions and court suits, and sometimes sought divorces. Others were midwives and had influence over the well-being of others, often to the chagrin of their male competitors, medical doctors. Still others exhibited a female pride and assertiveness, refusing to defer to their male neighbors.

Karlsen goes on to offer one of the most powerful explanations of the New England witchcraft trials.[10] She argues that at the heart of the hysteria was an underlying anxiety about inheritance. The inheritance system was designed to keep property in the hands of men. When there were no legitimate male heirs, women inheritors became aberrations who threatened the orderly transmission of property from one male generation to the next. Many of the witches were potential inheritors. Some of them were already widowed and without sons. Others were married but older, beyond their childbearing years, and therefore no longer likely to produce male heirs. They were also "disposable" since they were no longer performing the "essential" functions of a woman, as reproducer and, in some cases, helpmate. Many of the witches were charged just shortly after the death of the male family member, and their witchcraft convictions meant that their lands could easily be seized. Seen in this light, persecution of "witches" was an attempt to maintain the patriarchal social structure and prevent women from becoming economically independent. These early examples of the use of criminal charges in the social control of women may be seen as precursors to the punitive institutions of the 1800s. Up until this time, there were few carceral institutions in society. However, with the rise of capitalism and urbanization come the burgeoning of prisons in the United States.[11] It is to those initial days of systematic imprisonment that we now turn.

The Emergence of Prisons for Women

The relatively few women who were imprisoned at the beginning of the 19th century were confined in separate quarters or wings of men's prisons. Like the men, women suffered from filthy conditions, overcrowding, and harsh treatment. In 1838 in the New York City Jail (the "Tombs"), for instance, there were 42 one-person cells for 70 women. In the 1920s at Auburn Penitentiary in New York, there were no separate cells for the 25 or so women serving sentences up to 14 years. They were all lodged together in a one-room attic, the windows sealed to prevent communication with men.[12] But women had to endure even more. Primary among these additional negative aspects was sexual abuse, which was reportedly a common occurrence. In 1826, Rachel Welch became pregnant while serving in solitary confinement as a punishment and shortly after childbirth she died as a result of flogging by a prison official. Such sexual abuse was apparently so acceptable that the Indiana state prison actually ran a prostitution service for male guards, using female prisoners.[13]

Women received the short end of even the prison stick. Rather than spend the money to hire a matron, women were often left completely on their own, vulnerable to attack by guards. Women had less access to the physician and chaplain and did not go to workshops, mess halls, or exercise yards as men did. Food and needlework were brought to their quarters, and they remained in that area for the full term of their sentence.

Criminal conviction and imprisonment of women soared during and after the Civil War. In the North, this is commonly attributed to a multitude of factors, including men's absence during wartime and the rise of industrialization, as well as the impact of the dominant sexual ideology of 19th-century Victorianism.[14] The double standard of Victorian morality supported the criminalization of certain behaviors for women but not for men. In New York in the 1850s and 1860s, female "crimes against persons" tripled while "crimes against property" rose 10 times faster than the male rate.

Black people, both women and men, have always been disproportionately incarcerated at all times and all places. This was true in the Northeast and Midwest prisons before the Civil War. It was also the case in the budding prison system in the western states, where Blacks outstripped their very small percentage of the population at large. The only exception was in the South where slavery, not imprisonment, was the preferred form of control of African-American people.[15] Yet while the South had the lowest Black imprisonment rate before the Civil War, this changed dramatically after the slaves were freed. This change took place for African-American women as well as men. After the Civil War, as part of the re-entrenchment of Euro-American control and the continuing subjugation of Black people, the post-war southern states passed infamous Jim Crow laws that made newly freed Blacks vulnerable to incarceration for the most minor crimes.[16] For example, stealing a couple of chickens brought three to ten years in North Carolina. It is fair to say that many Blacks stepped from slavery into imprisonment. As a result, southern prison populations became predominately Black overnight. Between 1874 and 1877, the Black imprisonment rate went up 300 percent in Mississippi and Georgia. In some states, previously all-white prisons could not contain the influx of African-Americans sentenced to hard labor for petty offenses.[17]

These spiraling rates in both the North and South meant that by mid-century there were enough women prisoners, both in the North and South, to necessitate the emergence of separate women's quarters. This practical necessity opened the door to changes in the nature of the imprisonment of women. In 1869, Sarah Smith and Rhoda Coffin, two Indiana Quakers, led a campaign to end the sexual abuse of women in that state's prison, and in 1874 the first completely separate women's prison was constructed. By 1940, 23 states had separate women's prisons.[18] The literature refers to these separate prisons for women as "independent" women's prisons.[19] This is ironic usage of the word since they were independent only in their physical construction. In every other way they fostered all forms of dependency in the incarcerated women and were an integral part of the prison system. Although these prisons were not initiated as separate institutions until almost a century after men's prisons, it is not so much this time lag that differentiates the development of prisons for women from those for men. The difference comes from the establishment of a bifurcated (two-part) system, the roots of which can be found in the patriarchal and white supremacist aspects of life in the United States at the time. Understanding this bifurcation is a step towards understanding the incarceration of women in the United States.

On the one hand, there were custodial institutions that corresponded by and large to men's prisons. The purpose of custodial prisons, as the name implies, was to warehouse prisoners. There was no pretense of rehabilitation. On the other hand, there were reformatories that, as the name implies, were intended to be more benevolent institutions that "uplifted" or "improved" the character of the women held there. These reformatories had no male counterparts. Almost every state had a custodial woman's prison, but in the Northeast and Midwest the majority of incarcerated women were in reformatories. In the South, the few reformatories that existed were exclusively white. However, these differences are not, in essence, geographical; they are racial. The women in the custodial institutions were black whether in the North or the South, and had to undergo the most degrading conditions, while it was mainly white women who were sent to the reformatories, institutions that had the ostensible philosophy of benevolence and sisterly and therapeutic ideals.[20]

The Evolution of Separate Custodial Prisons for Women

In the South after 1870, prison camps emerged as penal servitude and were essentially substituted for slavery. The overwhelming majority of women in the prison camps were Black; the few white women who were there had been imprisoned for much more serious offenses, yet experienced better conditions of confinement. For instance, at Bowden Farm in Texas, the majority of women were Black, were there for property offenses, and worked in the field. The few white women who were there had been convicted of homicide and served as domestics. As the techniques of slavery were applied to the penal system, some states forced women to work on the state-owned penal plantations but also leased women to local farms, mines, and railroads. Treatment on the infamous chain gangs was brutal and degrading. For example, women were whipped on the buttocks in the presence of men. They were also forced to defecate right where they worked, in front of men.[21]

An 1880 census indicated that in Alabama, Louisiana, Mississippi, North Carolina, Tennessee, and Texas, 37 percent of the 220 Black women were leased out whereas only 1 of the 40 white women was leased. Testimony in an 1870 Georgia investigation revealed that in one instance "There were no white women there. One started there, and I heard Mr. Alexander (the lessee) say he turned her loose. He was talking to the guard; I was working in the cut. He said his wife was a white woman, and he could not stand it to see a white women worked in such places."[22] Eventually, as central penitentiaries were built or rebuilt, many women were shipped there from prison farms because they were considered "dead hands" as compared with the men. At first, the most common form of custodial confinement was attachment to male prisons; eventually independent women's prison evolved out of these male institutions. These separate women's prisons were established largely for administrative convenience, not reform. Female matrons worked there, but they took their orders from men.

Like the prison camps, custodial women's prisons were overwhelmingly Black, regardless of their location. Although they have always been imprisoned in smaller numbers than African-American or Euro-American men, Black women often constituted larger percentages within female prisons than Black men did within men's prison. For instance, between 1797 and 1801, 44 percent of the women sent to New York state prisons were African-Americans as compared to 20 percent of the men. In the Tennessee state prison in 1868, 100 percent of the women were Black, whereas 60 percent of the men were of African descent.[23] The women incarcerated in the custodial prisons tended to be 21 years of age or older. Forty percent were unmarried, and many of them had worked in the past.[24]

Women in custodial prisons were frequently convicted of felony charges; most commonly for "crimes" against property, often petty theft. Only about a third of female felons were serving time for violent crimes. The rates for both property crimes and violent crimes were much higher than for the women at the reformatories. On the other hand, there were relatively fewer women incarcerated in custodial prisons for public order offenses (fornication, adultery, drunkenness, etc.), which were the most common in the reformatories. This was especially true in the South where these so-called morality offenses by Blacks were generally ignored, and where authorities were reluctant to imprison white women at all. Data from the Auburn, New York prison on homicide statistics between 1909 and 1933 reveal the special nature of the women's "violent" crime. Most of the victims of murder by women were adult men. Of 149 victims, two-thirds were male; 29 percent were husbands, 2 percent were lovers, and the rest were listed as "man" or "boy" (a similar distribution exists today). Another form of violent crime resulting in the imprisonment of women was performing "illegal" abortions.[25]

Tennessee Supreme Court records offer additional anecdotal information about the nature of women's violent crimes. Eighteen-year-old Sally Griffin killed her fifty-year-old husband after a fight in which, according to Sally, he knocked her though a window, hit her with a hammer, and threatened to "knock her brains out." A doctor testified that in previous months her husband had seriously injured her ovaries when he knocked her out of bed because she refused to have sex during her period. Sally's conviction stood because an eyewitness said she hadn't been threatened with a hammer. A second similar case was also turned down for retrial.[26]

Southern states were especially reluctant to send white women to prison, so they were deliberately screened out by the judicial process. When white women were sent to prison, it was for homicide or sometimes arson; almost never did larceny result in incarceration. In the Tennessee prison, many of the African-American property offenders had committed less serious offenses than the whites, although they were incarcerated in far greater numbers.[27] Frances Kellor, a renowned prison reformer, remarked of this screening process that the Black female offender "is first a Negro and then a woman—in the whites' estimation."[28] A 1922 North Carolina report describes one institution as being "so horrible that the judge refuses to send white women to this jail, but Negro women are sometimes sent."[29] Hundreds of such instances combined to create institutions overwhelmingly made up of African-American women.

The conditions of these custodial prisons were horrendous, as they were in prisons for men. The southern prisons were by far the worst. They were generally unsanitary, lacking adequate toilet and bathing facilities. Medical attention was rarely available. Women were either left totally idle or forced into hard labor. Women with mental problems were locked in solitary confinement and ignored. But women suffered an additional oppression as well.

> The condition of the women prisoners is most deplorable. They are usually placed in the oldest part of the prison structure. They are almost always in the direct charge of men guards. They are treated and disciplined as men are. In some of the prisons children are born... either from the male prisoners or just "others"... One county warden told me in confidence, "That I near kill that woman yesterday..." One of the most reliable women officials in the South told me that in her state at the State Farm for women the dining room contains a sweat box for women who are punished by being locked up in a narrow place with insufficient room to sit down, and near enough to the table so as to be able to smell the food. Over the table there is an iron bar to which women are handcuffed when they are strapped.[30]

Generally speaking, the higher the proportion of women of color in the prison population, the worse the conditions. Therefore, it is not surprising that the physical conditions of incarceration for women in the custodial prisons were abysmal compared to the reformatories (as the following section indicates). Even in mainly Black penal institutions, Euro-American women were treated better than African-American women.

Early 20th Century: Female Reformatories

Reformatories for women developed alongside custodial prisons. These were parallel, but distinct, developments. By the turn of the century, industrialization was in full swing, bringing fundamental changes in social relations: shifts from a rural society to an urban one, from a family to market economy; increased geographic mobility; increased disruption of lives; more life outside the church, family, and community. More production, even for women, was outside the home. By 1910, a record high of at least 27 percent of all women in New York state were "gainfully" employed.[31] Thousands of women worked in the New York sweatshops under abominable conditions.

There was a huge influx of immigration from Southern and Eastern Europe, many of these were Jewish women who had come straight from Czarist Russia and brought with them a tradition of resistance and struggle. The division between social classes was clearly widening and erupted in dynamic labor struggles. For example, in 1909, 20,000 shirt-waist makers, four-fifths of whom were women, went on strike in New York.[32] Racism and national chauvinism were rampant in the United States at the turn of the century in response to the waves of immigrants from Europe and Black people from the South. The Women's Prison Association of New York, which was active in the social purity movement, declared in 1906 that:

> If promiscuous immigration is to continue, it devolves upon the enlightened, industrious, and moral citizens, from selfish as well as from philanthropic motives, to instruct the morally defective to conform to our ways and exact from them our own high standard of morality and legitimate industry... Do you want immoral women to walk our streets, pollute society, endanger your households, menace the morals of your sons and daughters...? Do you think the women here described fit to become mothers of American citizens? Shall foreign powers generate criminals and dump them on our shores?[33]

Also at the turn of the century various currents of social concern converged to create a new reform effort, the Progressive movement, that swept the country, particularly the Northeast and Midwest, for several decades.[34] It was in this context that reformatories for women proliferated. Reformatories were actually begun by an earlier generation of female reformers who appeared between 1840 and 1900, but their proliferation took place during this Progressive Era as an alternative to the penitentiary's harsh conditions of enforced silence and hard labor.[35] The reformatories came into being as a result of the work of prison reformers who were ostensibly motivated to improve penal treatment for women. They believed that the mixed prisons afforded women no privacy and left them vulnerable to debilitating humiliations.

Indeed, the reformatories were more humane and conditions were better than at the women's penitentiaries (custodial institutions). They did eliminate much male abuse and the fear of attack. They also resulted in more freedom of movement and opened up a variety of opportunities for "men's" work in the operation of the prison. Children of prisoners up to two years old could stay in most institutions. At least some of the reformatories were staffed and administered by women. They usually had cottages, flower gardens, and no fences. They offered discussions on the law, academics, and training, and women were often paroled more readily than in custodial institutions.[36] However, a closer look at who the women prisoners were, the nature of their offenses, and the program to which they were subjected reveals the seamier side of these ostensibly noble institutions.

It is important to emphasize that reformatories existed for women only. No such parallel development took place within men's prisons. There were no institutions devoted to "correcting" men for so-called moral offenses. In fact, such activities were not considered crimes when men engaged in them and therefore men were not as a result imprisoned.[37] A glance at these "crimes" for women only suggests the extent to which society was bent on repressing women's sexuality. Despite the hue and cry about prostitution, only 8.5 percent of the women at the reformatories were actually convicted of prostitution. More than half, however, were imprisoned because of "sexual misconduct." Women were incarcerated in reformatories primarily for various public order offenses or so-called "moral" offenses: lewd and lascivious carriage, stubbornness, idle and disorderly conduct, drunkenness, vagrancy, fornication, serial premarital pregnancies, keeping bad company, adultery, venereal disease, and vagrancy. A woman might face charges simply because a relative disapproved of her behavior and reported her, or because she had been sexually abused and was being punished for it. Most were rebels of some sort.[38]

Jennie B., for instance, was sent to Albion reformatory for five years for having "had unlawful sexual intercourse with young men and remain[ing] at hotels with young men all night, particularly on July 4, 1893."[39] Lilian R. quit school and ran off for one week with a soldier, contracting a venereal disease. She was hospitalized, then sentenced to the reformatory. Other women were convicted of offenses related to exploitation and/or abuse by men. Ann B. became pregnant twice from older men, one of whom was her father, who was sentenced to prison for rape. She was convicted of "running around" when she was seven months pregnant.[40] One woman who claimed to have miscarried and disposed of the fetus had been convicted of murdering her illegitimate child. There was also the increasing practice of abortion that accounted for at least some of the rise in "crime against persons."[41]

As with all prisons, the women in the reformatories were of the working class. Many of them worked outside the home. At New York State's Albion Reformatory, for instance, 80 percent had, in the past, worked for wages. Reformatories were also overwhelmingly institutions for white women. Government statistics indicate that in 1921, for instance, 12 percent of the women in reformatories were Black while 88 percent were white.[42]

Record keeping at the Albion Reformatory in New York demonstrates how unusual it was for Black women to be incarcerated there. The registries left spaces for entries of a large number of variables, such as family history of insanity and epilepsy. Nowhere was there a space for recording race. When African Americans were admitted, the clerk penciled "colored" at the top of the page. African-American women were much less likely to be arrested for such public order offenses. Rafter suggests that Black women were not expected to act like "ladies" in the first place and therefore were reportedly not deemed worthy of such rehabilitation.[43]

The program of these institutions, as well as the offenses, was based on patriarchal assumptions. Reformatory training centered on fostering ladylike behavior and perfecting housewifely skills. In this way it encouraged dependency and women's subjugation. Additionally, one aspect of the retraining of these women was to isolate them, to strip them of environmental influences in order to instill them with new values. To this end family ties were obstructed, which is somewhat ironic since the family is at the center of the traditional role of women. Letters might come every two months and were censored. Visits were allowed four times a year for those who were on the approved list. The reformatories were geographically remote, making it very difficult for loved ones to visit. Another thorn in the rosy picture of the reformatory was the fact that sentencing was often open-ended. This was an outgrowth of the rehabilitative ideology. The incarceration was not of fixed length because the notion was that a woman would stay for as long as it took to accomplish the task of reforming her.

Parole was also used as a patriarchal weapon. Ever since the Civil War, there was a scarcity of white working-class women for domestic service. At the same time, the "need for good help" was increasing because more people could afford to hire help.[44] It was not an accident that women were frequently paroled into domestic jobs, the only ones for which they had been trained. In this way, vocational regulation went hand-in-hand with social control, leading always backwards to home and hearth, and away from self-sufficiency and independence. Additionally, independent behavior was punished by revoking parole for "sauciness," obscenity, or failure to work hard enough. One woman was cited for a parole violation for running away from a domestic position to join a theater troupe; another for going on car rides with men; still others for becoming pregnant, going around with a disreputable married man, or associating with the father of her child. And finally, some very unrepentant women were ultimately transferred indefinitely to asylums for the "feeble-minded."

Prison reform movements have been common; a reform movement also existed for men. However, all these institutions were inexorably returned to the role of institutions of social control.[45] Understanding this early history can prepare us to understand recent developments in women's imprisonment and indeed imprisonment in general. Although the reformatories rejected the more traditional authoritarian penal regimes, they were nonetheless concerned with social control. Feminist criminologists claim that in their very inception, reformatories were institutions of patriarchy. They were part of a broad attack on young working-class women who were attempting to lead somewhat more autonomous lives. Women's sexual independence was being curbed in the context of "social purity" campaigns. [46] As more and more white working-class women left home for the labor force, they took up smoking, frequenting dance halls, and having sexual relationships. Prostitution had long been a source of income for poor women, but despite the fact that prostitution had actually begun to wane about 1900, there was a major morality crusade at the turn of the century that attacked prostitution as well as all kinds of small deviations from the standard of "proper" female propriety.[47]

Even when the prisons were run by women, they were, of course, still doing the work of a male supremacist prison system and society. We have seen how white working-class women were punished for "immoral behavior" when men were not. We have seen how they were indoctrinated with a program of "ladylike" behavior. According to feminist criminologists such as Nicole Hahn Rafter and Estelle Freedman, reformatories essentially punished those who did not conform to bourgeois definitions of femininity and prescribed gender roles. The prisoners were to embrace the social values, although, of course, never to occupy the social station of a "lady." It is relevant to note that the social stigma of imprisonment was even greater for women than men because women were supposedly denying their own "pure nature." This stigma plus the nature of the conditions of incarceration served as a warning to all such women to stay within the proper female sphere.

These observations shed some light on the role of "treatment" within penal practice. Reformatories were an early attempt at "treatment," that is, the uplifting and improvement of the women, as opposed to mere punishment or retribution. However, these reforms were also an example of the subservience of "treatment" to social control. They demonstrate that the underlying function of control continually reasserts itself when attempts to "improve" people take place within a coercive framework.[48] The reformatories are an illustration of how sincere efforts at reform may only serve to broaden the net and extend the state's power of social control. In fact, hundreds and hundreds of women were incarcerated for public order offenses who previously would not have been vulnerable to the punishment of confinement in a state institution were it not for the existence of reformatories.

By 1935, the custodial prisons for women and the reformatories had basically merged. In the 1930s, the United States experienced the repression of radicalism, the decline of the progressive and feminist movements, and the Great Depression. Along with these changes came the demise of the reformatories. The prison reform movement had achieved one of its earliest central aims, separate prisons for women. The reformatory buildings still stood and were filled with prisoners. However, these institutions were reformatories in name only. Some were administered by women but they were women who did not even have the progressive pretenses of their predecessors. The conditions of incarceration had deteriorated miserably, suffering from cutbacks and lack of funding.

Meanwhile, there had been a slow but steady transformation of the inmate population. Increasingly, the white women convicted of misdemeanors were given probation, paroled, or sent back to local jails. As Euro-American women left the reformatories, the buildings themselves were transformed into custodial prisons, institutions that repeated the terrible conditions of the past. As custodial prison buildings were physically closed down for various reasons, felons were transferred to the buildings that had housed the reformatories. Most of the women were not only poor but also were Black. African-American women were increasingly incarcerated there with the growth of the Black migration north after World War I. These custodial institutions now included some added negative dimensions as the legacy of the reformatories, such as the strict reinforcement of gender roles and the infantilization of women. In the end, the reformatories were certainly not a triumph for the women's liberation. Rather they can be viewed as one of many instances in which U.S. institutions are able to absorb an apparent reform and use it for continuing efforts at social control.

Women and Prison Today

Women are an extremely small proportion of the overall U.S. prison population, approximately 5 percent.[49] [Roughly 7.4 percent in 1996—*E.R.*] At the end of 1988, there were 32,691 women in state and federal prisons.[50] Although imprisonment rates for women are low, they are rising rapidly, after having remained more or less constant for the previous 50 years. According to government statistics, the number of women prisoners has mushroomed from 13,420 in just eight years, a 244 percent increase, as compared to an increase of 188 percent for men during the same period.[51] The rate for women has grown faster than that for men each year since 1981.[52] During 1987 alone, there was a 9.3 percent increase in the rate of imprisonment for women while the figure for men rose 6.6 percent.[53] In New York City jails, the rate for women rose a staggering 33 percent in 1989 alone, more than twice the rate of men.[54] There is a good deal of speculation about the causes of this rate increase. Although the disproportionate rise in the imprisonment rate of women has not yet been satisfactorily explored, there are some existing explanations and hypotheses. Some say there has been a jump in violent crime perpetrated by women as a result of the women's movement and the associated empowerment of women. In other words, increased gender equality brings more violence by women. However, there is no evidence to support either the allegation that female violent crimes have increased, nor that equality leads to more violent crime by women.

In fact, by most if not all accounts, violent crimes by women have remained constant or, in some cases, actually declined. For instance, a comparison of female crime rates between 1977 and 1987 indicates that violent personal crimes actually declined while alcohol and drug-related crimes tripled.[55] A study by Ralph Weisheit specifically compared "gender equality" in various states with the female homicide rates in these states.[56] The results indicated that those states with the highest degree of gender equality also have the lowest rate of homicide by women.

If feminism is not the explanation for those spiraling imprisonment rates, what is? The rising rates can be explained, to a large extent, by many of the same factors that influence the rates of males imprisoned for substance abuse offenses. In one southern prison, 77 percent of the women are there on drug- or alcohol-related offenses. In another state, the number of new admissions for such offenses has jumped from 5 to 56 percent in the last 10 years.[57] Not only are drug- and alcohol-related offenses more frequent, but the nature of the charges tends to be more severe. That is, we are now seeing felony drug charges as compared to past misdemeanors for substance abuse.[58]

Why the rates are rising more quickly for women remains an unanswered question. It is possible that deteriorating economic conditions are now pushing women to the brink faster than men; as the primary caretakers of children, women may be driven by poverty to engage in more "crimes" of survival. Changes in sentencing laws and practices, such as mandatory minimum-sentencing, are commonly referred to as a main factor in rising imprisonment rates for women.[59] Many commentators have indicated that judges are less hesitant than ever to send women to prison. Offenses that used to get probation are now drawing prison time and sentences are harsher. Some observers state that if there was ever a shred of "chivalry" in the white male criminal justice system, that is no longer true today. For instance, an administrator of a Texas women's prison was quoted by the *New York Times* as stating that "Chivalry is dead... It's equal rights, dog-eat-dog, no woman at home with an apron on anymore."[60] Whatever the reason, it seems certain that women are being treated more punitively than in the past by the criminal justice system.

Who are the women in prison? The profile that emerges in study after study is that of a young, single mother with few marketable job skills, a high school dropout who lives below the poverty level. Seventy-five percent are between the ages of 25 and 34, are mothers of dependent children, and were unemployed at the time of arrest. Many left home early and have experienced sexual and physical abuse. Ninety percent have a drug or alcohol-related history.[61] Another extremely significant factor is the race of incarcerated women. In 1982:

> The population of women's prisons was 50 percent black, although blacks comprised only 11 percent of the total population in this country; 9 percent Hispanic [*sic*, Latino], when [they] were only 5 percent of the total population; and 3 percent Native American, although this group comprises only 0.4 percent of the total population.[62]

In fact, African-American women are eight times more likely than white women to go to prison. Although a greater proportion of white women are arrested, a smaller proportion are incarcerated. A 1985 Michigan study reported that 10.5 percent of all arrests were those of white women, while non-white women accounted for 6.1 percent of all arrests. On the other hand, Euro-American women were just 1.8 percent of those incarcerated, while women of color were 4.5 percent.[63] It is not clear, of course, what other factors are involved, such as the distribution of arrestable offenses or the role of prosecutorial discretion. What seems certain is that there is a different set of dynamics at work for white and non-white women. And as Karl Rassmussen, Executive Director of the Women's Prison Association of New York, says, "150 years ago it was poor whites, their names often Irish—and alcohol abuse. Today, it's poor minorities and drug abuse."[64]

Numerous studies have indicated that women of color, Black women in particular, are, when compared with white women, over-arrested, over-indicted, under-defended, and over-sentenced. African-American women are seven times more likely to be arrested for prostitution than women of other ethnic groups. A California study demonstrated that white female drug violators represent the primary group arrested for this offense (65. l percent) but are far less likely to be imprisoned (39.4 percent) than any minority female group. Over a 16-year period, Black women incarcerated in Missouri received significantly longer sentences for crimes against property, and served longer periods in prison. White women were generally given much longer sentences for crimes against persons, in fact, almost double those of Black women. However, actual time served for African-American women was longer. For both murder and drug offenses, Euro-American women ended up serving one-third less time for the same offenses. The study concluded that "differential treatment is definitely accorded to female offenders by race."[65]

Assata Shakur, the once-imprisoned leader of the Black Liberation Army who was liberated from a New Jersey prison in 1979 and granted political asylum in Cuba, has offered this description:

> There are no criminals here at Riker's Island Correctional Institution for Women (New York), only victims. Most of the women (over 95 percent) are black and Puerto Rican. Many were abused children. Most have been abused by men and all have been abused by "the system." There are no big time gangsters here, no premeditated mass murderers, no godmothers. There are no big time dope dealers, no kidnappers, no Watergate women.

> There are virtually no women here charged with white-collar crimes like embezzling and fraud. Most of the women have drug-related cases. Many are charged as accessories to crimes committed by men. The major crimes that women here are charged with are prostitution, pickpocketing, shop lifting, robbery, and drugs. Women who have prostitution cases or who are

doing "fine" time make up a substantial part of the short-term population. The women see stealing or hustling as necessary for the survival of themselves or their children because jobs are scarce and welfare is impossible to live on.[66]

As Shakur paints the picture, women's offenses are rarely vicious, dangerous, or profitable. Their crimes arise from difficult circumstances within society at large. Most women are in prison for relatively minor offenses; property crimes, sometimes referred to as poverty crimes, are the most frequent. According to 1983 Bureau of Justice statistics, 43 percent of women were in for larceny, fraud, or forgery as compared with 15 percent of men. Additionally, women are less likely to be imprisoned for violent offenses; 35 percent of the men were in for violent crimes as compared with 24 percent of women. In general, women are less likely to be involved in homicide than are men. For the years 1980-1984, women were found guilty of only 14 percent of all homicides.[67]

Another important factor is that when women do engage in violent crime, it is often a fundamentally different sort of act. Women are much more likely to kill a male partner than to kill anyone else. Men are much more likely to perpetrate homicides against individuals outside the partner relationship, although the rate of male-perpetrated homicide against intimate partners is still nearly double the rate for female perpetrated homicides of male partners.[68] Women are much more likely to kill in self-defense in response to their male partners' physical aggression and threats, and the recidivism rates for such crimes are extraordinarily low. That is, it is unlikely for a woman to repeat a homicide. This "female use of lethal counter-force" has been documented in numerous studies.[69] Other authors point out that besides the provocation that immediately triggers the female homicide and is recognized by the court of law, female homicide is often in response to preceding years of male abuse.[70]

According to Shelley Bannister, over one-third of all women have been or will be abused as children by males within and outside of their families. Annually, over two million women are battered by male partners.[71] Although no one knows exactly how many women are in prison for killing an abusing husband or boyfriend, Charles Patrick Ewing, a psychologist and attorney, believes that as many as a thousand women a year are convicted for such acts. He states that "This small but increasingly visible minority of battered women are in many cases doubly victimized: once by the men who have battered them and again by a system of criminal justice which holds them to an unrealistic standard of accountability." Moreover, Angela Brown, a Denver social psychologist who conducted research in this area, concludes that "women often face harsher penalties than men who kill their partners."[72]

In the early 1970s, when there was an active women's movement, several strong campaigns were waged regarding individual cases in which women physically defended themselves and their children against attack. Yvonne Wanrow, a Colville Indian, was convicted by an all white jury for the self-defense killing of a man who had molested her nine-year-old son as well as several other children. Inez Garcia struck back against the men who raped her and threatened her life, while the judge insisted that the allegations of rape were not even an issue in the case.[73] Dessie Woods was found guilty of murder and robbery of a white insurance agent who tried to rape her and a friend.[74] The influence of feminist thinking and agitation can be seen today. Bannister argues in a current criminal justice journal that "women who kill or attempt to kill their abusers are incarcerated for several reasons: 1) to deter other women from believing that they can similarly resist; 2) to reinforce in women the belief that they have no right to their own bodies' integrity and no right to defend against or resist male attack; and 3) to protect and assert men's power over women."[75] Even the Governor of Ohio felt compelled to pardon 35 women who had been imprisoned as a result of violence towards husbands and other men who had abused them.

What are the conditions women face when they are imprisoned? Women are confined in a system designed, built and run by men for men, according to a fall 1990 issue of *Time Magazine*. Prison authorities rationalize that because the numbers of women have been so relatively low, there are no "economies of scale" in meeting women's needs, particularly their special needs. Therefore, women suffer accordingly, they say. There are a wide range of institutions that incarcerate women and conditions vary. Some women's prisons look like "small college campuses," remnants of the historical legacy of the reformatory movement. Bedford Hills state prison in New York is one such institution; Alderson Federal Prison in West Virginia is another. Appearances, however, are deceptive. For instance, Russell Dobash describes the "underlying atmosphere [of such a prison] as one of intense hostility, frustration, and anger."[76]

Many institutions have no pretenses and are notoriously overcrowded and inadequate. The California Institution for Women at

Frontera houses 2,500 women in a facility built for 1,011.[77] Overcrowding sometimes means that women who are being held for trivial offenses are incarcerated in maximum-security institutions for lack of other facilities. Women's prisons are often particularly ill-equipped and poorly financed. They have fewer medical, educational, and vocational facilities than men's prisons.[78] Medical treatment is often unavailable, inappropriate, and inconsistent.[79] Job training is also largely unavailable; when opportunities exist, they are usually traditional female occupations. Courses concentrate on homemaking and low-paid skills like beautician and launderer.[80] Other barriers exist as well. In an Alabama women's prison, there is a cosmetology program but those convicted of felonies are prohibited by state law from obtaining such licenses.[81]

In most prisons, guards have total authority, and the women can never take care of their basic intimate needs in a secure atmosphere free from intrusion. In the ostensible name of security, male guards can take down or look over a curtain, walk into a bathroom, or observe a women showering or changing her clothes.[82] In Michigan, for instance, male guards are employed at all women's prisons. At Huron Valley, about half the guards are men. At Crane prison, approximately 80 percent of the staff is male and there are open dormitories divided into cubicles. In one section the cubicle walls are only four feet high and there are no doors or curtains on any cubicles anywhere at Crane. The officers' desks are right next to the bathroom and the bathroom doors must be left open at all times. Male guards are also allowed to do body shakedowns where they run their hands all over the women's bodies.[83]

Incarceration has severe and particular ramifications for women. Eighty percent of women entering state prisons are mothers. By contrast 60 percent of men in state prisons are fathers and less than half of them have custodial responsibility. These mothers have to undergo the intense pain of forced separation from their children. They are often the sole caretakers of their children and were the primary source of financial and emotional support.[84] Their children are twice as likely to end up in foster care than the children of male prisoners.[85] Whereas when a man goes to prison, his wife or lover most often assumes or continues to assume responsibility for the children, the reverse is not true. Women often have no one else to turn to and are in danger of permanently losing custody of their children. For all imprisoned mothers the separation from their children is one of the greatest punishments of incarceration, and engenders despondency and feelings of guilt and anxiety about their children's welfare.[86]

Visiting with children often is extremely difficult or impossible. At county jails where women are awaiting trial, prisoners are often denied contact visits and are required to visit behind glass partitions or through telephones.[87] Prisons are usually built far away from the urban centers where most of the prisoners and their families and friends live. Where children are able to visit, they have to undergo frightening experiences like pat-downs under awkward and generally anti-human conditions. When women get out of prison, many states are supposed to provide reunification services, but in fact most do not.[88] Although even departments of corrections admit that family contact is the one factor that most greatly enhances parole success, the prison system actively works to obstruct such contact.[89]

Reproductive rights are nonexistent for the 10 percent of the women in prison who are pregnant. Massachusetts is one of the few states to provide Medicaid funds for poor women to get abortions, but these funds are unavailable for imprisoned women.[90] All the essentials for a healthy pregnancy are missing in prison: nutritious food, fresh air, exercise, sanitary conditions, extra vitamins, and pre-natal care. Women in prison are denied nutritional supplements such as those afforded by the Women Infants and Children (WIC) program.[91] Women frequently undergo bumpy bus rides, and are shackled and watched throughout their delivery.[92] It is no wonder than that a 1985 California Department of Health study indicated that a third of all prison pregnancies end in late-term miscarriage, twice the outside rate. In fact, only 20 percent have live births. For those women who are lucky enough to have healthy deliveries, forced separation from the infant usually comes within 24 to 72 hours after birth.[93]

Many commentators argue that, at their best, women's prisons are shot through with a viciously destructive paternalistic mentality. According to Rafter, "women in prison are perpetually infantilized by routines and paternalistic attitudes."[94] Assata Shakur describes it as a "pseudo-motherly attitude… a deception which all too often successfully reverts women to children."[95] Guards call prisoners by their first names and admonish them to "grow up," "be good girls," and "behave." They threaten the women with a "good spanking." Kathryn Burkhart refers to this as a "mass infancy treatment."[96] Powerlessness, helplessness, and dependency are systematically heightened in prison while what would be most therapeutic for women is the opposite—for women to feel their own power and to take control of their lives. Friendship among women is discouraged, and the homophobia of the prison system is exemplified by rules in many prisons that prohibit any type of physical contact between women prisoners.[97] A woman can be punished for hugging a friend who has just learned that her mother died.[98] There is a general prohibition against physical affection, but it is most seriously enforced against known Lesbians. One Lesbian received a disciplinary ticket for lending a sweater and was told she didn't know the difference between compassion and passion. Lesbians may be confronted with extra surveillance or may be "treated like a man." Some Lesbians receive incident reports simply because they are gay.[99]

Many prison administrators generally agree that community-based alternatives would be better and cheaper than imprisonment. However, there is very little public pressure in that direction. While imprisonment rates for women continue to rise, the public outcry is deafening in its silence. Ruth Ann Jones of the Division of Massachusetts Parole Board says her agency receives no outside pressure to develop programs for women.[100] However, around the country small groups of dedicated people are working to introduce progressive reforms into the prisons. In Michigan, there is a program that buses family and friends to visit at prisons. In New York, at Bedford Hills, there is a program geared towards enhancing and encouraging visits with children. Chicago Legal Aid for Imprisoned Mothers (CLAIM), Atlanta's Aid to Imprisoned Mothers, and Madison, Wisconsin's Women's Jail Project are just some of the groups that have tirelessly and persistently fought for reforms as well as provided critical services for women and children.

The best programs are the ones that can concretely improve the situation of the women inside. However, many programs that begin with reform-minded intentions become institutionalized in such a way that they are disadvantageous to the population they are supposedly helping. Psychological counselors may have good intentions, but they work for the departments of corrections and often offer no confidentiality.[101] And of course, even the best of them tend to focus on individual pathology rather than exposing systematic oppression. Less restrictive alternatives like halfway houses often get turned around so that they become halfway in, not halfway out. That is, what we are experiencing is the widening of the net of state control. The results are that women who would not be incarcerated at all wind up under the supervision of the state rather than decreasing the numbers of women who are imprisoned.[102]

Prison Resistance

One topic that has not been adequately researched is the rebellion and resistance of women in prison. It is only with great difficulty that any information was found. We do not believe that is because resistance does not occur, but rather because those in charge of documenting history have a stake in burying this herstory. Such a herstory would challenge the patriarchal ideology that insists that women are, by nature, passive and docile. What we do know is that as far back as 1943 there was a riot in Sing Sing Prison in New York, which was the first woman's prison. It took place in response to overcrowding and inadequate facilities.[103]

During the Civil War, Georgia's prison was burned down, allegedly torched by women trying to escape. It was again burned down in 1900.[104] In 1888, similar activity took place at Framingham, Massachusetts, although reports refer to it as merely "fun." Women rebelled at New York's Hudson House of Refuge in response to excessive punishment. They forced the closing of "the dungeon," basement cells and a diet of bread and water. Within a year, similar cells were reinstituted. The story of Bedford Hills is a particularly interesting one. From 1915 to 1920 there were a series of rebellions against cruelty to inmates. The administration had refused to segregate Black and white women up until 1916, and reports of the time attribute these occurrences to the "unfortunate attachments formed by white women for the Negroes."[105] A 1931 study indicated that "colored girls" revolted against discrimination at the New Jersey State Reformatory.

Around the time of the historic prison rebellion at Attica Prison in New York State, rebellions also took place at women's prisons. In 1971, there was a work stoppage at Alderson simultaneous with the rebellion at Attica.[106] In June of 1975, the women at the North Carolina Correctional Center for Women staged a five-day demonstration "against oppressive working atmospheres, inaccessible and inadequate medical facilities and treatment, and racial discrimination, and many other conditions at the prison."[107] Unprotected, unarmed women were attacked by male guards armed with riot gear. The women sustained physical injuries and miscarriages as well as punitive punishment in lockup and in segregation, and illegal transfers to the Mattawan State Hospital for the Criminally Insane. In February of 1977, male guards were for the first time officially assigned to duty in the housing units where they freely watched women showering, changing their clothes, and performing all other private functions. On

August 2, 1977, a riot squad of predominantly male guards armed with tear gas, high pressure water hoses, and billy clubs attacked one housing unit for five hours. Many of the women defended themselves and were brutally beaten; 28 women were illegally transferred to Mattawan where they faced a behavior modification program.[108]

This short exposition of the rebellions in women's prisons is clearly inadequate. Feminist criminologists and others should look towards the need for a detailed herstory of this thread of the women's experience in America.

Conclusion

We began this research in an attempt to understand the ways that patriarchy and white supremacy interact in the imprisonment of women. We looked at the history of the imprisonment of women in the United States and found that it has always been different for white women and African-American women. This was most dramatically true in the social control of white women, geared toward turning them into "ladies." This was a more physically benign prison track than the custodial prisons that contained Black women or men. But it was insidiously patriarchal, both in this character and in the fact that similar institutions did not exist to control men's behavior in those areas. We also saw that historically the more "Black" the penal institution, the worse the conditions. It is difficult to understand how this plays out within the walls of prisons today since there are more sophisticated forms of tracking. That is, within a given prison there are levels of privileges that offer a better or worse quality of life. Research is necessary to determine how this operates in terms of white and African-American female prisoners. However, we can hypothesize that as women's prisons become increasingly Black institutions, conditions will, as in the past, come more and more to resemble the punitive conditions of men's prisons. This is an especially timely consideration now that Black women are incarcerated eight times more frequently than white women.

Although the percentage of women in prison is still very low compared to men, the rates are rapidly rising. And when we examine the conditions of incarceration, it does appear as if the imprisonment of women is coming more and more to resemble that of men in the sense that there is no separate, more benign, track for women. Now more than ever, women are being subjected to more maximum-security, control units, shock incarceration; in short, everything negative that men receive. We thus may be looking at the beginning of a new era in the imprisonment of women. One observation that is consistent with these findings is that the purpose of prisons for women may not be to function primarily as institutions of patriarchal control. That is, their mission as instruments of social control of people of color generally may be the overriding purpose. Turning women into "ladies" or "feminizing" women is not the essence of the mission of prisons. Warehousing and punishment are now enough, for women as well as men.

This is not to suggest that the imprisonment of women is not replete with sexist ideology and practices. It is a thoroughly patriarchal society that sends women to prison; that is, the rules and regulations, the definition of crimes are defined by the patriarchy. This would include situations in which it is "okay" for a husband to beat up his wife, but that very same wife cannot defend herself against his violence; in which women are forced to act as accessories to crimes committed by men; in which abortion is becoming more and more criminalized. Once in prison, patriarchal assumptions and male dominance continue to play an essential role in the treatment of women. As discussed previously, women have to deal with a whole set of factors that men do not, from intrusion by male guards to the denial of reproductive rights. Modern day women's imprisonment has taken on the worst aspects of the imprisonment of men. But it is also left with the sexist legacy of the reformatories and the contemporary structures of the patriarchy. Infantilization and the reinforcement of passivity and dependency are woven into the very fabric of the incarceration of women.

The imprisonment of women of color can be characterized by the enforcement of patriarchy in the service of the social control of people of color as a whole. This raises larger questions about the enormous attacks aimed at family life in communities of color, in which imprisonment of men, women, and children plays a significant role. However, since this area of inquiry concerns the most disenfranchised elements of our society, it is no wonder that so little attention is paid to dealing with this desperate situation. More research in this area is needed as there are certainly unanswered questions. But we must not wait for this research before we begin to unleash our energies to dismantle a prison system that grinds up our sisters.

NOTES

1. Gerda Lerner, *The Creation of Patriarchy*, (London/New York: Oxford University Press), 1986, p. 239.

2. Audre Lorde, "Age, Race, Class, and Sex: Women Redefining Difference," *Racism and Sexism: An Integrated Study*, Paula S. Rothenberg, ed., (New York: St. Martin's), 1988, p. 179.

3. It was the life of the fetus that had value, not the life of the woman herself, for "women were merely the vessels of the unborn soul." See Russell P. Dobash, R. Emerson Dobash, and Sue Gutteridge, *The Imprisonment of Women*, (New York: Basil and Blackwell Publishers), 1986.

4. Dobash, Dobash, and Gutteridge.

5. Carol F. Karlsen, *The Devil in the Shape of a Woman*, (New York: W. W. Norton), 1987, p. xii.

6. William J. Chambliss and Milton Mankoff, *Functional and Conflict Theories of Crime*, (New York: MSS Modular Publications), 1973.

7. John D'Emilio and Estelle B. Freedman, *Intimate Matters: A History of Sexuality in America*, (New York: Harper and Row Publishers), 1988.

8. Karlsen, p. xii.

9. Karlsen, p. xii.

10. Karlsen, p. xii.

11. David J. Rothman, *The Discovery of the Asylum*, (Boston: Little, Brown, and Co.), 1971.

12. Nicole Hahn Rafter, *Partial Justice: Women in State Prisons 1800-1935*, (Boston: New England University Press), 1985.

13. Estelle B. Freedman, *Their Sisters' Keepers: Women's Prison Reform in America, 1830-1930*, (Ann Arbor: University of Michigan Press), 1981, p. 15.

14. Victorian ideology maintained that the woman's world was a separate sphere, albeit a morally superior one. Women reportedly had little or no natural sexual desire; sexuality, on their parts, served only the function of reproduction. This was in contrast to men, who were viewed as being lustful. An interesting psychological speculation is that in the United States, Jacksonian male reformers were obsessed with notions of sexual purity that stemmed from a deep fear of social disorder. As social and economic relations were transformed by capitalism, Jacksonians experienced "psychological tensions." "Uncontrolled" sexuality for women equaled chaos in the popular mind of this period; Jacksonians relied on "pure" women to "keep the lid on" since men could not be expected to do so by their very "natures." See Freedman, pp. 19-20.

15. Rafter.

16. W. E. B. DuBois, *Black Reconstruction in America*, (New York: Athenaeum Press), 1979.

17. Rafter.

18. Freedman.

19. Freedman. Also see Rafter.

20. In the West, little attention was paid by the authorities to systematic prison development until well into the 20th century. California established the only women's reformatory, which remained the region's sole independent prison for women until the 1960s. In 1930, Washington built a women's building.

21. Freedman.

22. Freedman, p. 151.

23. At least one-quarter of Tennessee's black women prisoners were recently emancipated slaves and part of the post-war northward migration. They were young, uneducated, separated from their families, and unprepared for employment. Freedman, p. 139.

24. Freedman, p. 128.

25. Freedman, p. 112.

26. Freedman, p. 110.

27. Freedman, p. 144.

28. Freedman, p. 134.

29. Freedman.

30. Freedman, Chapter 4, Note 44, quoting Frank Tannenbaum.

31. Rafter, p. 160.

32. Richard O. Boyer and Herbert M. Morais, *Labor's Untold Story*, (New York: UE Press), 1972.

33. Rafter, pp. 93-94.

34. Robert L. Allen, *Reluctant Reformers: Racism and Social Reform Movements in the United States*, (Washington, DC: Howard University Press), 1974.

35. These women were middle- to upper-class, of Protestant liberal sects, and from the Northeast. They belonged to women's religious and educational groups that fed their sense of sisterhood and fueled their mission. Some were abolitionists. Some were feminists. They were generally believers in a separate women's sphere and did not seek equality in the public arena. These early reformers were, however, critical of the double standard for men and women, and called for women's solidarity. Their faith that women, with their moral superiority, could be redeemed led them to demand policy changes and eventually to fight for the establishment of all-women's prisons, run by women. After the Civil War, the movement grew and changed, and eventually led to the founding of the women's reformatories. See Freedman.

36. Freedman.

37. Freedman.

38. Rafter, p. 161.

39. Rafter, p. 118.

40. Rafter, p. 161.

41. Freedman, p. 13.

42. Custodial prisons, discussed earlier, were 64.5 percent Black and 33.5 percent white during that time. An alternative explanation seems to be that the proportion of Black women imprisoned in reformatories may have corresponded to their actual proportion within New York state society at large. The number seems small because we are accustomed to enormously disproportionate imprisonment rates for Black women. See Rafter, p. 146.

43. Rafter, p. 134.

44. Rafter, p. 13.

45. Allen.

46. Rafter, p. 164.

47. Rafter, p. 118.

48. Dobash, Dobash, and Gutteridge.

49. U.S. Bureau of the Census, *Statistical Abstract of the United States 1990*, (Washington, DC: U.S. Government Printing Office), 1990, p. 198.

50. *Statistical Abstract of the United States 1990*.

51. *Statistical Abstract of the United States 1990*.

52. George J. Church, "The View from Behind Bars," *Time Magazine*, (Special Issue on Prisons), Fall 1990.

53. Elaine De Costanzo and Helen Scholes, "Women Behind Bars, Their Numbers Increase," *Corrections Today*, June 1988.

54. *New York Times*, April 17, 1989.

55. De Costanzo and Scholes, p. 106.

56. Ralph A. Weisheit, "Structural Correlates for Female Homicide Patterns," unpublished paper delivered at the American Society of Criminology Annual Conference, Illinois State University, Normal, November 9, 1988.

57. De Costanzo and Scholes.

58. William Bennett, statement on *CNN News* Program, August 23, 1989.

59. Linda Rocawich, "Lock 'em Up," *The Progressive*, August 1987.

60. Peter Appleborne, "Women in U.S. Prisons: Fast-Rising Population," *New York Times*, June 15, 1987.

61. See Imogene Moyer, "Mothers in Prison," *Journal of Contemporary Criminal Justice*, 1987, pp. 54-55. Also see Tatiana Schreiber and Stephanie Poggie, "Women in Prison: Does Anyone Out Here Hear?" *Resist Newsletter*, no. 206, May 1988; and Jana Schroeder, "Fifth Annual Roundtable on Women in Prison: Advocates and Activists," *Off Our Backs*, October 1989.

62. Joycelyn M. Pollock-Byrne, *Women, Prison, and Crime*, (Pacific Grove, CA: Brooks/Cole Publishing), 1990, p. 3. The author is citing R. B. Flowers, *Women and Criminality: The Woman as Victim, Offender, and Practitioner*, (Westport, CT: Greenwood Press), 1987, p. 150.

63. Robin Walters, "Women Behind Bars," *The Tri-State Peace and Justice Journal*, vol. 2, June/July 1988.

64. See Sherrye Henry, "Women in Prison," *Parade Magazine*, April 10, 1988.

65. *In U.S. Prisons and in Southern Africa, Women Fight a Common Enemy*, (Berkeley, CA: Coalition for International Women's Week), 1989.

66. Assata Shakur, "Women in Prison," *The Black Scholar*, vol. 9, no. 1, April 1978, p. 9.

67. Angela Brown and Kirk Williams, "Resource Availability for Women at Risk," unpublished paper presented at the American Society of Criminology Annual Meeting, Chicago, November 1987.

68. Brown and Williams, p. 14.

69. Brown and Williams, p. 3. Also see Shelley Bannister, "Another View of Political Prisoners," *Critical Criminologist*, vol. 1, no. 4.

70. Nancy Rubin, "Women Behind Bars," *McCall's*, August 1987. Also see Rocawich.

71. Rubin.

72. Sandy Rovner, "Abused Women Who Kill," *Judgment*, vol. 10, no. 2, June 1987.

73. *In U.S. Prisons and in Southern Africa, Women Fight a Common Enemy*.

74. *Bar None*, no. 7, 1989.

75. Bannister argues that women who respond to male violence with physical resistance, and are incarcerated as a result, should be viewed as political prisoners.

76. Dobash, Dobash, and Gutteridge, p. 5.

77. See Church.

78. Dobash, Dobash, and Gutteridge; Rubin.

79. Schreiber and Poggie.

80. Church.

81. Schroeder.
82. *Resistance at Bedford Hills,* (New York: Solidarity with Sisters Inside Committee), 1990.
83. Letter to the Editor, *Off Our Backs,* October 1989.
84. Ellen Barry, "Children of Prisoners: Punishing the Innocent," *Youth Law News,* March/April 1985.
85. Walters.
86. Phyllis Jo Baunach, *Mothers in Prison,* (New Brunswick, NJ: Transaction Books), 1985.
87. Barry.
88. Rubin.
89. Schroeder.
90. Schreiber and Poggie; Schroeder
91. Schroeder.
92. Schreiber and Poggie; Schroeder.
93. Walters.
94. Rafter, p. 10.
95. Shakur, p. 10.
96. Kathryn Burkhart, *Women in Prison,* (New York: Doubleday Publishers), 1973.
97. Schroeder, p. 7; Burkhart, p. 77.
98. Schroeder.
99. Schreiber, p. 5.
100. Schreiber, p. 3.
101. Schreiber, p. 5.
102. Rocawich.
103. Freedman, p. 48.
104. Rafter, p. 48.
105. Rafter, pp. 80, 153, 170.
106. *In U.S. Prisons and in Southern Africa, Women Fight a Common Enemy.*
107. *Bar None,* p. 17.
108. *Resistance at Bedford Hills.*

15

THE POLITICS OF CONFINEMENT AND RESISTANCE

The Imprisonment of Women

Karlene Faith[1]

The Victimization-Criminalization Continuum

Poverty and racist discrimination are significant factors in criminalization processes. However, since most poor people and most people of color do not engage in crime, then neither poverty nor racial designation (alone or in combination) can account for criminal behavior. Those who are held accountable for criminal behaviors are often those who are already under the eye of the law and who have little voice.

Women constitute the most impoverished group of every Western society, yet women commit by far the least crime. Sexual, biological, and physiological explanations for female crime are increasingly being abandoned. Deterministic economic theories are also discredited, in favor of those that stress the broader social environment, or that deconstruct and demystify dominant discourses that define crime and deviance. Gender socialization and stratification may explain why women steal one item rather than another (for example, cosmetics rather than stereo equipment), but other factors must be considered to explain why anyone steals at all, or, more to the point, why so many do not. It is of particular interest when women commit serious crime precisely because it is so rare.

Certainly much crime stems from victimization of every kind, but victimization cannot be named as "the" cause of crime. That is, although most abusers were abused, most victims of childhood sexual abuse do not become abusers. Most victims of racism do not similarly victimize other people. Most poor people do not steal. Most battered women do not kill their abusive mates. Although women who get in trouble with the law have higher rates of prior victimization than women at large, they constitute a very small percentage of the totals of women who have been physically, sexually, and psychologically assaulted.

The continuum, then, does not follow deterministically from victimization to criminalization. Rather, social victims *en masse* serve as the very large pool from which women who sell sex, steal, or hurt people and get caught are candidates for prosecution. The continuum from victimization to criminalization is arbitrarily drawn according to power relations as constructed through racially-divided and class-based social structures, in tandem with the authority of law and other dominant discourses such as medicine, social sciences, and welfare, which all serve selective law enforcement practices.

Involuntary Confinement

Prison planners, administrators, and staff prefer soft jargon to hardline language because it suggests a distinction between the brutal institutions of yore and modern penal philosophies. However, to the women themselves, the euphemisms are offensive. To the person who is forcibly confined within them, these places are prisons and they are prisoners, and that is how I refer to them. These words are the most direct means of describing a situation where people are held captive, locked behind bars, walls, and fences, under constant surveillance, their every move regulated by guards operating under the authority of the state. I commonly speak of guards rather than *correctional officers* because, whatever other function they might serve, the bottom line is that they must literally watch and scrutinize these women to maintain the security and custodial functions of any prison.

The most poignant argument against euphemistic language has been reiterated to me from time to time over the years by bewildered women who hadn't realized they were being sent to prison: they were shocked to discover that the *correctional* institution or *treatment* center to which the judge sentenced them was not a hospital, or a therapeutic environment, or a temporary *assessment* or *reception* facility, but rather a cold, undisguised prison from which they could not escape.

The history of unruly, defiant women is the history of men's efforts to control them[2] and this translates into practical terms in the context of criminal justice. "Criminal law has been codified by male legislators, enforced by male police officers and interpreted by male lawyers and judges."[3] Agreed. It is generally men who put women in prison, but more specifically it has been particular laws, particular men, and particular women who are implicated. And certainly men are much more likely to imprison other men than to imprison women outside the confines of the home.

In their experience of the pains and degradations of segregation, and in other features of incarceration, women share almost everything in common with men in prison. During the 1970s, male prisoners in North America took the first initiatives in filing one court case after another to protest the inhumane conditions of the institutions in which they were incarcerated. Paradoxically, in this same era, female prisoners began to file gender discrimination appeals in the courts, pleading for reforms on the grounds that they lacked equal rights with incarcerated men relative to, for example, classification; vocational, educational and recreational programs; condition and diversity of facilities; visitation rights; and health care. Given that women cannot be seen as "similarly situated" with men in the larger society, given their special needs as an historically oppressed group and, especially, as primary caretakers of children, there has been considerable merit to the spirit of these legal challenges. However, if we view prisons in their concrete totality and recognize the sustained conditions of dehumanization in men's institutions, one can only conclude that imprisonment is one arena in which it is foolhardy to plead for gender equality. Equal misery cannot be perceived as a social advance for women or anyone.

Elie Wiesel, the renowned author and survivor of the mid-20th-century Holocaust (in which an estimated six million Jews and uncounted homosexuals, gypsies, mentally ill, and physically disabled people were tortured, burned, slaughtered, and starved to death), speaks of how, in order to detach themselves from the horror, people learned to hold their spirit separate from their body. Therapists working with survivors of childhood sexual abuse also attest to the pervasiveness of this ability to "dissociate" as a psychic survival strategy. Indeed, it is a familiar adage in prison communities that "they can take my body but they can't take my mind or soul." But this is often more a battle cry than a statement of fact. Despite the prevalence of such testimony, for many women the body/mind/soul can't be separated, and for such women one of the most devastating aspects of imprisonment is indeed losing control over one's own body. A woman in California in the first year of a five-years-to-life sentence for selling marijuana, for whom incarceration was intolerable, was unsuccessful in a suicide attempt. The response of the authorities was to teach her just how complete was her loss. As she recounted to me in an interview:

As soon as the hospital released me, I was sent before the Disciplinary Board. It's against the rules to attempt to kill yourself, and the Board sentenced me to 30 days in solitary detention—a very long, lonely 30 days. The only human being I saw in that time was the matron who brought the food around. By the time I was released from the "quiet room" I was so withdrawn I couldn't communicate with other people, so my closed custody status, where I could only leave my cell to go to work and to the Central Feeding Unit, was extended by six months.

The claiming of the prisoner's body begins with admission and is unremitting for the duration of imprisonment. As Christina Jose-Kampfner noted from interviews with women serving life sentences in the United States, "cavity searches" cause a "humiliation that they never get used to."[4] Russell Dobash, Rebecca Dobash, and Sue Gutteridge similarly note that women imprisoned in the United Kingdom "found body searches increasingly hard to bear."[5] For the women who experience it, a forced vaginal exam is tantamount to state-authorized rape, and torturing and shaming women in this way seems clearly intended to reinforce their dehumanized prisoner status. The following excerpted text, by Lyn MacDonald, accompanied "a collaborative sculptural installation" by Vancouver artist Persimmon Blackbridge:

> When I was transferred from one jail to another, they gave me a vaginal "exam"—whole hand style... The full exam went like this—vaginal (speculum and bi-manually) and checks through all your body hair, nose, mouth, ears, between toes, bottoms of feet. We had lice shampoo squirted into our hands and had to rub it into our pubic hair and shampoo with it while one or two guards watched. We stood naked and spread-eagled while these guards circled us with clipboards noting our various scars, birthmarks and tattoos. I flipped out when the nurse stuck her hand in me and stated, "You've been pregnant." I COULDN'T STAND her having that knowledge without me telling her. I felt like they could start peeling me in layers, down to my raw nerves... I started screaming at her/them, backing into the wall, hugging myself, threatening them. Fortunately, another nurse quickly covered me with a robe and led me to a chair. I got myself together... these outbursts are usually punished with isolation or worse.[6]

The prevailing, time-worn assumption that female prisoners have low self-esteem may well be a blaming or condescending projection by class-biased people who can't imagine that women with so many problems could think well of themselves. My experience with many women inside is that they do not take on judgements against themselves offered by people whose authority or personal character they do not respect. Ruth Glick and Virginia Neto, in a national survey in the United States, found that "the majority of incarcerated women felt relatively good about themselves."[7] This perception is consistent with the findings of Marion Earnest who, in 1978, concluded that prisoners adopted a self-conception of themselves as "criminals" only if their most "significant others" viewed them as criminal.[8]

Certainly a history of abuse can have the effect of producing torment, including shame, self-blame, and self-injury, but it can also produce anger and the sense that "I'm okay, it's the world that's messed up." It's a safe assumption that lack of self-confidence is not more prevalent among women inside than outside prisons. Given that most incarcerated women have had to hustle in some way to survive, many of these women might well have a greater sense of their resourcefulness than is the norm among women, even when their means of survival appears self-destructive to others.

Federal Prison for Women in Canada—a.k.a. P4W

P4W, until 1995, was the only exclusively federal prison for women in Canada. A guard sitting in a wire cage just inside the prison checks the credentials of everyone seeking entry, and on the other side of a metal detector is a maze of staff offices, stairwells, long corridors with stained walls and shiny linoleum-tile floors that lead to and run past the tiny, barred cell in the tiered "range" units, a separate section of dorm-like rooms in the "wing" (to which well-behaved women can graduate after several months), a cafeteria, the isolated segregation and hospital areas, and rooms, upstairs and down, for the limited work, school, recreational, counseling, and health programs and services.

The issue of centralization has been raised by each of the 13 reports commissioned by the government since the opening of P4W. The federal government has had dozens of male institutions throughout the country to accommodate prisoners' proximity to family members, and to meet various official requirements. It is a futile and foolish exercise to suggest that women would do better if they were granted a range of "choices" equivalent to those offered to men in the system. Men's prisons are no more constructive than women's prisons; programs in men's institutions do not represent real choices for men, and have not proven any particular use in terms of so-called "rehabilitation" or post-prison employment. Nevertheless, differences among men are at least theoretically taken into account, whereas women are blatantly denied any recognition as individuals with distinct identities and needs.

At P4W, all prisoners are subject to maximum-security custody even though prison officials agree that less than 15 percent of approximately 150 women require surveillance in the interests of public safety.[9] Given the small numbers of women, a commensurate budget, and the constraints of the physical layout, programs are necessarily limited. This combination of high-level security, great distance from families and communities, and few choices for daily activity or movement—together with individual reasons for despair— results in lethargy, claustrophobia, depression, self-injurious behavior, and suicide. From informal tallies it seems that at least 12 women killed themselves at P4W between 1977 and 1991, of whom 8 were Native women.

In February of 1995, the Canadian (and later U.S.) public got a rare look at the racist and sexist brutality running rampant in P4W. The Canadian Broadcast Company aired a clandestine copy of a routine videotape made by Correctional Services Canada (CSC) to document a search conducted on eight segregation-unit women on the night of April 26, 1994. CSC's male Emergency Response Team was caught on tape brutalizing, harassing, and ripping the clothes off of women, all unarmed, several of whom were actually asleep.[10]

Ostensibly to allow women to be incarcerated closer to home, the system has built five new smaller prisons, spread out through the provinces, to replace P4W. To the extent that the regional replacements for P4W are simply new prisons, rather than genuine alternatives, the problems that have characterized P4W will be compounded five-fold. Five prisons for women cannot be perceived as an advance over one centralized institution. Writing on these new prisons, Kelly Moffat emphasizes that the problems of geographic dislocation cannot be solved by five new regional institutions in the geographically largest country in the world.[11] Most incarcerated women will still not be within visiting proximity of their families. To underscore Moffat's arguments, and as the history of prisons has demonstrated, if institutions are available, judges send people to them, and with increased beds the likelihood is that more women will be imprisoned for lesser offenses than is currently the case. And when those beds are filled, advocates of carceral "solutions" will propose the construction of yet more women's facilities. Nothing short of a radical readjustment in "correctional" thinking will break this cycle, and the underlying problems of female "offenders" will remain unaddressed except on the most superficial levels.

New Prisons, Same Repression

Prisons are small totalitarian societies, with rules and regulations affecting every intimate detail of life. The prisoner is reduced to a number, one unit in the vast "correctional" enterprise. Personal testimonies from prisoners produce a jumbled accumulation of agonies:

- the stigma of incarceration;
- the claustrophobia of confinement;
- craving fresh air or the feeling of rain on the face;
- deadly boredom;
- strict limitations on physical movement and the aggravation of needing an "inmate pass" to move from one part of the institution to another;
- anxiety about one's children (and frequently the devastation of losing them);
- loneliness for close family members, sweethearts, and community support systems;
- nervousness from being under constant scrutiny and supervision;
- physical and emotional problems that accompany withdrawal from alcohol and street drugs;
- lack of anyone to advocate for one's needs;
- lack of privacy and the tensions that erupt between people who haven't chosen to be confined together;
- endless line-ups;
- inability to get straight answers to questions;
- paranoia about breaking arbitrary, tyrannical, or, at best, coercive institutional rules;
- fears of being punitively isolated for behavioral infractions, or segregated in a prison-within-the-prison for "medical observation" or "protective" or "administrative" custody;
- insensitivities and abuses of power both by staff and other prisoners;
- mail and phone censorship and the risk of losing these "privileges;"

- lack of choice in such simple matters as when to eat, sleep, or watch television;
- little or no choice of diet;
- weight gain;
- chain-smoking as a coping mechanism;
- having to be locked in one's cell periodically for routine "body counts;"
- the inability to escape from the cacophony of radios, television, people hollering at each other, the rattling of keys, and clanging of electronic doors;
- never getting a good night's sleep because of the noise, and because it's never fully dark;
- depressions and mood swings produced by prescribed behavior-modifying drugs;
- not knowing how or whether to show feelings (if you laugh too much you must be stoned on contraband drugs; if you're too quiet you must be depressed and in need of medicine);
- the dependency and infantilization that result from being denied the right to make any decision concerning one's own life;
- uncertainty of when you will be released and the realization of very limited choices in the "free" world when the time comes.

These and other conventional features of life in prison can wound the spirit or rupture the already wounded, sometimes irreparably. However, women may also become stronger through sheer anger and their will to survive with their self-respect intact:

> [O]ne thing prison's taught me is to be very strong, and that I am a worthwhile person. Nobody likes to have their freedom taken away from them, but all the abuse and everything they threw at me—it just made me stronger each time.[12]

Headlines of sensational cases to the contrary, even most women who have killed do not represent a danger to society[13] and there is no concrete benefit at all to be derived from incarcerating people unless there is empirical reason to judge them as dangerous. Generally, the perceived benefits of prisons to society are entirely symbolic. They are an exercise in scapegoating.

Prison as punishment legitimizes inherently destructive institutions, and because prisons are omnipresent as a legal option they displace efforts toward more practical solutions to both "crime" and the problems of people who are criminalized. Penal philosophies focus on the medicalized and criminalized individual instead of the root social causes of illegal actions. The practices of incarceration, and the hegemonic authority of prison planners, stifle the imagination of policy makers.

Prison abolitionists, or those who call for community centers as a replacement for centralized institutions, have existed since the beginnings of prisons. The Archambault Commission in Canada recommended that the Kingston Prison for Women should be closed in the very year, 1938, that it was fully operational. In 1972, in England, critics who opposed expansion of the Holloway Prison for women argued that its primary function was to hold women on remand who had not even been sentenced.[14] The movement by social critics toward advocacy of "alternatives to prison" is accelerating even as more institutions are being constructed and greater numbers of women and men are being sent to them.[15]

Most women in prison spend time cleaning, doing institutional laundry, or otherwise assisting with the maintenance of the institution. Men in institutions must also do this sort of "women's work" to earn their keep, but without the gender-based ideological pretense that it is a rehabilitative program. This premise is an historical constant that has been applied to even the youngest of "female offenders." For example, in 1928, the Matron of the British Columbia Industrial Home for Girls stated that "[s]ince marriage is the greatest trade open to women, household training is her greatest necessity. The successful married life of many of our girls is due largely to this training in 'domestic efficiency.'"[16]

As applied to contemporary adult women,

> The emphasis upon the inculcation of domestic skills and the relative lack of realistic education and training in skills relevant to the job market serves to reinforce the women's own feelings of entrapment as well as their practical dependency upon the welfare state and the men who pass through their lives.[17]

With or without explicit articulation, most contemporary women's prison programs are based on the vestigial bourgeois assumption that women don't need to earn a living. In California, per capita funding to the institution increases according to whether a program or work assignment qualifies as "training." Thus, a woman who pulled weeds day after day, and behaved herself, could be rewarded with a useless certificate in "Landscape Gardening." Or she could spend years mopping floors and scrubbing toilets and in return could receive a certificate in "Vocational Housekeeping." The best she could hope for, upon release, would be a job as a motel maid. The heavy emphasis on sanitation in women's institutions is also symbolic of the historic presumption that all women, but especially "criminal women," are dirty, and need to be purified in body and soul while, at the same time, cleaning up everyone else's dirt.

Education for Empowerment: The Santa Cruz Project

Radical and Black Power politics in the United States in the late 1960s and early 1970s, and a series of uprisings in prisons for men, resulted in critical analyses of prisons, the creation of prisoners' rights organizations and unions, and new communications between prisoners, academics, and community activists. By the early 1970s, prisoners' writings were required reading in numerous university courses, and some universities began teaching courses inside prisons. In California, almost all of this activity was centered on African-American male prisoners, who were (and are) seriously over-represented in the imprisoned population. African-American women were similarly over-represented at 40 percent of the California female prison population, while constituting only 10 percent of the female population in the state. Yet women in prison had received virtually no attention from activists: they constituted less than 4 percent of all state prisoners, they were not generally as politicized as the men, and they did not engage in the kinds of protest actions that attracted media attention.

In 1970, while teaching a political science course with prisoner-students at the Soledad maximum-security men's institution, I was startled to discover that even they knew nothing at all of women in prison, not even the location of the one state facility for women. These men knew all about the dozens of state and federal male prisons that dotted the state, and among them they had served time in many of these institutions, but female prisoners were as invisible to them as they were to the broader public.

Out of frustration that there was so little community knowledge of incarcerated women (and so few library references), I turned my focus to "women behind bars." Beginning in the spring of 1972, I virtually lived at the California Institution for Women (CIW) during most weekdays for a five-month period, doing participant-observation research up to 14 hours a day. I also gathered data from prison files, administered questionnaires and did life history interviews with 100 women. Dozens more participated in small-group interviews on the experience of incarceration. A recurrent complaint among the women was the lack of programs with relevance to their own life experience, and some wanted to know specifically about "women's lib," then a hot topic in the media. Thus began the work of organizing the first university-level course to be taught in a women's prison, on the topic of "Women in Society."

Many women and some men from all over the state, including other community activists, performers, graduate and law students, and university faculty (mostly from Santa Cruz, but from other universities as well, including Stanford, San Jose, and UCLA), let us know they would like to participate. The Santa Cruz Women's Prison Project (SCWPP) evolved rapidly from an interdisciplinary academic initiative to a statewide educational, political, cultural, artistic, spiritual, and entertainment network that converged on weekends at the women's prison. From the beginning, the volunteers included many feminists and other revolutionaries on the cutting edge of post-1960s cultural and political resistance movements. Some had spent time in jail, or would in the future, for actions against the Vietnam War and against investment in South Africa, and for their support of other radical causes.

The work of the Santa Cruz project was coordinated by a fluctuating number of women, generally between seven and ten of us, located in Santa Cruz, Los Angeles, and San Francisco. As unpaid but often full-time coordinators, working with dozens of other volunteers at any given time, our activities included: liaising with the university and the prison; working with women inside in designing accredited arts, humanities, and social science curricula; recruiting university professors, graduate students, and community activists as volunteer instructors; providing academic advice to prisoners enrolling in the program; arranging classrooms and other basic logistics; setting up poetry readings, concerts, dances, and other cultural events in the prison according to the women's interests, and doing the same on the outside to introduce people to the work of the project; setting up art shows of work done by women in the institution; working on projects with in-prison groups such as a three-day Black Culture Marathon cosponsored by the African-American sisterhood; providing sponsorships for new self-help groups such as the Long-Termers Organization that, in our third year, sponsored an historic in-prison public forum on alternatives to incarceration, attended by over 200 guests from the outside; supporting projects such as family days and the construction of a playground through the mothers' support group; soliciting donations of textbooks from publishers; writing small-grant proposals for modest funding from progressive social change foundations such as Vanguard and Liberty Hill; organizing prisoners' rights benefits on the outside in collaboration with diverse community groups, such as the Vietnam Veterans Against the War, Women Against Rape and the Women's Health Center; maintaining contact and coalition work with a myriad of political activist groups around the state, and with graduate students and dissident faculty from the School of Criminology at the University of California at Berkeley, which was shut down by then-Goveror Ronald Reagan as a result of social justice work and student/faculty protest activity; assisting prisoner-students when they were released on parole (which over time became increasingly time-consuming, involving a statewide network of support contacts); writing admission recommendation letters and arranging transfer credit for parolees enrolling in other colleges and universities; an enormous amount of public speaking, writing articles, and radio, television and film work to raise and maintain statewide interest in and support for the project; and, generally, balancing our goals for the program with the demands of the university, those of the prison authorities, and the prisoners' own priorities.

The SCWPP was a collectively organized, statewide network, for the most part united in our socialist-feminist outlook but with diversity amongst us. The collective process was challenging. Some of us had more experience and knowledge of the institution and a more sustained commitment than others. The prison authorities could not grasp the collective concept and wanted some of us to speak for everyone else. The distance between the three central locations of activity caused some communication delays and difficulties. But we never lost the ideal of working collectively; we routinely engaged in the process of criticism/self-criticism, and there were few actual conflicts over the years. The coordinators from all three locations cooperated with each other's initiatives, and although we didn't always arrive at a consensus concerning program policies and had to make compromises, we avoided most of the problems of centralized power that serve to subvert the principles of collective decisionmaking. We didn't model ourselves after any existing program, but in form and content we resembled (and sometimes worked in coalition with) the "People's Colleges" and "Universities Without Walls" that operated out of storefronts in the San Francisco Bay Area during the late

1960s and into the 1970s. Apart from very small grants, we all covered expenses out of our own pockets; volunteers who could afford it would sometimes contribute a few hundred dollars to assist with gas expenses, postage, teaching materials, telephone, film rentals, and so on. We sought donations for everything we needed: IBM, for example, donated a typewriter to our work.

In the 1990s, most prison officials, as well as critics, acknowledge the contradictions of attempts to "rehabilitate" someone within the punitive, custodial environments of prisons, but in the 1970s, when the SCWPP was formed, this goal still dominated "correctional" rhetoric in North America.

The program established by the SCWPP broke with all assumptions of traditional penal philosophy. We did not assume that people in prisons are in any greater need of rehabilitation than any other segment of society. Rather, we analyzed crime as a socially constructed condition, and criminal justice as a discriminatory system that criminalized people from the least socially empowered groups. We rejected patriarchal and class-based presumptions of fixed gender roles, thus we did not accept the common view that women in conflict with the law *de facto* suffer from non-conformity to "feminine" standards. We also didn't presume to know better than the women inside what they needed to make sense of their lives during incarceration or when they were released. We recognized that women in prison are adults who are no less aware of the world they live in than anyone else, and despite popular mythology, no less intelligent by any discernible standard. This perception was validated by my review, in 1972, of 100 randomly selected California Institution for Women files that revealed that Stanford-Binet IQ tests, which were administered to all the women, produced an average score of 110. This score, already at the high end of the free world norm, would probably have been even higher outside the exceptionally stressful conditions of the prison, especially if the scores were adjusted for cross-cultural discrepancies in the test.

It was perhaps inevitable, given mutual antagonisms between some of the more aggressive male guards and SCWPP volunteers who refused to be intimidated by them, that problems would erupt. In a political climate that drew negative attention to the state prison system at large, any outside group seeking to ameliorate the harshness of the prison environment was perceived as potentially threatening to the routine of the institution and the authority of the guards. During this period many outside groups, conservative and progressive alike, had been barred from various prisons for what to outsiders seemed like trivial reasons. Many participants in our group, in particular, were correctly identified as radical rabble-rousers, and although some of the staff strongly defended our presence, others were unrelenting in their intolerance. That we were affiliated with the university, and had the support of liberal state officials as well as the prison administration, only served to exacerbate resentments against the group as a whole. As one of the coordinators I was frequently alerted by prisoners to ways that the project was kept under surveillance, with unfriendly guards lying in wait for someone to trip up and discredit the program so as to justify our expulsion from the institution.

We in the SCWPP went to the prison with the idea that anyone, ourselves included, can benefit from becoming critically aware of social reality, and confident enough to act on that awareness. Education is for raising social consciousness as much as for gaining marketable skills. We believed social responsibility to be the purpose and the prerequisite for empowerment and liberation. We saw both universities and prisons as agencies of social control. The curricula (programs), student (prisoner) selection, and reward (punishment) processes are all determined by hierarchies, through which men and women are made to fit their class-divided niches as human commodities. We understood that schools have systematically deprived the majority of education without which political power (self-rule) is impossible. Our purpose was to facilitate rather than obstruct the learning process.

No one expects a prison to be an easy-going environment, but volunteers with the SCWPP who were novices to the prison system were invariably shocked at the level of power held by both male and female guards, and the perceived pettiness of their concerns. Traditionally, teachers have been similarly perceived as holding unilateral power over students, but our experience at the unusually progressive University of California at Santa Cruz had inculcated notions of genuine democracy in education. When subjected to what they interpreted as unreasonable controls over their classes and workshops, instructors and facilitators reacted with visceral if not vocal indignation. When prisoners were treated in humiliating fashion by guards, the outsiders wanted to defend them, to somehow empower them against insults and cruelties. The prisoners, for their part, took a certain pleasure in these outraged reactions by volunteers. For the prisoners, the pettiness and arbitrariness of prison discipline was par for the course and they would shrug it off with the attitude that "it's no big deal; we live with this every minute of every day."

The intended purpose of the SCWPP was to extend to women in prison the benefits of higher education and the empowerment that accrues from gaining political knowledge, recognizing constructive life choices (despite structural goal limitations), and acquiring skills to act on them. However, the program had at least as much educational value for the volunteers as it did for the prisoners. The volunteers came to understand who is in prison, and why, beyond the fact of having been convicted of breaking a law. The volunteers also received an education in the power of the state to delimit options for those judged criminal. Most of the volunteers, male and female, had never encountered such utter lack of control over one's own environment as is represented by the structure of prisons, but they also commonly experienced the women themselves as exuding exceptional strengths. It was an education in the politics of punishment. It was also an education in education.

One of the values of the program was that it linked those associated with the most elitist and the most disreputable of social institutions and located common denominators among them. It created a bridge across which people from very different social elements could walk, and meet, and engage in discourse related to social change. This happened for women who were incarcerated together, and for the volunteers among themselves, just as it happened between insiders and outsiders. Some of the volunteers had more in common with prisoners than with other volunteers, but differences among other participants were pronounced and in other contexts could have been the basis for mistrust. Instead, in the prison environment, potential antagonisms based on real power differences of culture, class, race, ethnicity, age, gender, sexual orientation, and social status were deconstructed through the unifying processes of building the program. The women inside either initiated or were consulted about every decision concerning academic curriculum and cultural workshops; their priorities affected and often dictated the program's direction. It was a collective investment, and whenever the program's continuity was disrupted for another investigation or penalty, everyone's education was at stake. At no time did the volunteers assume that they were giving more to the women inside than they were receiving from them.

Still defending the right of the SCWPP to continue the work at CIW after years of conflict, we pointed to the positive effect the program was having on the women's chances for a successful parole. Given the unorthodox nature of the program, we were not always able to persuade authorities of its value as a countercultural model. We could, however, boast of success based on low recidivism, the most conventional (if flawed) means of evaluating the success of any prison program. Of approximately 100 women who completed the credit courses and with whom we remained in touch for at least five years following their release on parole, only 5 were returned to prison for a new crime or a violation of the terms of parole, compared to the normal CIW recidivism rate that exceeded 70 percent. It was partially on these grounds that the coordinators of the project, immediately following our expulsion and for many years thereafter, were invited by state officials to serve as consultants on matters pertaining to women in prison. At the time, this struck us as ironic (or, more cynically, as a means of trying to co-opt us before we tried some other "revolutionary" project inside prisons), but in fact it was consistent with the contradictions in the ways that policies and power relations are constructed within the broader "correctional" enterprise.

It is reasonably argued, given the social obstacles that face anyone with a prison record, that recidivism should not be a measure of whether or not an in-prison program is worthwhile. At the same time, even given the self-selection of these highly motivated students, one cannot discount the value of a program that clearly does cultivate strengths with which to face and overcome those obstacles. In the 1990s, the word "empowerment" has become a catch-phrase, and those who use this word bring many different meanings to it. The Santa Cruz workshops were symbolically empowering in that they challenged the relationship of criminal justice to social divisions based on class and race. They generated understanding of abuses of power based on institutionalized hierarchies of authority. And simultaneously they opened up empowering understandings of ways that life choices are expanded to the extent that individuals can maximize their abilities within the context of collective and community support systems, even given structural obstacles.

As integral to the work of the SCWPP as the courses and cultural events inside the prison was the public education work of demystifying prisons and serving advocacy for prisoners, and the cultivation of community outgrowths from our work. The network of support groups grew through the four years of the program, and through these contacts women gained assistance in exiting from and staying out of prison, with focus on practical issues such as finding jobs and housing, regaining child custody, and gaining admission to college/university. Women coming out on parole also found emotional support through these contacts, and they entered into the organizational work of the

Santa Cruz project. They did radio talk shows, spoke at community forums, and joined in the work of coalitions.

Given that so few women, relative to men, are convicted of serious crimes that endanger others, we have a strong basis with women prisoners for setting up models of decarceration, which could be extended to male prisoners. Whatever her (or his) illegal offense, unless a woman (or man) is clearly a danger to society it makes much more sense to provide community services to address the reasons for the offense than to lock someone away in an institution that can only exacerbate or postpone addressing the problems that put the person in prison in the first place. In particular, there is a clear need to address economic inequities and gender relations, especially as they affect women.

The women who participated in the Santa Cruz program became conscious of themselves as political subjects in their own educational process. Although they were living in conditions not of their own choosing, they were learning ways by which the choices they did have could work not only to their own advantage but could also bring them closer to community with other women who likewise resisted confinement. Outsiders in the project who lacked prior knowledge of criminal justice were similarly recognizing choices, and ways by which they had themselves been confined by self-serving dichotomies: good people and bad people; the right way to live and the wrong way to live; the right way to think/look/act and the wrong way. Such judgements set up walls that are concretized by the very existence of prisons.

State policies, particularly those engendered by criminal justice systems, rarely empower the least privileged populations in any meaningful way. Specifically, there is little cause for hope that state agencies and institutions will themselves ever take the initiative to deconstruct the bureaucracies that sustain penal traditions. It is also dubious whether educators who receive substantial grants for prison education or research programs are likely to promote empowering grassroots initiatives as enacted by the volunteers of the SCWPP. The liberal democratic state educates not for independence, freedom, and equality, but for the duties of citizenship accorded to one's (usually inherited) social position. The rhetoric of the liberal state is the guarantee of individual rights, but it is the rights of individuals within politically dominant groups that are protected. The state, in its hierarchical modes of social organization, has a vested interest in discouraging dissident political minority populations from demanding the same guarantees for themselves.

One of the paradoxes of the Santa Cruz program was that, in offering university credits and feminist pedagogy to imprisoned women, we were explicitly challenging the class privilege that normally excludes low-income people from educational advancement, but it was working-class guards and security officials, themselves excluded from higher education, who were most directly obstructive to this process. When the Santa Cruz project was just forming, one of the CIW guards had asked if our group would be willing to let staff take the classes, also for credit. We said no, because one of the reasons the women were keen on the program was that it was independent of the custody, security, and punitive functions of the institution, and we knew if guards were in the classes the prisoners wouldn't enroll

In retrospect, I regret that we did not set up a separate program for the staff, or appeal to the women to open up certain classes. Certainly, in the broader picture, the guards were not our enemy, and if they had had a vested interest in the program's continuance, more of them would have supported it. It would have been a process of demystification, on both sides, if the guards and volunteers had gotten to know one another within an egalitarian and collaborative study environment. As it was, numerous male and female guards who were assigned to handle security at non-credit evening cultural celebrations (which were attended not just by the students but by a majority of the prisoners) became among our strongest allies.

Education for liberation and empowerment of confined groups, wherever and however rarely it occurs, is an exercise in counter-hegemony that calls for a more equitable and transformative share in social power and decision-making. As Catherine Cusic and Debra Miller summed up our work, we engaged in "education as the practice of freedom, as opposed to education as the practice of domination." People sent to prison may have offended society, but by virtue of their incarceration (together with inmates of mental illness institutions), they signify the least socially empowered of all adult human groups. When these people are also women, they are the least visible and the most silenced of all. As women and men who in the early 1970s were finding our voices as feminists and feminist allies, we could do no better for ourselves than to support their reclamation of their lives.

NOTES

1. While this piece does cover a range of issues, for a deeper view I highly recommend the original book: Karlene Faith, *Unruly Women: The Politics of Confinement and Resistance,* (Vancouver: Press Gang), 1993.

2. See, for example: Meda Chesney-Lind, "Rediscovering Lilith: Misogyny and the 'New' Female Criminal," *The Female Offender: Selected Papers from an International Symposium,* C. Griffiths and M. Nance, eds., (Burnaby: Simon Fraser University Criminology Research Centre), 1980.

3. Imogene L. Moyer, "Crime Conflict Theory, and the Patriarchal Society," *The Changing Role of Women in the Criminal Justice System: Offenders, Victims, and Professionals,* I. Moyer, ed., (Prospect Heights: Waveland Press), 1992, p. 18.

4. Christina Jose-Kampfner, "Coming to Terms with Existential Death: An Analysis of Women's Adaption to Life in Prison," *Social Justice,* vol. 17, no. 2, 1990, p. 112.

5. Russell P. Dobash, R. Emerson Dobash, and Sue Gutteridge, *The Imprisonment of Women,* (New York: Basil and Blackwell Publishers), 1986, p. 204.

6. Persimmon Blackbridge with Geri Ferguson, Michelle Kanashiro-Christense, Lyn MacDonald, and Bea Walkus, "A Collaborative Sculptural Installation: Doing Time," *Matriart: A Canadian Feminist Art Journal,* vol. 3, no. 1, 1992, p. 23.

7. Ruth Glick and Virginia Neto, *National Study of Women's Correctional Programs,* (Washington, DC: U.S. Dept. of Justice), 1977, pp. 171-172.

8. Marion R. Earnest, *Criminal Self-Conception in the Penal Community of Female Offenders: An Empirical Study,* (San Francisco: R&E Associates), 1978, p. 79.

9. Liz Elliot and Ruth Morris, "Behind Prison Doors," *Too Few to Count: Canadian Women in Conflict with the Law,* E. Adelberg and C. Currie, eds., (Vancouver: Press Gang), 1987, p. 150.

10. For more on these human rights violations at P4W and their aftermath, see: Karlene Faith, "Aboriginal Women's Healing Lodge: A Challenge to Penal Correctionalism?" *The Journal of Human Justice,* vol. 6, no. 2, 1995; *Prison News Service* issues for 1994 and 1995.

11. Kelly (Hannah) Moffat, "Creating Choices or Repeating History: Canadian Female Offenders and Correctional Reform," *Social Justice,* vol. 18, no. 3, 1991, pp. 196-197.

12. Una Padel and Prue Stevenson, *Insiders: Women's Experience of Prison,* (London: Virago Press), 1988, p. 193.

13. See, for example, Bonnie Walford, *Lifers: The Stories of Eleven Women Serving Life Sentences For Murder,* (Montreal: Eden Press), 1987.

14. Frances Heidensohn, *Women and Crime,* (London: Macmillan), 1985, p. 62.

15. See, for example, Russ Immarigeon, "Women in Prison," *The Journal of the National Prison Project,* (Washington, DC: ACLU), 1987; and Bureau of Justice Statistics, *Prisoners in 1989,* (Washington, DC: Department of Justice), 1990.

16. Jody K. Gordon, "The 'Fallen' and the Masculine: A Feminist Historical Analysis of the BC Industrial Home for Girls, 1914-1946," unpublished honors thesis, (Burnaby: Simon Fraser University), pp. 45-46.

17. Elaine Genders and Elaine Player, "Women in Prison: The Treatment, the Control and the Experience," *Gender, Crime, and Justice,* P. Carlen and A. Worrall, eds., (Bristol, PA: Open University Press), 1987, p. 171.

16

SISTERS INSIDE

Prologues and Social Control

Prisons and Social Control

Collective piece by the staff of *Kinesis*

The judicial/prison system most often comes up in feminist discussion in deciding how to deal with men who commit crimes against women. The urgency of ending violence against us has compelled women to implicitly support this system.

However, in doing this, we cut ourselves off from the struggles of women who are imprisoned. We also lose sight of our long-term goal of a society not based in coercion, a goal that requires the dismantling of the prison system. We need to remember how women's issues and prison issues are part of the same struggle.

Prison issues are important for feminists, both because individual women are being oppressed by prison and, in a wider context, because the judicial/prison system exists to support the larger power structure that oppresses us all.

Women in prison are fighting to maintain a sense of self within a system that isolates and degrades, one that attempts to teach submission to authority through the constant exercising of power, in both serious and petty ways, over prisoners. What is generated is not obedience but anger, and since a prisoner risks punishment such as being sent to segregation if she directs her anger at the system that's hurting her, that anger is often directed inward or at other prisoners.

Because the most brutal methods of social control are directed at a society's most oppressed groups, the women most likely to be incarcerated are poor and/or women of color. In North America, a very high proportion are Native.

That the great majority of prisoners are in for crimes against property shows the system's role in maintaining the economic order. Prison is a type of violence that enforces a state's power over its citizens, in the same way that rape and battering enforce the power of men over women. Since this kind of power by coercion is antithetical to feminism, we need to make prison abolition part of our feminist analysis.

One implication of this is that we must reevaluate the strategy of trying to have abusive men put in prison. For now, it's one of the only strategies available to protect women and children from particularly violent men. What other approach could be used remains a difficult question. However, this doesn't have to stop us from opposing the prison system as a whole; we can recognize that if we use the system to convict violent men, it is an unsatisfactory and short-term solution.

We have to stop trying to inject feminist values into an essentially patriarchal system. We've seen in our recent anti-pornography work how our demands, even when clearly articulated, are twisted and used in the state's interests.

We've implicitly supported the system by trying to change it using its own terms. Since the severity of the penalty for an action is supposed to express society's amount of disapproval for that action, feminists have pushed for stronger penalties for crimes against women as a way of increasing the expressed disapproval for these crimes. This doesn't work for several reasons.

First, the justice system is controlled through government by the economic elite. It therefore supports that elite's interests (retaining power) and will continue to reflect their values and not those of feminists. An example of these values is a recent sentencing by Supreme Court Judge Samuel Toy. Finding a British Columbia man guilty of rape and murder of a teenage woman, Toy sentenced him to 15 years to be served concurrently with the sentence he had already received for the rape and murder of a second teenager. In 1984, this same judge imposed a life sentence on political activist Ann Hansen for her part in actions with the Wimmin's Fire Brigade and Direct Action.

This raises another point. When we support the state's imprisonment of a rapist, we support the state's right to imprison, period. And this is used against us when we challenge the system. In the last decade or so, women in prison have also faced the backlash against feminism. Previously, the court held women less responsible for our actions than it did men and thus women got shorter sentences. But this is one of the few places where disparity between women and men decreased quickly. One of the state's first responses to our demands for equal legal rights has been to hand out longer sentences to women.

Another problem is the whole approach of responding to someone's violent or irresponsible behavior with various degrees of punishment. It implies that revenge is the most important response to a wrong-doing, rather than supporting the victim or trying to prevent the behavior from happening again. It also suggests that people have to be coerced to behave responsibly.

Feminists must participate in the search for alternate ways of dealing with those who oppress. With the awareness that the judicial/prison system is not our ally in the long run, we'll be more reluctant to ask one part of the patriarchy to protect us from other parts.

Our other task is to learn about and support the struggles of prisoners. Women inside fight back and resist all the time. And although there are few methods of resistance open to prisoners, some of them are: talking back to guards; breaking rules; destroying prison property; participating in sit-ins, occupations, work or hunger strikes; and exposing brutality through the media and through lawsuits.

Support from the outside is a crucial factor in the success of prisoners' campaigns. The knowledge that people outside care about what's happening contributes to prisoners' strength and makes prison administrators respond much more quickly to demands.

We can express our support for particular campaigns against unfair court decisions or treatment of prisoners through letter writing, protest phone calls and faxes, demonstrations, and education campaigns in our communities. We can also work for reforms of the prison system, keeping in mind that this is an interim measure to abolishing prisons. This includes lobbying governments to fund more prison programs with as many options available to female as male prisoners and training in a variety of jobs.

On an ongoing basis, we need to strengthen connections with our sisters inside. We must recognize women prisoners' struggles as an essential part of our movement. We can do this by:

- Visiting women in prison when possible—meeting with individual women who want visits; organizing informational or skill-sharing workshops; sharing our talents (e.g., musicians can play gigs at prisons), and so on.

- Writing to imprisoned women who request letters of support or correspondence.

- Sharing our resources—sending money to defense funds and prisoner support or action groups; donating books, musical instruments, art supplies to prisoners.

- Sharing information—sending periodicals free to prisoners; soliciting articles from prisoners; and providing material support to prisoner publications.

17

WOMEN'S CONTROL UNIT

Marianna, FL

Silvia Baraldini, Marilyn Buck,
Susan Rosenberg, and Laura Whitehorn

Shawnee Unit, at the Federal Correctional Institution in Marianna, Florida, was opened by the Federal Bureau of Prisons (BOP) in August 1988, after the small group-isolation experiment at Lexington High Security Unit (HSU) was shut down in response to a lawsuit by prisoners housed there and a national and international campaign. The political and security mission of Shawnee is the same as that of the HSU: to control, isolate, and neutralize women who, for varying reasons, pose either a political, escape, or disruption threat. Neutralization ensures that the women imprisoned here will never leave prison with the full capacity to function. Central to the mission is the understanding that Washington can decide at any point to transfer any female political prisoner or prisoner of war here. The recent transfer of Laura Whitehorn is a case in point.

The unit serves as a public admonishment to those who would challenge the supremacy of the United States—deterrence and isolation are central to its mission. It also serves to maintain control over all women in BOP prisons: 12 women who were targeted as leadership of the recent demonstration against police violence by women at Lexington were transferred here in less than 24 hours.

Once a control unit is set up, it fulfills many needs. The BOP operates Shawnee with some flexibility. Protected witnesses, disciplinary cases, high profile individuals, members of various Colombian cartels, and women with successful escape histories are imprisoned here. What distinguishes them from the political prisoners is their ability to transfer out of Shawnee. Over the past year, there has been a massive movement out of the unit. But political prisoners, despite repeated requests to be transferred, have been excluded from this.

Psychological Control

To wash away the brutal image of the HSU, the BOP has created the deception that life at Shawnee is normal, not designed or manipulated. The physical plant is designed to deflect any concern from the outside about human rights abuses—it looks comfortable and attractive. This appearance is a lie.

The women of Shawnee live in a psychologically assaultive environment that aims at destabilizing women's personal and social identities. This is true of the prison system as a whole; here it has been elevated to a primary weapon, implemented through a physical layout and day-to-day regimen that produce inwardness and self-containment. The unit is a small triangle with a small yard. Within this severely limited space, women are under constant scrutiny and observation. In the unit, cameras and listening devices (the latter are installed in every cell) ensure constant surveillance and control of even the most intimate conversation. Lockdown is not necessary because there is nowhere to go, and individuals can be observed and controlled better while having the illusion of some mobility.

The fences around the yard—the only place where one could have any sense that an outside world existed—were recently covered with green cloth, further hammering into the women the sense of being completely apart and separate. It is one thing to be imprisoned in this tiny isolation unit for a year or two, another to be told one will be here for three more decades—that this small unit will be one's world for the rest of one's life.

Compared to the other federal prisons for women, Shawnee is like being in a suffocating cocoon. What replaces visual stimulation and communication is TV. As in the Marion control unit, there is a TV in every cell—the perfect answer to any complaints about isolation or boredom. TV provides the major link to the world—a link that conveniently produces passivity and inculcates "family values."

The intense physical limitations are compounded by a total lack of educational, training, or recreational programs. At a time when such programs are being expanded at other women's prisons, here, at the end of the line, women are not worthy of even the pretense of rehabilitation. The geographical location of Shawnee makes contact with family and community an almost impossible task. Gradually, women here begin to lose their ability to relate to the outside world. As time moves on, frustration sets in, accompanied by alienation and despair. The result is the creation of dysfunctional individuals who are completely self-involved, unable to participate in organized social activities, and unprepared for eventual reintegration into life on the outside: women who resist less, demand less, and see each other as fierce competitors for the few privileges allowed.

Competition and individualism become the defining characteristics of personality distortion here. The staff seeks out the most needy personalities and molds them into informants. Unit life has been rocked by a number of internal investigations begun when individual prisoners "confided" in ambitious staff members. Snitching and cooperation are the pillars of the "justice system." Those who refuse to go along are isolated and targeted by those who do. In the tiny world of the unit, this can have a massive effect on one's daily life.

A system of hierarchical privileges governs the unit and destroys any potential unity. Small comforts, such as pieces of clothing, have become the mechanism through which cooperation and collaboration are obtained. The latest wrinkle is the institution of "privileged housing"—the arbitrary designation of a limited number of cells on the upper tier as a reward for acceptable behavior. This is classic behavior modification. The unit is in a constant state of uproar over the daily moves that enforce the fall from privileged status.

White Supremacy and Racism

There are close to 90 women imprisoned at Shawnee: one-third Black women from various parts of the world, one-third Latin women, one-third white women, and a very small number of Native-American women. The numerical balance belies the hegemony of white supremacist ideology. As outside the walls, a permanent conflict exists between Black people and those in power. Prisoners experience and are affected by the sharpening of conflict on the outside and the increasing national oppression experienced by Black people in particular. Events in California have given focus to the discontent and heightened the contradictions. Since May 1992, an unprecedented number of Black women have been put in the hole—more than the total for the past two years. Currently, five women from the unit are in the hole; all are Black. And while the administration says that they do not deal with gangs, "Boyz 'N the Hood" and "Jungle Fever" were banned from the prison after the Aryan Brotherhood protested.

A strict segregationist policy determines who gets the jobs. After four years, no Black women have ever worked for education or recreation, except for janitorial jobs. It has taken as long to place a

Black woman in commissary and to promote one woman to be a trainer in the UNICOR factory. All Black staff have left the unit, eliminating the small cushion they provided. This is significant, as staff in the federal system determine everything from access to family to release conditions.

Racism governs how religion can be practiced. Islam, Judaism, and Native-American religions are either totally ignored or marginalized. One cannot help but notice this, since there is a daily diet of fundamentalist Protestant and Catholic services, seminars and retreats.

Superexploitation of Women's Labor

Like B block at Marion, there is no productive labor at Shawnee besides UNICOR. Unit life is organized to facilitate the functioning of the Automated Data Processing (ADP) factory. Nearly 40 women work here, 12 hours a day and 5 more hours on Saturday. The forced rhythm of this work has made the ADP factory the most profitable UNICOR operation in the BOP for its size. The complete lack of any other jobs, the need for funds, the lack of family support, the enormous expense of living in Shawnee, all push women into UNICOR, into intense competition and into an acceptance of their exploitation. Unlike general population prisons, Shawnee prisoners are not even permitted to work in jobs maintaining the physical plant. Removing productive labor is an element in destroying human identity and self-worth.

Increasing Violence, Misogyny and Homophobia

The recent physical attacks by male guards at Lexington, and a similar incident here at Shawnee, illustrate the marked tendency towards using greater force to control women prisoners. While lower security women are being sent to minimum-security facilities, those left in high-security prisons will be more and more vulnerable to physical attack—justified by being characterized by the BOP as "dangerous."

Women in prison are at the very bottom. The misogyny and contempt for women in the society as a whole are compounded by the way the prison system is organized to exploit and utilize women's oppression. The BOP characterizes some women as "dangerous" and "terrorist" (having gone beyond the bounds of acceptable female behavior in the United States), making them the target of particularized repression, scorn, and hatred. To be classified maximum-security is to be seen as less than human, by definition not eligible for "rehabilitation."

All women's prisons operate based on the all-pervasive threat of sexual assault, and the dehumanizing invasion of privacy. Throughout the state and federal prison system in the United States, invasive "pat searches" of women by male guards ensure that a woman prisoner is daily reminded of her powerlessness: she cannot even defend her own body.

In the control unit, there is absolutely no privacy: windows in cell doors (which cannot be covered), patrolling of the unit by male guards, and the presence of the bathrooms in the cells guarantee this. The voyeuristic nature of the constant surveillance is a matter of record: in the past year alone, there have been three major internal investigations of sexual harassment and misconduct by male officers—including rape.

Programs that exist in other women's prisons, addressing the particular needs of women, are deemed frivolous at Shawnee. Most women here are mothers, but no support at all is given to efforts to maintain the vital relationship between mother and child. Similarly, if Shawnee were not a control unit, then education, recreation, religious, and cultural programs should be on a par with those at Lewisburg, Leavenworth, and Lompoc (three men's high-security prisons). But not a single program available in those prisons is available here.

The median age of the women here is 37—a situation distinct from any other women's prison. Nearly everyone is doing more than 15 years; more than 10 women are serving life sentences without parole. Menopause is the main medical problem in the unit. Menopause is an emotional as well as a physiological process. Ignoring this is a pillar of misogynist Western medicine. In the repressive reality of Shawnee, refusal to recognize and treat the symptoms of menopause becomes a cruel means of punishment and an attack on the integrity of one's personality.

Security determines all medical care. Two women who have suffered strokes here were both denied access to necessary treatment in a hospital, a life-threatening decision, made solely for "security reasons."

Intense isolation and lack of activities mean that the loving relationships that provide intimacy and comfort to women in all prisons are of heightened importance here. Until recently, a seemingly tolerant attitude towards Lesbian relationships was actually a form of control. For Lesbian relationships to function without disciplinary intervention by the police, the women had to negotiate with, and in some instances work for, the staff. This tolerance was viewed as necessary because the relationships served as a safety valve for the tensions and anger in the population. As a result of the system of police-sanctioned tolerance, people tended to elevate the individual relationships above any collective alliances that might endanger the administration's rule over the unit.

This situation served to increase the already intense homophobia in the population. A new administration has now ended the tolerance, and Lesbian women are now suffering greater harassment and discrimination. A witch hunt is underway to identify Lesbians and couples engaging in homosexual behavior.

Misogyny and homophobia, together with racism, define conditions here. When coupled with the repressive practices of a control unit, psychological disablement can result—fulfilling the Shawnee mission.

Conclusion

Partly as a result of the astronomic rise in the number of women in prison and the resulting public interest in women's prisons, and partly as a result of the struggle against the Lexington HSU, the BOP has to be very careful not to appear to be brutal in its treatment of women prisoners. The investigations of the HSU by Amnesty International, the Methodist Church, the American Civil Liberties Union and others struck a nerve in Washington. The experiment carried out within the walls of the HSU failed because of the personal and political resistance of those inside and outside the walls. But this defeat did not deter the BOP-stated goals. It just drove them to hide those goals cosmetically behind a veneer of new paint and the momentary elimination of the most notorious abuses. The BOP always denies the truth of its workings. It denies the existence of control units and this unit in particular, not even listing it in the BOP Register of Prisons. Nevertheless, Shawnee is the present women's version of the Marionization of the prison system. The next one is supposed to be opened in North Carolina in 1994. [At the time of publication, this prison has not opened.—E.R.] The movement should not fall into the trap and ignore the particular control strategy aimed at women. Uncovering and exposing the reality that Shawnee Unit is a control unit will contribute to the movement against all control units.

Anti-imperialist Political Prisoners
Marianna, Florida
Fall 1992

SECTION FOUR

THE DEATH PENALTY IS DEAD WRONG

In his philosophical study, *Discipline and Punish: The Birth of the Prison*, Michel Foucault details the historical process by which all punishment, but especially capital punishment, has been "humanized" by the state. He analyzes how penal establishments have adopted supposedly more civilized methods, leaving behind the public spectacle of torture.

But the punishment-body relation is not the same as it was in the torture during public executions. The body now serves as an instrument or intermediary: if one intervenes upon it to imprison it, or make it work, it is in order to deprive the individual of a liberty that is regarded both as a right and as a property. The body, according to this penality, is caught up in a system of constraints and privations, obligations, and prohibitions. Physical pain, the pain of the body itself, is no longer the constituent element of the penality. From being an art of unbearable sensations punishment has become an economy of suspended rights. If it is still necessary for the law to reach and manipulate the body of the convict, it will be at a distance, in the proper way, according to strict rules and with a much "higher" aim. As a result of this new restraint, a whole army of technicians took over from the executioner, the immediate anatomist of pain: warders, doctors, chaplains, psychiatrists, psychologists, educationalists... The modern rituals of execution attest to this double process: the disappearance of the spectacle and the elimination of pain. [1]

So while the trappings and outward appearance of executions have been transformed and made to appear more humane, little has changed regarding the ultimate imperative: the state sees itself as the collective vehicle of revenge and the dispatcher of some necessary foreboding message to the criminal.

Even if the state were morally correct and its message to the criminal necessary, the penalty is simply not working. All the statistics bear this out.

The first piece, a compilation of facts collected from materials by Death Penalty Focus of California, assembles some good arguments to counter common rationalizations for the death penalty. I *would* caution that we may not want to make *all* of these arguments our rallying cry. The failure to challenge the life-without-parole "alternative"—in itself something akin to a penalty of death—is, I believe, a grave error. This piece does, however, arm us with explicit and detailed challenges to the myths that sustain capital punishment, with which we can begin to expose the racism, scapegoating, and class prejudice—the roots and essence of the modern execution—that fuel the death penalty.

A great deal of strong abolitionist work in recent years has shown that there are many options for action. Besides compiling the informational packet, Death Penalty Focus has organized demonstrations and vigils, organized religious communities to actively oppose state killing, put on educational presentations, and been a vocal lobbyist, pressuring lawmakers and California's governor to stop executions.

The American Civil Liberties Union (ACLU) has also been a force for galvanizing legal communities to oppose the death penalty. They have filed appeals on behalf of death row inmates, consistently reaffirming that the death penalty is cruel and unusual. Though it overlaps with some of the information cited in the Death Penalty Focus compilation, the ACLU's Capital Punishment Project piece, "The Case Against the Death Penalty," contains key theoretical and philosophical arguments that complement the other selection quite well. While it makes what I see as false assumptions regarding our "democratic system" and our "civilized society," and it, too, fails to challenge life-without-parole, it nonetheless provides a clear and well-defined moral and political critique.

Also included here is an insightful, incisive essay by Mumia Abu-Jamal, a political prisoner on Pennsylvania's death row. Mumia began his career as a journalist in the 1960s, when he was Minister of Information for the Black Panther Party. Later, as a supporter of the MOVE organization, he exposed the criminal conduct of the Philadelphia police in their infamous 1978 pre-dawn raid of the MOVE household. This journalism made him a target of local authorities, who railroaded Mumia in a 1982 trial in which he was convicted of killing a police officer despite evidence that Mumia was innocent.

First appearing in the *Yale Law Journal* of January 1991, the article moves from exposé to legal primer to survey of the political landscape. More recently, this article appeared in Abu-Jamal's book *Live from Death Row* (Addison-Wesley, 1995), the publication of which has caused further repression for his candid journalism. The piece lays bare the massive contradictions on which capital punishment operates, not only for the general populace but for the people whose hands are more directly on the switch—politicians, wardens, guards, police, district attorneys, attorneys general, judges, and governors. Many careers have been and continue to be built on the backs of people sentenced to death.

"Killing Justice: Government Misconduct and the Death Penalty" shows the pervasiveness of illegal and unethical tactics, and the lengths to which agents of the state will go to secure death sentences and executions. This piece is excerpted from a report by the Death Penalty Information Center in Washington, DC.

NOTES

1. Michel Foucault, *Discipline and Punish: The Birth of the Prison* (New York: Vintage), 1979, p. 11.

18

DEATH PENALTY FACTS
AND FIGURES

Exploding the Myths

MYTH: The death penalty is just punishment for murder.

FACT: Killing is not a just punishment for killing. We do not burn the homes of arsonists or sexually abuse those who rape; it does not make sense to kill someone who has killed. There is no question that a murderer should be dealt with—but not by executing him or her.

MYTH: Other countries use the death penalty "like us."

FACT: The vast majority of countries in Western Europe and North and South America have abandoned capital punishment. South Africa abolished the death penalty in 1995.

MYTH: Execution is cheaper than imprisonment.

FACT: It costs more to execute a person than to keep him or her in prison for life. In March 1988, the *Sacramento Bee* reported that it costs at least $1 million to prosecute a capital case at the trial and appellate levels. The *Bee* concluded that California could save $90 million a year if the death penalty were abolished. The costly process of appeals is necessary to prevent the execution of innocent people, and even with our system of judicial review, in capital cases, more than 23 innocent people have been executed nationwide in this century, and over 319 people revealed to be innocent have been convicted of capital crimes.

A few cyanide pellets or jolts of electricity versus a lifetime of imprisonment looks like a great savings to taxpayers. But virtually every study on the issue of cost proves that executions are far more expensive than life in prison without parole. From the moment a capital murder investigation begins, through the trial stages, and finally to the punishment phase, a capital case is more expensive than a non-capital charge at every level. The potential savings are dramatic.

In a 1992 study, the *Dallas Morning News* determined that executions in Texas cost $1.55 million to $2.3 million more than 40 years in Texas' highest security prison. The *Miami Herald* calculated that one execution in Florida costs $3.2 million. The New York State Public Defenders Association concluded executions in that state were three times as expensive as life in prison. Capital cases are an expensive luxury in the criminal justice system.

Since 1990, the California state government has shifted most of the financial burden of death cases to the county level. In the current economic climate, counties in California are planning or are in the process of cutting essential social services to pay for exorbitantly expensive death penalty trials. Monterey County is pursuing three capital trials with a total price tag of $1.5 million for the county. Simultaneously, the county is considering cuts in sheriff and police protection to cover a projected $2.5 million budget shortfall.

Streamlining the appeals process will not result in substantial savings. It is unlikely to save much money or markedly reduce the time to execution. When the Supreme Court reintroduced the death penalty in 1976, it was with the understanding that "death is different." Because of its severity and finality, the court insisted on systematic guarantees the trial would be as unbiased as possible. These guidelines, known as "Super Due Process," are expensive. Simply put, the time-honored, constitutionally-protected right of due process is irreconcilable with inexpensive capital trials.

MYTH: The death penalty deters crime.

FACT: Scientific studies have repeatedly shown that the death penalty does *not* deter crime any more than other punishments. Former U.S. Supreme Court Justice Thurgood Marshall has said, "The death penalty is no more effective a deterrent than life imprisonment."

In fact, some studies point to higher murder rates following executions. The widely respected Sellin studies conducted in the U.S. in 1962, 1967, and 1980 concluded the death penalty has no deterrent effect. Furthermore, FBI statistics from 1978 to 1988 show that murder rates in 12 states that routinely carried out executions were exactly twice that of murder rates of 13 states with no death penalty (106 per million versus 53 per million).

If the death penalty did deter potential offenders more effectively than other punishments, then jurisdictions with the death penalty could be expected to have a lower rate of crime than those without. Similarly, a rise in the rate of crimes punishable by death would be expected in jurisdictions that abolish executions and a decline in crime rates would be expected among those that introduce it. Finally, one would anticipate a drop in homicide rates immediately following executions, particularly highly publicized ones. Yet, study after study has failed to establish any such link between the death penalty and homicide rates.

In California during the four months of 1992 preceding Robert Alton Harris' highly publicized execution, the average number of monthly homicides was 306. In the four months following the execution, the average number of homicides per month was 333. This suggests the presence of a "brutalization effect" noted in previous studies. The average annual increase in homicides was twice as high during years in which the death penalty was being carried out than in years during which no one was executed.

In a comparison of retentionist and abolitionist countries, homicide rates have been found to be greater in countries that use the death penalty than those which do not. In an analysis of selected countries, the five abolitionist countries with the highest homicide rate averaged a rate of 11.6 per 100,000. The five retentionist countries with the highest homicide rate averaged a rate of 41.6 per 100,000. In other words, countries that have capital punishment appear to have higher murder rates than those countries than do not.

MYTH: To be safe, we must execute murderers.

FACT: Since 1978, California has provided for life sentences without the possibility of parole. That means that the public can be assured that those who commit atrocious murders and receive life-without-parole will never be free again. In the meantime, executions have a brutalizing effect on society and divert our attention from addressing the root causes of crime.

Beyond this, not even proponents of the death penalty have ever advocated that we execute all murderers. Thus, there must be a determination of which murderers are so dangerous they must be put to death. In 1971, the U.S. Supreme Court invalidated all existing death penalty statutes because the Court determined they were arbitrarily applied. Six years later the Court allowed for its re-introduction if states engaged in a rigorous "Super Due Process" to assure that there would be no arbitrary assignment of the death penalty. Despite the supposed heightened scrutiny, the death sentence remains a roll of the dice.

Of every 100 people arrested for murder in this country, just one is executed. In California, where only a small percentage of murder cases would allow a sentence of death, just 10 out of every 100 capital cases end with a death judgment.

"It would be one thing to say that ten murderers deserve to be executed for their crimes," says David Bruck of the South Carolina Office of Appellate Defenders. "But it is quite another thing to say that of those ten we will choose three at random, allow one to live because he is white and another because his victim was black, and then execute only the one who remains. In essence that is what the death penalty does today."

Approximately 23,000 people commit murder in the U.S. every year. The approximately 280 persons sentenced to death are not necessarily the most dangerous criminals. Ninety percent of those on Death Row had no involvement in a prior killing and many are first-time criminal offenders. Death Row also includes many people who never intended to kill anyone, though a murder occurred in the course of a robbery or other offense. Their accomplices in the crime did the actual killing.

For example, in August 1987, Beauford White was executed in Florida although he did not kill or intend to use lethal force. In fact, he objected to any killing before his accomplices started shooting. In July 1992, Willy Andrews was executed for a murder he did not commit. He was in another room at the time of the shooting.

The arbitrariness of the death penalty system has led to case after case where the triggerman was sentenced to life imprisonment, while the accomplice was sentenced to die. The actual killer often plea bargains his case, in exchange for a life sentence and testifying against his codefendant.

MYTH: The death penalty is fair.

FACT: Local politics, money, race, and place where the crime is committed can play a more decisive part in sending a defendant to the death chamber than the circumstances of the crime itself. Additionally, innocent people have been executed and this injustice can *never* be rectified. And evidently, such "mistakes" are more likely to happen to the poor, mentally retarded, and Black.

The Poor. "Too often the death penalty is punishment not for committing the worst crime but for being assigned the worst lawyer," said Georgia attorney Stephen Bright. More than 90 percent of those on Death Row were financially unable to hire an attorney to represent them at trial. As a result, poor defendants are often represented by young, inexperienced or incompetent counsel—lawyers willing to accept the low fees provided by many states, particularly those in the South.

Evidence supporting this travesty of justice is conclusive. The *Houston Chronicle* reported that in Kentucky, one-quarter of the attorneys who represented the 26 convicts on Death Row in 1990 had been either disbarred or suspended. Other cases are illustrative:

- In a Louisiana case, the defense attorney for Freddie Kirkpatrick had not noticed until the trial was underway that the murder victim was an old friend. The attorney missed this obvious conflict of interest earlier because he failed to do the appropriate pre-trial preparation. Obligated to finish, the defense attorney told jurors they would be "justified" in sentencing the defendant to death. They did. Kirkpatrick's co-defendant, represented by a different lawyer, received a life sentence for the same crime.

- Judy Haney and her family were abused by her husband for 15 years before her resistance had fatal results. The jury, however, was unaware of this mitigating circumstance because her attorney did not bring the evidence to trial. He was ordered to spend the night in jail because he was drunk in court. The attorney was released from jail the following morning to return to court but had been unable to prepare for the trial. Haney was sentenced to death.

- A Georgia lawyer who represents many poor defendants facing the death penalty was unable to give a judge the name of one death penalty case. He could name only two cases at all, one of which, the *Dred Scott* decision, was not a criminal case. Although precedents are the basis of practicing law, this attorney was not judged to be incompetent.

Given the U.S. Supreme Court's stance on refusing death penalty appeals to federal courts on the grounds of having had an incompetent lawyer, adequate trial-level counsel becomes critical. The high court maintains this position even though federal judges have found constitutional errors in more than 40 percent of the death penalty cases that reached them through the *habeas corpus* petitions in the last 16 years.

The Mentally Disabled. Despite permanent limitations on their ability to learn and reason, hundreds of mentally disabled prisoners sit on Death Row. The mentally disabled, due to often immature notions of cause and blame, often accept responsibility for acts in which they had little involvement. They are more susceptible both to coercion and a desire to please, making them considerably more likely to confess to crimes they didn't commit.

The case of Jerome Bowden, a young Black man charged with murder in Georgia, is typical. Bowden had been consistently diagnosed over many years as severely retarded. All the physical evidence implicated a co-defendant—who agreed to testify against Bowden in exchange for a life sentence. With no physical evidence, fingerprints, or eyewitnesses implicating Bowden, the entire case was based on his own confession and the plea-bargained testimony of his co-defendant. Bowden later explained that the detective who had interrogated him said he was a "friend" who would help Bowden. The detective asked him to "sign here" and Bowden did. The court determined that Bowden was competent to waive his constitutional right against self-incrimination and that his confession—which he could not write—was voluntary and reliable. He was executed in 1986.

In February 1989, the American Bar Association adopted a resolution that the mentally disabled should not be subject to execution; they argued that executing "a person with mental retardation violates contemporary standards of decency."

At least 15 people diagnosed as mentally disabled have been executed in the United States since the reinstatement of the death penalty. In the general population, 2.5 percent are mentally disabled. On Death Row, the numbers range between 10 and 30 percent. Eleven states now expressly prohibit the execution of the mentally disabled. In June 1989, the U.S. Supreme Court held that the Constitution does not bar the execution of the mentally disabled.

Other Innocent. Since 1900, 350 innocent people have been sentenced to death, according to a study in the *Stanford Law Journal*. At least 23 were executed for crimes they did not commit. Since 1970, 67 innocent people have been released from Death Row with evidence of their innocence.

For example, deliberate misconduct by Los Angeles law enforcement officials secured capital murder convictions for Clarence Chance and Benny Powell. Powell and Chance served 17 years in prison for a murder they did not commit. In 1972, all Death Row inmates—including Powell and Chance—had their death sentences commuted after the U.S. Supreme Court struck down capital punishment as "freakish" and arbitrarily applied. Capital punishment was reinstated in 1976 after the laws were rewritten. Had Chance and Powell been tried today, they probably would have received death sentences. Both

Chance and Powell were released from prison in the spring of 1992. Despite the safeguards these new laws are supposed to provide, defendants aren't protected from willful miscarriages of justice by an overzealous prosecution system. (For more on police misconduct, see Chapter 21, "Killing Justice.")

Discovery of these judicial errors is often cited as proof that the system works. In truth, most of these problems were found accidentally and only through the persistence of volunteer investigators. Standard legal procedures designed to safeguard against such lethal errors failed. Today, even the meager protection for the innocent that time provides is threatened. Congress is speeding up the appeals process and cutting spending to the crucial resource centers that assist in and conduct the appeals for thousands of indigent Death Row prisoners.

MYTH: Race has nothing to do with capital punishment.

FACT: Racism is an important factor in determining who is sentenced to die. In 1987, the U.S. Supreme Court case of *McCleskey v. Kemp* established that in Georgia, someone who kills a white person is more than four times more likely to be sentenced to death than someone who kills a Black person. The race of the defendant as well as the race of his or her victim plays a decisive role in who gets the death penalty. More than half of the individuals on California's Death Row are people of color.

The evidence is clear: justice isn't color-blind when it comes to the death penalty. Blacks who commit murder are far more likely to be put to death than whites. The Government Accounting Office reviewed all the recent studies on this subject and concluded: "Our synthesis of the 28 studies shows a pattern of evidence indicating racial disparities in the charging, sentencing, and imposition of the death penalty after the (1976) *Furman* decision," which reinstated capital punishment in this country.

Studies reveal:

- Only three whites have been executed for killing a Black in the past 50 years. Of the 16,000 recorded executions in U.S. history, only 33 involved a white killing a Black.

- More than 83 percent of those executed in this country since 1976 had killed whites, while almost half of all victims were Black.

- A 1973 study of 1,265 cases from Florida, Georgia, Louisiana, South Carolina, and Tennessee demonstrated nearly seven times as many Blacks were sentenced to death as were whites. Of 882

Blacks convicted of rape, 110 were sentenced to death. Among the 442 whites convicted of the same crime, only 9 received a death sentence.

- In Florida, between 1972 and 1977, Black offenders who killed whites were four times more likely to be sentenced to death than those who murdered Blacks. Blacks who killed whites were five times more likely to receive the death penalty than whites who killed whites.

- In South Carolina, over a four-year period, in murder trials involving white victims and Black killers, prosecutors sought the death sentence in 38 percent of the cases. When the killer was white and the victim was Black, the figure dropped to 13%.

- A study of sentencing patterns in Texas in the 1970s showed that, where a Chicano killed a white, 65 percent of the defendants were tried for capital murder while only 25 percent of whites who killed Blacks or Chicanos faced the death penalty.

MYTH: Most Americans support the death penalty.

FACT: Despite political posturing and common perceptions, the public's desire for capital punishment is far weaker than initial readings of opinion polls suggest. Most Americans accept the death penalty in principle when asked "do you favor or oppose the death penalty for convicted murderers." However, the results change dramatically when people are given an option. A widely quoted poll conducted shortly before Robert Harris' execution in April 1992 indicated that 80 percent of Californians supported the death penalty. A Northeastern University researcher challenged these findings with another survey. When specific alternatives to the death penalty are offered, support for the death penalty drops below 50 percent. Two out of three Californians said they preferred life in prison without parole plus restitution over the death penalty. The findings are consistent with those in other states:

- In Florida, 70 percent said they preferred a sentence of life without parole and financial restitution to the victim's family.

- In Virginia, 59 percent preferred a sentence of 25 years before parole, plus financial restitution; in Nebraska, 58 percent preferred this arrangement.

- Even where restitution is not part of the life without parole option, a plurality of those polled in Kentucky and Oklahoma still prefer it over the death penalty.

Other evidence that public support for the death penalty is waning includes:

- In Louisiana, where eight people were executed in as many weeks in 1987, the number of jury verdicts for death remained nearly zero for a long period following this wave of executions.
- In March 1991, New Mexico became the fifth state—after Georgia, Maryland, Kentucky, and Tennessee—to prohibit the execution of the mentally disabled, a significant population on any Death Row.

Because most Americans assume that killers will be out on the streets again in a few years, apparent support for the death penalty is exaggerated. However, 31 states—most recently Oregon, Florida, Maryland, and Oklahoma—have adopted a life prison term with no chance of parole for certain offenses. According to the California governor's office, not a single prisoner sentenced to life without parole has walked out of prison since the state provided for that option in 1977.

MYTH: The death penalty offers justice to victims' families.

FACT: Families of murder victims undergo severe trauma and loss that no one should minimize. But executions do not help family members heal their wounds. The extended process prior to executions prolongs the agony of the family. It would be far more beneficial to the families of murder victims if the funds now being used for the costly process of executions were diverted to provide them with counseling and other assistance.

Opponents of the death penalty have been accused of not having sympathy for the victims of crime, even though many of the most outspoken abolitionists are crime victims. Most abolitionist groups favor comprehensive support services for victims' families—especially financial support when an income earner has been killed. But these groups oppose any further manipulation of the sorrow we all feel for victims' families to justify executions. Instead, abolitionists encourage real assistance to victims' families, more effort to address the underlying roots of criminal activity and proven policies that protect us all from violent crime.

For information on victims, readers are encouraged to contact Murder Victims Families for Reconciliation (MVFR). MVFR is an organization of persons who have lost family members to violent crime and advocate the abolition of the death penalty. MVFR is a diverse and all-inclusive group that believes that healing happens not by vengeance, but by reconciliation—with society, the community, the act of murder itself, and sometimes even the offender. For more information contact:

> *MVFR*
> PO Box 208
> Atlantic, VA 23303
> (804) 824-0948

SOURCES

David Baldus, George Woodworth, and Charles Pulaski, Equal Justice and the Death Penalty: A Legal and Empirical Analysis, (Boston: Northeastern University Press), 1990.

Hugo Adam Bedau and Michael L. Radelet, "Miscarriages of Justice in Potentially Capital Cases," Stanford Law Review, vol. 40, 1987, pp. 21-179.

John Blume and David Bruck, "Sentencing the Mentally Retarded to Death: An Eighth Amendment Analysis," Arkansas Law Review, vol. 41, 1988, pp. 725-764.

William Bowers, "The Pervasiveness of Arbitrariness and Discrimination under Post-Furman Capital Statutes," Journal of Criminal Law and Criminology, vol. 74, no. 3, Fall 1983, pp. 1067-1100.

Robert Bryan, "The Execution of the Innocent," NYU Review of Law and Social Change, vol. 18, no. 3, 1991.

Capital Losses: The Price of the Death Penalty for New York State, (Albany, NY: New York State Defenders Association, Inc.), 1982.

Marcia Coyle et al., "Fatal Defense: Trial and Error in the Nation's Death Belt," The National Law Journal, June 11, 1990.

Joe Morris Doss, "The Death Penalty—Law and Morality," (Cincinnati: Forward Movement Publications), 1988.

Sheldon Ekland-Olson, "Structured Discretion, Racial Bias, and the Death Penalty: The First Decade After Furman in Texas," Social Science Quarterly, vol. 69, December 1988, pp. 853-873.

Margot Garey, "The Cost of Taking a Life: Dollars and Sense of the Death Penalty," U.C. Davis Law Review, vol. 18, no. 4, 1985, pp. 1221-1273.

Samuel Gross and Robert Mauro, "Patterns of Death: An Analysis of Racial Disparities In Capital Sentencing and Homicide Victimization," Stanford Law Review, vol. 37, 1984, pp. 27-153.

Richard Lacayo, "You Don't Always Get Perry Mason," Time, June 1, 1992.

Kent S. Miller and Michael Radelet, *Executing The Mentally Ill*, (Newbury Park, CA: Sage Publications), 1993.

Barry Nakell and Kenneth Hardy, *The Arbitrariness of the Death Penalty*, (Philadelphia: Temple University Press), 1987.

Robert Spangenberg and Elizabeth Walsh, "Capital Punishment or Life Imprisonment: Some Cost Considerations," *Loyola of Los Angeles Law Review*, vol. 23, November 1989, pp. 45-58.

Ronald J. Tabak and J. Mark Lane, "The Execution of Injustice: A Cost and Lack-of-Benefit Analysis of the Death Penalty," *Loyola of Los Angeles Law Review*, vol. 23, November 1989, pp. 59-146.

John Howard Yoder, *The Christian and Capital Punishment*, (Newton, KS: Faith and Life Press), 1961.

Howard Zehr, "Death as a Penalty: A Moral, Practical and Theological Discussion," (Ekhart, IN: MCC U.S. Office of Criminal Justice).

19

THE CASE AGAINST
THE DEATH PENALTY

Hugo Adam Bedau

The American Civil Liberties Union (ACLU) holds that the death penalty inherently violates the constitutional ban against cruel and unusual punishment and the guarantee of due process of law and the equal protection of the laws. The imposition of the death penalty is inconsistent with fundamental values of our democratic system. The state should not arrogate unto itself the right to kill human beings, especially when it kills with premeditation and ceremony, under color of law, in our names, and when it does so in an arbitrary and discriminatory fashion. In the judgment of the ACLU, capital punishment is an intolerable denial of civil liberties. We shall therefore continue to seek to prevent executions and to abolish capital punishment by litigation, legislation, commutation, or by the weight of a renewed public outcry against this brutal and brutalizing institution.

In 1972, the Supreme Court declared that under then existing laws "the imposition and carrying out of the death penalty... constitutes cruel and unusual punishment in violation of the Eighth and Fourteenth Amendments" (*Furman v. Georgia*, 408 U.S. 238). The majority of the Court concentrated its objections on the way death penalty laws had been applied, finding the result so "harsh, freakish, and arbitrary" as to be constitutionally unacceptable. Making the nationwide impact of its decision unmistakable, the Court summarily reversed death sentences in the many cases then before it, which involved a wide range of state statutes, crimes, and factual situations.

But within four years after the *Furman* decision, more than 600 persons had been sentenced to death under new capital punishment statutes that provided guidance for the jury's sentencing discretion. These statutes typically require a bifurcated (two-stage) trial procedure, in which the jury first determines guilt or innocence and then chooses imprisonment or death in the light of aggravating or mitigating circumstances.

In July 1976, the Supreme Court moved in the opposite direction, holding that "the punishment of death does not invariably violate the Constitution." The Court ruled that these new statutes contained "objective standards to guide, regularize, and make rationally reviewable the process for imposing the sentence of death" (*Gregg v. Georgia*, 428 U.S. 153). Thus the states and Congress have for some years had constitutionally valid statutory models for death penalty laws, and more than three dozen state legislatures have enacted death penalty statutes patterned after those the Court upheld in *Gregg*. In recent years, Congress has enacted death penalty statutes for peacetime espionage by military personnel and for drug-related murders.

Executions resumed in 1977. By the early 1990s, nearly 3,000 persons were under sentence of death and more than 180 had been executed.

Despite the Supreme Court's 1976 ruling in *Gregg v. Georgia*, the ACLU continues to oppose capital punishment on moral and practical, as well as on constitutional, grounds:

- Capital punishment is cruel and unusual. It is a relic of the earliest days of penology, when slavery, branding, and other corporal punishments were commonplace. Like those other barbaric practices, executions have no place in a civilized society.

- Opposition to the death penalty does not arise from misplaced sympathy for convicted murderers. On the contrary, murder demonstrates a lack of respect for human life. For this very reason, murder is abhorrent, and any policy of state-authorized killings is immoral.

- Capital punishment denies due process of law. Its imposition is arbitrary and irrevocable. It forever deprives an individual of benefits of new evidence or new law that might warrant the reversal of a conviction or the setting aside of a death sentence.

The death penalty violates the constitutional guarantee of the equal protection of the laws. It is applied randomly at best and discriminatorily at worst. It is imposed disproportionately upon those whose victims are white, on offenders who are people of color, and on those who are themselves poor and uneducated.

The defects in death penalty laws, conceded by the Supreme Court in the early 1970s, have not been appreciably altered by the shift from unfettered discretion to "guided discretion." These changes in death sentencing have proved to be largely cosmetic. They merely mask the impermissible arbitrariness of a process that results in an execution.

Executions give society the unmistakable message that human life no longer deserves respect when it is useful to take it and that homicide is legitimate when deemed justified by pragmatic concerns.

Reliance on the death penalty obscures the true causes of crime and distracts attention from the social measures that effectively contribute to its control. Politicians who preach the desirability of executions as a weapon of crime control deceive the public and mask their own failure to support anti-crime measures that will really work.

Capital punishment wastes resources. It squanders the time and energy of courts, prosecuting attorneys, defense counsel, juries, and courtroom and correctional personnel. It unduly burdens the system of criminal justice, and it is therefore counterproductive as an instrument for society's control of violent crime. It epitomizes the tragic inefficacy and brutality of the resort to violence rather than reason for the solution of difficult social problems.

A decent and humane society does not deliberately kill human beings. An execution is a dramatic, public spectacle of official, violent homicide that teaches the permissibility of killing people to solve social problems—the worst possible example to set for society. In this century, governments have too often attempted to justify their lethal fury by the benefits killing would supposedly bring to the rest of society. The bloodshed is real and deeply destructive of the common decency of the community; the benefits are illusory.

Two conclusions buttress our entire case: capital punishment does not deter crime, and the death penalty is uncivilized in theory and unfair and inequitable in practice.

Deterrence

The argument most often cited in support of capital punishment is that the threat of executions deters capital crimes more effectively than imprisonment. This claim is plausible, but the facts do not support it. The death penalty fails as a deterrent for several reasons.

ONE: Any punishment can be an effective deterrent only if it is consistently and promptly employed. Capital punishment cannot be administered to meet these conditions.

Only a small proportion of first-degree murderers is sentenced to death, and even fewer are executed. Although death sentences since 1980 have increased in number to about 250 per year,[1] this is still only 1 percent of all homicides known to the police.[2] Of all those convicted on a charge of criminal homicide, only 2 percent—about one in fifty—are eventually sentenced to death.[3]

The possibility of increasing the number of convicted murderers sentenced to death and executed by enacting mandatory death penalty laws was ruled unconstitutional in 1976. (*Woodson v. North Carolina*, 428 U.S. 280)

Considerable delay in carrying out the death sentence is unavoidable, given the procedural safeguards required by the courts in capital cases. Starting with empaneling the trial jury, murder trials take far longer when the death penalty is involved. Post-conviction appeals in death penalty cases are far more frequent as well. All these factors increase the time and cost of administering criminal justice.

The sobering lesson is that we can reduce such delay and costs only by abandoning the procedural safeguards and constitutional rights of suspects, defendants, and convicts, with the attendant high risk of convicting the wrong person and executing the innocent.

TWO: Persons who commit murder and other crimes of personal violence either premeditate them or they do not. If the crime is premeditated, the criminal ordinarily concentrates on escaping detection, arrest, and conviction. The threat of even the severest punishment will not deter those who expect to escape detection and arrest. If the crime is not premeditated, then it is impossible to imagine how the threat of any punishment could deter it. Most capital crimes are committed during moments of great emotional stress or under the influence of drugs or alcohol, when logical thinking has been suspended. Impulsive or expressive violence is inflicted by persons heedless of the consequences to themselves as well as to others.

Gangland killings, air piracy, drive-by shootings, and kidnapping for ransom are among the graver felonies that continue to be committed because some individuals think they are too clever to get caught. Political terrorism is usually committed in the name of an ideology that honors its martyrs; trying to cope with it by threatening death for terrorists is futile. Such threats leave untouched the underlying causes and ignore the many political and diplomatic sanctions (such as treaties against asylum for international terrorists) that could appreciably lower the incidence of terrorism.

The attempt to reduce murders in the illegal drug trade by the threat of severe punishment ignores this fact: anyone trafficking in illegal drugs is already betting his life in violent competition with other dealers. It is irrational to think that the death penalty—a remote threat at best—will deter murders committed in drug turf wars or by street-level dealers.

THREE: If, however, severe punishment can deter crime, then long-term imprisonment is severe enough to cause any rational person not to commit violent crimes. The vast preponderance of the evidence shows that the death penalty is no more effective than imprisonment in deterring murder and that it may even be an incitement to criminal violence in certain cases.

(a) Death penalty states as a group do not have lower rates of criminal homicide than non-death penalty states. During the 1980s, death penalty states averaged an annual rate of 7.5 criminal homicides per 100,000 of population; abolition states averaged a rate of 7.4.[4]

(b) Use of the death penalty in a given state may increase the subsequent rate of criminal homicide in that state. In New York, for example, between 1907 and 1964, 692 executions were carried out. On the average, over this fifty-seven-year period, one or more executions in a given month added a net increase of two homicides to the total committed in the next month.[5]

(c) In neighboring states—one with the death penalty and the others without it—the one with the death penalty does not show a consistently lower rate of criminal homicide. For example, between 1972 and 1990, the homicide rate in Michigan (which has no death penalty) was generally as low as or lower than the neighboring state of Indiana, which restored the death penalty in 1973 and since then has sentenced 70 persons to death and carried out two executions.[6]

(d) Police officers on duty do not suffer a higher rate of criminal assault and homicide in states that have abolished the death penalty than they do in death penalty states. Between 1973 and 1984, for example, lethal assaults against police were not significantly more or less frequent in abolition states than in death penalty states. There is "no support for the view that the death penalty provides a more effective deterrent to police homicides than alternative sanctions. Not for a single year was evidence found that police are safer in jurisdictions that provide for capital punishment."[7]

(e) Prisoners and prison personnel do not suffer a higher rate of criminal assault and homicide from life-term prisoners in abolition states than they do in death penalty states.[8] Between 1984 and 1989, 17 prison staff were murdered by prisoners in 10 states; of these murders, 88 percent (15 of 17) occurred in death penalty jurisdictions—just as about 88 percent of all the prisoners in those 10 states were in death penalty jurisdictions.[9] Evidently, the threat of the death penalty "does not even exert an incremental deterrent effect over the threat of a lesser punishment in the abolitionist state."[10]

Actual experience establishes these conclusions beyond a reasonable doubt. No comparable body of evidence contradicts them.

Three investigations since *Furman*, using methods pioneered by economists, reported findings in the opposite direction.[11] Subsequently, several qualified investigators have independently examined these claims, and all have rejected them.[12] The National Academy of Sciences, in its thorough report on the effects of criminal sanctions on crime rates, concluded: "It seems unthinkable to us to base decisions on the use of the death penalty" on such "fragile" and "uncertain" results. "We see too many plausible explanations for [these] findings... other than the theory that capital punishment deters murder."[13]

Furthermore, cases have been clinically documented where the death penalty actually incited the capital crimes it was supposed to deter. These include instances of the so-called suicide-by-execution syndrome—persons who wanted but feared to take their own life and committed murder so that society would kill them.[14]

It must, of course, be conceded that inflicting the death penalty guarantees that the condemned person will commit no further crimes. This is an incapacitative, not a deterrent, effect of executions. Furthermore, it is too high a price to pay when studies show that very few convicted murderers ever commit another crime of violence.[15] A recent study examined the prison and post-release records of 533 prisoners on Death Row in 1972 whose sentences were reduced to life by the Supreme Court's ruling in *Furman*. The research showed that six had committed another murder. But the same study showed that in four other cases, an innocent man had been sentenced to death.[16]

Recidivism among murderers does occasionally happen. But it happens less frequently than most people believe; the media rarely distinguish between a paroled murderer who murders again and other murderers who have a previous criminal record but not for homicide.

There is no way to predict which convicted murderers will kill again. Repeat murders could be prevented only by executing all those convicted of criminal homicide. Such a policy is too inhumane and brutal to be taken seriously. Society would never tolerate dozens of executions daily, yet nothing less would suffice.

Unfairness

Constitutional due process as well as elementary justice require that the judicial functions of trial and sentencing be conducted with fundamental fairness, especially where the irreversible sanction of the death penalty is involved. In murder cases (since 1930, 99 percent of all executions have been for this crime), there has been substantial evidence to show that courts have been arbitrary, racially biased, and unfair in the way in which they have sentenced some persons to prison but others to death.

Racial discrimination was one of the grounds on which the Supreme Court relied in ruling the death penalty unconstitutional in *Furman*. Half a century ago, Gunnar Myrdal, in his classic *American Dilemma* (1944), reported that "the South makes the widest application of the death penalty, and Negro criminals come in for much more than their share of the executions." Statistics confirm this discrimination, only it is not confined to the South. Between 1930 and 1990, 4,016 persons were executed in the United States. Of these, 2,129 (or 53 percent) were Black. For the crime of murder, 3,343 were executed; 1,693 (or 51 percent) were Black.[17] During these years African Americans were about 12 percent of the nation's population.

The nation's Death Rows have always had a disproportionately large population of African Americans, relative to their fraction of the total population. Over the past century, Black offenders, as compared with white, were often executed for crimes less often receiving the death penalty, such as rape and burglary. Between 1930 and 1976, 455 men were executed for rape, of whom 405 (or 90 percent) were Black. A higher percentage of the Blacks who were executed were juveniles; and Blacks were more often executed than were whites without having their conviction reviewed by any higher court.[18]

In recent years, it has been widely believed that such flagrant discrimination is a thing of the past. Since the revival of the death penalty in the mid-'70s, about half of those on Death Row at any given time have been Black[19]—a disproportionately large fraction given the Black/white ratio of the total population, but not so obviously unfair if judged by the fact that roughly 50 percent of all those arrested for murder were also Black.[20] Nevertheless, when those under death sentence are examined more closely, it turns out that race is a decisive factor after all.

An exhaustive statistical study of racial discrimination in capital cases in Georgia, for example, showed that "the average odds of receiving a death sentence among all indicted cases were 4.3 times higher in cases with white victims."[21] In 1987 these data were placed before the Supreme Court in *McCleskey v. Kemp* and the Court did not dispute the statistical evidence. The Court did hold, however, that the evidence failed to show that there was "a constitutionally significant risk of racial bias..." (*McCleskey v. Kemp*, 481 U.S. 279)

In 1990, the U.S. General Accounting Office (GAO) reported to the Congress the results of its review of empirical studies on racism and the death penalty. The GAO concluded: "Our synthesis of the 28 studies shows a pattern of evidence indicating racial disparities in the charging, sentencing, and imposition of the death penalty after the *Furman* decision" and that "race of victim influence was found at all stages of the criminal justice system process..."[22]

These results cannot be explained away by relevant non-racial factors (such as prior criminal record or type of crime), and they lead to a very unsavory conclusion: in the trial courts of this nation, even at the present time the killing of a white person is treated much more severely than the killing of a Black person. Of the 168 people executed between January 1977 and April 1992, only 29 had been convicted of the killing of a non-white, and only one of these 29 was himself white.[23] Where the death penalty is involved, our criminal justice system essentially reserves the death penalty for murderers (regardless of their race) who kill white victims.

Both sex and socioeconomic class are also factors that enter into determining who receives a death sentence and who is executed. During the 1980s and early 1990s, only about one percent of all those on Death Row were women,[24] even though women commit about 15 percent of all criminal homicides.[25] A third or more of the women under death sentence were guilty of killing men who had victimized them with years of violent abuse.[26] Since 1930, only 33 women (12 of them Black) have been executed in the United States.[27]

Discrimination against the poor (and in our society racial minorities are disproportionately poor) is also well established. "Approximately ninety percent of those on death row could not afford to hire a lawyer when they were tried."[28] A defendant's poverty, lack of firm social roots in the community, inadequate legal representation at trial or on appeal—all these have been common factors among Death

Row populations. As Justice William O. Douglas noted in *Furman,* "One searches our chronicles in vain for the execution of any member of the affluent strata in this society" (*Furman v. Georgia,* 408 U.S. 238). The demonstrated inequities in the actual administration of capital punishment should tip the balance against it in the judgment of fair-minded and impartial observers. "Whatever else might be said for the use of death as a punishment, one lesson is clear from experience: this is a power that we cannot exercise fairly and without discrimination."[29]

Justice John Marshall Harlan, writing for the Court, noted:

...the history of capital punishment for homicides... reveals continual efforts, uniformly unsuccessful, to identify before the fact those homicides for which the slayer should die... Those who have come to grips with the hard task of actually attempting to draft means of channeling capital sentencing discretion have confirmed the lesson taught by history... To identify before the fact those characteristics of criminal homicides and their perpetrators which call for the death penalty, and to express these characteristics in language which can be fairly understood and applied by the sentencing authority, appear to be tasks which are beyond present human ability. (*McGautha v. California,* 402 U.S. 183 (1971))

Yet in the *Gregg* decision, the majority of the Supreme Court abandoned the wisdom of Justice Harlan and ruled as though the new guided-discretion statutes could accomplish the impossible. The truth is that death statutes approved by the Court "do not effectively restrict the discretion of juries by any real standards. They never will. No society is going to kill everybody who meets certain preset verbal requirements, put on the statute books without awareness of coverage of the infinity of special factors the real world can produce."[30]

Even if these statutes were to succeed in guiding the jury's choice of sentence, a vast reservoir of unfettered discretion remains: the prosecutor's decision to prosecute for a capital or lesser crime, the court's willingness to accept or reject a guilty plea, the jury's decision to convict for second-degree murder or manslaughter rather than capital murder, the determination of the defendant's sanity, the final decision by the governor on clemency.

Discretion in the criminal justice system is unavoidable. The history of capital punishment in American society clearly shows the desire to mitigate the harshness of this penalty by narrowing its scope. Discretion, whether authorized by statutes or by their silence, has been the main vehicle to this end. But when discretion is used, as it always has been, to mark for death the poor, the friendless, the uneducated, the members of racial minorities, and the despised, then discretion becomes injustice.

Thoughtful citizens, who in contemplating capital punishment in the abstract might support it, must condemn it in actual practice.

Inevitability of Error

Unlike all other criminal punishments, the death penalty is uniquely irrevocable. Speaking to the French Chamber of Deputies in 1830, years after the excesses of the French Revolution, which he had witnessed, the Marquis de Lafayette said, "I shall ask for the abolition of the punishment of death until I have the infallibility of human judgment demonstrated to me."[31] Although some proponents of capital punishment would argue that its merits are worth the occasional execution of innocent people, most would also insist that there is little likelihood of the innocent being executed. Yet a large body of evidence shows that innocent people are often convicted of crimes, including capital crimes, and that some of them have been executed.

Since 1900, in this country, there have been on the average more than four cases per year in which an entirely innocent person was convicted of murder. Scores of these people were sentenced to death. In many cases, a reprieve or commutation arrived just hours, or even minutes, before the scheduled execution. These erroneous convictions have occurred in virtually every jurisdiction from one end of the nation to the other. Nor have they declined in recent years, despite the new death penalty statutes approved by the Supreme Court.[32] Consider this handful of representative cases:

- In 1975, only a year before the Supreme Court affirmed the constitutionality of capital punishment, two African-American men in Florida, Freddie Pitts and Wilbert Lee, were released from prison after 12 years awaiting execution for the murder of two white men. Their convictions were the result of coerced confessions, erroneous testimony of an alleged eyewitness, and incompetent defense counsel. Though a white man eventually admitted his guilt, a nine-year legal battle was required before the governor would grant Pitts and Lee a pardon. Had their execution not been stayed while the constitutional status of the death penalty was argued in the courts, these two innocent men probably would not be alive today.[33]

- Just months after Pitts and Lee were released, authorities in New Mexico were forced to admit they had sentenced to death four white men—motorcyclists from Los Angeles—who were innocent. The accused offered a documented alibi at their trial, but the prosecution dismissed it as an elaborate ruse. The jury's verdict was based mainly on what was later revealed to be perjured testimony (encouraged by the police) from an alleged eyewitness. Thanks to persistent investigation by newspaper reporters and the confession of the real killer, the error was exposed and the defendants were released after 18 months on death row.[34]

- In Georgia in 1975, Earl Charles was convicted of murder and sentenced to death. A surviving victim of the crime erroneously identified Charles as the gunman; her testimony was supported by a jailhouse informant who claimed he had heard Charles confess. Incontrovertible alibi evidence, showing that Charles was in Florida at the very time of the crime, eventually established his innocence but not until he had spent more than three years under death sentence. His release was owing largely to his mother's unflagging efforts.[35]

- In 1989, Texas authorities decided not to retry Randall Dale Adams after the appellate court reversed his conviction for murder. Adams had spent more than three years on Death Row for the murder of a Dallas police officer. He was convicted on the perjured testimony of a 16-year-old youth who was the real killer. Adams's plight was vividly presented in the 1988 docudrama, *The Thin Blue Line*, which convincingly told the true story of the crime and exposed the errors that resulted in his conviction.[36]

- Another case in Texas from the 1980s tells an even more sordid story. In 1980, a Black high school janitor, Clarence Brandley, and his white co-worker found the body of a missing 16-year-old white schoolgirl. Interrogated by the police, they were told, "One of you two is going to hang for this." Looking at Brandley, the officer said, "Since you're the nigger, you're elected." In a classic case of rush to judgment, Brandley was tried, convicted, and sentenced to death. The circumstantial evidence against him was thin, other leads were ignored by the police, and the courtroom atmosphere reeked of racism. In 1986, Centurion Ministries—a volunteer group devoted to freeing wrongly convicted prisoners—came to Brandley's aid. Evidence had meanwhile emerged that another man had committed the murder for which Brandley was awaiting execution. Brandley was not released until 1990.[37]

Each of the five stories told above has a reassuring ending: the innocent prisoner is saved from execution and is released. But when prisoners are executed, no legal forum exists in which unanswered questions about their guilt can be resolved. In May 1992, Roger Keith Coleman was executed in Virginia despite widely publicized doubts surrounding his guilt, and evidence that pointed to another person as the murderer—evidence that was never submitted at his trial. Not until late in the appeal process did anyone take seriously the possibility that the state was about to kill an innocent man, and then efforts to delay or nullify his execution failed. Was Coleman really innocent? At the time of his execution, his case was marked with many of the features found in other cases where the defendant was eventually cleared. Were Coleman still in prison, his friends and attorneys would have a strong incentive to resolve these questions. But with Coleman dead, further inquiry into the facts of the crime for which he was convicted is unlikely.

Overzealous prosecution, mistaken or perjured testimony, faulty police work, coerced confessions, the defendant's previous criminal record, inept defense counsel, seemingly conclusive circumstantial evidence, community pressure for a conviction—such factors help explain why the judicial system cannot guarantee that justice will never miscarry. And when it does miscarry, volunteers outside the criminal justice system—newspaper reporters, for example—and not the police or prosecutors are the ones who rectify the errors. To retain the death penalty in the face of the demonstrable failures of the system is unacceptable, especially as there are no strong counterbalancing factors in favor of the death penalty.

Barbarity

The traditional mode of execution, still available in a few states, is hanging. Death on the gallows is easily bungled: if the drop is too short there will be a slow and agonizing death by strangulation. If the drop is too long, the head will be torn off.

Two states, Idaho and Utah, still authorize the firing squad. The prisoner is strapped into a chair, and hooded. A target is pinned to the chest. Five marksmen, one with blanks, take aim and fire.

Electrocution has been the most widely used form of execution in this country in this century. The condemned prisoner is led—or dragged—into the death chamber, strapped into the chair, and electrodes are fastened to head and legs. When the switch is thrown the body strains, jolting as the voltage is raised and lowered. Often smoke rises from the head. There is the awful odor of burning flesh. No one knows how long electrocuted individuals retain consciousness.

In 1983, the electrocution of John Evans in Alabama was described by an eyewitness as follows:

> At 8:30 p.m., the first jolt of 1,900 volts of electricity passed through Mr. Evans' body. It lasted thirty seconds. Sparks and flames erupted... from the electrode tied to Mr. Evans' left leg. His body slammed against the straps holding him in the electric chair and his fist clenched permanently. The electrode apparently burst from the strap holding it in place. A large puff of grayish smoke and sparks poured out from under the hood that covered Mr. Evans' face. An overpowering stench of burnt flesh and clothing began pervading the witness room. Two doctors examined Mr. Evans and declared that he was not dead.
>
> The electrode on the left leg was refastened... Mr. Evans was administered a second thirty-second jolt of electricity. The stench of burning flesh was nauseating. More smoke emanated from his leg and head. Again, the doctors examined Mr. Evans. [They] reported that his heart was still beating, and that he was still alive. At that time, I asked the prison commissioner, who was communicating on an open telephone line to Governor George Wallace, to grant clemency on the grounds that Mr. Evans was being subjected to cruel and unusual punishment. The request... was denied.
>
> At 8:40 p.m., a third charge of electricity, thirty seconds in duration, was passed through Mr. Evans' body. At 8:44, the doctors pronounced him dead. The execution of John Evans took fourteen minutes.[38]

Afterwards, officials were embarrassed by what one observer called the "barbaric ritual." The prison spokesman remarked, "This was supposed to be a very clean manner of administering death."[39]

An attempt to improve on electrocution was the gas chamber. The prisoner is strapped into a chair, a container of sulphuric acid underneath. The chamber is sealed, and cyanide is dropped into the acid to form lethal gas. Here is an account of the 1992 execution in Arizona of Don Harding, as reported in the dissent by U. S. Supreme Court Justice John Paul Stevens:

> When the fumes enveloped Don's head he took a quick breath. A few seconds later he again looked in my direction. His face was red and contorted as if he were attempting to fight through tremendous pain. His mouth was pursed shut and his jaw was clenched tight. Don then took several more quick gulps of the fumes.
>
> At this point Don's body started convulsing violently... His face and body turned a deep red and the veins in his temple and neck began to bulge until I thought they might explode.
>
> After about a minute Don's face leaned partially forward, but he was still conscious. Every few seconds he continued to gulp in. He was shuddering uncontrollably and his body was racked with spasms. His head continued to snap back. His hands were clenched.
>
> After several more minutes, the most violent of the convulsions subsided. At this time the muscles along Don's left arm and back began twitching in a wavelike motion under his skin. Spittle drooled from his mouth.
>
> Don did not stop moving for approximately eight minutes, and after that he continued to twitch and jerk for another minute. Approximately two minutes later, we were told by a prison official that the execution was complete.
>
> Don Harding took ten minutes and thirty-one seconds to die. (*Gomez v. U.S. District Court*, 112 S.Ct. 1652)

The latest mode of inflicting the death penalty, enacted into law by nearly two dozen states, is lethal injection, first used in Texas in 1982. It is easy to overstate the humaneness and efficacy of this method. There is no way of knowing that it is really painless. As the U.S. Court of Appeals observed, there is "substantial and uncontroverted evidence... that execution by lethal injection poses a serious risk of cruel, protracted death... Even a slight error in dosage or administration can leave a prisoner conscious but paralyzed while dying, a sentient witness of his or her own asphyxiation" (*Chaney v. Heckler*, 718 F.2d 1174 (1983)).

Nor does the execution always proceed smoothly as planned. In 1985, "the authorities repeatedly jabbed needles into... Stephen Morin, when they had trouble finding a usable vein because he had been a drug abuser."[40] In 1988, during the execution of Raymond Landry, "a tube attached to a needle inside the inmate's right arm began leaking, sending the lethal mixture shooting across the death chamber toward witnesses."[41]

Indeed, by its veneer of decency and by subtle analogy with lifesaving medical practice, death by lethal injection makes killing as punishment more acceptable to the public. Even when it prevents the struggles of the condemned person and avoids maiming the body, it is no different from hanging or shooting as an expression of the absolute power of the state over the helpless individual.

Most people observing an execution are horrified and disgusted. "I was ashamed," writes sociologist Richard Moran, who witnessed an execution in Texas in 1985. "I was an intruder, the only member of the public who had trespassed on [the condemned man's] private moment of anguish. In my face he could see the horror of his own death."[42] Revulsion at the duty to supervise and witness executions is one reason why so many prison wardens—however unsentimental they are about crime and criminals—are opponents of capital punishment.

In some people, however, executions seem to appeal to strange, aberrant impulses and give an outlet to sadistic urges. Warden Lewis Lawes wrote of the many requests he received to watch electrocutions, and told that when the job of executioner became vacant, "I received more than seven hundred applications for the position, many of them offering cut-rate prices."[43]

Public executions were common in this country during the 19th century; one of the last was in 1936 in Kentucky, when 20,000 people gathered to watch a young African-American male hanged.[44] Delight in brutality, pain, violence, and death may always be with us. But surely we must conclude that it is best for the law not to encourage these impulses. When the government sanctions, commands, and ceremoniously carries out the execution of a prisoner, it lends support to this destructive side of human nature.

More than two centuries ago, the Italian jurist Cesare Beccaria, in his highly influential treatise, *On Crimes and Punishments* (1764), asserted: "The death penalty cannot be useful, because of the example of barbarity it gives men." And even if the death penalty were a "useful" deterrent, it would still be an "example of barbarity." No society can safely entrust the enforcement of its laws to torture, brutality, or killing. Such methods are inherently cruel and will always mock the attempt to cloak them in justice. As Supreme Court Justice Arthur J. Goldberg wrote, "The deliberate institutionalized taking of human life by the state is the greatest conceivable degradation to the dignity of the human personality."[45]

Retribution

Justice, it is often insisted, requires the death penalty as the only suitable retribution for heinous crimes. This claim will not bear scrutiny. All punishment by its nature is retributive, not only the death penalty. Whatever legitimacy, therefore, is to be found in punishment as just retribution can in principle be satisfied without recourse to executions.

It is also obvious that the death penalty could be defended on narrowly retributive grounds only for the crime of murder, and not for any of the many other crimes that have frequently been made subject to this mode of punishment (rape, kidnapping, espionage, treason, drug kingpins). Few defenders of the death penalty are willing to confine themselves consistently to the narrow scope afforded by retribution.

It is also often argued that death is what murderers deserve, and that those who oppose the death penalty violate the fundamental principle that criminals should be punished according to their deserts—"making the punishment fit the crime."

If this principle is understood to require that punishments are unjust unless they are like the crime itself, then the principle is unacceptable. It would require us to rape rapists, torture torturers, and inflict other horrible and degrading punishments on offenders. It would require us to betray traitors and kill multiple murderers again and again, punishments impossible to inflict. Since we cannot reasonably aim to punish all crimes according to this principle, it is arbitrary to invoke it as a requirement of justice in the punishment of murderers.

If, however, the principle of just deserts is understood to require that the severity of punishments must be proportional to the gravity of the crime, and that murder being the gravest crime deserves the severest punishment, then the principle is no doubt sound. But it does not compel support for the death penalty. What it does require is that crimes other than murder be punished with terms of imprisonment or other deprivations less severe than those used in the punishment of murder.

Criminals no doubt deserve to be punished, and punished with severity appropriate to their culpability and the harm they have caused to the innocent. But severity of punishment has its limits—imposed both by justice and our common human dignity. Governments that respect these limits do not use premeditated, violent homicide as an instrument of social policy.

Some whose loved one was a murder victim believe that they cannot rest until the murderer is executed. But the feeling is by no means universal. Coretta Scott King observed:

> As one whose husband and mother-in-law have died the victims of murder assassination, I stand firmly and unequivocally opposed to the death penalty for those convicted of capital offenses. An evil deed is not redeemed by an evil deed of retaliation. Justice is never advanced in the taking of a human life. Morality is never upheld by a legalized murder.[46]

And Kerry Kennedy, daughter of the slain Senator Robert Kennedy, has written:

> I was eight years old when my father was murdered. It is almost impossible to describe the pain of losing a parent to a senseless murder... But even as a child one thing was clear to me: I didn't want the killer, in turn, to be killed. I remember lying in bed and praying, 'Please, God. Please don't take his life, too.' I saw nothing that could be accomplished in the loss of one life being answered with the loss of another. And I knew, far too vividly, the anguish that would spread through another family—another set of parents, children, brothers, and sisters thrown into grief.[47]

Financial Costs

It is sometimes suggested that abolishing capital punishment is unfair to the taxpayer, as though life imprisonment were obviously more expensive than executions. If one takes into account all the relevant costs, the reverse is true. "The death penalty is not now, nor has it ever been, a more economical alternative to life imprisonment."[48]

A murder trial normally takes much longer when the death penalty is at issue than when it is not. Litigation costs—including the time of judges, prosecutors, public defenders, and court reporters, and the high costs of briefs—are all born by the taxpayer.

A 1982 study showed that were the death penalty to be reintroduced in New York, the cost of the capital trial alone would be more than double the cost of a life term in prison.[49]

In Maryland, a comparison of capital trial costs with and without the death penalty for the years 1979 to 1984 concluded that a death penalty case costs "approximately 42 percent more than a case resulting in a non-death sentence."[50] In 1988 and 1989, the Kansas legislature voted against reinstating the death penalty after it was informed that reintroduction would involve a first-year cost of "more than $11 million."[51] Florida, with one of the nation's largest Death Rows, has estimated that the true cost of each execution is approximately $3.2 million, or approximately six times the cost of a life-imprisonment sentence.[52]

The only way to make the death penalty a "better buy" than imprisonment is to weaken due process and curtail appellate review, which are the defendant's (and society's) only protections against the grossest miscarriages of justice. The savings in dollars would be at the cost of justice: in nearly half of the death penalty cases given review under federal *habeas corpus*, the conviction is overturned.[53]

Public Opinion

The media commonly report that the American public overwhelmingly supports the death penalty. More careful analysis of public attitudes, however, reveals that most Americans would oppose the death penalty if convicted murderers were sentenced to life without parole and were required to make some form of financial restitution. In California, for example, a Field Institute survey showed that in 1990, 82 percent approved in principle of the death penalty. But when asked to choose between the death penalty and life imprisonment plus restitution, only a small minority—26 percent—continued to favor executions.[54]

A comparable change in attitude toward the death penalty has been verified in many other states and contradicted in none.

Abolition Trends

The death penalty in the United States needs to be put into international perspective. In 1962, it was reported to the Council of Europe that "the facts clearly show that the death penalty is regarded in Europe as something of an anachronism"[55]

Today, 28 European countries have abolished the death penalty either in law or in practice. In Great Britain, it was abolished (except for treason) in 1971; France abolished it in 1981. Canada abolished it in 1976. The United Nations General Assembly affirmed in a formal resolution that, throughout the world, it is desirable to "progressively restrict the number of offenses for which the death penalty might be imposed, with a view to the desirability of abolishing this punishment."[56]

Conspicuous by their indifference to these recommendations are nations generally known for their disregard for the human rights of their citizens: China, Iraq, Iran, South Africa, and the former Soviet Union.[57] Americans ought to be embarrassed to find themselves linked with the governments of such nations in retaining execution as a method of crime control. [South Africa abolished the death penalty in 1995, after the new administration, led by Nelson Mandela, gained office—E.R.]

Once in use everywhere and for a wide variety of crimes, the death penalty today is generally forbidden by law and widely abandoned in practice. The unmistakable worldwide trend is toward the complete abolition of capital punishment.

NOTES

1. U.S. Bureau of Justice Statistics, *Capital Punishment*, annually, 1980 to present.
2. Federal Bureau of Investigation, *Uniform Crime Reports*, (Washington, DC: GPO), annually, 1980 to present.
3. *Uniform Crime Reports.*
4. *Uniform Crime Reports*, annually, 1980-1989.
5. William J. Bowers and Glenn L. Pierce, "Deterrence or Brutalization," *Crime and Delinquency*, vol. 26, October 1980.
6. *Capital Punishment*, 1972-1990; *Uniform Crime Reports*, annually, 1972-1990; National Association for the Advancement of Colored People Legal Defense and Educational Fund (NAACP LDF), *Death Row, USA*, Spring 1992.
7. William C. Bailey and Ruth D. Peterson, in *Criminology*, 1987, p. 22.
8. U.S. Bureau of Justice Statistics, *Sourcebook of Criminal Justice Statistics*, (Washington, DC: GPO), 1990.
9. U.S. Bureau of Justice Statistics, "Prisons and Prisoners in the United States," (Washington, DC: GPO), 1992, p. 1.
10. Wendy P. Wolfson, "The Deterrent Effect of the Death Penalty on Murder," The Death Penalty in America, 3rd ed., Hugo Adam Bedau, ed., (London: Oxford University Press), 1982, p. 167.
11. Ehrlich, *American Economic Review*, 1974; Phillips, *American Journal of Sociology*, 1980; and Stephen K. Layson, "Homicide and Deterrence: a Reexamination of the United States Time-Series Evidence," *Southern Economic Journal*, vol. 52, July 1985.
12. M. Lempert, "The Effects of Executions on Homicides: a New Look in an Old Light," *Crime and Delinquency*, vol. 29, January, 1983; Ruth D. Peterson and William C. Bailey in *Criminal Law in Action*, 2nd ed., Chambliss, ed., 1984; W. J. Bowers, "The Effect of

Execution is Brutalization, Not Deterrence," *Challenging Capital Punishment*, Kenneth C. Haas and James A. Inciardi. eds., (Newbury Park, CA: Sage Publications), 1988; Ruth D. Peterson and William C. Bailey, "Murder and Capital Punishment in the Evolving Context of the Post-Furman Era," *Social Forces*, vol. 66, March 1988; Michael Radelet *et al.* in *Loyola of Los Angeles Law Review*, vol. 23, November 1989.

13. Alfred Blumenstein *et al.*, eds., *Deterrence and Incapacitation: Estimating the Effects of Criminal Sanctions on Crime Rates*, (Washington, DC: National Academy of Sciences), 1978, p. 358.

14. Louis West, "Psychiatric Reflection on the Death Penalty," *Capital Punishment in the United States*, Hugo Adam Bedau *et al.*, eds., 1976; George F. Solomon, "Capital Punishment as Suicide and as Murder," *Capital Punishment in the United States*; Bernard L. Diamond, "Murder and the Death Penalty: a Case Report," *Capital Punishment in the United States*.

15. Hugo Adam Bedau, "Recidivism, Parole, and Deterrence," Death Penalty in America.

16. James W. Marquart *et al.*, "National Study of the Furman-Commuted Inmates," *Loyola of Los Angeles Law Review*, vol. 23, November 1989.

17. *Capital Punishment*, 1977; NAACP LDF, *Death Row, USA, Spring 1992*.

18. William J. Bowers, Legal Homicide: Death as Punishment in America, 1864-1982, (Boston, Northeastern University Press), 1984; Victor L. Streib, *Death Penalty for Juveniles*, (Bloomington, IN: Indiana University Press), 1987.

19. NAACP LDF, *Death Row, USA*, 1976 to present.

20. *Uniform Crime Reports*, 1972, 1990.

21. David Baldus, George Woodworth, and Charles Pulaski, *Equal Justice and the Death Penalty: A Legal and Empirical Analysis*, (Boston: Northeastern University Press), 1990, p. 401.

22. U.S. General Accounting Office, "Death Penalty Sentencing," (Washington, DC: GAO), 1990, pp. 5, 6.

23. NAACP LDF, Death Row, USA, Spring 1992; *Sourcebook of Criminal Justice Statistics*, 1990.

24. Capital Punishment, 1980-1990.

25. *Uniform Crime Reports*, 1980-1990.

26. Memorandum, National Coalition to Abolish the Death Penalty, January 1991.

27. *Capital Punishment*, 1979; NAACP LDF, *Death Row, USA*, Spring 1992.

28. Ronald J. Tabak and Mark J. Lane, "The Execution of Injustice: A Cost and Lack-of-Benefit Analysis of the Death Penalty," *Loyola of Los Angeles Law Review*, vol. 23, November, 1989, pp. 59-146.

29. Samuel R. Gross and Robert Mauro, *Death and Discrimination*, (Boston: Northeastern University Press), 1989, p. 224.

30. Charles L. Black, *Capital Punishment: The Inevitability of Caprice and Mistake*, 2nd ed., (New York: W. W. Norton), 1982.

31. Lucas, *Recueil des debats*, part 2, 1831, p. 32.

32. Michael L. Radelet *et al.*, *In Spite of Innocence: Erroneous Convictions in Capital Cases*, (Boston: Northeastern University Press), 1992; Hugo Adam Bedau and Michael L. Radelet, "Miscarriages Of Justice in Potentially Capital Cases," *Stanford Law Review*, vol. 40, 1987, pp. 21-179.

33. Gene Miller, *Invitation to a Lynching*, (Garden City, NY: Doubleday), 1975; The New York Times, September 10, 1975, p. 1.

34. "Capital Punishment," Senate Hearings, 1981, pp. 713-20.

35. Atlanta Weekly, May 30, 1982.

36. Randall Adams et al., *Adams v. Texas*, (New York: St. Martin's Press), 1991.

37. Nick Davies, *White Lies: Rape, Murder, and Justice Texas Style*, (New York: Pantheon Books), 1991.

38. *Glass v. Louisiana*, 471 U.S. 1080 (1985).

39. *Boston Globe*, April 24, 1983, p. 24.

40. *The New York Times*, December 14, 1988, p. A29.

41. *The New York Times*, December 14, 1988, p. A29.

42. *Los Angeles Times*, March 24, 1985, pt. IV, p. 5.

43. Lewis Lawes, *Twenty Thousand Years in Sing Sing*, (New York: R. Long & R. R. Smith), 1932.

44. M. Teeters, *Journal of the Lancaster County Historical Society*, 1960.

45. *The Boston Globe*, August 16, 1976, p. 17.

46. Coretta Scott King, speech to National Coalition to Abolish the Death Penalty, Washington, DC, September 26, 1981.

47. Foreword to Ian Gray *et al.*, *A Punishment In Search of A Crime: Americans Speak Out Against the Death Penalty*, (New York: Avon), 1989.

48. Robert Spangenberg and Elizabeth Walsh, "Capital Punishment or Life Imprisonment: Some Cost Considerations," *Loyola of Los Angeles Law Review*, vol. 23, 1989, p. 47.

49. *Capital Losses: The Price of the Death Penalty for New York State*, (Albany, NY: New York State Defenders Association, Inc.), 1982.

50. U.S. Government Accounting Office, *Limited Data Available on Costs of Death Sentences*, (Washington, DC: GAO), 1989.

51. Spangenberg and Walsh.

52. *Miami Herald*, July 10, 1988.

53. *New York Times*, September 22, 1989.

20

TEETERING ON THE BRINK BETWEEN DEATH AND LIFE

Mumia Abu-Jamal

For there to be equivalence, the death penalty would have to punish a criminal who had warned his victim of the date at which he would inflict a horrible death on him and who, from that moment onward, had confined him at his mercy for months. Such a monster is not encountered in private life.[1]

—Camus[2]

"Yard in!"

The last "yard" of the day is finally called. "Capitals! Fourth, fifth, and sixth tier—YARD UP!" the corpulent correctional officer bellows, his rural accent alien to the urban ear.

One by one, cells are unlocked for the daily trek from cell to cage. Each man is pat-searched by guards armed with batons, then scanned by a metal detector.

Once the inmates are encaged, the midsummer sky rumbles, its dark clouds swell, pregnant with power and water. A bespectacled "white shirt" turns his pale face skyward, examining nature's quickening portent. The rumbles grow louder as drops of rain sail earthward, splattering steel, brick, and human.

"Yard in!," the white shirt yells, sparking rumbling murmurs of resentment among the men.

"Yard in?!—shit, man—we just got out here!"

The guards adopt a cajoling, rather than threatening, attitude. "C'mon, fellas—yard in, yard in. Ya know we can't leave y'uns out here when it gits ta thunderin' an' lightning."

"Oh—why not? Y'all 'fraid we gonna get ourself electrocuted?" a prisoner asks.

"Ain't thatta bitch?" another adds. "They must be afraid that if we do get electrocuted by lightning they won't have no jobs and won't get paid!"

A few guffaws, and the trail from cage to cell thickens.

Although usually two hours long, today's yard barely lasts ten minutes, for fear that those condemned to death by the state may perish, instead, by fate.

For approximately 2,400 people locked in state and federal prisons, life is unlike that in any other institution. For these are America's "condemned," those who bear a stigma far worse than "prisoner." These are America's Death Row residents: men and women who walk the razor's edge between half-life and certain death in 34 states or under the jurisdiction of the United States.[3] The largest Death Row is in Texas (324 people: 120 African Americans, 144 whites, 52 Hispanics, 4 Native Americans, and 4 Asian Americans); the smallest are in Connecticut (2 whites), New Mexico (1 Native American, 1 white), and Wyoming (2 whites).[4]

You will find a Blacker world on Death Row. African Americans, a mere 12 percent of the national population, compose about 40 percent of the Death Row population.[5] There, too, you will find this writer.

Control

It is from Pennsylvania's largest Death Row at the State Correctional Institute at Huntingdon, in rural south-central Pennsylvania, that I write. In the Commonwealth, I am but one of 123 persons who await death. I have lived in this barren domain of death since the summer of 1983. For several years now I have been assigned "DC" (disciplinary) status for daring to abide by my faith, the teachings of John Africa, and in particular, for refusing to cut my hair.[6] For this I have been denied family phone calls, and on occasion, I have been shackled for refusing to violate my beliefs.[7]

Life here oscillates between the banal and the bizarre.

Unlike other prisoners, Death Row inmates are not "doing time." Freedom does not shine at the end of the tunnel. Rather, the end of the tunnel brings extinction. Thus, for many here, there is no hope.

As in any massive, quasi-military organization, reality on the Row is regimented by rule and regulation. As against any regime imposed on human personality, there is resistance, but far less than one might expect.

For the most part, Death Row prisoners are the best behaved and least disruptive of all inmates. It is also true, however, that there is little opportunity to be otherwise, given that many "death units" operate on the "22 + 2" system: 22 hours locked in cell, followed by 2 hours of recreation out of cell. Outdoor recreation takes place in a cage, ringed with double-edged razor wire—the "dog pen."

All Death Rows share a central goal: "human storage" in an "austere world in which condemned prisoners are treated as bodies kept alive to be killed."[8] Pennsylvania's Death Row regime is among America's most restrictive, rivaling the infamous San Quentin death unit for the intensity and duration of restriction. A few states allow four, six, or even eight hours out-of-cell, prison employment, or even access to educational programs. Not so in the Keystone State.

Here, one has little or no psychological life. Here, many escape death's omnipresent specter only by way of common diversions— television, radio, or sports. Here, TVs are allowed, but not typewriters: one's energies may be expended freely on entertainment, but a tool essential for one's liberation through judicial process is deemed a "security risk."

One inmate, more interested in his life than his entertainment, argued forcefully with prison administrators for permission to buy a non-impact, nonmetallic, battery-operated typewriter. Predictably, permission was denied for "security" reasons. "Well, what do y'all consider a thirteen-inch piece of glass?" the prisoner asked. "Ain't thatta 'security risk?'"

"Where do you think you'll get that from?" the prison official demanded.

"From my TV!"

Request for typewriter denied.

TV is more than a powerful diversion from a terrible fate. It is a psychic club used to threaten those who dare resist the dehumanizing isolation of life on the Row. To be found guilty of an institutional infraction means one must relinquish it.

After months or years of non-contact visits, few phone calls, and ever decreasing communication with one's family and others, many use TV as an umbilical cord, a psychological connection to the world they have lost. They dread its separation and depend on it, in the way that lonely people turn to TV for the illusion of companionship. For many, loss of TV is too high a price to pay for any show of resistance.

Humiliation

Visits are an exercise in humiliation.

In Pennsylvania, as in many other death states, non-contact visits are the rule.[9] It is not just a security rule; it is a policy and structure which attempts to sever emotional connection by denying physical connection between the visitor and the inmate. Visits are conducted in a closed room, roughly 80 square feet in size. The prisoner is handcuffed and separated by a partition of shatterproof glass, steel trim, and wire mesh.

What visitors do not see, prior to the visit, is a horrifying spectacle—the body-cavity strip search. Once the prisoner is naked, the visiting-room guard spits out a familiar cadence:

"Open yer mouth—
Stick out your tongue—
You wear any dentures?
Lemme see both sides of your hands—
Pull your foreskin back—
Lift your sac—
Turn around—
Bend over—
Spread your cheeks—
Bottom of yer feet—
Get dressed."

Several prisoners have protested administratively that such searches are unreasonable, arguing that body-cavity strip searches before and after non-contact visits cannot be justified. Either allow contact visits, they argue, or halt the body-cavity strip searches. But prison officials have responded to this proposal in the same manner with which they have responded to repeated calls by the condemned for allowance of typewriters: refusal, due to the "security risk."

For the visitor, too, such visits are deeply disturbing.

In *Rhem v. Malcolm*,[10] the often-cited case on prison conditions in New York, Judge Lasker quoted expert testimony from Karl Menninger, the late psychiatrist, who described non-contact visiting as "the most unpleasant and most disturbing detail in the whole prison," and a practice which constitutes "a violation of ordinary principles of humanity."[11] Dr. Menninger stated:

> [I]t's such a painful sight that I don't stay but a minute or two as a rule. It's a painful thing... I feel so sorry for them, so ashamed of myself that I get out of the room.[12]

The ultimate effect of non-contact visits is to weaken, and finally to sever, family ties. Through this policy and practice, the state skillfully and intentionally denies those it condemns a fundamental element and expression of humanity—that of touch and physical contact—and thereby slowly erodes family ties already made tenuous by the distance between home and prison. Thus a prisoner is as isolated psychologically as he is temporally and spatially. By state action, he becomes "dead" to those who know and love him, and therefore, dead to himself. For who is a person, but for his relations and relationships?

Hurled by judicial decree into this netherworld of despair, forcefully separated from relationships, overcome by the dual shame of their station and the circumstances of the crime which led them to death's door, a few succumb to the shady release of suicide.[13] Some fight Sisyphian battles, struggling to prove their innocence and reverse unjust convictions. Others live as they are treated—as "shadows of [their] former selves, in a pantomime of life, human husks."[14]

To such men and women, the actual execution is a *fait accompli*, a formality already accomplished in spirit, where the state concludes its premeditated drama by putting the "dead" to death a second time.

Politics and "Justice" of Death

Although it might be said fairly that many people, both inside and outside of prison, are utterly uninformed as to the workings of the U.S. Supreme Court, there are some among those on Death Row who watch the Court with acute attention. For them, the sudden resignation of Justice William J. Brennan, Jr. comes as crushing news after a season of sorrow. The recent spate of losses suffered by capital litigators spells all but certain doom for those who continue to petition the present Court for legal relief.[15]

Where the issue of the death penalty is concerned, law follows politics, and conservatives won the sociopolitical battles of the 1980s on the basis of an agenda which included a ringing endorsement of capital punishment. The venerated principle of *stare decisis*[16] meant little in the politically charged judicial arena. Statistical methodology and scientific and sociological studies, once valued tools for challenging state practice, now serve as meaningless academic exercises.

McCleskey v. Kemp[17] was the clincher. The Supreme Court majority, Justice Powell writing, assumed the validity of the so-called Baldus study, which presented mounds of powerful statistical data demonstrating gross racial disparity in Georgia's death penalty tallies, but rejected the study's clear implications.[18]

Justice Brennan's dissent telescoped the Baldus study's meaning: defendants charged with killing whites are 4.3 times more likely to be sentenced to die as defendants charged with killing Blacks; six of every eleven defendants convicted of killing a white would not have received a death sentence had their victim been Black.[19] Thus the study showed that "there was a significant chance that race would play a prominent role in determining if [a defendant] lived or died."[20]

The majority's perambulations to its eventual rejection of that which it could hardly deny—that the race of the victim is a primary factor in determining whether a defendant lives or dies—proved the potency of the old adage offered by the satirical character, Mr. Dooley, who shrewdly observed: "No matther whether th' constitution follows th' flag or not, th' supreme coort follows th' iliction returns."[21]

McCleskey's claim, based on sophisticated statistical and multiple regression analysis, buttressed by "our understanding of history and human experience,"[22] was not disproved by the *McCleskey* court; rather, it was rejected out of fear. In rejecting the conclusion that the facts established an unconstitutional infirmity, Justice Powell noted with alarm, that "McCleskey's claim, taken to its logical conclusion, throws into serious question the principles that underlie our entire criminal justice system."[23]

Precisely.

Because McCleskey dared question the fundamental fairness of the entire system, his claims were answered with rejection.

Delbert Tibbs, an African-American divinity student, once found himself tossed in with Death Row prisoners in Florida. Convicted by an all-white jury in 1974 for a rape and related murder, he spent three harrowing years in death's shadow before appellate reversal. In speaking about his jury, he observed:

"PEER: one of equal rank; one among equals." I knew the definition of that word, and there was nothing remotely akin to this meaning existing between me and these seven hard-eyed White Men and five cold-eyed White Women who made up this jury of my "peers."

I knew that any peerage that they comprised, as indeed they did comprise such a thing, totally excluded me, at least, in their eyes...

...Peers, indeed.

I'm sure that in the eyes of that jury I was not just another human being. Oh, no. I was dangerous, because, darker. I didn't belong...[24]

On the *McCleskey* decision, Tibbs noted:

Apparently, that Justice of the United States, writing for the majority, thinks that the United States is not two separate societies, one black and one white, and quite unequal...

...Justice is not meted out without regard to race, sex, economics, or previous condition of servitude...

That Justice was speaking as if there were no Civil War and no chattel slavery. He spoke as if there were no history of lynchings, as if there were no *Dred Scott* decision, no Medgar Evers, Little Rock, nor "Bombingham." Memphis didn't happen in that "America."[25]

What does happen, in this America, is the cheapening of Black life and the placing of a premium upon white life. As Justice Brennan's eloquent dissent in *McCleskey* argues, the fact that this practice may be customary does not make it constitutional.

To do justice, one must consistently battle, in Brennan's words, "a fear of too much justice."[26] Finding that fear firmly entrenched, he framed his arguments, not merely as counters to positions with which he passionately disagreed, but also as warnings for the future, a day not yet dawned:

It is tempting to pretend that minorities on death row share a fate in no way connected to our own, that our treatment of them sounds no echoes beyond the chambers in which they die. Such an illusion is ultimately corrosive, for the reverberations of injustice are not so easily confined....

The Court's decision today will not change what attorneys in Georgia tell other Warren McCleskeys about their chances of execution. Nothing will soften the harsh message they must convey, nor alter the prospect that race undoubtedly will continue to be a topic of discussion. McCleskey's evidence will not have obtained judicial acceptance, but that will not affect what is said on death row. However many criticisms of today's decision may be rendered, these painful conversations will serve as the most eloquent dissents of all.[27]

Ironically, perhaps, the "eloquent dissents" of *pro se* Court-watchers are commonly delivered in the winning or losing of a bet: inmates on the Row often wager with one another on the outcome of judicial decisions. But as the real stakes riding on any given outcome are high, objective predictions are rarely possible.

By viewing every decision through the prism of politics, I never lost a bet even in cases where "jailhouse lawyers" claimed to have "the law" on their side. There is, of course, no satisfaction in such victories: every bet won has been a case lost; every case lost a step closer to death. My predictions, based on political winds rather than law, have earned me the enmity of those jailhouse lawyers who continue to place faith in legal precedents and principles despite their growing pile of lost wagers.

Death March and Lessons Unlearned

There is a quickening upon the nation's Death Rows of late, a picking up of the pace of the march toward death. The political prod is sparking movement, and judges in death cases are beginning to find themselves under increasing pressure to make the final judgment.

As murder rates rise in American cities, so too does the tide of fear. Both politicians and judges continue to ride that tide that washes towards the execution chamber's door. No matter that of the ten states with the highest murder rate, eight of them lead the country in executions which supposedly deter; no matter that of the ten states with the lowest murder rate, only one (Utah) has executed anyone since 1976.[28] No matter that the effectiveness of the death penalty is not really debated; no matter that the contention that the death penalty makes citizens "safer" is no longer seriously argued.

Habeas corpus, fundamental to English law since the reign of King Charles and to the United States Constitution since its inception, now faces evisceration under the hand of the Chief Justice of the Supreme

Court,[29] a possibility unthinkable just a few years ago. Many of the "condemned," with constitutional error rife throughout their records, will soon be executed without meaningful review.

States that have not slain in a generation now ready their machinery: generators whine, poison liquids are mixed and gases are measured and readied, silent chambers await the order to smother life. Increasingly, America's northern states now join the rushing pack, anxious to re-link themselves with their pre-*Furman*[30] heritage.

Deterrence?

The March 1988 Florida execution of Willie Darden, exceedingly well publicized here and abroad, should have had enormous deterrent effect according to capital theories. But less than eleven hours after 2,000 volts coursed through Darden's manacled flesh, a Florida corrections officer, well-positioned to absorb and understand the lessons of the state ritual, erupted in a jealous rage and murdered a man in the maternity wing of a hospital.[31]

Seems like a lesson well learned to me.

NOTES

1. *Editor's note:* Reading this quote, activists in the movement against domestic violence have pointed out that such a monster does exist, in millions of homes across the country and throughout the world. The testimony of survivors attests to the fact that the terror under which many battered women live daily is akin to the type of Death Row experience outlined here. See Judith Lewis Herman, *Trauma and Recovery: The Aftermath of Violence from Domestic Abuse to Political Terror*, (New York: Basic Books), 1992.

2. Albert Camus, "Reflections on the Guillotine," *Resistance, Rebellion, and Death,* (O'Brien, trans), (New York: Knopf), 1961.

3. National Association for the Advancement of Colored People Legal Defense and Educational Fund (NAACP LDF), *Death Row, U.S.A.,* September 21, 1990.

4. NAACP LDF, *Death Row, U.S.A.*

5. NAACP LDF, *Death Row, U.S.A.*

6. John Africa is the founder of MOVE, an organization formed in 1972 as the "Christian Movement for Life." Adherents to MOVE ideology reject the social order and its legal authority. Followers of the teachings of John Africa place faith in "God-given natural law," wear their hair in dreadlocks, and reject technology, formal education, and other products of an unequal, unjust society. See Washington, "MOVE: A Double Standard of Justice?," *Yale Journal of Law and Liberation,* no. 1, 1989.

7. MOVE members incarcerated in Pennsylvania prisons are often given disciplinary status for refusing to cut their hair; some have been denied parole for refusing to agree to stipulations forbidding them to associate with other members upon release. See

Washington; e.g., Moushey, "Inmate's Rehabilitation Counts for Little," *Pittsburgh Post-Gazette*, September 4, 1990. MOVE supporter Richard Garland, considered a rehabilitated model prisoner by corrections officials, was denied parole based on refusal to disassociate himself from MOVE members including his wife. Such actions by the state violate constitutional rights to freedom of religion, speech, and association. See, e.g., *Garland v. Sullivan*, 2 Civ. Trial Manual (BNA) no. 5, at 108-09, Apr. 9, 1986 (E.D. Pa., no. 80-2350, Mar. 5, 1986) (jury in civil case brought by inmate against prison guards finds MOVE is religious organization within meaning of First Amendment); *Contra Africa v. Pennsylvania*, 662 F.2d 1025 (3d Cir. 1981) (upholding state prison's rejection of MOVE member's special dietary request on ground that MOVE fails to qualify within meaning of First Amendment).

8. Johnson and Carroll, "Litigating Death Row Conditions: The Case for Reform," *Prisoners and the Law*, I. Robbins, ed., 1988 (quoting R. Johnson, "Death Row Confinement: The Psychological and Moral Issues," unpublished paper presented at colloquium on the death penalty at Towson State University, March 10, 1983).

9. Inmates on Death Row in Georgia, Florida, California, and Alabama are permitted contact visits. See R. Johnson. The late Florida Corrections Chief, Louis Wainwright, consistently defended the efficacy of contact visits for noncapital-offense state prisoners. See *Miller v. Carson*, 401 F. Supp. 835, 884 (M.D. Fla. 1975), affirmed in part, 563 F.2d 741 (5th Cir. 1977): "It was defendant Wainwright's opinion that contact visits are desirable and an effective rehabilitative tool."

10. 371 F. Supp. 594 (SDNY 1974).

11. 371 F. Supp. 594 (SDNY 1974).

12. 371 F. Supp. 594 (SDNY 1974).

13. NAACP LDF, *Death Row, USA*.

14. Johnson and Carroll.

15. These cases, even with Justice Brennan sitting, reveal an ill-disguised judicial hostility to issues which once seemed meritorious. See *Saffle v. Parks*, 110 S. Ct. 1257 (1990)—scope of collateral review does not include finding that instruction to jury to "avoid any influence of sympathy" is unconstitutional; *Boyde v. California*, 110 S. Ct. 1190 (1990)—instruction that jury "shall impose a sentence of death" (if it finds that aggravating circumstances do not outweigh mitigating circumstances) does not violate defendant's constitutional right to individualized assessment of appropriateness of death penalty; *Blystone v. Pennsylvania*, 110 S. Ct. 1078 (1990)—statute requiring imposition of death penalty where aggravating circumstances outweigh mitigating ones is not unconstitutional; *McCleskey v. Kemp*, 481 U.S. 279 (1987)—statistical data showing, *inter alia*, that Blacks convicted of killing whites being more likely to receive death penalty than other defendants did not demonstrate violation of petitioner's constitutional rights since petitioner failed to establish evidence that racial considerations played a role in his case; *Lockhart v. McCree*, 476 U.S. 162 (1986)—removal for cause persons opposed to death penalty does not violate petitioner's right to jury selected from a fair cross-section of the community; *Wainwright v. Witt*, 469 U.S. 412 (1985)—removal for cause of person opposed to death penalty does not violate petitioner's Sixth and Fourteenth Amendment rights to trial by impartial jury where judge made finding that excused juror's views would prevent or substantially impair the performance of her duties.

16. "To stand by that which was decided; rule by which common law courts 'are slow to interfere with the principles announced in the former decision and often uphold them

even though they would decide otherwise were the question a new one.'" *Barron's Law Dictionary.*

17. *McCleskey v. Kemp*, 481 U.S. 279 (1987).

18. In support of his claim that the Georgia capital sentencing process was administered in a racially discriminatory manner in violation of the Eighth and Fourteenth Amendments, McCleskey submitted a statistical study (the Baldus study) which examined over 2,000 Georgia murder cases from the 1970s. The Court's majority assumed the study's statistical validity for purposes of decision. *McCleskey v. Kemp*, 481 U.S. 279 (1987). The dissenters, however, were persuaded that the statistical evidence was valid.

19. *McCleskey v. Kemp*, 481 U.S. 279 (1987).

20. *McCleskey v. Kemp*, 481 U.S. 279 (1987).

21. F. Dunne, "The Supreme Court's Decisions," *Mr. Dooley on the Choice of Law*, E. Bander, ed. 1963 (collection of newspaper essays from the turn of the century). On capital punishment, Mr. Dooley observed: "I don't believe in capital punishment... but 'twill niver be abolished while th' people injye it so much." Dunne, "The Law's Delays," *Mr. Dooley on the Choice of Law.*

22. *McCleskey v. Kemp*, 481 U.S. at 328 (J. Brennan, dissenting).

23. *McCleskey v. Kemp*, 481 U.S. at 314-15.

24. Delbert Tibbs, "From Seminary to Cell Block," *A Saga of Shame: Racial Discrimination and the Death Penalty*, (Hyattsville, MD: Let Live, Quixote Center), 1989, p. 16.

25. Tibbs.

26. *McCleskey v. Kemp*, 481 U.S. 339 (J. Brennan, dissenting).

27. *McCleskey v. Kemp*, 481 U.S. 339.

28. "Murder in the City," *USA Today*, August 6, 1990 (FBI and U.S. Department of Justice data on murder rates by state); "United States Executions" (data sheet of September 25, 1990—National Coalition to Abolish the Death Penalty, listing executions by state and names and dates of execution of people put to death since 1976).

29. Rehnquist has long been impatient with the slow pace of state executions, stating that persistent challenges by capital defendants undermine the "rule of law" and make a "mockery" of the criminal justice system. Robert A. Burt, "Disorder in the Court: The Death Penalty and the Constitution," *Michigan Law Review*, vol. 85, August 1987, pp. 1741-1819. Recently Rehnquist has been in the forefront of legislative efforts to "reform" *habeas corpus* in order to grease the skids to death. See "Chief Justice Endorses Powell Committee Report on *Habeas* Reform in Capital Cases," *Criminal Law Reporter*, no. 47 at 1159, May 23, 1990 (endorsement of proposal to restrict capital defendants to single opportunity at federal level for collateral review of sentence).

30. *Furman v. Georgia*, 408 US 238 (1972) *(per curiam)* (imposition and carrying out of death penalty in cases before the Court would constitute cruel and unusual punishment in violation of Eighth and Fourteenth Amendments).

31. Breslin, "State Shouldn't Be in the Killing Business," *The Sunday News*, (Lancaster, PA), March 20, 1988.

21

KILLING JUSTICE

Government Misconduct and the Death Penalty

Death Penalty Information Center

"(...the prosecutor) is the representative... of a sovereignty... whose interest... in a criminal prosecution is not that it shall win a case, but that justice shall be done."

—Berger v. United States, 295 U.S. 78 (1935)

"That requirement, in safeguarding the liberty of the citizen against deprivation through the action of the State, embodies the fundamental conceptions of justice which lie at the base of our civil and political institutions."

—Herbert v. Louisiana, 272 U.S. 312 (1926)

Prosecutorial Misconduct: An Overview

When Jimmy Carter was in the White House, Gary Nelson was convicted and sentenced to die for the 1978 rape and murder of a six-year-old child in Chatham County, Georgia, the kind of high visibility crime that exerts great pressure on police and prosecutors to solve quickly.

On November 6, 1991, after more than 11 years protesting his innocence—watching time forever slip away behind him while it moved him closer and closer to the electric chair—Nelson was released. A free man.

It had taken his appellate lawyers, working without pay, that many years to prove that the government's capital case against their client rested on a foundation of official lies, the knowing use of false testimony, and the willful suppression of evidence in the state's possession that not only tended to support Nelson's claim of innocence, but which pointed to the guilt of another.

Although he spent more than a decade of his life on Death Row, Nelson might still be considered lucky. Others with equally compelling evidence of official government misconduct remain imprisoned in every state in the country and on every Death Row. Some, like Roger Coleman in Virginia and Barry Fairchild in Arkansas, faced execution despite the misconduct. [Barry Lee Fairchild was executed on August 31, 1995—E.R.]

For others, like Warren McCleskey and Bobby Francis, it is already too late. Both men were executed in 1991.

Misconduct by the government in the pursuit of a death sentence can take many forms. But whether it involves the use of threats and intimidation to obtain a "confession," the use of jailhouse informants who secretly enter into deals with the prosecution for their testimony, or the government's unrevealed promise of leniency for one co-defendant in exchange for his or her testimony against another, the resulting death sentence is fundamentally unfair, and cannot be tolerated in a society which honors the principle that no person is above the law.

Police Abuse

Misconduct often begins with the police. It can be as subtle as an implied threat for failing to cooperate or as overt as the beating of Rodney King. Often, the police are under great pressure to act quickly, especially when the murder victim is white, prominent, a child, or a police officer. As former head of Philadelphia's organized-crime homicide squad Frank Friel says, "The supervisor wants your report in. There's pressure from the victim's family. You're working for 36 hours straight. It becomes a challenge to prevail—a good guy versus bad guy thing."[1]

Often, the police develop a theory of the crime and then search out evidence—and suspects—that support that theory. Then, when they arrest someone, they proceed as if the suspect is already guilty. "The mentality and the pressure are to not let the guilty guy go free," Friel, now chief of police in Bensalem, Pennsylvania, explains. "When you see shortcomings, you hedge. You block out anything that doesn't fit... You feel you have no obligation to bring up evidence pointing to others. Why cloud the issue?"[2]

Sometimes, the scenario is not so benign. "Two men who claimed to have been the only witnesses to the 1978 San Bernardino murder of a police officer's son now say they actually saw nothing, but were pressured by police into giving false testimony that has kept an innocent man in prison for 13 years," begins a recent article in the *Los Angeles Times*. The fact that the victim was the son of a police officer greatly increases the likelihood of such misconduct. According to the article, one of the witnesses gave the police what they wanted only after being handcuffed to a motel room bed during 24 hours of questioning. Before trial he recanted, but the district attorney allegedly covered it up so the defense never learned of the recantation.[3]

In the case of Barry Fairchild, the evidence is that the sheriff and his deputies engaged in overt brutality, both verbal and physical, against a succession of Black suspects until one of them gave in to the intimidation and signed a confession. As is often the case, Fairchild was the least able to withstand the assault. Mentally disabled, he finally told the police what they wanted to hear.

Racism

Racism is often the motive for official misconduct. When the U.S. Court of Appeals for the Eleventh Circuit reversed the death sentence of Jimmy Lee Horton in September 1991, they singled out District Attorney of the Ocmulgee Judicial Circuit Joe Briley for special censure. In a succession of death penalty cases, Briley has used his peremptory jury strikes to ensure that Black defendants continue to be tried by all-white juries. In one case, Briley instructed the Putnam County clerk on how to underrepresent Blacks and women in the jury pool and not get caught. The court noted that since becoming DA in 1974, Briley has used 89.9 percent of his jury strikes against Blacks in capital cases involving Black defendants. Where the defendant is Black and the victim white, that figure rises to 94.1 percent. In overturning Horton's death sentence, the court reminded the prosecutor of his duty to do justice, and held that the prosecutor acted unconstitutionally to deny Blacks the "right and opportunity to participate in the administration of justice."[4]

In January 1990, Clarence Brandley was released after spending nearly a decade on Death Row in Texas for a crime he did not commit. The misconduct in that case involved every level of government, from the police who threatened witnesses to prevent them from testifying for Brandley, to the trial judge and the prosecutor who held secret meetings to rehearse objections and rulings, to the state attorney general who lied about the results of a lie detector test. What enabled

Texas officials to pursue Brandley with such single-minded disregard for facts, fairness and basic justice was that the victim in the case was a white school girl who had been raped and murdered. The likely suspects were the school's janitors, one of whom—Clarence Brandley—is Black.

In 1987, U.S. District Court Judge Perry Pickett held that Brandley

> did not receive a fair trial, was denied the most basic fundamental rights of due process of law, and did not commit the crime for which he now resides on death row... The court unequivocally concludes that the color of Clarence Brandley's skin was a substantial factor which pervades all aspects of the State's capital prosecution... In the 30 years this court has presided over matters in the judicial system, no case has presented a more shocking scenario of the effects of racial prejudice, perjured testimony, witness intimidation, an investigation the outcome of which was predetermined, and public officials who, for whatever motives, lost sight of what is right and just.[5]

Jailhouse Snitches

One of the most common features of death penalty cases involves the testimony of jailhouse informants or snitches—inmates who swear in court that the defendant confessed to them. For people in prison or jail, such testimony can be a powerful bargaining chip: in exchange for it, the state will often reduce the time they are serving or dismiss charges pending against them. Because the possibility of leniency is a strong inducement to lie, the prosecutor is required to tell the defense—who, in turn, will tell the jury—when such deals are made. With that knowledge the jury can weigh the credibility of the testimony. Misconduct occurs when such deals are kept secret.

Warren McCleskey was singled out from among four co-defendants by a cellmate who testified that McCleskey had admitted to him that he was the one who pulled the trigger. The prosecutor, when asked by McCleskey's attorney, denied that anything had been offered in exchange for his testimony. That was a lie discovered inadvertently 10 years after he had been sent to Death Row. When it was revealed, two jurors came forward to say they would never have sentenced Warren McCleskey to death if they had known of the deal.

His attorneys petitioned the federal court to remedy the clear misconduct of the prosecutor. Instead, the Supreme Court took the opportunity to announce a new rule: except under rare circumstances, prisoners can petition the federal courts for redress but once. If they fail to raise constitutional abuses the first time through—even if the failure is due to the government's misconduct—the federal court is closed to them.

McCleskey had been through the federal court system once before, losing 5-4 on the issue of whether the death penalty is applied in a racially discriminatory way.[6] His attorneys did not raise the issue of the prosecutor's illegal acts at that time, relying on official assurances that no deal had been offered. The Court's new rule made clear that lawyers who trust the government to tell the truth do so at their own peril. Or, more precisely, at their clients' peril. Warren McCleskey was executed September 25, 1991.

The unreliability of this kind of testimony was dramatically brought home when jailhouse informant Leslie White showed how a prisoner with intelligence and a telephone can learn enough details about a pending case to sound convincing even if he has never met the person he testifies against. His admission to reporters in Los Angeles that he had fabricated a dozen confessions of others in exchange for lenient treatment led the Los Angeles County Grand Jury to investigate. In 1990, the grand jury's special counsel, Douglas Dalton, reported that "Despite all the warnings of misconduct—by admissions of the informants, notice by the courts, and even an internal campaign within the district attorney's office—the district attorney's office deliberately rejected taking the necessary action which would have effectively ended these practices." The grand jury concluded that the Los Angeles County District Attorney's Office had "failed to fulfill the ethical responsibilities of a public prosecutor."[7]

Despite this, in a subsequent capital case in which the condemned maintained that the informant's testimony against him was perjured, the California Supreme Court held he had no right to see the DA's files on "mere speculation." In a stinging dissent, two justices called the ruling a "Catch-22"—prohibiting the accused from seeing the files without concrete facts while denying him the opportunity to get those facts. The dissenters described the majority opinion as "a miscarriage of justice which may return to haunt us."[8]

Since prosecutors do not have to open their files for inspection, no one can be sure how widespread the practice is. After canvassing post-conviction cases in California, however, attorneys for the California Appellate Project estimate that "close to a third of those individuals suffering death judgments have had jailhouse informants involved in some capacity in their cases." That translates to roughly 100 people under sentence of death in California and, extrapolating to the entire country, more than 800 condemned prisoners nationwide!

Deals with the Devil

A deadly variation of the undisclosed deal involves the use of co-defendants. Here, instead of jailhouse informants providing the testimony essential for a conviction or a death sentence, it is provided by someone else implicated in the crime. It is a common practice for prosecutors to promise leniency to—or threaten more serious punishment for—one defendant in exchange for testimony against another.

On the eve of Thanksgiving 1991, Texas officials were gearing up to execute Justin Lee May on the basis of just such testimony. At May's trial, co-defendant Richard Miles testified that it was May who pulled the trigger. May was found guilty and sentenced to death. In exchange for his testimony, Miles was allowed to plead guilty to a non-capital offense. Just four days before the execution, overcome by a guilty conscience, Miles recanted his damning testimony. In his affidavit, Miles stated:

> While I was present, and was an eyewitness to the offense, Justin Lee May was not present, nor did he participate in the offense in any manner. All of my testimony concerning his involvement in this crime was untrue... (The police) told me that I could be executed if I didn't cooperate, so I decided to cooperate with the police and tell them what they seemed to be after... Before the trial I was afraid that if I didn't point the finger at May, they would pin me on capital murder and I would be executed... Even now, I am afraid the police will come after me and find some way to have me locked up again. But my conscience is eating at me, and it's time to tell the truth regardless of what may happen to me.[9]

May is lucky. Not only did his accuser come forward to clear his conscience, the Fifth Circuit Court of Appeals stayed the execution, providing time to examine the new evidence. Bobby Francis was not so lucky.

A judge sentenced Francis to death in Florida in 1983 despite a jury-recommended life sentence. It was Francis' third trial for the offense. (Two earlier trial results had been set aside because of flawed proceedings.) In the first trial, a co-defendant, Charlene Duncan, had been convicted and sentenced to life in prison. By the time Francis was tried a third time, Ms. Duncan, who was serving her life sentence, was represented by the same man then prosecuting Francis. Just before trial, as reward for her testimony against Francis, the prosecutor filed a motion to have Duncan's conviction and sentence vacated. When Francis was convicted and sentenced to death, the motion on Duncan's behalf was granted. She pled guilty to third-degree murder, was sentenced to "time served," and was released.

State Supreme Court Justice Ben F. Overton observed that he was "deeply concerned about the conduct of the prosecutor... Such conduct adversely affects the credibility of our justice system."[10] It also adversely affected Bobby Francis, who was executed in Florida on June 25, 1991.

Jim McCloskey, director of Centurion Ministries, spends all his time investigating claims of wrongful convictions by the imprisoned. He estimates that half the cases he sees involve alleged confessions by one defendant to another that later prove to be false. When he first came across this aspect of homicide cases, he could not understand what prompted an individual to lie about someone confessing to murder. It was explained to him quite simply by a defendant who, like Richard Miles in the case of Justin Lee May, had falsely testified about such a confession and later recanted. "It's a matter of survival. Either I go away or your guy goes away. And I ain't going away."[11]

Occasionally, the unreliability and unfairness of death sentences secured on this basis reaches the conscience of elected officials with the power to act. Anson Avery Maynard was scheduled to die in North Carolina on January 17, 1992. Just one week before the execution, on January 11, Governor Jim Martin commuted Maynard's sentence to life in prison because of doubts about his guilt. The governor's office noted that there was no physical evidence linking Maynard to the 1981 murder for which he was sentenced to die, and that the eyewitness testimony came from someone who admitted his participation in the murder and, for his testimony, was given full immunity from prosecution.[12]

Governor Martin's commutation requires a political courage rare in most elected officials these days. It was the first commutation in North Carolina since that state reinstated the death penalty in 1976. The irony is that although Maynard is no longer under threat of execution because of doubts about his guilt, he is confined to prison for life despite those same doubts. At least, however, if he is later proven innocent, the state can partially rectify its error.

C.Y.A.

There is another motive for a form of misconduct that all of us probably engage in from time to time. It might be described as "Cover Your Ass." When we make mistakes, even inadvertently, it is often difficult to own up. But when those mistakes lead to a sentence of death, covering them up adds another layer of misconduct, deadly and deliberate.

In the U.S. government's non-capital prosecution of Leonard Peltier for the murder of two FBI agents in 1975, the case rests largely on the testimony of a mentally ill woman, Myrtle Poor Bear, who swore she saw Peltier kill the agents in cold blood. Later, she recanted the testimony, claiming the FBI threatened to take her daughter from her if she did not testify. But when she came forward to speak the truth, the judge ruled her incompetent, and refused to take her testimony.

When asked about the use of the coerced testimony by "60 Minutes" reporter Steve Kroft, Assistant U.S. Attorney Lynn Crooks, who prepared the government's case against Peltier, said, "It doesn't bother my conscience one bit… He got convicted on fair evidence. Doesn't bother my conscience one whit. I don't agree that there's anything wrong with that, and I can tell you, it don't bother my conscience if we did."[13]

Unfortunately, this willingness to defend the indefensible is all too common in capital cases, as a number of the examples discussed in this report make clear.

Conclusion

This report is not meant to be the definitive study of prosecutorial misconduct in capital cases. Rather, it is designed to call attention to the fact that such misconduct is widespread, is not confined to a single region of the country, and often leads to wrongful convictions and even to the execution of the innocent. It is designed to remind us that we are all implicated when the government is guilty of illegalities, when it forgets the constitutional mandate to "establish justice" and engages in the same kind of acts which, if committed by individuals, could be criminally prosecuted. It is designed to remind us that every aspect of a legal process that ends in the sentence of death for a fellow citizen cries out for deliberate, careful review to ensure that the sentence was obtained legally—and to prevent "the people" from executing an innocent person.

The prosecutor in a criminal case is usually a politician—the elected local district attorney or state attorney general—whose client is the people as a whole. Unlike a defense attorney, whose task it is to provide the most effective advocacy possible for the accused, whether innocent or guilty, the people's representative is not tasked to win a case but to do justice. When the government sacrifices justice for a courtroom victory, the entire judicial process is corrupted.

As a federal appeals court judge wrote in overturning a Louisiana death sentence because the prosecutor had exculpatory evidence in his possession that he did not reveal, "Such conduct would be reprehensible in an ordinary case; where a man's life is at stake, it is beyond reprehension."[14]

NOTES

1. Ted Rohrlich, "Minister of Justice," *Los Angeles Times Magazine*, December 23, 1990.
2. Rohrlich.
3. Ted Rohrlich, "Murder Witnesses Now Say They Lied," *Los Angeles Times*, August 14, 1991, A3.
4. *Horton v. Zant*, 941 F.2d 1449 (1991).
5. Nick Davies, *White Lies: Rape, Murder, and Justice Texas Style*, (New York: Pantheon Books), 1991.
6. *McCleskey v. Kemp*, 481 U.S. 279, 107 S.Ct. 1756 (1987).
7. Report of the 1989-90 Los Angeles County Grand Jury: "Investigation of the Involvement of Jail House Informants in the Criminal Justice System in Los Angeles County".
8. Philip Hager and Ted Rohrlich, "Justices Limit Access to Informant Files," *Los Angeles Times*, December 4, 1990, p. A3.
9. Affidavit of Richard Miles, *May v. Collins*, "On Application for a Certificate of Probable Cause" in the United States Court of Appeals for the Fifth Circuit, No. 91-6273, December 18, 1991.
10. *Francis v. State*, 473 So. 2d 672 at 677 (1985).
11. Ted Rohrlich, "Minister of Justice."
12. Bruce Henderson, "Martin Commutes Man's Death Sentence," *The Charlotte Observer*, January 11, 1992.
13. James Stolz, "The Last Sioux Brave," *60 Minutes*, September 22, 1991.
14. *Lindsey v. King*, 769 F.2d 1034 (1985).

SECTION FIVE

POLITICAL IMPRISONMENT IN THE UNITED STATES

Many political organizers have made (and continue to make) the contention that all prisoners are political prisoners. In some senses, this is true. It is not necessarily that all prisoners are themselves politically active, or publicly identified with a particular movement or cause, but that the context in which human beings are caged is extremely political. The legal machinery that brings a person to be locked up is never objective or indiscriminatory; there are a multitude of socioeconomic, racial, and political factors that play into each case. So many prisoners are convicted, sentenced, incarcerated, and subjected to legal and physical harassment based on reasons clearly beyond the facts of the case: from their race or class backgrounds, to their associations or political beliefs.

"Justice" is far from blind. The unbiased administration of just laws, described in civics classes or shown on television, does not exist. Poor people and people of color routinely receive harsher penalties from judges and juries than do white middle-class folk, for the exact same crimes. The whole process is riddled with DA, cop, judge, guard, and prison official misconduct. Framing of suspects, coercion of witnesses, and the gang-jacketing[1] of defendants are commonplace. Arbitrary and unfair rulings and procedures are rampant. Thus, many activists assert that all prisoners, whether politicized or not, should be considered in the political context within which they were caged. However, the point of using the term "political prisoner" is to draw attention to the huge variance in the treatment of different prisoners. It is to highlight the fact that people who have committed heinous acts while not articulating an agenda the state finds threatening are often released within months or years of their sentencing, while people who challenge state authority are held for decades, lied to, harassed, abused, and ridiculed as "terrorists."

Recognizing and raising awareness about political prisoners is also about drawing attention to the government's true agenda: quashing the opposition of people who dare challenge either particular institutions or the whole economic and political system. The state's rationale is that if it is able to keep these activists, agitators, and revolutionaries out of sight and out of mind, then it will be easier to keep the rest of the populace complacent. The goal is to make an example of political prisoners, to crush further resistance by intimidating those who would articulate the nature of and fight against their oppression. This rationale ignores the fact that wherever there is repression, there will always be resistance.

While the U.S. government denies that it holds political prisoners and prisoners of war, it cages hundreds of people who have been identified by all international standards to be clearly deserving of this status. Amnesty International has repeatedly called on the U.S. government to discontinue torture of its citizens; representatives from this human rights monitoring group have found the federal government and state prisons to be in violation of the United Nations' Standard Rules for the Treatment of Prisoners (see Section Six on control unit prisons and Chapter Six, "In Critical Condition").

Imprisonment in general is highly political. Yet, Mumia Abu-Jamal, for instance, is considered a political prisoner because the governments of Pennsylvania and the United States have treated him the way they have as a direct result of his work with the Black Panther Party, his support for the MOVE organization, and for his religious practices. Norma Jean Croy has been targeted for a crime she did not commit, not only because she is Native American, but because of her vocal resistance as a woman and as a Lesbian. Federal grand juries have been used as a tool to disrupt the Left—not the Right—for decades.[2]

Many of the essays in this section are available through groups such as the Prison Activist Resource Center (PARC) and the International Anarchist Black Cross, as well as papers such as *Prison News Service*. The Freedom Now! network, now largely defunct, concentrated its efforts on those prisoners explicitly identified with particular liberation movements, or particular struggles. Other groups have continued where they left off. This is vital work, explored more fully in the readings that follow. Besides the national liberation and anti-imperialist movements discussed here, political prisoners also came from a variety of backgrounds, including anarchists, tax resisters, and activists in the animal liberation and disarmament movements. For more information, see the *Organizers' Guide* from PARC (order form on the last page of this book). Please also note that *Prison News Service* has, in the last several years, been a unique and valuable resource on detailed information regarding the subtle and controversial political and tactical issues surrounding political prisoner support and the role of groups such as Freedom Now! See especially issues 21-29.

Included here are analyses of the practice of political imprisonment and highlights of specific cases. Most activists who address issues of political prisoners also provide a critique of the prison system as a whole, and specific abuses within it. For reasons of brevity and to avoid redundancy, this critique has largely been edited out of the following chapters.

NOTES

1. Gang-jacketing is the practice of creating public knowledge or conjecture of a person's affiliation to a gang. The practice was used widely by the FBI in its infamous COINTELPRO, and is used today by agents of the state at various levels to condemn prisoners and activists.

2. For example, *Underground: The Magazine of the North American Animal Liberation Front Supporters Group*, PO Box 8673, Victoria, BC, Canada V8W 3S2, and "Defense Lawyer is Jailed Over Client Confidentiality," *New York Times*, February 15, 1991. For many others, contact PARC or search the alternative press index, available in most libraries, and on-line through the Institute for Global Communications. Contact igc-info@igc.org.

22

PRISONS AS CONCENTRATION CAMPS

It Can't Happen Here—or Can It?[1]

José López

Since the social upheavals of the '60s, the number of political prisoners in the United States has grown dramatically, with over 100 behind bars today. The number of prisoners has also spiraled upwards. These increases take place in a particular context: prisons are increasingly being used as tools of counterinsurgency and population control by a U.S. government that faces serious economic, social, political, and military crises.

Who's in Prison?

According to the Bureau of Criminal Justice Statistics, at year-end 1991 the number of prisoners in this country reached 823,414. The bloating of the imprisonment rate is expected to continue. By 2000, the total prison population will double. Over the next few years the prison population, excluding jails, probation, and parole will reach one million. The United States is becoming a nation of prison houses.

A closer look at the statistics shows that rates of imprisonment began zooming upwards after the social upheavals of the late 1960s. (In 1969, 120 cities burned in Black rebellions.) In 1925, when the United States began keeping these statistics, the imprisonment rate was 79 per 100,000. The rate stayed more or less constant until 1972, when it started to rise dramatically. By 1991, the rate had skyrocketed to 310!

Counterinsurgency

The Crisis of Democracy was a major ruling-class policy statement on domestic affairs, written principally by Samuel Huntington and issued by the Trilateral Commission in 1973. The book described the U.S. political crisis of the '60s and '70s as being caused by the excessive demands of "ungovernable sectors," Black, Chicano, and Native-American movements, along with women and youth. In the words of Samuel Huntington, "The demands on democratic government grow, while the capacity of democratic governments stagnates. This, it would appear, is the central dilemma of the governability of democracy..." He lamented that society had become too democratic: "There are potentially desirable limits to the indefinite extension of political democracy." The Trilateralist remedy was more authoritarianism to ensure "a more balanced existence."

In the 1970s, U.S. military and intelligence circles closely studied the work of Frank Kitson and Robin Eveleigh, two British colonels who articulated the need for permanent counterinsurgency. These theorists insisted that since insurgency was a stable feature of the political landscape, governments must implement permanent low-intensity repressive strategies to "nip revolutionary movements in the bud." In this model, prisons serve as an important tactic to contain political leaders and organizers.

Recent studies support the understanding of prisons as tools for population control, for detaining the "undesirables." William Nagel, a well-known criminologist, analyzed many factors in various states to determine which factors were related to rapidly increasing imprisonment rates. He found no relationship between the crime rate (or violent crime rate) and the imprisonment rate, and no relationship between the crime rate (or violent crime rate) and the proportion of Black people in a state.

However, he discovered a very strong relationship between the imprisonment rate and the proportion of Black people. In other words, people go to prison in increasing numbers because they are Black, not because of a rise in the crime rate. Two British criminologists, Steven Box and Chris Hale, found similar results and concluded that people are sent to prison during times of economic instability, not because of an increase in crime, but because they are perceived as a threat by those who hold power in society. Thus, prisons have become a tool of those in power to contain and control Blacks, as well as Mexicans, Puerto Ricans, and Native Americans.

What makes this government's program for social "stability" work? Law and order. More police. More prisons. Longer prison terms. The death penalty. The "ungovernables"—those who cannot be controlled, those who will not submit to living in the areas designated for Third World peoples, those who refuse to work for low wages, and those who rebel and try to organize their people—will end up in prison where they can be controlled.

Political Prisoners

In the 1960s, as the civil rights and Black Power movements grew, the number of Black political prisoners swelled and the prison struggle became a major part of the Black liberation struggle. Political prisoners like George Jackson stated that prisons are an important tool in the government's effort to contain Black people and destroy their freedom.

Although the government refuses to admit it, there are over 100 political prisoners and prisoners of war in U.S. prisons today. They come from the Puerto Rican, Black/New Afrikan, and Native-American liberation movements. They include progressive Christians, white anti-imperialists, draft resisters, and grand jury resisters. The movements that these people represent honor, love, and respect them. Yet the government contends that they are criminals or terrorists, and reserves for them, as well as for prisoners showing leadership and political direction, the harshest treatment.

Control Units

Control units are designed to totally control the lives of the prisoners in them, and to ultimately break the spirit of these prisoners. In the case of political prisoners and POWs (prisoners of war), the control units are part of a calculated strategy to weaken the movements and intimidate others from taking a stand. The United States Penitentiary at Marion in southern Illinois is the most maximum security prison in the country, serving as an experimental laboratory and trendsetter for the whole prison system; 36 states now have control units in operation or under construction.

At Marion, the Bureau of Prisons (BOP) established the first control unit where prisoners are subjected to sensory deprivation and solitary confinement. In the early years of the prison, officials experimented with the use of drugs on control unit prisoners. For punishment, Marion puts prisoners in "boxcars"—small, enclosed, soundproof boxes. In October 1983, the entire prison was locked down. For many years (as is the case for most control units), prisoners were locked in tiny cells for more than 22 hours a day. They were denied contact with each other and forced into total idleness; punished by being shackled naked and spread-eagled to cement beds; denied all contact visits; and deprived of work programs, group educational activities, and congregational religious worship. Squads of guards in riot gear routinely beat prisoners who broke the rules.

The Bureau of Prisons tries to perpetuate the myth that Marion contains "the most vicious, predatory prisoners in the system." The truth is that the criteria for placement in and out of Marion are intentionally vague. In fact, 80 percent of the men in Marion are eligible for placement at less restrictive prisons. Although some infamous felons are placed there, the prison also houses people sentenced to short terms for victimless crimes, people imprisoned for their political beliefs and activities, and prisoner leaders.

A control unit for women was built at the Lexington Federal Correctional Institute in Kentucky in October 1986. This was a behavior modification unit in which the Bureau of Prisons used sensory deprivation, extreme isolation, and sexual degradation to control the prisoners. The director of the Bureau said that the conditions in the unit were necessary to provide adequate security for the women. He said their radical politics made them a threat to the community and "escape prone." Other prison officials told the women that their only avenue out of the unit was to renounce their political associations, to repudiate a lifetime of political principle. After a national protest campaign, in October 1987 the Bureau announced that it would close the unit, stating that it was not big enough to house all the female political "terrorists" in the country. In June 1988, three of the prisoners sued the Bureau. A federal judge agreed that the Bureau had persecuted them for their political beliefs and ruled that they be transferred out of the unit immediately. By August 1988, all of the women had finally been moved out of the unit and it was closed. In August 1988, the Bureau opened a new federal prison in Marianna, Florida. It contained a special women's unit which the Bureau said would "continue the mission" of the Lexington Control Unit.

Women in Prison

The number of women in prison has increased enormously in the last 10 years, at a faster rate than the number of men in prison, to over 50,000. These women are disproportionately Black, Latina, and Native American. Two-thirds are under the age of 35, and 90 percent are single mothers. They are poor, with 85 percent reporting incomes of less than $2,000 in the year prior to their arrest. Most are in prison for economic crimes. Of the few imprisoned for violent crimes, the vast majority were convicted for defending themselves or their children from abuse. Their imprisonment is not a reflection of their criminal characters, but rather of the role of women in this society.

Once in prison, women face a kind of brutality that is more psychological and sexual than physically violent. Women are sexually harassed by male guards and subject to sexual blackmail, pressured to trade sex with guards in return for protection or "favors" (which often means the necessities of life). In co-educational prisons, female prisoners are heavily outnumbered and surrounded by male prisoners. These men, though powerless themselves, can still create an atmosphere of sexual and physical intimidation. Prison authorities treat women like children, calling them "girls." Women are not even offered the inadequate kinds of job training available to men prisoners; they are disrespected in every way. Lesbians and Lesbian relationships are subject to additional manipulation and attack. Female prisoners lose not only their freedom, but often face loss of contact with their children, sometimes forever.

All over the world and in the United States, the last two decades have seen a dramatic rise in the proportion of women involved in revolutionary and progressive movements. This has been reflected in the growing proportion of female political prisoners. In the United States, roughly 25 percent of political prisoners are women. How can these leaders be controlled and prevented from acting as examples to others? Female political prisoners have been subjected to intense campaigns of psychological manipulation and sexual abuse, including vaginal and rectal finger probes by male guards, constant video surveillance (even in shower areas), and the threat of rape by male guards or prisoners. The Lexington Control Unit was an experiment in this vein and Marianna federal prison is its extension.

Immigrants

Immigrants are another group of "undesirables" the government is trying to contain. During brighter economic times, immigrants, mostly Mexican, were considered desirable because they were cheap labor for industrial production. Now, however, the government perceives them as undesirables taking jobs away from U.S. citizens. In addition, the government fears that some immigrants, such as Palestinians, Central Americans, Haitians, and Irish Republicans, will spread the truth about the U.S.-sponsored persecution in their home-lands, where liberation struggles are rising. And the government has tried to exclude immigrants from countries that are not allies of the United States, such as Libya and Iran.

To control these immigrant populations, the government passed the Immigration Reform and Control Act in 1986, which stated that only immigrants who can prove that they have lived and worked in the United States may apply for residency, and that it is illegal for employers to hire immigrants. As part of the Federal Emergency Management Agency's REX '84 training program, mechanisms were created and exercised for detaining thousands of immigrants, as well as North American dissidents, if the government should deem it necessary in a political emergency. A recent example illustrates all of this painfully well. When thousands of people rebelled in Los Angeles in May 1992, following the racist verdict that let off the four cops who brutalized Rodney King, the L.A. police forces mobilized themselves and deported thousands of Mexicans and Salvadorans, many of them, it was later revealed, "in error."

The Bureau of Prisons intentionally builds walls of silence around its prisons in hope that the public will never learn about the people living within the prison walls, nor the BOP's brutal policies. The wall of silence must be torn down.

Despite the denial of the United States, there are scores of political prisoners in this country, and hundreds, maybe thousands, of people now choosing political work that might involve prison as punishment. And there is no sign that this trend will stop. In addition, organizations and individuals on the outside are trying to expose the reality of political prisoners in the United States and to make them visible. Within this context, assembling a book such as *Can't Jail The Spirit* seemed to us to be a particularly important task. We feel that only when we listen to the prisoners' own voices can we begin to understand who they are and why they have acted the way they did.

Who Is a Political Prisoner?

Political prisoners exist as a result of real political and social conflicts in the society. There is no society free of contradictions, and therefore no society that does not have political prisoners. The absurd position of the U.S. government that it alone has no political prisoners is consistent with its position that there are no legitimate social or political movements struggling for fundamental change. The strategy of criminalization and isolation of political prisoners, i.e., the denial of their existence, in part allows the United States to propagate the lie that U.S. society has achieved social peace, and that whatever dissent there is functions solely within the existent bourgeois democratic framework.

There is a notable group of political prisoners called prisoners of war. These people are members of oppressed nations who consider their nations to be at war with the United States, or who are building towards such a war. That is, they are members of national liberation struggles who have participated in pursuits similar to political prisoners, except that they have been involved in the use of organized revolutionary violence and/or are members of clandestine organizations that may utilize revolutionary violence. POWs usually take the position, consistent with international law, that U.S. courts have no jurisdiction over them, and therefore they may and often do refuse to participate in legal proceedings, including their own trials. There is a great deal of documented international law to support this position, including the Geneva Convention Protocols One and Two, and Resolution 1514 of the United Nations General Assembly (passed on December 14, 1960), which states that colonialism is a crime against humanity and that those captured fighting against it are prisoners of war.

Special conditions are often constructed for the attack on political prisoners. Laws are created to repress them. Often they are given longer sentences than other people convicted of similar crimes. When inside prison, they are often treated worse. Control unit prisons have been used against them with great vengeance. For example, male political prisoners are often sent to Marion Federal Penitentiary straight from court. This violates the Bureau of Prisons' own regulations, which maintain that prisoners be sent to Marion only after they have been disruptive in another prison. And, finally, the United States has resorted to outright murder as in the case of Puerto Rican prisoner of war Angel Rodriguez Cristobal and Black revolutionary George Jackson. These repressive acts are designed not so much to punish political prisoners for their actions, but to brutalize them and others into turning against their political causes. Simply deny your beliefs and you will be relieved of this burden, they are told. With startling regularity and courage, the vast majority of them refuse this "option" and remain steadfast, beacons to those of us who believe that a new society must be created.

Prisoners Who Are Not Political Prisoners

In one sense, most prisoners are political prisoners insofar as their incarceration is directly related to oppressive conditions within our society. However, to say this is to leave no room for distinctions among people who are arrested for murder, rape, or burglary on the one hand, and expropriations, bombing U.S. installations, attending demonstrations, or disabling nuclear weapons, on the other. To say that most prisoners were oppressed before they were incarcerated, or even that all prisoners of color were oppressed before they were incarcerated, is true but inadequate. Not all people have the same consciousness, willingness, or ability to struggle.

These are distinctions that become relevant when defining political prisoners and prisoners of war. Although we believe that we should not call everyone a political prisoner or a prisoner of war, this does not mean that we regard other prisoners with the disgust and horror that is held out for them by many North Americans. Not only are most prisoners oppressed by societal conditions, they are also subjected to unimaginably barbaric prison conditions. The Bill of Rights does not exist for most of them. In fact, the 13th Amendment, which ended chattel slavery in the United States, actually legalized it behind the prison walls: "Neither slavery nor involuntary servitude, except as a punishment whereby the party shall have been duly convicted, shall exist in the United States."

More importantly, we recognize that prisons are instruments of population control for people of color. The act of incarcerating huge numbers of prisoners is a fundamental political act by the United States. This is an act that is central in sustaining the system of white supremacy, a system we are dedicated to destroying. Many people are sent to prison for "crimes" that are acts of self-defense or survival. These would include women who attack or even kill men who brutalize them, people who steal to survive, prostitutes, and other similar groups of people. Some feminists challenge the above definitions and assert that women who attack and even kill men who brutalize them are indeed political prisoners. This is certainly a reasonable perspective.

Although these people are not political prisoners according to the definition employed in this essay, they deserve our support for their struggle to survive and, in many cases, resist. In addition, the

United States has always imprisoned huge numbers of people because they were "foreigners" of one sort or another. This process started during the labor struggles around the turn of the century, continued through the internment of the Japanese people during World War II, and still exists today for many Central Americans and citizens of other countries. Again, while we do not consider them political prisoners, we recognize the political nature of their imprisonment.

Finally, we must mention here prisoners who have engaged in right-wing political activity against the government. We are interested in building a new and humane society, one that will be free of the system of white supremacy, of male supremacy, and of all other forms of exploitation. Since the right wing is fighting to reinforce the system that commits these crimes, we do not consider right-wing prisoners to be political prisoners, and certainly not our political prisoners.

A Brief Historical Overview

From the turn of the century until about 1950, there were mass upsurges in political activity, and each was met with repression and imprisonment. From about 1915 to 1920, there was massive repression of the Industrial Workers of the World (the Wobblies). Then came the Palmer Raids against the Communist Party and its sympathizers. In the 1940s, many war resisters were sent to prison; in the next decade more people were once again imprisoned during the McCarthy period. In 1950, the people of Puerto Rico rose up against the United States in pursuit of their independence, in the Grito de Jayuya. This rebellion was met with massive repression, which in turn was met by attacks against the U.S. government in Washington, DC, by the Puerto Rican Nationalists. And these attacks in turn resulted in their imprisonment.

Then came the '60s. The government attacked the Black Liberation Movement, murdering more than 30 Black Panthers and incarcerating dozens upon dozens of Black revolutionaries. In the following decade, there was an upsurge in nationalist activity around the question of oppressed nations within the borders of the United States. Several major organizations were either formed, or reached the height of their activity, during this period. These organizations engaged in every aspect of struggle against the United States in efforts to end the hundreds of years of colonial rule over their respective nations, and have met with enormous repression. They include: the Provisional Government of the Republic of New Afrika, a Black organization founded in 1968 to seek five southern states for a New

Afrikan national territory; the Black Liberation Army (BLA), a clandestine political/military organization, which was most active during this period; the American Indian Movement (AIM), which occupied Wounded Knee for 71 days in 1973, and demanded sovereignty of its national territories; the Movimiento de Liberación Nacional Puertorriqueño (MLN-PR), founded in 1977, and the Fuerzas Armadas de Liberación Nacional (FALN), founded in 1974, both of which were formed to seek independence for Puerto Rico.

This rise of nationalist organizations coincided with two essential dimensions of imprisonment within the United States. First, the imprisonment rate, which had been constant at about 100 prisoners per every 100,000 population since 1925, began to rise dramatically. This rise, which started in 1972, has resulted in a doubling of the U.S. prison population, with another doubling expected by the year 2000.

Second, this period of nationalist activity led to a sharp increase in the number of political prisoners. As these nationalist organizations intensified their struggles, the state intensified its repression and brutality. But it was not only members of oppressed nations who became political prisoners. North American anti-imperialists acted in solidarity with these nationalist struggles and in pursuit of their own visions of a new society. In addition, religious communities began a series of attacks on nuclear weapons that eventually grew into the Ploughshares movement and generated many other North American political prisoners. There are currently over 100 political prisoners, and their sentences are longer than ever before. Whereas in the past, most political prisoners were sentenced to a few years, they are now receiving sentences of 30 years and more, and in some cases as many as several lifetimes! We are thus looking at a situation in which many political people will spend the rest of their lives in prison—unless we do something about it. And, gradually, people are beginning to do something about it.

In the past couple of years, significant efforts have been made to support political prisoners in the United States There is the defense work to free Puerto Rican political prisoners and prisoners of war; the work that eventually freed Dhoruba Bin Wahad and the New York 8; the continuing efforts to free Leonard Peltier, the Native-American leader, Mumia Abu-Jamal, who is facing the death penalty, and geronimo ji Jaga (Pratt), the Black Panther leader who is now one of the longest-held political prisoners in the world; and the work of the Ploughshares movement, the anti-nuclear movement, and the draft resistance movement.

Three Important Accomplishments

Highlighting this work around political prisoners have been three extraordinary accomplishments:

1. *Cuba grants political asylum to Assata Shakur.* Targeted as the supposed leader of the Black Liberation Army, Assata was hunted down and arrested in 1973. She was tried seven times, found not guilty six times, finally framed and convicted, and sent to prison on a sentence of life plus thirty-three years. In 1979, the revolutionary movement liberated Assata from Clinton Prison in New Jersey. A few years later, Assata appeared in Cuba. Several people have been accused of helping her to escape. They include Sekou Odinga, Mutulu Shakur, Marilyn Buck, and Silvia Baraldini, who are now all political prisoners themselves.

2. *Mexico refuses to extradite William Morales; Cuba grants political asylum.* FALN leader William Morales was captured in 1978, and during his trial he became the first person to take a prisoner of war position in a U.S. court. He subsequently escaped, fled to Mexico, and was arrested by Mexican authorities. In July 1988, the Mexican government refused to extradite him to the United States, and he was granted asylum in Cuba. When Mexico released Morales, he was escorted to his plane for his trip to Cuba by Rafael Cancel Miranda, the Puerto Rican National Hero who spent 25 years in prison, and was finally freed in 1979 after a long campaign led by the National Committee to Free Puerto Rican Prisoners of War. Morales was also escorted by Pablo Marcano, another ex-political prisoner and *independentista.* This victory was the result of a major campaign launched within Mexico and internationally. The breadth and depth of that campaign continued the tradition established by the Puerto Rican independence movement to support and defend their political prisoners.

3. *Control unit shut down; judge recognizes political prisoners.* The Lexington Control Unit for Women was opened in Kentucky in October 1986 to torture, brutalize, and break female political prisoners. The first three women sent there were Alejandrina Torres, Puerto Rican prisoner of war, Susan Rosenberg, North American anti-imperialist political prisoner, and Silvia Baraldini, Italian national anti-imperialist political prisoner. After a two-year campaign, these women and the movements they represent achieved a major victory in federal court. In August 1988, the U.S. government and the Bureau of Prisons were forced to shut down the Lexington Control Unit. Not only did the

judge admit that the women had been sent to Lexington unjustifiably, but he stated in his decision that the women were sent there because of their political beliefs. To our knowledge this is the first time that any arm of the U.S. government has ever admitted that this country detains political prisoners.[2]

These three important achievements show how sustained struggle succeeds, and why support of political prisoners must be a central part of our pursuit of a new society.

An Historical Juncture

It is always difficult to recognize the shape of an historical development in progress. One can easily fall prey to false predictions based upon an inadequate understanding of unfolding processes. Nonetheless, we believe that we are currently in the midst of a newly emerging consciousness around political prisoners in the United States. This period was initiated by the work and great success that freed the Puerto Rican Nationalists in 1979. The Nationalists had suffered in prison for 25 years (Oscar Collazo, one of them, actually served over 29 years) until a deliberate, determined effort to free them was generated. This effort was led in the United States by a group of people who would later form the National Committee to Free Puerto Rican Political Prisoners and Prisoners of War.

In the 15 years since the freeing of the Nationalists, there has been an increase in work involving political prisoners in this country. Fifteen Puerto Ricans have asserted that they are POWs; Black/New Afrikan Freedom Fighters like Sundiata Acoli, geronimo ji Jaga (Pratt), Sekou Odinga, and many others have done the same; Leonard Peltier has become an international symbol of the struggle against U.S. oppression; there has been a huge increase in the number of North American political prisoners, both anti-imperialist freedom fighters and Ploughshares activists [and animal liberation activists!—E.R.] and dozens of people have gone to prison for refusing to collaborate with grand juries. In addition, the Lexington Control Unit for Women was opened and closed; Assata Shakur and William Morales were liberated and granted asylum by Cuba; a federal judge acknowledged the existence of political prisoners in the United States and granted that their rights were being violated.

The U.S. Left has been painfully slow in responding to these events. However, other progressive sectors in this country have begun to move around these issues. For example, the fight against the

Lexington Control Unit included large sectors of the Episcopal and Methodist churches and the United Church of Christ; parts of the women's movement, most notably Lesbians; and parts of the Puerto Rican legislature. The international situation with regard to political prisoners in the United States has also changed. We have already referred to the roles of Mexico in freeing Morales, and Cuba in granting asylum to Shakur and Morales.

For years, the United States criticized Cuba for its prison policies. In response, Cuba opened its prisons to U.S. human rights activists. They returned to the United States with a report that documented that conditions in Cuba's prisons were vastly better than those in the United States, including such characteristics as full employment at minimum wage, educational opportunities for all, and widespread conjugal visits. The report received inadequate and distorted media attention but the debate about the United States denying visas to the Cuban delegation, which wished to reciprocally visit U.S. prisons, forced itself onto the "op-ed" pages of the *New York Times* and generated considerable interest.

A Call for Action and Support

Those of us who are concerned with social justice must be concerned with prisons and political prisoners in this country. We cannot only demonstrate and agitate for the freedom of South African and Salvadoran political prisoners but we must also agitate for the freedom of geronimo ji Jaga (Pratt), Leonard Peltier, Alejandrina Torres, Susan Rosenberg, and the many other political prisoners that the United States has imprisoned.

We believe that a fundamental restructuring of society is necessary. In the course of pursuing such a restructuring, some will go to prison. They must be supported—one and all. Political prisoners are not just virtuous and courageous people. They are representatives of movements, and when we fight for political prisoners, we are fighting for those movements. We believe that many progressive people have refused to recognize the importance of political prisoners and that they have made this mistake most often and most intensely when the question of political violence is involved. In the '60s, many people were willing to defend Black political prisoners who were being framed or attacked, but once they began to fight back, many of their supporters disappeared. Other examples abound.

When Puerto Rican Nationalists rose up against the United States in an effort to gain their independence in 1950 during the Grito de Jayuya, the United States responded with incredible brutality, strafing towns by air, murdering many *independentistas*, imprisoning over 3,000 of them, and generally repressing the entire nation. In response to this massacre, and in an effort to call international attention to the continuing colonization of Puerto Rico, Oscar Collazo and Griselio Torresola attacked President Truman's residence. Torresola was killed during the attack. The Communist Party wrote that they were "profoundly shocked" by the Puerto Ricans' action and that they "condemn and reject all acts of violence and terror." The attack on Truman, they said, "*can only be the act of terrorists, deranged men, or agents...*" (our emphasis). How interesting, then, that the nation of Puerto Rico regards these men as national heroes.

When William Morales was captured by the United States in 1978, he was called a "terrorist" and an "ultra-leftist" by the *Guardian* newspaper, which certainly did not work for his freedom. Yet now here is a mass campaign in Mexico calling him a political prisoner and a freedom fighter and Cuba giving him political asylum.

Finally, it is clear that many progressive people appreciate the fact that Assata Shakur is free. They read her recent autobiography and proclaim her and her freedom. All of this is, of course, wonderful. What is not so wonderful is that virtually no one has stepped forward to defend Sekou Odinga, Mutulu Shakur, Silvia Baraldini, and Marilyn Buck who are in prison for militarily freeing Assata. In fact, these people are often attacked by the Left for being militarist or ultra-Left.

There are dozens of other examples like this, but our purpose here is not to engage in polemics or to attack other organizations. We don't want to minimize the role that others will play in work around political prisoners—we want to maximize the role. But we do think that it must be made clear how the progressive movement in this country has traditionally responded to political prisoners as a way of pointing out how that response must change. One purpose of this book is to try to improve this situation. We take up this question of political violence because it is here that much division takes place. Amnesty International, for example, will not declare as a political prisoner anyone who has engaged in armed struggle. And, as noted above, many others have a similar view. Our position is that we support all political prisoners—and demand freedom for all of them. We believe such a position is the only principled one.

The question of political prisoners must always be prominent on the agenda of all of our movements. If we don't stand side by side with our comrades and colleagues when they are taken prisoner, then what does this say to the prisoners and to all those who might dare to struggle in the future? And what does it say to the U.S. government that would so badly like to incarcerate all those who it perceives as a threat? Many of us know and understand this, but not enough of us act on this understanding. Enabling such activity is the purpose of this book and the work being done by the organizations listed [in the *Organizers' Guide*]. We hope that you will become involved.

What You Can Do

- Contact the organizations listed for information or to invite them to speak to your organizations, unions, women's groups, churches, house parties, etc.;
- Write to political prisoners and POWs;
- Start your own work around political prisoners.

NOTES

1. This piece is excerpted from *Can't Jail the Spirit*, (Chicago: Editorial El Coqui), 1992. The book contains the biographies/autobiographies of dozens of political prisoners and prisoners of war, including photos, addresses, and essays about the movements from which they come. A very handy resource and an excellent introduction to the issue, it is, unfortunately, difficult to locate due to a limited print run.

2. Despite the enduring political advances made during the Lexington campaign, the judicial victory has since been overturned. The United States government immediately appealed the decision, and on September 8, 1989, the Washington, DC, appellate court reversed Judge Parker's courageous ruling. The court endorsed the government's position that it can use a prisoner's political associations and beliefs in making security decisions and in determining conditions of confinement. By implication, the government is now authorized to send political prisoners directly to control units like Marion, simply on the basis of their political histories.

23

SPEAKING TRUTH
TO POWER

Political Prisoners in the United States[1]

Dhoruba Bin Wahad

I spent 19 years of my life in prison for something I didn't do basically because I was very vocal about my political beliefs. I believe that African-American people have the right to defend themselves against racist attacks by any means necessary. Because I publicly advocated that position as a leader of the Black Panther Party, I was targeted and framed by the U.S. government through a racist and political counter-insurgency program, known as the Counter-Intelligence Program (COINTELPRO), aimed against political (mostly Black) activists in the '60s.[2] Popular myth holds that COINTELPRO was an aberration, the result of the sick mind of an individual named J. Edgar Hoover—that it never would have occurred if Hoover wasn't head of the Federal Bureau of Investigation (FBI). But the Central Intelligance Agency (CIA) had a similar program, known as Operation Chaos, which also utilized domestic surveillance techniques in its efforts to suppress the anti-war movement, the Black nationalist movement, and the so-called New Left in the United States. The CIA engaged in this type of activity even though it had no legal mandate to. So much for the sanctity of the law. As U.S. history amply attests, the rule of law is merely the rule of privileged white men.

Most of you weren't even born when the so-called civil rights movement began. Some of you were just babies when the Black Panther Party came on the scene. The few of you who have heard of the Black Panther Party probably have an image of us as a bunch of crazy Black men and women running around with guns, sporting black leather jackets and berets. In October 1966, the Black Panther Party came out with a 10-point program. Point one of that program was decent housing fit for human beings. We demanded relevant education that taught Black people about slavery (our holocaust), the role we have played in this society. Then we got to point number seven, which said that we wanted an end to the racist murder and brutality committed by the police against Black people. Everybody went bananas. The minute Black folks stood and said, "Hey, hold up, Homes, you ain't going to be shooting me with that gun or hitting me with that stick. Because I got a stick, I got a gun, too and I'm not with that turn-the-other-cheek program. I'm not goin' out chump-style. I can and will get to whippin' and shootin'," the police said, "What? You're a cop killer." And that is how the press characterized us.

That characterization stuck because white folks were scared to death of Black men and women with guns. For whites, Black folks advocating self-defense translates to unprovoked, random, senseless violence. The minute that we talked about defending ourselves from racist police brutality, we were beyond the pale. We were open game; we became criminals.

One of the ways that the government begins to mobilize the forces of repression against dissidents in the United States is by setting the parameters of political debates, limiting discussion of a particular issue. The first thing that the system does when it decides to repress a particular segment of society is to create the impression that certain individuals are crazy, and that they are criminals. In other words, the system criminalizes political dissent. Once that happens, you become fair game for the law enforcement agencies who can say, "We're not repressing him or her because of his or her politics; we're repressing him or her because he or she broke the law."

In all of the infamous Panther 21 trials, there was always a conspiracy charge. The Panther 21 trials lasted about two years and were, at that time, the longest political trials in New York City history. In 1969, the entire leadership of the New York chapter of the Black Panther Party was indicted on 150 counts of conspiracy to commit murder and arson. They arrested us and charged us with a conspiracy to blow up the Botanical Gardens (a conspiracy to destroy flowers and trees), and accused us of conspiring to bomb department stores frequented by poor Black people—on Easter, no less. (Now everyone knows that department stores are closed on Easter, but we were supposed to be planning to set the bombs to explode right in the middle of the Easter shopping rush hour.) They painted us as a bunch of shameless fanatics who were down to blow up white Easter bunnies.

They raided us. They snatched me out of my bed at 3:30 in the morning and dragged me downtown. I was totally traumatized. They took me downtown, indicted me, and set my co-defendants' and my bail at $100,000. Then began the process of vilifying us in the press. The media said, "Panthers Arrested for Plot to Overthrow the Government and Destroy Department Stores." There was an editorial in the New York Daily News saying that evidence existed that the Panthers were tied to the Cubans who were paying the Panthers to disrupt and destroy New York City. It was suggested that there be a senatorial investigation to see whether the Panthers were being funded by Communists abroad. The media created the image that we were criminals, that we were crazy, that we were out to destroy people, that we had no respect for life.

They did this for an entire year. But, because it was the 1960s, it had the complete opposite of its intended effect. The more they said bad things about us, the more people seemed to believe in us. When we went to court the room was overpacked with people who loved us. The prosecution never came up with one stick of dynamite. They said the reason they couldn't find a stick of dynamite was because we had, at the last minute, switched the real dynamite for fake dynamite! In 45 minutes, the jury acquitted us of all charges. That infuriated the New York District Attorney. As a result, the DA targeted me for a rerun.

COINTELPRO changed the political environment. It changed how people perceived those individuals who fought for change. Police agents infiltrated the Panther Party and caused the leadership to abandon the struggle. We were placed in jail. We had to fight constantly to raise bail. Once the atmosphere changed, the support that had been there initially disappeared. When I was finally convicted, there was nobody in court but the police, district attorneys, and the prosecutors. They were successful because there was no one in court for me. They believed the hype.

The United States has a history of destroying those individuals who they cannot control and to whom people have begun to listen. They destroyed the Reverend Dr. Martin Luther King, Jr., they destroyed Marcus Garvey. They have destroyed numerous African-American leaders and working-class white leaders who have struggled for the rights of working-class people. We need to learn from these things, so we don't make mistakes again. Reverend Dr. Martin Luther King once said that he did not believe that an unjust law was worthy of being obeyed. We have a moral obligation to speak truth to injustice.

As a revolutionary, you must vigilantly counter the negative spin those in power will put on your politics. Check out how the system manipulates information to delegitimize you. As an example, look at how they have defined the Puerto Rican Nationalists: "unreasonable terrorists who refuse to deal with the given political landscape." They don't supply you with important facts that place the Puerto Rican Nationalist struggle in an historical context. By confining the parameters of the debate, they are attempting to isolate the Puerto Rican Nationalists. So when the government murders or imprisons them, it would have you believe that it is "only enforcing the law against people who are completely crazy and unreasonable."

America's solution for the economic problems of a particular region is two-fold: either build a military base and/or a prison. We need to understand that we are living in a society based on war—or at least the fear of war—and the repression and alienation of people who do not buy into the accepted standards or conform to the acceptable molds.

In New York State, there was a prison movement in 1972, right after the Attica Rebellion. What made the movement short-lived was the fact that it was proposing to unionize labor. The inmates in prison were beginning to organize for a minimum wage. Understand that right now in New York prisons, prisoners are making pretty good money if they make 50 cents per hour. The average prisoner makes $7.50 every two weeks. Industries like Correctional Craft (COR-CRAFT) in New York sell prisoner-made products on the regular market. There is quite a profit margin when you employ prisoners at slave wages and sell their products at market rates. So when prisoners tried to unionize they were viewed as a threat to profits and as an obstruction in the military production line. Prisoners who attempt to organize other prisoners or to raise their consciousness are viewed as interfering with the orderly running of the prisons.

In New York State, 85 percent of all prisoners are Black or Latino, yet Blacks and Latinos make up something like 20 percent of the state's population. The majority of prisons in New York are located in rural white communities that generally are economically depressed and lack a viable tax base. These communities have an outflow of youth who go to college, receive valuable training, and then seek employment in urban areas. Prisons are being built in these types of areas at a phenomenal rate. The prison industry is doing a booming business and, in some areas, has virtually replaced the farm industry. During the last three years in New York State, for instance, they have built about fifteen prisons. We are talking about a conscious effort to create an industry and subsidize certain rural areas in this country. You should see the prisons today. Kids going in, 17, 18 years old, who have sentences like 65 years to life. Young people who will never get out. And for every prisoner in New York, you have five state employees.

There is also a relationship between the fact that prisons are becoming privatized centers of production for business corporations and the fact that the U.S. government is transforming prisons like Marion into isolation centers (for political prisoners). The moment that prisons are made into centers for producing wealth, you're going to create an incentive for prisoners to unionize. The only people in prison who are in a position to provide leadership for that union building are the political prisoners. So one of the government's solutions is to take the political prisoners away from the rest of the prison population and to isolate them.

When I say isolation, I'm talking about 23 hours of lock-up. Although supposedly you have a right to one hour of recreation, often you don't get it. You get it if the guard feels like giving it to you. If he gets mad at somebody on the outside, he may walk in and decide he wants to give you a half hour or he might just forget about you all together. Even within that hour you have to make a choice between making a telephone call or taking a shower. If you take a shower, you can't make a phone call. If you make a phone call, you can't take the shower. Isolation units are not just about the removal of prisoners, but also about destroying people's psychological and physical integrity. This occurs with any prisoner who is seen as uncooperative or does not want to participate in the slave-wage system in prison.

One example of how this works is the United States penitentiary at Marion.[3] Marion is the most maximum-security prison in the country; the only level six prison. It has been a trendsetter in terms of repressive technology and human cruelty. How do you get into Marion? You get there by earning your way, by proving that you "can't adjust in a more open environment." The government says you're the worst of the worst. But that's a lie. Marion has more political prisoners than any other prison in the country. Many are there not because they "couldn't adjust" but because of their political beliefs.

Marion has a program known as "lockdown" where you're in a cell 22½ hours a day. The only way you get out is by jumping through hoops. They have a program that you have to satisfy to show you have "clear conduct."

HUMAN RIGHTS AND THE WAR
AGAINST AFRICAN PEOPLE

We must recognize that we exist in a society that employs its most influential institutions to promote indifference and hostility towards the incarcerated, in general, and towards African-American males, in particular, whether incarcerated or not. In such a milieu, institutional abuse is an inevitability and the profoundly demonized elements of the society—African-American males—will be disproportionately affected by this institutional abuse of power... We must be prepared to declare, as a matter of principle, that an individual does not forfeit his/her fundamental human rights merely as a result of having violated the law and ending up incarcerated. We must not be timid about asserting that even the patently guilty are entitled to human rights protections... Our movement must win minds in order to achieve its objectives. This is the primary front of struggle. The onus on those of us who understand the struggle in these terms is to impel people to examine their fallacious beliefs and attitudes and to offer them an analysis that may result in their repudiation of these same false beliefs and attitudes...

A war against African people has been and is being waged. The Mississippi jail and prison murders are manifestations of this war. The war is being carried on in the public school system where our children cannot even learn their own history as documented by their ancestors, elders, and scholars and where they will never learn how to apply their talents to the enhancement of the quality of life in their communities. The war is being fought in the criminal justice system that will put our young men and women behind bars for drug trafficking—an economy that thrives because there is no Drug Enforcement Administration (DEA) "war on drugs" and because there is no licit employment for these young people. As a matter of fact, drugs are a major weapon in this war. This war means startling infant mortality rates among African Americans. It means that young African-American women of childbearing age are being encouraged to use inadequately-tested contraceptive technology because no one in a position of power has any interest in developing creative solutions to the problem of adolescent pregnancy. It is a war whose primary target is the young people of our communities—a brutal, multifaceted assault on our future, on our capacity to survive and reclaim greatness as a people, on our ability to protect and preserve for generations to come the best of our way of life. It is a war that is being maintained on the global plane wherever African people are. It's happening in the Sudan, in Angola, in Mozambique. This is how genocidal intent works!

But as we have always done—and long before the period of our captivity in the lands of the Western Hemisphere began—we will continue to resist! We will not be erased from the historical record, nor will we be reduced to the content of an historical footnote. So we have no choice but to resist! And we welcome the support of allies who will work with us on our terms. Amen-Ra.

—*Kanika Ajanaku, organizer of the Committee*
Against Mississippi Jail Lynchings

If you are good enough, you win your way to the "pre-release unit" where they have the UNICOR program, a Federal industry that makes cable and other material for the U.S. military. Now some of the political prisoners are there because of acts against the United States government and military. They will never compromise their political principles by working for the U.S. military. Therefore, because part of the program at Marion is successfully completing this "pre-release unit," political people who refuse to enroll in UNICOR will never get out.

What is the main cause of this build-up of the prison system? Today the major justification is the "war on drugs." Back in the '60s, the code word for getting the Black folks off the street was "law-and-order." Now it is "war on drugs." Under the guise of fighting drugs, various states and cities and municipalities are passing laws that are blatantly unconstitutional. They are passing stop-and-frisk laws. Police SWAT teams are kicking in doors in African-American communities. People are more terrified of the drug dealers in our communities than they are of the police and Drug Enforcement Administration who play a more pivotal role as drug traffickers than the low-level street dealers. People are so uptight about the nihilistic behavior of these drug dealers and our youth that they are calling for more police. That is like someone calling for more arsenic. If we agree that drug dealing is a reprehensible crime that should be punished, then all perpetrators should be dealt with and stricter punishment reserved for law enforcement officers. But in our eagerness to deal with the "drug problem," the legislation that is getting passed is heralding the way for fascism. Laws are being passed that allow, under the guise of fighting the war on drugs, for the police to kick down your door without a warrant. If you are a political organizer, they just kick down your door and say, "We just thought he was a drug dealer." These laws are testing the limits of our tolerance for fascism—if it comes disguised as something else.

The de-criminalization of drugs is essential to freeing us. We have to take law enforcement out of the picture. That doesn't mean legalizing drugs or that I advocate cocaine and heroin should flow freely in the Black community. But in the end, the Black community is responsible for its own integrity; we can't rely on others to enforce it for us. A cop with an Uzi can't solve the drug problem. As long as law enforcement, on the one hand, is in the business of dealing drugs itself, and on the other, is involved with the suppression of drugs, we are going to have the problem of an expanding national security complex.

However, just because the war on drugs is political does not mean that Joe Drugdealer becomes a political prisoner when he is arrested. The important thing to remember is that the U.S. government has criminalized political dissent and therefore characterizes political activists it incarcerates as merely criminals rather than political prisoners or POWs. In this way, the government keeps the myth alive that there are no political prisoners in the United States and that the U.S. criminal justice system is not used as a tool of repression.

Drugs were introduced in a massive way into the African-American community. Heroin in particular was introduced around the time that Malcolm X was beginning to speak publicly. Drugs were aimed primarily at the youth in order to depoliticize them and rock them to sleep. They began to break down familial and social institutions in the African-American community. Drugs have historically been used to derail oppressed people's struggles. They were used against the Chinese during the so-called Boxer Rebellion in Southeast Asia, in Malaysia, and in the Sudan in Africa. Drugs started out in the African-American community as a conscious political ploy.

Drugs have had the most devastating impact on the African-American community because the African-American community is so vulnerable to destabilization. There are few economic opportunities for African-American labor. The African-American family is under enormous pressure. We don't control educational and economic institutions. The political power of African Americans does not correspond to our numbers. Furthermore, we are led by individuals who are opportunistic, and not accountable to the community. Anything like drugs becomes devastating to a community that doesn't have the support networks and infrastructure to resist it.

We have to create a moral and ethical environment in which others cannot prey on us by selling drugs. We need to do that without collaborating with the police, because the police, right now, are part of the problem. At the same time we need to wage a campaign to make the police responsive to our needs politically. So long as you lack political power, the police can come into your neighborhood and do whatever they want. Can you imagine them doing that in Scarsdale? Picture the police racing into Scarsdale, sealing off one end of the block lined with $300,000 to $2,000,000 homes and rounding everybody up, putting them in police vans, and then searching the houses, kicking in doors and looking for drug dealers. They wouldn't do that, because Scarsdale has political clout.

The African-American community shouldn't go the route of Scarsdale, but we do need to create an environment that makes Black elected officials responsible to the needs of our community—and if they are not, we need to remove them from office. We need to create an infrastructure that takes youth off the drug track and puts them to work as social activists, building our community. We need to create a climate that says that we will not tolerate certain types of behavior, and we don't need the police to enforce it. We'll enforce it. The Black Panther Party advocated community control of the police in 1969 and that's still what we need today: the police should live in, train in, and be a part of the community that they police. That is one political struggle.

The drug dealers are another political struggle. We have to raise the consciousness of our community so that those individuals who have the strength, stamina, and physical capacity can hook up with those individuals who have the experience, principles, and organizing abilities to rid our communities of these people. And we've got to begin fighting by creating relevant organizations whose leadership is accountable to the people and whose agendas we determine.

Lastly, we need to be building a movement around the issue of political prisoners. We need to create a movement to challenge the myth that there are no political prisoners in the United States. Because as long as the United States can get away with saying that there are no political prisoners within its borders, those of us who stand up and take a position risk becoming a target of political repression and face the possibility of arbitrary imprisonment by those individuals in power who disagree with us and feel that it's all right, in fact, believe it is their moral obligation to oppress us.

> Speech delivered at a forum of the
> *Yale Journal of Law and Liberation*,
> April 30, 1990

NOTES

1. A word about these terms:

Prisoner of War: those combatants struggling against colonial domination and racist regimes captured as prisoners are to be accorded the status of prisoners of war and their treatment should be in accordance with the provisions of the Geneva conventions Relative to the Treatment of Prisoners of War of August 12, 1949. (Geneva Assembly Resolution 3101 (XXVIII)).

Political Prisoner: a person incarcerated for actions carried out in support of legitimate struggles for self-determination or for opposing illegal policies of the United States government and/or its political subdivisions. The Campaign (see note on author) takes objection to the use of the term "illegal policies" in the definition above since the United

States has defined all of its actions from slavery to the oppression of women as "legal." (Definition adopted at the International Tribunal on Human Rights Violations of Political Prisoners and Prisoners of War in the United States, which was held in New York City, December 1990.)

2. COINTELPRO was an FBI counter-intelligence program initiated in 1968 under the leadership of J. Edgar Hoover. According to a memo issued by Hoover on March 4, 1968, COINTELPRO's central aim was, "To prevent the coalition of militant black nationalist groups which might be the first step toward a real mau mau in America," and "To prevent (nationalist) groups and leaders from gaining 'respectability' by discrediting them to the 'responsible' Negro community, to the white community and to Negro radicals" (FBI memo to Special Agent-in-Charge [SAC] Albany from the FBI director, March 4, 1968). During 1968 and 1969, the FBI covertly worked to undermine the supply of financial and material resources to Black nationalist organizations. COINTELPRO also explicitly strove to discredit the legality and legitimacy of targeted nationalists. In April 1969, members of the New York Black Panther Party were arrested on bomb conspiracy charges. BPP chairman Bobby Seale was arrested and indicted for the murder of a police informant in New Haven. In December 1969, the Chicago police raided a BPP apartment, killing party leader Fred Hampton and Mark Clark.

3. See Section Six and Jan Susler, "The Women's High Security Unit in Lexington, KY," *Yale Journal of Law and Liberation,* vol. 31, 1989.

24

WHITE NORTH AMERICAN POLITICAL PRISONERS

Collective statement by members of
Out of Control: Lesbian Committee to
Support Women Political Prisoners
and Prairie Fire Organizing Committee

Speech delivered by B♀ (rita d. brown)

I am very honored to be here today, at this tribunal condemning
500 years of genocide and celebrating 500 years of resistance. I came
to speak about some 35 white political prisoners presently being held
in U.S. prisons and jails—many of whom are imprisoned because of
their solidarity with oppressed nations and peoples in the United
States and around the world. I speak from experience and deep feeling
for I am a former political prisoner myself having spent eight-and-a-
half years in federal prisons around the country because of my actions
as a member of the George Jackson Brigade. In those years I was
moved from prison to prison. During that time I spent almost a year
in isolation in Davis Hall at Alderson. This was the first special control
unit for political women in the federal system. Sister Assata Shakur
and I were held there along with reactionary and Nazi prisoners—the
government's threat to us was very clear. I was also kept for extra long
periods in isolation and threatened and harassed specifically because
I am a Lesbian. This was not all that unusual treatment, however, for
my experience mirrors that of all the political prisoners. Yet our very
existence is still denied by the U.S. government and not seen or
understood by most people in this country.

The strategy of the U.S. government towards all political prisoners and POWs held in prisons is to criminalize them—to disguise their
political identities under the rhetoric of criminal activity. But they are

not criminals. All of these white North American political prisoners have been convicted of and imprisoned for activities that are strictly political in nature. These political prisoners and POWs are not a new phenomenon but are part of the history of the resistance in the Americas. In fact, under international law as well as the Constitution of the United States, people not only have the right, but the absolute responsibility to resist the illegal policies and practices of the oppressor and colonizing nation. And that's what they have done.

The North American political prisoners draw on a history of resistance that includes the anti-slavery/abolitionist movement, those who helped in the Underground Railroad, women's rights activists, labor and working-class organizers, and supporters of anti-colonialism and anti-militarism. Some of their names are familiar: John Brown, Emma Goldman, Eugene Debs, Ruth Reynolds, and Ethel and Julius Rosenberg; but most of the names of our historical grandmothers and grandfathers remain unknown to us because the historians don't want us to know about them. Some of these political prisoners come from working-class or poor communities, some were already ex-cons, and still others were college students, but a common thread runs through all their stories—the decision to take action. Action in support of self-determination; action against racism; action against U.S. military and nuclear policy; action against apartheid in South Africa and action in solidarity with workers and poor people around the world. In order to understand them and their situation better we have to go back a little in history.

If you were living in this country in the '60s and '70s, you had to be affected by the struggles for freedom and social justice. Products of those times, many of the women and men in prison today were active in support of the civil rights movement and were influenced by the demand for self-determination by Malcolm X and the organizing of Martin Luther King, both of whom would be assassinated by 1968. Others worked with the Black Panther Party (BPP), often in defense of BPP members who were imprisoned for political activities. Many came to work also with Native-American, Mexicano/Chicano, and other Third World liberation struggles. Along with millions of others, they consistently opposed U.S. policy in Vietnam and were part of the anti-war movement. There were mass demonstrations throughout the country, marches on Washington, student strikes, sit-ins, and the burning of draft cards. There were also thousands of acts of sabotage against academic, corporate, military, and government targets that ranged from property damage to bombings. This was also the period when women began to be more conscious about their own oppression and began to demand liberation and when Lesbians and gay men came out of the closet and went into the streets demanding an end to gay oppression. During these years a prisoner's rights movement developed, led mostly by Black prisoners and with close ties to the BPP and other community groups. Many of the white political prisoners worked with these organizations and thus came to better understand the integral part that prisons play in this society. They came to understand this country needs to control its people and criminalize, jail, or kill those whom it either can't control or doesn't need. The government's response to this legitimate protest and sense of empowerment was swift, repressive and violent. COINTELPRO, the FBI's counter-intelligence program, was responsible for the destruction of the BPP and the disruption of the American Indian Movement. Hundreds of BPP members and other Black activists, like Fred Hampton and Bunchy Carter, were killed or jailed. The same was true for Native people struggling for sovereignty.

This period also saw the killing of students at Kent and Jackson State universities and the widespread use of grand jury witch hunts that were designed to further disrupt legal organizations. Out of these experiences came the understanding that U.S. society is based on the rape and plunder of Native lands, the expropriation of the life and labor of African slaves, and the class exploitation of European, Asian, and Mexican workers. People were enraged at the racism so basic to this country and were determined not be a part of it. Many began to see that there was a connection between the colonialism here at home and the war of imperialism in Vietnam.

It was during this time that activists in various parts of the country independently decided to begin armed resistance, expropriations, and sabotage. These were difficult steps to take but were all done in pursuit of their vision for change. This vision included changing centuries-old oppressive practices that promote hatred and that create psychological and physical damage and destruction. It meant creating a society based on self-determination for oppressed peoples both inside and outside the United States, based on an end to white supremacy, a society that was not based on class divisions. It meant creating a society where Lesbians and gay men could be proud of who they were. And it meant creating a non-sexist society where women could be equal, free, and unafraid. Finally all these people are driven by a vision of a future based not on greed and profit but one that truly answers people's needs.

This vision and spirit of resistance continued to move North Americans to action during the '70s and '80s. Thousands of people organized to resist the building of nuclear weapons, the intervention in Nicaragua and El Salvador, and in solidarity with Black forces against apartheid in South Africa. Many whites demonstrated and organized against racism and the growth of the Klan and other white supremacist groups. Thousands of people signed pledges of resistance to participate in civil disobedience if Nicaragua was invaded and participated in these acts as intervention in Central America increased. Women marched *en masse* against cutbacks in reproductive rights and protected abortion clinics against attacks. Lesbians and gay men demanded that the society deal with the AIDS pandemic and pushed for broader acceptance of Lesbian and gay rights. Again, during the Gulf War, thousands of white people joined in the streets protesting U.S. policy.

Not much has changed. We can understand the desire to resist very well. Genocidal conditions are increasing for Black and other communities of color. There is a rise of police brutality, drugs, and jailings and, as we all know, dramatic cuts to social services. Violence against women is increasing—a woman gets raped every two minutes. The right-wing scapegoats and whips up hysteria against gays and Lesbians with a propaganda campaign for their "family values." Abortion is all but gone; the courts are making one right-wing decision after another; and if we don't look out, soon we won't even have air we can breathe or earth we can stand on.

Before we get more specific about who the prisoners are, we'd like to take time to define what we mean by political prisoner. For some of us, this definition means those in prison as a direct result of their political actions, affiliations, and beliefs. Still others wish to extend that definition to those imprisoned for social crimes who have become politicized while inside prison and who therefore suffer extra repression for it. Some of us also think it important to extend the definition of political prisoner to those imprisoned for their sexual orientation (adopted by Amnesty International in 1992) and to those imprisoned for defending themselves against and/or fighting their abusers, such as women imprisoned for killing their batterers.

So let's get down to specifics. First, there are prisoners who consider themselves to be revolutionary anti-imperialists. The Jonathan Jackson-Sam Melville Brigade and United Freedom Front (UFF) were armed clandestine organizations that emerged from the experiences of working-class people in poor communities, in the military, and in prison. The Jackson-Melville Brigade was held responsible for a number of bombings of government and corporate offices in the mid- to late-'70s. These actions raised the demands of independence for Puerto Rico and an end to U.S. support for apartheid in South Africa, among other issues. The UFF operated from the early to mid-'80s and demanded the end of governmental and corporate support for South Africa, an end to U.S. intervention in Central America, and freedom for all political prisoners and POWs in U.S. prisons. Today the people charged with these acts are known as the "Ohio 7." They include Raymond Levasseur, Thomas Manning (both Vietnam Vets who had spent years in prison for social crimes), Jaan Laaman, Carol Manning, Richard Williams, Barbara Curzi, and Pat Gros Levasseur (these last two are both out on parole).

Other North American anti-imperialists were imprisoned for their direct aid to armed clandestine Black organizations in the early '80s. Judy Clark, David Gilbert, and Kathy Boudin are serving life sentences in prison. They are charged with aiding an attempted expropriation (robbery for political reasons) of an armored truck in New York State in 1981. This action was claimed by the Revolutionary Armed Task Force. Marilyn Buck was also charged as a result of this action, as well as for assisting in the escape of Assata Shakur. Susan Rosenberg and Timothy Blunk were captured in 1984 on charges of conspiracy to possess explosives. Later they, along with Alan Berkman, Laura Whitehorn, Linda Evans, and Marilyn Buck, were charged with a number of bombings claimed by the Armed Resistance Unit and the Red Guerrilla Resistance. Included in these is the 1983 bombing of the Capitol in solidarity with the people of Grenada and in retaliation against the U.S. invasion that year. Other actions were taken against corporate and military targets in solidarity with the peoples of Central America and against intervention, against the Zionist occupation of Palestine, and to protest police killings of Black and Latino people in New York City.

Once again I come to my own background as a former member of the George Jackson Brigade. We were a multi-racial, armed organization that operated in the Northwest in the mid- to late-'70s. We took our name from George Jackson, the Black revolutionary who was assassinated in prison on August 21, 1971. We were composed mainly of working-class ex-convicts, and engaged in acts of armed resistance in solidarity with the struggle of Native people for sovereignty, in support of a strike by Seattle Auto Workers, and in support of struggles by Washington State prisoners for basic human rights. I've already told you that I was in prison for eight-and-a-half years. My comrades, Mark Cook, a Black prisoner, and Ed Meade, a white prisoner, remain in prison to this day for these actions. [Ed Meade was released in 1994.—*E.R.*]

There are also anti-authoritarian prisoners. Bill Dunne and Larry Giddings have been in prison since 1979 for participating in expropriations and the liberation of a comrade from jail. Richard Picarielo has been in prison since 1977 for armed actions against U.S. oppression and imperialism. Due to be released after fifteen years, the state is scrambling to extend his sentence because he's dared to continue struggling from inside. [Released in mid-1995, Picariolo was promptly re-imprisoned for supposed parole violations after only four months of "freedom."—*E.R.*]

· Next, I'd like to talk about those people who consider themselves part of the Ploughshares. Taking their name from the famous biblical quote about turning swords into ploughshares, these antinuclear and anti-military activists come from a religious conviction and tradition that insists that they must not sit by while weapons of destruction are being made and used. Over the last 10 years many have entered military bases and destroyed military property directly, while others have borne witness and engaged in symbolic acts. The most recent case is that of Peter Lumsdain and Keith Kjoller, who destroyed the Navstar computer—part of the United States's first strike capability—to the tune of two-and-a-half million dollars. They received 18 months for this "crime."

Throughout the '80s, the government also prosecuted members of the sanctuary movement. These include clergy, church workers, and lay activists who have "illegally" provided refuge to Central and South American refugees fleeing U.S.-sponsored repression in their homelands. Following an historic tradition, there are also military resisters. For example, Gilliam Kerley was sentenced to three years in prison plus a $10,000 fine not merely for refusing to register but because he persisted in organizing against registration and the draft. Military resisters continue to sit in jail as a result of their refusal to serve in the Gulf War. [After hard-fought campaigns, all of the military resisters—or at least those whose cases were publicized—were released by the end of 1994.—*E.R.*] The U.S. legal system is also used to serve the government's allies in effecting their own counter-insurgency programs. In so doing, it echoes and enforces U.S. foreign policy.

Along with Haitians, Central and South Americans, and other Third World people, there are several European nationals being held in U.S. prisons. Silvia Baraldini, a citizen of Italy, received a 40-year sentence for aiding in the escape of Assata Shakur. Although the Italian government has said that it wants her back in Italy to serve her time in an Italian prison—in accord with the Straussberg Convention—the U.S. Justice Department refused to let her go, claiming the Italians won't be harsh enough. There are also nine alleged members or supporters of the IRA (Irish Republican Army) held in U.S. prisons by the U.S. government.

The same counter-insurgency tactics that have been detailed elsewhere have been used against white political prisoners. These include sophisticated spying and infiltration techniques, the jailing of many white activists for refusing to testify and/or cooperate with grand juries, the use of broad and vague conspiracy laws to criminalize people for association and belief and the use of preventative detention to deny bail. Laura Whitehorn was held without bail for four years before going to trial.

Finally, because they are political prisoners, they get some of the longest sentences in the world. Their political beliefs are used as a basis to impose sentences that are, in many instances, the equivalent of natural life in prison. The reason for this is that they are revolutionaries. For example, in 1986, a man convicted of planning and carrying out bombings—without making warning calls—of 10 occupied health clinics where abortions were performed, was sentenced to 10 years in prison and was paroled after 46 months. In contrast, Raymond Levasseur was convicted of bombing four unoccupied military targets in protest against U.S. foreign policies, and sentenced to 45 years in prison. A Ku Klux Klansman, charged with violations of the Neutrality Act and with possessing a boatload of explosives and weapons to be used in an invasion of the Caribbean island of Dominica received eight years. Yet Linda Evans, convicted of purchasing four weapons with false ID, was sentenced to 40 years—the longest sentence ever imposed for this offense.

Prisons are a horrible experience for everyone in this country. This was well documented in the Prison Discipline Study Report, issued in 1991. [See Chapter 7.] This national survey revealed that both physical and psychological abuse, so severe that it approaches the internationally accepted definition for torture, are the norm in maximum-security prisons throughout the United States. That's the case for all prisoners. In this context the North American prisoners—like political prisoners everywhere—are systematically singled out for particularly severe sentences and constant harassment once incarcerated. This includes particular abuse directed at the women and Lesbians, including sexual assault and threats, often at the hands of male guards.

One of the most brutal weapons in the government's arsenal is the control unit prison. Its goal is to reduce prisoners to a state of submission where it becomes possible to destroy their bodies, their spirit, their will, and ultimately their resistance and very self-definition. While officials claim that these units are only for the most violent disciplinary problems, more and more political prisoners are being placed there solely for their political beliefs. For instance, Alan Berkman, Raymond Levasseur, and Tom Manning were all sent directly to Marion Control Unit after sentencing. Silvia Baraldini and Susan Rosenberg, along with Puerto Rican POW Alejandrina Torres, were sent to the Lexington High Security Unit for two years in 1986. The justification: their political beliefs and associations. Once it was closed, as a result of a massive campaign inside and out, Susan and Silvia were sent to the new control unit for women at Marianna. Marilyn Buck was also sent there directly after sentencing.

In addition to isolation in control units, all political prisoners are more frequently subjected to cruel and inhumane punishment. This includes torture, sexual assault, strip and cavity searches (including those by male guards on women prisoners), punitive transfers, censorship, and denial of medical care, which has had grave consequences in several cases. Alan Berkman, suffering from Hodgkin's disease, nearly died several times while in prison because officials withheld necessary medical treatment. Silvia Baraldini's abdominal lumps, which anyone could feel, were ignored for months only to reveal that she had an aggressive form of uterine cancer. Silvia continues to have difficulty receiving medical attention.

Yet, imprisonment doesn't mean the end of these revolutionaries' organizing and political work. They continue once they're inside. For many of them, this has meant organizing resistance to oppressive prison policies, publishing prison newsletters, providing legal help and assistance, and facilitating courses, work stoppages and hunger strikes. For others it's also meant becoming AIDS activists. In fact, some of the women are responsible for developing the most comprehensive models (like AIDS Counseling and Education [ACE] at Bedford Hills and Pleasonton AIDS Counseling and Education [PLACE] at FCI-Dublin) for AIDS education and peer counseling in prisons in the country! But even in these cases, political prisoners are punished for being too successful in their work. For instance, Ed Meade, who organized Men Against Sexism at Walla Walla, was prevented from continuing his work on prisoner-on-prisoner rape. Bill Dunne was kept at Marion for years for publishing a newsletter there and David Gilbert was moved from place to place for developing work on AIDS in prison, and finally prevented from doing any work at all. Quite recently, Laura Whitehorn was transferred from Lexington to Marianna after she participated in the first women's prison uprising in 20 years. Tim Blunk was moved back to Marion from Lewisburg after there was a strike there of Black and Puerto Rican prisoners.

Why does the government so determinedly continue to attack and repress these women and men once they are incarcerated? It needs to break their spirits and prevent them from continuing to educate and mobilize from within the prison walls. On the one hand, these prisoners are used as examples to intimidate whole movements and communities from continuing their resistance. The government wants it made very clear the price one can pay for being a white person willing to take a stand against this racist and inhuman system is very high. On the other hand, they need these revolutionaries to be buried away and forgotten. We won't let that happen! Clearly now is a time for action. We too can follow the examples of these brave women and men who have given so much of their lives for freedom and justice. We must recognize who and what they are: political prisoners. We must demand their freedom so they can be back on the streets where they belong.

I know I speak for all the white political prisoners when I say that it's been a great honor to be able to speak to you today at this International Tribunal. All of us pledge to continue our resistance to the crimes outlined by today's speakers and commit ourselves to continue to work until there is a world where everyone can have true justice and freedom.

Speech delivered at the International Tribunal of Indigenous Peoples and Oppressed Nations in the United States, October 3, 1992

25

NATIVE-AMERICAN RELIGIOUS FREEDOM UNDER ATTACK

An Interview with Little Rock Reed

Deborah Garlin

It is our belief that Little Rock Reed, a part Lakota man and sundancer who has committed his life to working for the self-determination and the religious rights of the aboriginal peoples of this land, has been targeted by the Ohio government to be imprisoned and possibly murdered, in order to silence his voice which speaks to the injustices perpetrated on the aboriginal peoples and particularly our men, women, and children who are incarcerated throughout this land.

We demand that the government conduct a fair and unbiased investigation into the circumstances relating to the current imprisonment of this man so that he may be free to continue doing the work that Tunkasila (the Grandfather, Great Spirit) has put in his heart to do. If such an investigation is not done, this relative's imprisonment, much like the [political] imprisonment of Leonard Peltier, will stand as a symbol of the injustices meted out by the white man's government against our people who simply wish to live in accordance with the traditional teachings given to us by our grandfathers, and to them by Wakan Tanka, the Creator.

—Traditional Circle of Elders
Pine Ridge Indian Reservation, September 1994

In 1979, Little Rock Reed robbed a store with an unloaded gun in Texarkana, Texas. An 18-year-old kid, he had been living in the streets and hitchhiking around the country for over two years. He pled guilty to the robbery and because he wouldn't testify against his co-defendants, Little Rock was sentenced to five years of hard labor in the Texas Department of Corrections. He managed to survive the environment, especially brutal for anyone as young as Little Rock, but he had become a very calloused and bitter young man by 1982, when he was handed $75 and a set of clothes (coat not included), and released in the wintry month of January with nowhere to call home.

He only lasted three months before he was again charged with robbery—this time in Ohio. Pleading guilty once more, he was given an indeterminate sentence of 7 to 25 years, a grim prospect in the mind of this 21-year-old who had only experienced a few short months in the free world as an adult. But at the age of 22, Little Rock had a dream that changed him dramatically. In his words:

> I grew very bitter, until I thought the bitterness would destroy me. I was disgusted with myself for having thrown my life away, and I was disgusted with the world around me. Simply put, I wanted to escape or die.

> But then one day as I slept I had a dream. It was a very profound dream. A very, very old man came to me. He didn't say any words with his mouth, but with his eyes. His wizened old face was so filled with the love and understanding I had always yearned for. As he looked into my eyes, my heart, my soul, his message was very clear to me. He, too, had lived on the Mother Earth, and he was a warrior for his people, my people. He, too, had endured a long life—much longer than mine—of bitterness and pain. He knew my suffering. He had been through it all and gone beyond.

> This grandfather didn't speak with his mouth. He spoke with the love in his eyes. He told me that for me to find peace within myself, I must look to the traditions of my people (the Lakota), to the elders, and to the little ones. They would guide me back to the Good Red Road of peace, love and harmony. He said he would always guide me and guard me and would never forsake me, and I know it's true...

> I made a commitment that day, almost 15 years ago. I went out onto the prison yard, laid my face against my Mother Earth—and cried. I looked to the sky, and I promised the Great Spirit that I would always try my best to do all I could for my people and to try my best to live in accordance with the teachings of the Sacred Pipe. And I vowed to someday sundance for my people, for all my relations—the human race, the earth, the animals, and all that God created.

In keeping with his commitment to the Creator, Little Rock began to read voraciously. Within a few short years, this convicted felon with no high school education had trained himself to utilize the resources in the prison law library. He became an expert on treaty rights and Native-American studies, and not only began to publish essays in academic journals and newsletters, but also was asked to organize panels and sessions for the annual conferences of such notable organizations as the Academy of Criminal Justice Sciences, the Association for Humanist Sociology and the American Society of Criminology. He gained expertise in constitutional law and became a jailhouse lawyer celebrated for his commitment to prison reform on a national level.

Little Rock founded the Native American Prisoners' Rehabilitation Research Project (NAPRRP) while in prison, and through the NAPRRP did enormous research resulting in a nearly 500-page book titled *The American Indian in the White Man's Prisons: A Story of Genocide* (UnCompromising Books, 1993), now used primarily as a college text in criminology and criminal justice courses. As is true of all Little Rock's writings, the book powerfully documents gross misconduct by prison officials, government attorneys and judges in their systematic efforts to destroy American Indian religions and communities. Native Americans are incarcerated at a higher *per capita* rate than any other racial or ethnic group, and while practicing Christianity is encouraged by prison officials, Native-American spiritual ceremonies and sacred objects are often prohibited within the prison setting. Because of the profound positive influence his cultural values have had on his own life and those he has touched, Little Rock firmly believes that cultural programming for Native-American prisoners that instills these values will have great impact on the Native-American community in general. Thus, his greatest commitment has been to the establishment of Native-American spiritual and cultural programs within this country's prisons.

It is his commitment to these matters—and his powerful and honest manner of speaking and writing—that caused Little Rock to become targeted by Ohio prison and parole officials. First eligible for parole after less than four-and-a-half years, at the time of his initial appearance before the parole board, he was in solitary confinement in a control unit. Modeled on the brainwashing chambers used in North Korean and Chinese prison camps, control units now proliferate throughout the country, and are used especially against jailhouse lawyers and activists like Little Rock. At the time, he was serving six months in the control unit as punishment for fasting to protest the Ohio Department of Rehabilitation and Corrections' policy eliminating any kind of Native-American religious freedom, including the barring of all Native spiritual leaders from the prisons.

Little Rock was escorted before the parole board clad in leg irons and handcuffs for his hearing in December 1986. The board, according to Little Rock, let him know that he would be released right away if he agreed to drop the impending First Amendment lawsuit challenging the prison system's persecution of Indian prisoners. Little Rock refused, saying

> The guards have beaten me, spit on me, gassed me, sprayed me with a water hose, and left me naked for days on end with no bedding or clothing; they ridicule and call me names, have thrown their human feces and urine on me—only because I ask that my Native relatives and I be allowed to pray in accordance with the teachings given our people by God. I mean no disrespect, but I cannot forsake my brothers.

So the board denied him parole. It was virtually impossible, however, to prove that the parole board was keeping him in prison for speaking about abuses against prisoners—until the chairman of the parole board handed the proof to Little Rock in writing. In October 1990, Little Rock was granted parole and transferred to a pre-release center for parolees in Orient, Ohio, where he successfully completed a reintegration program. But Little Rock had filed a grievance regarding some constitutional violations by the Adult Parole Authority (APA), so they rescinded his parole and had him transferred back to maximum-security at the Southern Ohio Correctional Facility in Lucasville. The parole board chairman specified the reason for the parole rescission: Little Rock complained about the violation of his constitutional rights. The APA also made this admission in a court hearing; Little Rock was attempting to obtain an order for his release from prison on the grounds that he was no longer being detained as punishment for his original crime, but rather for asserting his First Amendment rights. Yet the judge dismissed the petition, claiming that since Little Rock's indeterminate sentence was a maximum of 25 years, he could not seek court review of the APA's actions until he had served the full 25 years in prison.

When Little Rock appealed the decision to another Ohio court, it appeared as though the higher court, under pressure from Little Rock's supporters worldwide, would order Little Rock's release from prison. But the appeal court never got a chance to rule on the appeal. On May 5, 1992 (a year-and-a-half after the unlawful parole rescission), the parole board released Little Rock on parole to render the issues addressed in the appeal moot. Thus, the decision could not benefit other prisoners in similar situations. Little Rock was now expected to serve one year on parole before receiving a final discharge.

While on parole, Little Rock continued his work with the NAPRRP as its full-time director, in addition to attending college full-time. In his capacity as NAPRRP director, he continued to write and speak out against prison conditions and discrimination against Native prisoners. After succeeding in arranging a meeting to force the Ohio prison officials to discuss religious policies with representatives of the Indian community, he was ordered by his parole officer to stop corresponding with prison officials and to stop speaking or writing articles about Ohio's prison/parole policies or the APA would revoke his parole and return him to prison to serve the remaining 15 years of his 25-year sentence. At the same time he was given this gag order, he received a hostile letter from the warden at the Lucasville prison stating that he "took personally" Little Rock's continued statements regarding prison officials' religious persecution of the Indian prisoners at Lucasville. Little Rock also received letters from two other high-ranking prison administrators (in charge of religious services for the Ohio prison system) in which they implied that Little Rock's parole would be revoked if he continued his activities on behalf of Native-American prisoners.

Despite these threats, Little Rock did continue to speak, write articles, and give radio interviews. Shortly thereafter, the acting chief of the APA issued a warrant for his arrest, based on a misdemeanor charge brought against Little Rock by a Kentucky man. Yet before the warrant was even issued, the man had contacted the APA and informed them that his charge was false. The effort was futile; as that man's wife later testified, Little Rock's parole officer admitted that the prison and parole officials "up at the top" wanted Little Rock back in prison so that they could defuse his protests, and if they needed to use a false charge to legitimize their actions, so be it.

Facing another possible 15 years in prison due to his political activity, Little Rock fled Ohio. He was apprehended in Taos, New Mexico in September 1994.

Signed by 65 of the traditional spiritual leaders and elders of the Oglala Lakota Nation, the demand that opens this chapter is similar to those made by hundreds of other citizens, lawyers, professors, and organizations. The governors of New Mexico and Ohio, however, ignored all demands. Little Rock remained in the Taos jail from October 1994 to January 20, 1995 and, with the aid of Taos attorney John Paternoster and myself, fought extradition to Ohio. We asserted—and provided ample evidence—that his extradition was sought in retaliation for his exercising his right to free speech. During the hearings, we were able to introduce an overwhelming amount of testimony and documentary evidence supporting Little Rock's claim that he was not a fugitive from justice and that Ohio officials had conspired to imprison and torture him in retaliation for his writing and speaking about corrupt activities within Ohio's criminal justice system.

Finally, on January 20, 1995, New Mexico District Court Judge Peggy Nelson ordered Little Rock's immediate release from jail, ruling that the evidence, uncontroverted by the government, proved that Little Rock's claims were valid. In an unprecedented decision, Judge Nelson essentially recognized Little Rock as a political prisoner, declaring that Ohio prison and parole officials' pursuit of Little Rock's extradition and imprisonment "is premised on their desire to silence [his] voice." Judge Nelson ruled further that Ohio's extradition request was unconstitutional and based on motives of bad faith, and that if returned to Ohio, Little Rock would likely suffer great bodily injury or harm at the hands of those who wish to silence him.

The New Mexico Attorney General's Office (AG) appealed Judge Nelson's decision to the State Supreme Court. The AG admits that "throughout the evidentiary presentation in these extradition proceedings, [Little Rock and his attorneys] presented considerable evidence concerning his... mistreatment by Ohio and New Mexico authorities, improper motive and wrongdoing by Ohio corrections and parole personnel, his struggle to urge prisoner issues and the duress which required him to abscond from parole supervision in Ohio." Despite this admission and the proof that Little Rock had *no* criminal charges pending against him, as well as that the Ohio officials had committed perjury and falsified documents in their efforts to capture Little Rock, the AG's office nevertheless contended in its appeal brief that this "considerable evidence" was entirely "irrelevant." Citing the extradition clause of the U.S. Constitution, the brief maintained that an alleged fugitive had no right to present evidence in court of wrongdoing by the state officials demanding extradition.

Should the higher courts reverse Judge Nelson's well-reasoned decision, they would send a clear message to the social activists and writers who dare speak out about government wrongdoing: their voices may be legally stifled during any extradition process. This is a very disturbing prospect, particularly since Little Rock is hardly the only person in this country who state and federal officials seek to silence through manipulation and abuse of their "criminal justice" machinery or what Little Rock refers to as the "criminal just-us cyst'm."

At the time of publication, Little Rock is still awaiting a decision from the New Mexico State Supreme Court. He continues to work on prison issues and to write regularly for the *Prison News Service*. What follows is an interview that took place in November 1995, in Taos, New Mexico.

Deborah Garlin: Judge Nelson of the New Mexico District Court ordered your release from jail because Ohio's demand for your extradition is based on their desire to silence your voice. Why would your voice cause such upheaval among prison officials?

Little Rock Reed: My voice speaks the truth, as do the voices of many prisoners faced with the same kind of persecution I've been subjected to. Not all, but a significant number of government officials—government attorneys, public defenders, state and federal judges, prison administrators, parole officials, legislators, and politicians, etc.— would prefer that the public not learn many of the truths we speak, because if these truths were known, the entire criminal justice system as we know it today would be abolished. The truth is, America's criminal justice system is a fraud. It's the largest industry on the planet, and if it collapsed, the resulting depression would make that of the 1920s seem quite insignificant.

DG: What kind of truth is the government hiding from the public?

LR: I can't begin to cover them all, but here are a few truths I do know and can prove: 1) Violent crime rates are lower today than they have been in 15 years. 2) Government attorneys consciously imprison innocent people because prisoners are doing slave labor and making billions of dollars a year for big corporations. 3) The American Correctional Association, the United States' largest accrediting agency for prisons, is comprised primarily of prison officials who accredit themselves; it's a fraudulent organization that thumbs its nose—with absolute impunity—at government agencies who ask them to file tax returns that they are required by law to file. (If a prisoners' rights organization refused to file tax returns, it would be closed down and its executive officers prosecuted.) 4) Whenever you hear of a prison riot or uprising, what you don't hear in the mainstream media is that the prison officials themselves are largely responsible for the riots. Prison officials create violence every day so that they can convince the legislatures that more funds are needed for new prisons. They want more prisons because prisons are big business. The list goes on and on.

DG: You have assisted Indian prisoners in establishing spiritual and cultural programming in many states over the years. Can you talk a little about your work in this area and the current status of the struggle for Native-American religious freedom?

LR: Native people in this country, both inside and outside the prisons, are still struggling for the right to religious freedom that most other people in this country take for granted. Unfortunately, many courts use Christian concepts in determining what religious practices, cere-monies, and sacred sites deserve constitutional protections. For exam-ple, I've never heard of a Christian cathedral being knocked down so that the government and multinational corporations can get to the coal, uranium, oil, or other mineral resources that lie beneath it. However, in the Indian spiritual system, sacred sites aren't so much man-made. Sacred sites are in certain lakes and rivers, mountains and other natural shrines. Because they're made by God instead of man, the courts have no respect for them. Hundreds of Native-American sacred sites, including burial grounds, are being desecrated by the government and big corporations with the blessing of the courts.

The same situation exists in the prisons. I've done time in about eight different state prisons in Texas and Ohio, and in those states, Native prisoners are forbidden to practice their spiritual beliefs. Cer-tain ceremonies and sacred objects are held sacred to Native people, and when used by the people, healing comes. This is very important for Native prisoners, because most of them are in prison because they need healing of the mind, heart, spirit, and body. Indian life isn't easy. There's a lot of despair and hopelessness among those who wind up in prison, usually as a result of alcoholism—which is a means of numbing the despair and pain that they suffer both on the reservations and in the cities. The greatest healing available to these people is the healing that can come from counseling with traditional Native spiri-tual leaders and elders, and tribal ceremonies. But in the prisons I've been to, virtually every ceremony was prohibited, as were sacred objects and herbs, such as the drum, the sacred pipe, cedar, sage, sweet grass, and medicine bags. The sweat lodge ceremony was prohibited. In the prisons I've been in, Native spiritual leaders are even forbidden from entering the walls to pray with the prisoners, and to counsel with them. Yet at the same time, these prison administrators who forbid Native spiritual practices give special privileges to prisoners who participate in Christian religious practices and prayer meetings.

DG: What reasons do the prison administrators give for prohibiting Native religious practice?

LR: Oh, they come up with some real dillies! There was a lawsuit in Pennsylvania in the mid-'80s regarding the deprivation of Native religious freedom. The prisoners wanted long hair and access to sacred ceremonies and objects used in prayer (the wearing of long hair is a sacred practice for most traditional Indians). In order to beat the lawsuit, the prison director swore under oath that in his expert opinion the wearing of long hair by male prisoners would make it easy for them to conceal contraband, such as drugs and weapons. He testified that to allow the sweat lodge would cause security problems also, as would access to medicine bags, cedar, sage, drums, and other sacred objects. The state prevailed in that lawsuit by asking the court to dismiss the Indian prisoners' claims based on the prison director's speculative "expert opinion." After that lawsuit, prison officials faced with identical lawsuits in other states, such as Ohio, Indiana, Missouri, Texas, and Utah, have testified identically to the prison director in Pennsylvania. None of these officials have supported their testimony with any evidence, yet the courts usually buy what the prison officials say and dismiss the lawsuits.

I conducted a survey of all the prison systems in the United States and Canada a couple years ago. I sent the officials a questionnaire to determine which of these claims by prison officials were actually valid. At that time, what I found was that about 70 percent of the state prison systems, as well as the federal prison system and every prison in Canada, have allowed the wearing of long hair by male prisoners for many years, and that there is not one documented instance in which contraband has been found in long hair. I also found that sweat lodges and sacred objects such as drums, the sacred pipe, cedar, sage, medicine bags, headbands, etc., are permitted in all the Canadian prisons, the federal prison system, and at least 22 state prison systems, and that these practices and objects have caused no more security problems than those associated with Christian or recreational activities, and that in fact, access to these practices has significantly reduced misconduct and recidivism rates among Native prisoners. So, it's clear to me that the only reason prison officials forbid these is that they want to maintain control and force their own cultural values on Indian people. They don't want to allow prisoners to exercise self-determination to any extent. Their attitudes and practices not only cause harm to the Indian community—by creating hatred and resentment—but they also cost the taxpayers a lot of money. Right now there are a lot of lawsuits pending in federal and state courts regarding the deprivation of religious freedom for Native-American prisoners.

The bottom line is that this world needs healing, and it's not going to come through the repression of religious freedom and the obvious lack of respect for human dignity that is apparent in prison policies and practices.

DG: What do you think is the real reason for the suppression of Native-American religious freedom?

LR: There are a number of reasons that the government suppresses Native religious freedom. Some prison officials want absolute control of every aspect of a prisoner's being. Some prison officials fear the prospect of prisoners empowering themselves, and spirituality is empowering. Many prison officials suppress Native religious freedom because they don't understand Native spirituality, and they fear what they don't understand. But these reasons are those that can be attributed to narrow-minded officials.

The greatest reason for suppressing Native spiritual ceremonies and practices is a political reason that can be traced back to the late 1800s, when American Indian religious practices were criminalized by the federal government. Government and Christian leaders put their minds together and came to the conclusion that the reason for tribal resistance to the theft of Indian lands had nothing to do with Indians having a concept of ownership of the land, but rather, that tribal resistance was rooted in a profound and abiding respect for the sanctity of the land and a spiritual obligation to protect it. Thus the idea was that if Indians could have their spiritual values and beliefs crushed out of them through forced assimilation, those values and beliefs could be replaced with values that would have Indians agreeing with the selling of the earth. Sacred sites would no longer be sacred, hence it would be easier to persuade the Indians to transfer those lands to non-Indians for development.

Many Indian prisoners have lost touch with their cultural and spiritual identity and values systems. Providing them access to spiritual leaders, medicine men, and ceremonies has a tendency to instill in them the spiritual obligation to stand (albeit nonviolently) against the United States' continuing theft of Indian lands, the violation of treaties and political injustices that continue to this day on a massive level. Thus it logically follows that the most effective way to repress political resistance is to repress American Indian religious freedom, no less today than a hundred years ago. That's the main political reason Native Americans still do not have the protection of religious freedom that other groups do in this country.

Editor's note: At the end of 1995, the Religious Freedom Restoration Act was signed into law by President Clinton. This law raised the constitutional standard, opening the door for Native Americans behind bars to seek relief from the courts for violations of their right to practice their religion. Much of the law was made specifically to apply to prisoners, and indeed prisoners have started using it. *Hamilton v. Schriro* (42 USC 2000bb) is an excellent example in which a Native-American prisoner has sued for the right to wear his hair long, and have access to sweat lodge ceremonies and sacred objects. Unfortunately the courts have been ruling against the Act across the board. For more information, contact the Native American Rights Fund at 1506 Broadway, Boulder, CO 80302; (303) 447-8760.

SECTION SIX

THE NATIONWIDE LOCKDOWN

Control Unit Prisons on the Rise

That foreign military intervention and domestic repression have most often been successfully framed by imperialist governments as the preservation of democracy says a great deal about the cultural and political power of elites and their institutions. As has been noted in many of the preceding chapters, the modern maximum-security prison is a key institution in the maintenance of elite power in the United States. Not only are these "super-max" dungeons effective in squelching a great deal of the righteous opposition to prison conditions, imprisonment strategies, and general social reality, but in the interest of elite agendas, they send a powerful message to the populace. That message is essentially that our solution to an individual's violence must be to silence and punish the individual, not to address the root causes of this violence.

The state's justification for these tortuous conditions is that these prisoners are the "worst of the worst." This rationale is shared by most of the 36 or more states that have created control unit prisons. Often the people confined to these institutions indeed represent extreme products of our violent culture. However, as a number of the authors point out, control units (and for that matter, segregation, isolation, or "security" units in mainline prisons) serve just as often to put away jailhouse lawyers, Queers, those with organizing potential, and others whom prison officials see as a threat to their order.

In their piece, "Supermax Prisons: High-Tech Dungeons and Modern-Day Torture," Erica Thompson and Jan Susler look closely at the history of Marion, which has been used as a model for prison construction and for creating the conditions of isolation. They detail reports assailing the prison and various efforts launched by justice-minded folks to expose Marion's brutality. Thompson is active with the Committee to End the Marion Lockdown, and her commitment to prisoner's rights is made clear in this piece.

The other pieces speak specifically to the conditions at other federal and state flagship institutions, such as the Lexington High Security Unit for women, which was closed due to public protest; California's Pelican Bay State Prison, heralded as the state of the art in maximum-security incarceration; and the newly opened federal lockdown in Florence, Colorado.

26

SUPERMAX PRISONS

High-Tech Dungeons and Modern-Day Torture

Erica Thompson and Jan Susler

The United States Penitentiary (USP) at Marion, Illinois, opened in 1963, the same year the federal prison at Alcatraz closed. In 1983, the whole prison was permanently locked down and turned into the first control unit. It is currently the highest security prison in the United States.

Since the imposition of the permanent lockdown at Marion, both the model itself and the methods it employs have been strongly and continually criticized by human rights organizations. Consider the following:

- *The 1984 convening of Congressional hearings about USP Marion* was prompted by allegations of widespread staff violence against prisoners and abusive lockdown conditions to "provide a full airing of the issues to help the subcommittee develop constructive ways to increase the safety of correctional employees and inmates and reduce tension."[1]

- *The 1985 convening of a Congressional oversight hearing about USP Marion* involved testimony from congressional consultants, including recommendations that a mental health unit be created for the prisoners to treat the "negative health consequences" that may flow from lockdown confinement, conditions so adverse that even staff operate under "combat mentality"; and that lockdown not be permitted to endure indefinitely, as well as evidence that 80 percent of the prisoners at Marion were not even classified as level six prisoners.[2]

- *The 1985 report of the American Friends Service Committee* observed that Marion represents choosing "a course that favors the continual escalation of repression as a means of control, even though it has never been demonstrated that repression brings its desired results."[3]

- *The 1987 John Howard Association Report* concluded that Marion "is not a normal maximum-security prison on lockdown status, but rather a firmly established, fully functioning behavior modification program..."; that "the Marion program seems to be designed to break the defiant spirit and behavior... through a year or more of sensory and psychological deprivation [in which] prisoners are stripped of their individual identities..."[4]

- *The 1987 Report of Amnesty International* stated that "[w]ithin Marion, violations of the [United Nations] Standard Minimum Rules [for the Treatment of Prisoners] are common... There is hardly a rule in the Standard Minimum Rules that is not infringed in some way or other."[5]

- *The 1990 Report of the National Interreligious Task Force on Criminal Justice* concluded that "[t]he absence of balance in the procedures at Marion prison, where security measures override the individual need for human contact, spiritual fulfillment, and fellowship, becomes an excuse for the constant show of sheer force. The conditions of Marion prison... constitute, in our estimation, psychological pain and agony tantamount to torture."[6]

- *The 1990 Report of the U.S. House of Representatives Subcommittee on Courts, Intellectual Property and the Administration of Justice* expressed "concern... about the amount of time inmates spend in their cells in relative isolation and the limited opportunity for productive and recreational activity that is available in the highly controlled environment" and the need to "continue to develop a more humane approach to the incarceration of the maximum-security prison population," particularly in light of Marion's function as a model for prisons in the United States and in other countries.[7]

Since 1983, the Marion model—total physical and psychological control—has spawned control units throughout this country. Indeed, Marion itself is soon to be replaced by a new federal control unit in Florence, Colorado—an area notorious for high levels of uranium contamination and listed as an EPA Superfund site. Human Rights Watch, in its 1991 annual survey of the United State's prison system, found that the single most disturbing aspect was the proliferation of control unit prisons:

> Human Rights Watch deplores the fact that 36 states have followed the example of the maximum-security prison in Marion, Illinois, to create super-maximum-security institutions. The states have been quite creative in designing their own "maxi-maxis" and in making the conditions particularly difficult to bear, at times surpassing the original model.
>
> As a result, inmates are essentially sentenced twice: once by the court, to a certain period of imprisonment; and the second time, by the prison administration to confinement in "maxi-maxis" under extremely harsh conditions and without independent supervision. This second sentencing is open-ended and limited only by the overall length of an inmate's sentence and is meted out without the benefit of counsel. The increasing use of "prisons within prisons" leads to numerous human rights abuses and frequent violations of the U.N. Standard Minimum Rules for the Treatment of Prisoners.[8]

Indeed, the control unit construct has bred unique abuses in the hands of state officials. For example, at Westville, Indiana's Maximum Control Complex (MCC), prisoners are frequently firehosed and then placed on "strip cell status" with all clothing and bedding removed from the cell for days at a time. At California's Pelican Bay Security Housing Unit (SHU), prison officials may subject prisoners to merciless hogtying for hours at a time. [Hogtying is shackling a prisoner's wrists and ankles together, either in front or in back. See articles on Pelican Bay.—E.R.]

Supermax prisons (control units, maxi-maxis) differ intrinsically from lesser security institutions in three principal respects. First, unlike maximum-security institutions, where prisoners are out of their cells an average of 13 hours per day, supermax prisons are permanent lockdown facilities. In other words, prisoners are caged in their single cells approximately 23 hours per day.

Second, supermax prisons employ isolation, control, and behavior modification techniques. Prisoners are not allowed to communicate with other prisoners. Since the trend in these institutions is to utilize solid steel doors, rather than bars, complete isolation is virtually assured. Prisoners must eat, sleep, and live their entire lives alone in a cell. There is no congregate exercise or religious service. Censorship of reading materials is strict, and educational programs via correspondence courses are severely restricted, if allowed at all.

Prison officials seek to curtail any expression of creativity or individuality by the prisoners. Prisoners are not allowed to put anything on the walls, and until public outcry mounted, prisoners at MCC-Westville were not even allowed to know the time of day or night. Basic human needs such as human contact, communication, and individuality are viewed by prison officials as a threat to the smooth running and security of the institution and are, therefore, proscribed.

Visits by family members, often critical to a prisoner's psychological well-being, are restricted and take place under such oppressive conditions that many family members refuse to return. At MCC-Indiana, for instance, after a two-hour delay while prison officials attempted to deny a pre-approved visit by a prisoner's father, the father suffered a heart attack when his son was finally brought out and he saw his son's deteriorated physical condition and abuse by MCC guards.

On the rare occasion when a prisoner has an opportunity to leave his cell, he is fully shackled (hands, feet, and waist) and flanked by several guards. Minor rule infractions result in severe punishment ranging from a prisoner being fully strapped down to his bed to a visit from a cell extraction team (guards in riot gear with mace and steel-tipped rib-spreaders).

Finally, in some jurisdictions, officials designate a prisoner for transfer into a supermax prison as an administrative measure, as opposed to a punitive measure. The legal effect of an administrative transfer is that the prisoner has no legal recourse to challenge the designation. A punitive transfer, on the other hand, would require at least the minimum requirements of due process.

Not only can a prisoner not challenge his administrative designation, but he can be held indefinitely in a supermax because of that designation. Supermax prisons are unique in this respect. Standard procedure in non-supermax prisons would require that a prisoner be returned, as of right, to the general prison population at the conclusion of his punitive segregation term.

It is critical to view the supermax explosion in context. Our "criminal justice system" is racist and politically repressive. And the racial disparities in supermax prisons tend to be even greater than in the rest of the prison population. Moreover, prisoners who file lawsuits, speak out against injustice, and fight for dignity and respect are targeted for transfer to control units.

What is going on in the United States in the name of "law-and-order" is obscene and unprecedented in history. We must educate ourselves, speak out, and take action immediately. We must make a concerted effort to reframe the debate on all fronts. We must be relentless. There are no excuses.

NOTES

1. Opening remarks by Hon. Robert W. Kastenmeier, Chair, House Judiciary Committee Subcommittee on Courts, Civil Liberties, and the Administration of Justice, 3-29-84, in Oversight Hearing, 98th Congress, 2d Session, Serial No. 106, p. 2.

2. Oversight Hearing before the Subcommittee on Courts, Civil Liberties and the Administration of Justice, 99th Congress, 1st Session, 6-6-1985, Serial No. 26, pp. 33, 35, 39.

3. Mauer and Motz, *The Lessons of Marion—The Failure of a Maximum Security Prison: A History and Analysis, with Voices of Prisoners*, (Philadelphia: American Friends Service Committee), 1985, p. 2.

4. John Howard Association, *Report on the USP at Marion*, October 1987, p. 1.

5. Amnesty International, "Allegations of Ill-treatment in Marion Prison, IL, U.S.A.," (London: Amnesty International), May 1987, p. 15.

6. L.C. Dorsey, "Marion Prison: Progressive Correction or Legalized Torture?," (New York: The National Interreligious Task Force on Criminal Justice), p. 6.

7. Subcommittee on Courts, Intellectual Property, and the Administration of Justice, Report on Visit to the Marion Federal Penitentiary, Washington, DC, pp. 5-6.

8. *Prison Conditions in the United States*, (New York: Human Rights Watch), 1991.

27

THE CRIME OF PUNISHMENT

Pelican Bay Maximum Security Prison

Corey Weinstein and Eric Cummins

With imprisonment rates towering grimly over those of the most infamous police states, the United States has abandoned the goal of rehabilitation touted from the 1950s through the 1970s, and turned to high-tech dungeons that violate basic standards of human decency and international law.[1] A recent survey by the Federal Bureau of Prisons found that 36 states now operate some form of super-maxi-mum-security prison or unit within a prison.[2] These "maxi-maxi" prisons have become social control tools to manage the nation's disposable populations. Ostensibly designed to control disruptions, punish inmates, and break up prison gangs, these new facilities actually engender more violence. By exploiting racial tensions, they are deepening the already profound fissures in the U.S. social order. The rage they spawn is unleashed first on the prison yard and then onto the public streets when the prisoners are paroled. This prison system makes visible, through the still-smoking embers of South Central L.A., the tinderbox we are creating for the 21st century.

The California Model

In the race toward mass imprisonment, no state has outdone California, the nation's leading jailer. Home to 11 percent of the U.S. population, California incarcerates more people than any other state, has more than twice as many inmates in its jails as any other state in the country, and confines an astounding 20 percent of this country's juvenile prisoners. From 1982 to 1990, while spending for schools and other social programs was savagely reduced, funding for the state's prisons soared 359 percent, doubling the number of prisons and tripling the number of prisoners.[3]

LOCKDOWN OF THE LOCKDOWN

Based on our investigative interviews and its own research, Pelican Bay Information Project (PBIP) estimates that Pelican Bay prisoners were locked down for 40 percent of 1994. For prisoners in the SHU, that means revoking of the few privileges they already had: no "yard" (in reality, a small covered concrete run with no recreational equipment), no law library, extremely limited showers, no canteen, and further delays in medical care. No official reasons have been given for these drastic measures. Prisoners told us that these lockdowns and multiple cell searches were ostensibly being conducted to locate a missing piece of metal or to search for holes in the walls, but all agreed that the length of lockdowns and the manner in which cells were disrupted were a form of retaliation for the Madrid lawsuit. PBIP detailed the reports from prisoners:

Whatever the reason, PBSP [Pelican Bay State Prison] administration is using the lockdown to harass and punish prisoners. In some cases prisoners are forced to go five weeks between showers. No yard means no exercise and also that those double-celled get no break from each other's company. During cell searches guards throw everything around, step on personal property and trample legal materials. Many personal items are taken by guards to further demoralize prisoners. Receipts are not given for property taken and previously allowed reading material is arbitrarily confiscated. Pornography is encouraged over political and legal reading material. When prisoner kitchen workers are kept in their cells, guards prepare the trays brought to the SHU for the two daily hot meals. The food is thrown onto often dirty trays and winds up being disgusting and even inedible. Perhaps most important is the interference with jailhouse legal challenges over the many matters the prisoners are fighting. Recently a legal newspaper was restricted and legal mail continues to be opened.

One of the daily degradations of life in the SHU is the administration's decision to deprive prisoners of the items necessary to clean their cells. No cleanser, mops, sponges, or rags are provided at all. The prison is intent in creating the perception that the prisoners kept there are animals and must therefore be made to wallow in filth and stench. There is no routine inspection for cleanliness. Prisoners are forced to use their body soap, shampoo, tooth powder and towels, tee shirts, or toilet paper to clean their cells and toilets. During lockdown when the SHU tier tender is not allowed to clean the showers and sweep the tiers, there is garbage and filth in all pod areas.

—*Eli Rosenblatt*

Readers not familiar with the conditions or lawsuits described should see the three most recent issues of the *Pelican Bay Express*, available from PBIP at 2489 Mission St. #28, San Francisco, CA 94110; (415) 821-6545.

California also leads in the trend to isolate prisoners in high-security prisons with special control units. Security Housing Unit (SHU), Level Four, maximum-security, administrative segregation, and other high-security cells housed about 10 percent of the California Department of Corrections (CDoC) prisoners in 1991.[4]

In the seven prisons recently opened or scheduled for opening in California, 25 percent of the cells are high security with 750 SHU cells and 3,000 more maximum-security cells.[5] This allocation ensures that punitive warehousing will remain the function of prisons well into the future.

Isolation and Violence

In 1989, the CDoC unveiled its state-of-the-art weapon against crime: a 1,056-cell SHU at Pelican Bay State Prison near Crescent City. Within the main unit, the X-shaped SHU is a high-tech replica of the nation's earliest prisons, which featured solitary cells. These bleak gray torture chambers are now showcased nationwide as a 21st-century prototype.

As with its 18th-century ancestor, the key to control within the SHU is to minimize human contact and maximize sensory deprivation. A Pelican Bay SHU inmate is guaranteed at least 22½ hours of bleak confinement. Almost half of the cells, designed for one prisoner, are now overcrowded with two men per cell. The SHU prisoner has little or no face-to-face contact with others—not even with guards, who have been largely replaced by round-the-clock electronic surveillance. The inmate sits in a windowless cell with a poured concrete sleeping slab, immobile concrete stool, small concrete writing platform behind a thick, honeycombed steel-plated door. Guards monitor him from control booths with video cameras and communicate through speakers. A SHU prisoner never sees the light of day. He may not decorate his white cell walls. He has no job, educational classes, vocational training, counseling, religious services, or communal activities. No hobbies are permitted to help pass the time. The prisoner eats in his cell from a dinner tray passed through a slot in the door. Once a day he may exercise alone in a small, indoor, bare "dog walk" without exercise equipment, toilet, or water. He is strip-searched before and after this strictly monitored exercise. Because each of the 132 eight-cell pods has its own exercise area, this procedure is more a ritual of humiliation than a security precaution. Whenever a prisoner is moved from place to place, he is handcuffed before exit from his cell, shackled hands to waist, hobble-chained ankle-to-ankle, accompanied by two guards, and observed on video monitors.[6]

Isolation is strictly enforced. The eight-cell pods are unconnected. The eight to twelve prisoners within each pod cannot pass anything from cell to cell or communicate easily. Even the tier tender, a SHU prisoner who sweeps the pod walkways, is not allowed to speak to anyone as he passes the cells.

Outside communications are also tightly controlled. Prison authorities delay mail for weeks, withhold it for trivial or inconsistent reasons, and open privileged attorney-client communication.[7] Televisions and radios are available for purchase, but since the TV brings in six Colorado cable stations and the radio only gets local stations, prisoners have a hard time getting hometown or even general California news. Authorities also severely restrict access to news and books; the Seattle-based Books to Prisoners protests, "We're unable to send books in there."[8]

Guards and administrative staff also leak false information to the media. In the late summer of 1992, for example, after a prisoner was murdered by another inmate at Pelican Bay, prison staff tried to deflect an investigation by blaming gang drug wars.[9]

The Silence of the Cells

CDoC authorities defend the near absolute control of communications and environment as necessary to suppress violence. And while inmate-to-inmate violence is certainly reduced within the SHU, the level of physical and mental abuse perpetrated by guards against prisoners is extreme. Minor offenses, such as refusing to return a cup in protest of cold coffee or declining to attend an optional hearing, can result in "cell-extraction." In this brutal procedure, a team of six to eight guards in combat gear—with face visors and riot shields—often shoots and wounds the prisoner with a pellet gun and then with a taser stun-gun before opening the cell door. Once the door is open, the guards rush inside, beat the prisoner, and fully restrain him with chains. Once restrained, the inmate is often beaten again, and then left hogtied for hours in the corridor or a cell.[10]

Verbal harassment is another common form of abuse. Guards taunt prisoners with threats, denial of simple requests, or by boasting about their latest beating. The largely Latin-American (approximately 59 percent) and African-American (approximately 23 percent) SHU population complain that the predominately white guards also commonly direct racial slurs against them.[11]

Faced with constant harassment, sensory deprivation, and isolation, some prisoners become enraged and aggressive. Others retreat into themselves, choose to sleep most of the day, refuse exercise, stop writing to family and friends, and turn on their lights only to get food or medication. Some enter a private world of madness, scream incessantly in their cells, and even cover themselves with their own feces. This psychological decay is worse for prisoners who cannot afford a state-issued TV or radio. The often confused and delusional prisoners who are on psychiatric medication and housed in what is called the "ding-block" are victims of an even higher frequency of abuse.

The devastating consequences of long-term solitary confinement are predictable and well-documented. In his 1980 study at Walpole, Massachusetts prison, Dr. Stuart Grassian confirmed the impact of isolation. Prisoners developed:

> ...vivid hallucinations of sight, sound, smell and touch; dissociative features including sudden recovery "as from a dream" with amnesia for the events of the psychosis; agitation and motor excitement with aimless violence; delusions, usually described as persecutory.[12]

Grassian's study suggests an ominous self-fulfilling prophecy: SHU will drive men mad, predispose them to violence, and thus legitimize their solitary confinement.

Snitch, Parole, or Die

The Institutional Classification Committee at Pelican Bay—essentially a kangaroo court—decides which prisoners are confined in the SHU. Their decisions range from vindictive to arbitrary, and are often based on vague information from confidential informants. Some SHU inmates have attacked guards and participated in fights (often after deliberate provocation), or have been caught with weapons.[13] Other prisoners are consigned to the SHU as punishment for exercising their legal rights, such as filing suits against the CDoC or engaging in political activity and resistance. Still others were simply in the wrong place at the wrong time.

In about half the cases, however, the decision to send a man to a SHU is based on a charge of gang affiliation or membership.[14] Consistent with the CDoC's intent to make the Pelican Bay SHU its first-line weapon against prison gangs, all gang-linked inmates receive an indeterminate sentence. Once linked to a gang, the prisoner's only hope for release from the SHU is to snitch, wait to be paroled, or die. Snitching requires that a prisoner confess violations of prison rules to the Criminal Activities Coordinator and implicate gang members in illegal acts. Since it is illegal, even in wartime, to isolate a prisoner to extract information, this policy violates not only U.S. law but the Geneva Convention.[15]

The SHU prisoner with an indeterminate sentence is in an untenable situation: if he snitches, he becomes a target for retaliation by those he implicates and must become a regular informant to maintain the protection of the guards. SHU inmates who choose not to snitch or have no information to trade for freedom remain confined indefinitely. Others use snitching to their advantage by falsely accusing enemies of being gang members, and recruit new inmates into gangs by threatening to snitch. Many who are pressured into snitching just try to name the lone wolf, the mentally unstable, the individual entrepreneurs (inmates who collect debts or sell drugs, sex, condoms, etc.) or anyone too weak to retaliate.[16]

Inmates released from SHU are automatically assumed to have gotten out because they snitched. The frequency of retaliation against inmates suspected of complicity has helped give B Yard (the exercise area in Pelican Bay's adjacent 2,200-man maximum-security section) the reputation as the most violent in California's 106,000-person prison system. Guards reported 67 stabbings there in a single three-month stretch during 1992.[17] In 1993, one inmate died and 21 were injured in Pelican Bay's largest gang fight to date, involving 23 men.[18]

"The way the system works," said one Pelican Bay prisoner, "is that the guards run it. Prisoners have no more power. Back in '84 to '85, prisoners had power, they ran the prisons, and the guards had to treat prisoners with respect. That's all changed because of Pelican Bay. Now you have to snitch to get any favors at all, even a phone call. Snitch or stay here [in SHU]. This is an atmosphere of total fear."[19]

Rehab and Race

Pelican Bay as prototype prison of the future is a clear repudiation of the "treatment era" prison. What is more, its misguided efforts to control gangs and violence in CDoC by returning to the tortures of the pre-treatment past have backfired and made Pelican Bay an extraordinarily violent place. The forces that sent the rehabilitative model to an early grave are complex. Perhaps the most important component—the racial inequity that pervades society—is reflected in the justice system, and then reproduced in prison.

Prisons are increasingly and disproportionately non-white, with the Pelican Bay SHU particularly targeting Latino-Americans. While only about 15 percent of the state population, in 1992 Latinos made up 37 percent of the CDoC prisoners and 59 percent of the Pelican Bay SHU population.[20] One rumored explanation for this dramatic discrepancy in the SHU is that in 1989 just before Pelican Bay was opened, officials at Folsom Prison cut a deal with African-American gangs: if they would control yard violence at Folsom, rival Latino gangs would be transferred to Pelican Bay.[21]

The percentage of Blacks in California prisons also far exceeds their representation in the population and the pattern goes back decades. Around World War II, a disproportionate number of African Americans—many of whom migrated to California for jobs in the aircraft and shipbuilding industries—ended up in prison. By 1970, African Americans made up only 7 percent of the state's population, yet prisons were 29.8 percent black. By 1993, in the United States as a whole, African-American men suffered an incarceration rate of over 3,000 per 100,000, six times the national average. South Africa was able to maintain apartheid at the much lower rate of 729 per 100,000.[22]

At every stage in the justice system—arrest, pre-trial hearing, conviction, sentencing, classification hearing during imprisonment, and parole hearing—California's African Americans and other minorities received harsher penalties than whites.[23] At the same time, no other group of prisoners showed more rage at the persecuting machinery of the state than California's Black inmates. In the early 1950s, in the relatively freer atmosphere of the "treatment era" prison, Black prisoners began to seize and dominate the state's prison yards as a means of fighting segregation and reversing their position at the bottom of the convict caste system. As the 1950s civil rights movement heated up outside the walls, the Nation of Islam mounted a nation-wide prisoner recruitment drive that made it the movement's in-prison arm. By 1960, the Nation had 65,000 to 100,000 members, many in prison.[24] Although the group originally advocated submission to authority, prison officials overreacted. They banned the group, broke up Muslim meetings, and segregated militants in solitary cells called Adjustment Centers (ACs). These ACs were predecessors to the SHU.

The Risk of Prison Gangs

In the early 1960s, these Adjustment Centers were showcased as humane alternatives to dungeons of the past. The state considered them the ultimate rehabilitative tool through which incorrigible prisoners could receive intensive daily rehabilitative psychiatric assistance as well as group counseling, quality education, and a specially designed work program. ACs soon evolved into prisons within prisons, with their own exercise yards, dining rooms, and schools. Although designed for a maximum of three-month "rehabilitation," they soon became a long-term solution to undermine inmate organization and isolate political agitators such as Muslims.

This repression peaked when Muslim temple minister Booker T. (X) Johnson was killed in 1963 by a gunrail officer in San Quentin's AC. His successor, Eldridge Cleaver, established links to radicals outside San Quentin, proving to California's prisoners that a radical convict political union could change power relations within the prison. A year later, as if inspired by this insight, the California prison gang system emerged. An increasingly vocal minority of politicized prisoners formed political "gangs" in an emerging revolutionary convict culture. They founded groups like the Black Family/Black Guerrilla Family, and the San Quentin chapter of the Black Panther Party. These prison gangs were an attempt by the disenfranchised to exercise control over their immediate environment and to reverse the effects of racial discrimination. Other gangs, including the Aryan Brotherhood, La Nuestra Familia, and La Eme (the Mexican Mafia), were political only to the extent that controlling the yard and the inmate *sub rosa* economy entailed reshuffling power relations within the prison.

All the gangs provided crucial social, economic, and security services that helped prisoners survive the human degradation, deprivation, violence of incarceration, and endemic racism.

With the advent of the California prison gang system, inmate fights and yard attacks escalated, resulting in the deaths of guards and prisoners. Inmate assaults against guards jumped from 32 systemwide in 1969 to 84 in 1973.[25]

Gang members, revolutionaries, prisoner union organizers, and jailhouse lawyers joined the radical Muslims in the AC. This AC was now a transformed unit, which no longer sought to rehabilitate, but to punish, to limit treatment and education, and to restrict human contact. By the end of the 1960s, the ACs—which became the proto-type for Pelican Bay—were filled with political "troublemakers."

In 1970, a Soledad, California prison AC gunrail officer killed three Black prisoners. Inmate George Jackson declared one-for-one vengeance on guard staff. Almost immediately, a young white guard's corpse was thrown from a cell tier. Responding in kind, California prisons came down swiftly on prisoners by beginning to control movement, access to information, visitors, and legal services. From his cell in San Quentin's AC, which was by now a hotbed of revolutionary thought, George Jackson secretly composed his book, *Blood In My Eye*, a call to guerrilla action.[26]

On August 21, 1971, the San Quentin AC inmates tried a take-over, ending in the deaths of Jackson, two other inmates, and three guards. Three wounded guards recovered. That autumn, prison riots swept the country. In the bloodiest of these, at Attica Correctional Institution in New York State, 32 prisoners and 11 staff died when police and a National Guard army put down the uprising with gas, helicopters, and heavy gunfire.

Authorities cracked down hard around the country. By 1972, cellblocks at San Quentin were subdivided for closer inmate scrutiny and inmate contact with outsiders was severely cut back. From the AC, reports of widespread beatings and other prisoner abuses began to reach the courts.[27] That same year, Governor Ronald Reagan called for the development of new, high-tech, maximum-security prisons to deal with what he termed "troublemakers." Moe Comacho, then president of the California Correctional Officers Association, sec-onded the call. And in 1973, the House Internal Security Committee began conducting hearings on revolution in U.S. prisons, Attica and San Quentin in particular, with a mind to devising ways of putting down the ongoing turmoil.[28]

The legacy of the August 21 San Quentin takeover and the subsequent uprisings fed the official drive to build the largest solitary confinement prison in the United States—the SHU at Pelican Bay.

Prisoner Resistance

The new SHU at Pelican Bay goes farther than the ACs, with physical and programmatic features that make it a more effective control unit. It is also far more inhumane. Conditions have provoked resistance and protest both inside and outside the prison walls. Equal Justice U.S.A., a Washington, DC-based human rights organization, catalogued more than 100 organized or spontaneous prison rebellions nationwide in 1989 and 1990. In 1992, protests, demonstrations, teach-ins, forums, marches, and rallies focused on control unit prisons and racism in the criminal justice system in at least 12 states and Canada.[29]

Prison authorities met protest with force rather than reform. In January 1991, for example, a Pelican Bay guard on a late night shift harassed Latino prisoners, swearing at them and making grossly racist comments. In the morning, the prisoners refused to return their breakfast trays until they could protest the abuse to a lieutenant. The prison responded by "cell-extracting" 20 prisoners, including those who were willing to return their trays. The guards left prisoners hogtied on the walkway outside their cells for eight hours, while the medical staff refused requests for medical attention. Wearing only underwear, the prisoners were then moved to different cells and deprived of soap, toilet paper, and other basic amenities. Those who protested were put in the Violence Control Unit.[30]

In another incident, during the spring of 1992, prisoners at the Westville, Indiana Maximum Control Complex went on a prolonged hunger strike to protest such abuses as lack of TV and clocks, being hosed with cold water in their cells, repeated strip searches, and five-point restraint for days at a time. A few even cut off the ends of their fingers and tried to send their flesh to the American Civil Liberties Union (ACLU) to dramatize their need for help. A year earlier, 53 inmates at the Southport Correctional Facility, a maxi-maxi facility in New York State, took four guards hostage. Their demands included an end to verbal and physical abuse, more mental and physical health care, more heat in winter, and improved grievance procedures. For 26 hours, the prisoners negotiated with prison offi-cials and finally agreed to release the guards unharmed and to return peacefully to their cells in exchange for a chance to air grievances to a camera crew from a local TV station.[31]

In April 1993, at the notorious maximum-security facility in Lucasville, Ohio, 450 men mounted an 11-day siege. This uprising again demonstrated prisoners' willingness to risk all to gain improve-ments in the conditions of confinement.

Outlook for the Future

The repression administered in the Pelican Bay SHU has long-term effects beyond the obvious racism and violence in the yard. The trauma of isolation felt by SHU prisoners leaves deep scars. Most lose

LAWSUIT CHALLENGES TERROR

Shortly after the Pelican Bay SHU opened in late 1989, prisoners sent out an avalanche of letters complaining about the conditions. Within months, jailhouse-lawyer suits were being sent to the Federal District Court alleging cruel and unusual punishment. So compelling and numerous were the legal documents that presiding Judge Thelton Henderson asked Wilson, Sonsini, Goodrich, and Rosati, a large Palo Alto law firm, to review the 250 suits and prepare a class action civil rights suit.

Madrid v. Gomez came to trial in the summer of 1993. It alleges that conditions at Pelican Bay violate the First, Sixth, Eighth, and Fourteenth Amendments of the U.S. Constitution.

Particularly egregious is the lack of medical care: even in crises such as acute appendicitis, prisoner-patients have been examined through the cell door or food port, if at all. Spanish-language translation is not provided despite the high number of Spanish-speaking prisoners. Psychiatric care is inadequate and prisoners suffering from severe psychiatric disorders are treated as disciplinary problems and thrown naked into the Violence Control Unit—a strip cell with a plastic cover on the steel door. Prisoners who engage in persistent violent and irrational behavior have been chained to their toilets for days and forced to eat like dogs, lapping food from their trays.

The suit further alleges that the administrations fails to investigate and discipline guards for violations such as staff use of force, routine cell-extraction, and hogtying for alleged rules infractions, which either did not occur or did not warrant the level of violence used. Guards use a shoot-to-kill policy when breaking up fights in the B Yard, adding to the atmosphere of fear and violence in the yard.

Further, Pelican Bay officials are charged with reading confidential legal mail, mishandling legal and personal mail, and denying access to the law library and legal assistance. Prisoners are improperly classified as gang members and subjected to unfair hearings. The suit challenges the entire snitch, parole, or die policy and characterizes Pelican Bay as a "system of terror, deprivation, and isolation" which constitutes cruel and unusual punishment. [*Madrid v. Gomez* (#C-90-3094)]

contact with family and friends who are deterred by distance and cost from visiting the often remote prisons. Besides, many prisoners say that they do not want their families to see the state they are in: nervous, insecure, and drawn, with shaved heads from crude self-administered haircuts. Those labeled gang members have special concerns: anyone who associates with them is suspected or presumed to be in the gang. This taint extends even to a prisoner's contacts in the community through the CDoC Gang Task Force's outside investigative network. Thus, prisoners are reluctant to write friends or ask them to visit.

Friends, and even family members, do not write for fear they will be labeled gang members by their local police department.

Mario's story is illustrative. He was married and had children. During his most recent incarceration, he was accused by informants of being in a gang and sent to Pelican Bay SHU. His wife, not wanting their son to be tainted by his father's gang tag, filed for divorce. Without any formal charges giving the prisoner the right to face his accusers, the judge granted the divorce and denied all rights of visitation and correspondence because of "gang affiliation."[32]

Pelican Bay is a nightmare fulfillment of widespread demands for more punitive prisons. This abandonment of rehabilitation imprisonment is the apotheosis of the Adjustment Center concept gone bad—the AC without treatment. The SHU demonstrates that the more cruel and overcrowded our prisons, the more violent the prison yard will become.

Indeed, prisoners subjected to imprisonment in a SHU return to their communities untrained, untreated, poorer, and more disenfranchised than when they left. This system of dehumanizing, high-tech torture promotes violence, exacerbates gang activity, and deepens the fissures of race and class that already divide the United States.

NOTES

1. In 1991, Human Rights Watch issued *Prison Conditions in the United States*. Findings were based on a review of 27 penal institutions, the last 8 years of prison litigation, and interviews with experts and journalists. The report documented "numerous human rights abuses and frequent violations of the U.N. Standard Minimum Rules for the Treatment of Prisoners." (New York: Human Rights Watch), p. 4.

2. Ward Churchill *et al.*, *Cages of Steel*, (Washington, DC: Maisonneuve Press), 1993, p. 140.

3. "More Prisons Don't Create a Safer Society," San Jose Mercury News, February 8, 1990.

4. Weekly Report of Population, Youth and Adult Correctional Agency, State of California, January 31, 1993. Seventy percent of planned prison construction for the 1990s is for medium- and maximum-security prisons.

5. California Department of Corrections, "1991-1996 Facilities Master Plan," April 1991, Section 3.

6. While Pelican Bay prisoners are all male, the Central California Women's Facility near Chowchilla, California has its own small modern SHU.

7. Corey Weinstein interviews with prisoners; also cited in *Madrid v. Gomez*, Case No. C-90-3094 (THE) in U.S. District Court California.

8. Letter sent by "Books to Prisoners" to prisoners. Pelican Bay Information Project (PBIP). PBIP (2489 Mission St., #28, San Francisco, CA 94110) has conducted many

investigative tours, interviewing inmates, prison staff, visitors, and Crescent City residents. Those tours and the continuing investigation and monitoring of Pelican Bay SHU conditions provide much of the information for this article.

9. Steve Selke, "Prison Staff Thinks Killing Was a Gang Hit," *Triplicate* (Crescent City, CA), September 11, 1992.

10. PBIP investigation, 1991-92.

11. Corey Weinstein interview, CDoC Public Information Office, Pelican Bay State Prison, April 22, 1992.

12. Stuart Grassian, "Psychopathological Effects of Solitary Confinement," *American Journal of Psychiatry*, November 1983, p. 1450. This study of men housed at Walpole also documents effects going back to 19th-century Germany.

13. Throughout 1988 and 1989, just before the opening of Pelican Bay, an unprecedented number of fights occurred at the California State Prison at Corcoran near the city of Fresno in the Central Valley. Prisoners housed in the Corcoran SHU (which still serves as a lesser SHU with 750 cells) reported that prison authorities exacerbated fighting in the yard by releasing known enemies at the same time and permitting unequal numbers of rival gang members to "exercise" together. They set up prisoners by putting enemies in the same cell, housing someone with a mentally-ill prisoner, or announcing a prisoner's crime of rape or child molestation. The guards then often stood by and watched the inevitable clashes, called "cock fights," as if they were sporting events. Prisoners allege that the cock fights—often directed against Latino-American prisoners—were instigated to "prove" that the Corcoran SHU was inadequate and to justify transfer of prisoners to the newly-constructed Pelican Bay SHU. (Prisoners Rights Union of California, Sacramento, CA, 1988-89.)

14. Independent investigation by PBIP based on interviews and available roster lists.

15. Nigel Rodley, *Treatment of Prisoners Under International Law*, (Oxford: Oxford University Press), 1987, p. 359.

16. Catherine Campbell, "A House of Cards, A Pack of Lies: Pelican Bay Debriefing," *The California Prisoner*, December 1991.

17. PBIP interviews with guards and reporters during 1992 investigative visit.

18. "Prison Fight Involves 23 in Level 1," *Triplicate* (Crescent City, CA), January 23, 1993.

19. Corey Weinstein interview, August 1992, San Francisco. An ex-political prisoner who served many years in the federal system blames the high-tech security innovations such as electronic surveillance for the increased brutality. Formerly, he explains, prisoners and guards in maximum-security prisons shared space and depended for their personal safety on a mutually understood, negotiated peace that allowed both groups to carry out their daily activities. Screened by high-tech security and authorized to punish and incapacitate prisoners, Pelican Bay guards now have no such restraints and, as a consequence, the physical and psychological abuse they deliver is extreme and routine.

20. Corey Weinstein interview, CDoC Public Information Office, Pelican Bay State Prison, April 22, 1992.

21. Unsubstantiated letters to Prisoners Rights Union, 1989.

22. Alan Ryan, "Preparing for the Twenty-First Century Blues," *New York Review of Books*, May 13, 1993, p. 23.

23. Many researchers have noted the ways in which U.S. criminal justice has codified and perpetuated the wrongs of the culture at large. See R. L. McNeeley and Carl E. Pope, eds., *Race, Crime and Criminal Justice*, (Newbury Park, CA.: Sage Publications), 1981;

Robert Staples, "White Racism, Black Crime, and American Justice: An Application of the Colonial Model to Explain Crime and Race," *Phylon*, vol. 36, no. 1, March 1975, pp. 14-23; Gary G. Koch and Stevens Clarke, "The Influence of Income and Other Factors on Whether Criminal Defendants Go To Prison," *Law and Society Review*, vol. 2, no. 1, Fall 1976, pp. 57-93; Leo Carroll and Margaret E. Mondrick, "Racial Bias in the Decision to Grant Parole," *Law and Society Review*, vol . 2, no.1, Fall 1976, pp. 93-109.

24. Manning Marable, *Race, Reform and Rebellion: The Second Reconstruction in Black America, 1945-1982*, (Jackson: University of Mississippi Press), 1984, p. 60.

25. "Task Force to Study Violence Report and Recommendations," Table 1, California Department of Corrections working paper, July 1974, now in the papers of James Park.

26. George Jackson, *Blood In My Eye*, (New York: Random House), 1972.

27. Eric Cummins, *The Rise and Fall of California's Radical Prison Movement*, (Stanford, CA: Stanford University Press), 1994; see House of Representatives, 92nd Congress, Hearings Before Subcommittee No. 3 of the Committee on the Judiciary, Edwin T. Caldwell, "Prisons, Prison Reform, and Prisoners' Rights: California," (Washington, DC: Government Printing Office), 1971, pp. 72-76; see also accounts of inmate beatings in *San Francisco Chronicle*, August 25-27, 1971.

28. Cummins.

29. Committee to End the Marion Lockdown, "Walking Steel," (Chicago, IL: CEML), Fall 1992, p. 6.

30. PBIP investigation, 1991-92.

31. "Attica in 1991: Southport Uprising," *USA: A Look At the Reality, A Human Rights Monitor*, (Hyattsville, MD: Quixote Center), October 1991.

32. PBIP investigation, 1990.

28

LEXINGTON PRISON HIGH SECURITY UNIT

U.S. Political Prison

Mary K. O'Melveny

On August 19, 1988, the United States Bureau of Prisons (BOP) closed the doors to a small underground women's prison in Lexington, Kentucky known as the "High Security Unit" (HSU). In the less than two years that the HSU was operational, this 16-bed control unit (which never housed more than six women) became a focus of national and international concern over human rights abuses by the U.S. government, and direct proof that political prisoners not only exist in the United States but are the targets of a well-organized counter-insurgency campaign.

Lexington's origins and opening were shrouded in secrecy, without congressional oversight or public scrutiny. By the time the HSU was closed 22 months later, it had been a formal agenda item at the U.S./USSR Summit Conference, had been condemned by national and international human rights advocates (including a 38-page report by Amnesty International in London), had been held by a U.S. federal judge to have been operated in violation of the First Amendment to the U.S. Constitution, and had come to symbolize America's hypocrisy on the issues of human rights and political prisoners.

However, the government's closing of Lexington is, in its view, a mere transferring of its "mission" to a larger women's facility in Marianna, Florida, a remote area near the Georgia and Alabama borders.[1] Thus, while the particular Lexington experiment may have ended, the government has not disbanded its mission. It is important to examine and analyze Lexington's lessons, particularly as they highlight counter-insurgency within U.S. borders against those who resist racism, genocide, colonialism, and imperialism and end up as political prisoners in U.S. jails and prisons.

My first visit to the Lexington "High Security Unit" occurred in December 1986. My client, Susan Rosenberg, an anti-imperialist North American political prisoner, and Alejandrina Torres, Puerto Rican *independentista* and proclaimed POW, were the first women prisoners in the federal prison system to go to the High Security Unit when it opened in October 1986. The "new" federal underground prison unit was a prison within a prison. Fundamentally, in intent and practice, the HSU was an isolation unit (although the Bureau of Prisons denies this label) intended to closely monitor and control its residents. The conditions were startling. The HSU was in the basement of an old building formerly owned by the Public Health Service. It was "remodeled" in 1986 to house 16 women at a taxpayer expense of approximately $735,000, and an annual per woman maintenance cost of over $55,000, more than the annual cost for women in all other federal prisons.

This modern dungeon bore little relationship to the larger (1,700 inmates) prison at Lexington that sat amidst rolling hills and green Kentucky grazing land. Its residents could not see the pastoral landscape that lies past the double-razor wire-shrouded building. Ceiling-high windows were so thickly screened that daylight was barely perceptible.[2] The HSU prisoners lived in constant artificial light. Their only link to the world above was a television set, an occasional 10-minute social telephone call, and less frequent visits from attorneys. The things we take for granted as basic components of human existence—natural light, fresh air, color, sound, human contact, various smells—were conspicuously, intentionally absent. Also denied were those equally important, slightly more subtle human needs—privacy spheres, intellectual stimulation, comradeship, continuing connections to family, friends, and caring others, undisturbed sleep, health care, educational and recreational options, and spiritual comforts.

The Political Basis of Assignment

The Bureau of Prisons made no secret of the political basis for the designation of the first women sent to this unique experimental control unit. Susan Rosenberg was said to be "associated with the FALN, Black Liberation Army and other terrorist groups" and one who had "threatened in open court to take her armed revolution behind prison walls."[3] Alejandrina Torres was also said to be associated with the FALN and with the militant struggle for an end to the colonial domination of Puerto Rico. Both women were to spend nearly three months alone in the underground silence of the HSU, surrounded by guards who were tutored to hate and fear them,[4] their every movement monitored by cameras and in log books, cut off from virtually all contact with families, friends, and political supporters.

In January 1987, Susan Rosenberg and Alejandrina Torres were joined by Silvia Baraldini, an Italian national who had worked for years in the U.S. anti-imperialist movement before her 1983 conviction for conspiracy to liberate Assata Shakur from a New Jersey prison. As with the others, politics formed the obvious basis for this transfer:

> Although Ms. Baraldini scores well enough on her Custody Scoring Sheet to be considered for a custody reduction, she is a member of the May 19th Communist Party which is sympathetic to other radical groups including the New African Freedom Front and the FALN.[5]

The Bureau of Prisons advanced two criteria for placing female prisoners in the HSU. The first was the one it used to try to justify sending all three political prisoners to the unit:

> Candidates for placement in this Unit are those females whose confinement raises a serious threat of external assault for the purpose of aiding the offender's escape.[6]

The second, said to be applicable on only a "space-available basis," was for those women with "serious histories of assaultive, escape prone or disruptive activity." Later, the BOP's criteria became even more explicitly political:

> [A] prisoner's past or present affiliation, association or membership in an organization which has been documented as being involved in acts of violence, attempts to disrupt or overthrow the government of the U.S. or whose published ideology includes advocating law violations in order to "free" prisoners...[7]

No one, once sent to the HSU, could get out unless "the original factors for placement in the Unit no longer apply and when placement in a less secure facility becomes appropriate."[8] For political prisoners, the message could not have been clearer—renounce the political affiliations and beliefs that had led the Federal Bureau of Investigation/Bureau of Prisons to define them as candidates for the HSU, and they could get out. Fail to do so and remain in isolation, denied all aspects of humane existence and political connection, for 35 to 58 years.

For nearly two years these women lived alone together, cut off from the rest of the world in all but the most superficial ways. Until their situation eventually provoked outcries from human rights groups, religious communities, families and friends, attorneys and political activists, they existed in a sort of physical and psychic limbo, buried but still very much alive.

The Strategy of Isolation and Denial

The defining feature of the Lexington HSU women's control unit was small-group isolation. Isolation as torture is not new. In fact, it began as part of the Nazi experiments at Dachau, used first on the Communists and homosexuals imprisoned there. There is a science to the use of isolation, as witnessed by the fact that all conditions in isolation are remarkably similar. Nelson Mandela's isolation in South Africa's Pollsmoor High Security Prison shared the same essential characteristics as those in Uruguay's "La Libertad" prison/interrogation center.[9] The isolation units in Italy and West Germany known as "white cells" or "dead wings" are likewise strikingly parallel to the Lexington HSU.

Nearly ten years ago, Amnesty International condemned the use of small-group isolation and solitary confinement against the Red Army Faction (RAF) and 2nd June Movement in West Germany's Stammheim high-security prison as "torture or other cruel, inhuman or degrading treatment or punishment" of prisoners, in violation of the 1977 United Nations Standard Minimum Rules for the Treatment of Prisoners, and the 1966 United Nations Covenant on Civil and Political Rights. The detailed Amnesty report on Stammheim chronicled the effects of long-term confinement of these political prisoners in extreme isolation and described the inhumane conditions they were subjected to in these "high-security" wings.

There can be no doubt that the Lexington HSU was conceived by U.S. authorities as an experimental version of Stammheim's isolation wings, as part of a deliberate effort to destroy revolutionary and radical political prisoners and their capacity to organize support for their politics. Thus, at the 1978 U.S.-sponsored "Special Seminar on Terrorism in Puerto Rico" workshop, participants were specifically encouraged to examine the "interesting lessons" from West Germany and Italy and the conditions employed against political prisoners at Stammheim which resulted in the deaths of four RAF leaders.[10]

The Conditions Underground

The severe isolation of the HSU was accompanied by sensory deprivation and by often extreme voyeurism and sexual harassment by the mostly male staff, as well as sleep deprivation, overt hostility by guards, and completely arbitrary rules and rules changes. No meaningful work, recreational opportunities, or educational programs were offered. Personal property was forbidden, or so severely restricted as to be meaningless, in helping to establish an independent identity in the midst of a totally controlled, sterile environment. Twenty-four-hour camera and visual surveillance recorded every word and every activity: moods, illnesses, menstrual cycles, eating patterns.

Correspondence was severely censored for many months. Prison guards prepared logs documenting the names and addresses of every person who corresponded with the HSU prisoners. Telephone calls were also very limited and were not only monitored, but were also the subject of detailed memos analyzing the conversations, listing the names of all persons referred to in the conversations, and describing the assertedly "relevant" portions of what was said. These memos went to other agencies for evaluation and follow-up.[11]

Effects on the Prisoners

The more time that passed underground, the more overwhelming the effects. Susan Rosenberg described the conditions as "existential death," Debra Brown as akin to being "in the grave."[12] Sleep deprivation experiments[13] led to insomnia, exhaustion and unvented rage, as did the denial of privacy or personal space, coupled with constant sexual harassment either in fact or in threat, and the effort to infantilize the women because of their enforced dependency on the hostile guards, who defined every aspect of their lives.

Early on, the women began to experience some of the predictable psychopathological effects of long-term isolation: vision impairment, memory loss, inability to concentrate, loss of appetite and weight, and lethargy.[14] In August 1987, Dr. Richard Korn, a clinical psychologist and correctional expert, issued his first report for the American Civil Liberties Union's National Prison Project based upon a tour of Lexington and interviews with the prisoners. His findings about the conditions of Lexington were stark. First, he observed that "the power of the institution over the prisoners was total, beyond questioning and accounting, even if it appeared to violate traditional fairness or common sense."[15]

Among the factors affecting the psycho-physical well-being of the prisoners were rules "tending to depersonalize and deny individuality." Dr. Korn concluded that the restrictions imposed upon the women's lives were nothing less than an ideological attack that was "carefully deliberate, in every detail."

The psychological consequences for the prisoners were "evident" to Dr. Korn: claustrophobia; chronic rage reaction; suppressed, low-level to severe depression; onset of hallucinatory symptoms; defensive psychological withdrawal; blunting of apathy. Likewise, there were concrete physical reactions: loss of appetite, marked loss of weight, exacerbation of pre-existing medical problems, general physical malaise, visual disturbances, dizziness, heart palpitations.

Finding that Lexington had "many similarities" to the federal prison at Marion, Illinois and to West Germany's Stammheim prison, Dr. Korn had "no question" that the intent was:

> ...to reduce prisoners to a state of submission essential for their ideological conversion. That failing, the next objective is to reduce them to a state of psychological incompetence sufficient to neutralize them as efficient, self-directing antagonists. That failing, the only alternative is to destroy them, preferably by making them desperate enough to destroy themselves.[16]

Lexington as a "Deterrent"

Bureau of Prisons officials referred endlessly to the "mission" of Lexington. Deterrence was clearly another central feature of that mission. Some political prisoners, such as Carol Manning and Marilyn Buck, were "designated" to Lexington long before they were eligible for transfer anywhere, while others were threatened with the prospect of being sent there. Even though in-prison behavior was obviously irrelevant to the designation decision, social prisoners at the Federal Correctional Institution in Pleasanton (FCI-Dublin), one of the BOP's general population prisons, were "threatened" with the specter of the HSU if they did not "behave."[17]

In addition to increasing the level of intimidation and control over women in the federal prison system, Lexington obviously served as a chilling deterrent to political activists on the outside, particularly as the BOP expanded its placement criteria to include actions that might "disrupt the government" or membership in groups that advocated "law violations."[18]

Political and Legal Opposition

Central to the movement against Lexington was the prisoners' determination not to be broken by the never-ending attempts to destroy them, even as their physical health evidenced the strain. They were joined first by their families and friends, and by lawyers who offered crucial support (including female lawyers in Kentucky who immediately mobilized to offer assistance). The Puerto Rican independence movement embraced the issue and played a critical role in bringing attention to the existence of the unit and the inhumane treatment of the prisoners. Religious leaders and thousands of other individuals responded to the issue as one of basic human rights, rejecting the Reagan rubric of "terrorism" as a justification for inhumane conditions or political persecution.

A tour in September 1987 by the General Board of Global Ministries of the United Methodist Church resulted in a highly condemnatory report that directly confronted Lexington's politics, and the concern that it was a secret experiment in political persecution.[19] Not only did the Methodists' report state that the "extreme isolation… from all meaningful human contact and from any hope of such contact in the future" was "cruel and unusual punishment," but it called for the US. government to officially recognize the existence of political prisoners.

In October 1987, the Bureau of Prisons announced that it would close Lexington and move its "mission" to a new, larger women's prison in Marianna, Florida. Yet, the BOP kept Lexington open, refused to transfer the women to general population facilities, and persisted in defending the HSU as "safe" and "humane," despite the reports by the National Prison Project condemning Lexington as a "living tomb" that is "incompatible" with constitutional guarantees, and the concerns raised by the Methodist Church, Amnesty International, and others.

A lawsuit was finally begun in March 1988 seeking injunctive relief to close the unit and transfer the women. After voluminous testimony obtained by deposition and at a trial in June 1988, a federal judge ruled on July 15, 1988 that the BOP and Justice Department had unlawfully designated prisoners to Lexington based on their past political associations and personal beliefs.

Judge Barrington Parker found that political views of Silvia Baraldini and Susan Rosenberg that were "unacceptable" to the government could not form a constitutional basis for sending them to Lexington, particularly when their in-prison conduct had demonstrated no basis for finding them to be escape risks. The court rejected the government's effort to make it a "crime" for prisoners to be "members of leftist political organizations, even if those groups have engaged in unlawful pursuits in the past," and found that the government had failed to document any basis for their assignment other than "their alleged past connections with leftist groups promoting ideas that some government officials did not favor."

While breaking ground on the matter of recognizing the political nature of Lexington—and thus the existence of U.S. political prisoners—the Court rejected the Fifth and Eighth Amendment claims in the lawsuit, finding that the treatment of the prisoners did not constitute cruel and unusual punishment. However, Judge Parker did admit that the finding was a close call, since the unit had at times "skirted elemental standards of human decency," particularly in light of the "exaggerated security, small group isolation, and staff harassment," all of which "constantly undermine the inmates' morale." He castigated the government for its "shameful delays in remedying some of the more egregious conditions," and for operating "a unit that in many respects, measures below acceptable standards for federal prisons."

Amnesty International monitored the Lexington lawsuit, sending an observer to the trial. In August 1988, Amnesty issued a report that defined the HSU as, "an experimental control unit," with a "deliberately and gratuitously oppressive" regime in which:

> The constant and unjustified use of security chains, the repeated strip searching, the almost total lack of privacy, the claustrophobic lack of sensory stimuli, freedom of movement, possessions, choice of activities, and incestuously small range of contacts cannot be other than debilitating. Whereas most small security units compensate for any necessary physical limitations by granting prisoners extra privileges and greater autonomy, the reverse appears to be the case at HSU."[20]

In addition, Amnesty's observer found "overwhelming evidence that the prisoners at HSU have deteriorated physically and psychologically during their custody there. There has to be a prospect that one or more will finally resort to suicide should their custody at

HSU be prolonged."[21] Amnesty recommended Lexington's immediate closing and made it clear that Marianna "should not replicate HSU."[22]

The Government's Response

The government responded to the court ruling by ignoring its direction to move the women to general population federal correctional institutions. Instead, it designated the three political prisoners to pre-trial holding facilities (Metropolitan Correctional Centers), ensuring that they would continue to experience many of Lexington's most serious health-threatening conditions. The government also appealed, a process which can take months, or even years.

The new "high-security" prison in Marianna, Florida opened for business in August 1988 without shower curtains, educational programs, or even adequate medical staffing. By October 1988, more than 50 women had been sent to Marianna, none of them political prisoners. However, the government was already arguing for an expedited appeal because of an "urgent" need to transfer four Puerto Rican POWs to Marianna based upon their "FALN membership."[23] The government's intent to send other women political prisoners to Marianna remains clear.

Greater control and repression of federal prisoners will be the hallmark of Marianna regardless of the outcome of the government's appeal from its loss on Lexington. The existence and public acceptance of control units was largely unaffected by the court case; Marion remains locked down, despite national and international criticism of its inhumane conditions, and increasing numbers of state control units are being opened and filled.[24]

The Lessons of Lexington

In addition to the experiment in new forms of psychological torture, Lexington was an intelligence-gathering mission. The government learned a great deal from the Lexington experiment—about the psychology of female political prisoners, about the effects of long-term small-group isolation and the denial system, and about the nature and content of the resistance mounted against the HSU. No surprise that every letter to the women was read, and the sender's name and address recorded. No surprise that analytical memoranda were made of every phone call. No surprise that the government never retreated from justifying the need for the unit or the appropriateness of its operating conditions.

Lexington opened, existed, and "closed" in the midst of increasing retreats from constitutional guarantees both for persons charged in political cases and for political prisoners. Preventive detention and house arrests, together with the imposition of exaggerated sentences in political cases and the deliberate silent complicity of the mainstream press, all set the stage for the inhumanity of a Lexington control unit, and the larger counter-insurgency strategy it represents.

In other countries, the number and operation of special political prisons has been directly affected by the level of public exposure and resistance. These countries at least recognize that political prisoners exist. Thus, the lessons of the Lexington experiment must always be premised on exposing the myth that the United States has none. This done, the political repression and violations of international law that Lexington symbolizes can be more easily recognized and resisted.

The political prisoners detained at Lexington, like their counterparts in isolation at Marion and elsewhere in U.S. prisons, were and are victims of psychological torture. They were saved from joining the ranks of the "neutralized" and "disappeared" through growing public education generated by unrelenting political organizing. This model can and should be applied to expose the larger issues of how the United States treats political resistance in the United States, and how to prevent more live burials.

Author's Postscript

In August 1995, I went to visit Dr. Mutulu Shakur, a political prisoner who has been transferred to the new BOP maximum-security unit in Florence, Colorado. Florence provides dramatic evidence that the Lexington HSU was a trial run for its operation. Many similarities reminded me of my first visit to the HSU—particularly the dehumanizing process in place from the moment one enters the gates and is directed toward the glossy new building at the farthest point in the compound. As with the Lexington HSU, prisoners at Florence are literally buried below the surface of the shiny, new buildings and one only reaches them after traveling a long and lonely underground route. Visitors must be photographed, even though there is virtually no chance of human contact with the prisoners; few officials allow for even the most minimal contact, and it must be requested in advance. The attorney visiting rooms are locked shut during the visit and the prisoner must be physically removed by the guards before any visitor movement—even a trip to the rest room—can be authorized. The table and bench provided are concrete; An eerie silence penetrates every corner. Guards speak of "the mission" of the unit, yet the politics and perceived political activities of prisoners clearly play a dominant role in transfer. Having learned from Lexington, Florence makes the isolation complete. Inhumanity is the dominant atmosphere. The psychic toll will be real. The need to penetrate the enforced silence is crucial.

NOTES

1. September 30, 1987 letter from BOP Director J. Michael Quinlan to Congressman Robert W. Kastenmeier (D—Wisc.).
2. There were two groups of cells separated by a corridor. The women were housed on the "dark side" of the corridor until summer of 1987 when a tour by the ACLU National Prison Project questioned the basis for the room assignments. Windows on the "light side" were still heavily screened, but were located at regular window height, permitting slightly more light to enter.
3. Memorandum from William A. Perrill, Warden, Federal Correctional Institution, Tucson, Arizona to Jerry T. Williford, Regional Director, Western Regional Office of the BOP dated August 19, 1986, designating Rosenberg for transfer to maximum-security custody status at the HSU. Also cited by Warden Merrill was Rosenberg's asserted "link" to the 1979 escape of Assata Shakur from prison in New Jersey, even though those charges had been dropped by the government in 1985.
4. The women reported several occasions where unit guards remarked on having studied them in a special "school" to prepare them for dealing with the "terrorists" who were to be their charges at the HSU. Photographs and profiles were apparently part of the materials studied. During later litigation about the HSU, the government never produced any documents or information about such special training, but one BOP official, Southeast Regional Director Gary R. McCune, admitted that he had attended a special course given by the FBI about how to deal with "terrorists" in prison.
5. December 23, 1986, Memorandum from Pleasanton FCI Case Manager, Terry R. Ennis to Acting Associate Warden Dave Wisehart.
6. September 2, 1986, Memorandum from G. L. Ingram, BOP Assistant Director, to BOP Regional Directors.
7. September 30, 1987 letter from BOP Director J. Michael Quinlan to Congressman Robert W. Kastenmeier (D—Wisc.).
8. September 30, 1987 letter from BOP Director J. Michael Quinlan to Congressman Robert W. Kastenmeier (D—Wisc.).
9. Maxwell Bloche, "Uruguay's Military Physicians: Cogs in a System of State Terror," *Report for the Committee on Scientific Freedom and Responsibility*, (Washington, DC: American Association for the Advancement of Science), pp. 6-8.
10. Terrorism Conference Background materials, pp. 25-26.

11. These telephone logs came to light in the litigation brought against the Justice Department in March 1988 (*Baraldini v. Merest* Civ. No. 88-0764).

12. Letter from Susan Rosenberg; *ABC 20/20* interview with Debra Brown.

13. Sleep deprivation tactics, another common torture technique, occurred sporadically over several week-long periods.

14. S. Grassian, "The Psychopathological Effects of Solitary Confinement," *American Journal of Psychiatry*, November 1983, pp. 1450-54; Amnesty Federal Republic of Germany Report; H. D. Nelson, "Long Term Health Effects of P. C.W. Incarceration" Paper, Resident Talk, December 7, 1987; The Center for Victims of Torture, "Therapeutic Models: A Beginning," Draft, April 26, 1988.

15. Richard Korn, "The Effects of Confinement in HSU," appended to *Report on The High Security Unit for Women, Federal Correctional Institution, Lexington, Kentucky*, (Washington, DC: National Prison Project of the ACLU), August 25, 1987, p. 3.

16. Korn, pp. 19-20.

17. Interviews with Linda Evans and Laura Whitehorn, political prisoners then at FCI-Dublin in Pleasanton, September 1987.

18. September 30, 1987 letter from BOP Director J. Michael Quinlan to Congressman Robert W. Kastenmeier (D—Wisc.).

19. "Report of Visit by General Board of Global Ministries Team to High Security Unit for Women, Federal Correctional Institution, Lexington, Kentucky," October 15, 1987.

20. Amnesty International: USA, "The High Security Unit, Lexington Federal Prison, Kentucky," (AI Index: AMR 51/34/88). Amnesty appended its 15-month correspondence with the BOP about Lexington to the report.

21. Amnesty International.

22. Amnesty International.

23. See government's Motion to Expedite Appeal, filed September 9, 1988 in *Thornburgh v. Baraldini*, C.A. 88-5275 (DC Court of Appeals), pp. 6-10.

24. Amnesty International Report on "Allegations of Ill-Treatment in Marion Prison, Illinois, USA," (AMR 51/26/87), May 1987; "An Uneasy Calm...," report on the U.S. Penitentiary at Marion by John Howard.

29

SHACKLED JUSTICE

Florence—The Cutting Edge of Social Control

Robert Perkinson

The local motel in sleepy Florence, Colorado pops up awkwardly from the expansive prairie, proudly beaming the display "Welcome FCI Visitors, Weekly Rates Now Available." Just over the hill lies the largest federal prison complex in the United States, prized for jobs and growth by this rural community in central Colorado. Local citizens held bake sales and sold T-shirts, raising $128,000 to purchase land for the economy-boosting site. Scrambling to contain an explosive prison population, the Bureau of Prisons (BOP) accepted their offer and began construction of the $200 million compound in 1990.

Prisoners and their advocates are not nearly as enthusiastic. Finished in early 1994, the entire complex incarcerates some 2,500 inmates at four different security levels: minimum, medium, maximum, and administrative maximum (ADX). While all of the units reflect the social disparity of U.S. criminal justice politics, it is the ADX (control unit) that has especially outraged human rights activists.

The BOP designed Florence to be a high-tech replacement of the infamous lockdown prison in Marion, Illinois. After a decade of stinging lawsuits and public protest there, prisoncrats promised a kinder, gentler super-maximum prison in Florence. As the 552-cell men's control unit nears completion, however, all indications are that the prison will not reform the punitive Marion model of total isolation and sensory deprivation, but intensify it. An understanding of the new prison and the gamut of social policies it embodies is crucial; Florence represents the cutting edge of social control. Not only have many political activists been moved to the prison, but its construction underlines broader law-and-order reaction to urban decay and a growing domestic underclass.

The Marion Model

The Marion model for control unit prisons originated within the BOP over 30 years ago. At a 1963 conference in Puerto Rico, the same year Marion opened and Alcatraz closed, prison administrators looked towards the German Stammheim example, approving a blueprint for coercive behavior modification units. With the rise of national liberation movements, no longer would prison be "medicalized," but more purely punitive. Following the murder of 39 rebelling Attica inmates and their hostages by New York state troopers in 1971, they moved to institutionalize their plans. The BOP began to concentrate "problem" inmates in a new long-term control unit, forcibly enrolling them in the systematic Control and Rehabilitation Effort (CARE) program, and Marion became the "end of the line." When Harold Miller became warden in 1979, BOP plans were underway to convert Marion into a permanent isolation facility. After three killings and a brutal shakedown in 1983, resulting in 110 unprosecuted complaints of guard abuse, Marion assumed its present status.

Today, Marion prisoners spend 23 hours each day in their cells alone. There is no central library, limited education and religious services, and no job training program. In the most controlled cell block, inmates are allowed only one ten-minute phone call each month, three showers per week, and can never move from their cells without shackles and handcuffs. At any sign of resistance, the prison's Special Operations Response Team (SORT) uses "whatever force is necessary" to restore order, including chaining prisoners to their beds for days at a time. All this at the cost of $40,000 per prisoner every year. Chicago Lawyer Jan Susler comments, "Marion is an experiment to see how much a prisoner can take before he breaks, to see how far they can dehumanize somebody before they completely lose their sanity."

The effects of ADX, and other control units, on prisoner psychology are, predictably, profound. As early as 1890, the U.S. Supreme Court ruled that extended solitary confinement was "infamous punishment," leading to severe mental impairment. More recently, the *American Journal of Psychiatry* reported significant psychological problems associated with solitary confinement, including hallucinations, anxiety attacks, problems with impulse control, self-mutilation, and other diagnosable disorders. An Iowa prisoner wrote of his fourth year of segregation, "I remember waking up... so full of stress that the veins in my head were vibrantly flexing... like muscles having an involuntary spasm." An isolation prisoner in Pelican Bay echoed, "It's like we're dead... They've taken away everything that might give a little purpose to your life."

The Florentine Solution

Prison officials and their media dupes have tried to distance Florence from its problematic predecessor and accompanying political baggage. Administrative maximum facilities, they say, are an unfortunate necessity, housing only the most "predatory" criminals. Their hype is mostly anecdotal, offering detailed accounts of proverbial prisoner brutality. The *Denver Post*, for example, introduced the ADX with mug shots of Manuel Noriega, John Gotti, and assorted neo-Nazis and serial killers. By concentrating such inmates in a single prison, a BOP Congressional Affairs memorandum argues, they decrease violence throughout the prison system. As evidence of their benevolent intentions, the BOP claims that most inmates have been downgraded from Marion since the 1983 lockdown. The 21 original prisoners who still remain, of course, have been locked down for more than a decade.

Prison officials assert that while Marion was perfectly fair and operated within Constitutional guidelines (they make no mention of international guidelines), Florence will be even better. Unlike Marion, the new ADX is designed as a super-maximum prison. BOP literature cites new technology as the key, allowing Florence to function securely without bed restraining loops and standard shackling. Like Marion, Florence will function on various security levels, ostensibly allowing inmates to work their way towards release through long-term subservient behavior. During construction, Russ Martin, the Florence project manager, summarized the Florence renaissance approach, "The entire design of the facility is to create a more humane environment, to take away the dungeon effect." Reading BOP media releases, one almost envisions Florence, where cells are "rooms," and prisoners work toward completion of their "institutional careers," as a harmonious beacon of new-age corrections. October 1993 was even "Hispanic Heritage Month" at the prison.

The actual conditions at Florence, however, hearken more to the Inquisition. Dan Dove, chief of BOP Public Affairs, admits that there is no judicial oversight in determining who will be sent to the Florence ADX. "Inmates may be represented by a staff member at these hearings," he writes, "but there is no provision for attorney representation." A 1985 congressional report on this completely arbitrary process determined that 80 percent of Marion inmates merited a less severe security rating.

Inside the walls, the rack only tightens. The Florence ADX penitentiary sits in the southeast corner of the four-prison complex. It is an imposing triangle of x-shaped cell-blocks, surrounded by double 20-foot fences interwoven with razor wire. Two perimeter roads, 8,000-watt lights, microwave sensors, and six sniper towers separate the ADX from the other facilities. Prisoners will never reach this dead space, as the prison walls themselves serve as the primary perimeter, containing the limited recreation areas and everything else. Guards and visitors will enter the prison through a tunnel.

Inside, guards control every door, light, intercom, and system with touch-screen computers and fiber-optic communication lines. Steel doors separate each of nine blocks from the others, and each triangle side represents a different security level. Four cell-blocks compare somewhat to standard maximum-security prisons and will probably serve as the pre-transfer unit. The B and C units, with room for over 150, are the most extremely isolated, the hole within the hole.

Countering charges of sensory deprivation at Marion, BOP officials have noted that the cells there close with open bars, allowing communication and free air flow. They have eliminated even this vestige of humanity at Florence. Cells in the six isolation units measure less than 16 by 8 feet each, and lock with a solid steel door. Each cell contains a three-foot-wide cement bed slab, a concrete stool and desk, a steel sink and toilet, and a three-by-three shower stall. A fluorescent light panel glares from the wall, illuminating other amenities like an electric cigarette lighter, an inmate duress switch (since the cells are sound-proof), an air grate, and, in some cells, a small television. Double doors shrink the cells by another three feet, trapping dead space between bars and the outer door. Only two window slits allow external light into the cage, one on the steel door staring into the empty hallway, and another body-length sliver facing an empty courtyard. The shower, along with food slots in the door and individual phone jacks, allows for total isolation.

When and if prisoners are allowed out of their cell, they will have little to celebrate. Visits in the control blocks will be tightly regimented and only allowed through Plexiglas dividers. There will be no joint religious services of any faith, and educational programs will be restricted beyond GED work. Not even demeaning UNICOR assignments will break the monotony of isolation. In the worst units, inmates will exercise alone in a pod barely twice the size of their cages.

Interlocking doors will allow only one prisoner out of his cell at a time. Totally alone, with nothing but an electronic escort, prisoners will move to the perma-steel mesh-covered coop for their one promised hour each day. Actually, it is difficult to imagine how inmates will even receive their hour; in the B unit, for example, there are only eight exercise pods for 78 cells, requiring that each be filled continually, 10 hours each day, to meet the quota.

Trapped in Toxicity

Florence shares not only cruelty with Marion, but also its environmental woes. At Marion, contamination surfaced as early as 1984, when the Environmental Protection Agency (EPA) placed Crab Orchid Lake, a nearby water source, on its National Priorities List for Superfund cleanup. Elevated PCBs and other toxins convinced the town to switch to an alternative water supply, and guards began carrying bottled water to work. Marion administrators took no action on behalf of the prisoners, however, until 1992, consistently denying any contamination or safety risks. Meanwhile, for over a decade Marion prisoners consumed contaminated water every day, ingesting chloroform levels more than 1,000 times higher than established safety limits. Several prisoners and their supporters filed lawsuits against the prison, including Robert Wyler, who has since died of kidney cancer.

Marion's history of environmental neglect may foreshadow similar events at Florence. Five miles due west of the new prison complex lies the Cotter Uranium Processing Facility, another EPA Superfund site. Cotter began operation of the mill in 1958, processing uranium ore into purified uranium oxide "yellowcake." Cotter stored the cakes, including original Manhattan project ore with some of the highest concentrations of Thorium-230 and Protactinium-231 known, in giant, unlined tailings ponds. Later, when the ponds were lined, there were over 70 leaks reported at Cotter between 1980 and 1986. Until its suspension of operations in 1987, Cotter accumulated approximately 3.5 million tons of radioactive tailings, storing them over 135 acres near Canon City and Florence.

The surrounding communities suffer contamination through both their water and air. Toxic compounds leak into the underground water supply through the unlined ponds, and also into the Arkansas River. According to a state-commissioned investigation, the nearby housing development of Lincoln Park has radioactive levels 2,000 times normal background. During the irrigation season, the drainage spills into the Fremont ditch, floating radioactivity directly towards the Florence water supply. Studies along the Fremont ditch found elevated levels of molybdenum, arsenic, lead, and other contaminants. Molybdenum levels here were even higher than those much closer to the mill site. Additional allegations that Cotter may have dumped tailings and other waste down abandoned mine shafts to circumvent federal safety standards raise the specter of even worse contamination, perhaps of the entire aquifer. The BOP's final Environmental Impact Statement worries that the prison's water supply may have to be re-routed in the future due to "pollution" problems.

The mill also endangers the surrounding communities and the prison population with airborne particulates. Cotter estimates that over 19.9 tons of radioactive dust escaped the plant during each year of its operation. In the arid plains, these particles are especially mobile, and the prison lies directly in Cotter's secondary wind pattern, subject to radium, uranium, thorium, and other hazardous materials. Cotter's continual negligence has prompted several lawsuits on behalf of the EPA, the state and local residents. There have been no suits, however, filed on behalf of Florence prisoners, and since carcinogens can take years to complete their work, any court action may be long delayed.

That the government has expressed little concern for prisoner, or even guard, environmental safety should come as no surprise. Dozens of prisons have even worse environmental records. The Michigan State Prison in Jackson, for example, was fined $160,000 for illegally storing DDT and Agent Orange. At a state prison in Arizona, a visiting room sign warns, "If you are pregnant or of child-bearing age, do not drink the water." Federal and state prisons mimic corporate behavior across the country, dumping their waste based on the given community's resources and ability to respond. Consequently prisoners, people of color, and poor communities like Florence bear the brunt of environmental degradation.

Shut It Down!

Prisoners and prison activists have not accepted human rights violations, racism, and toxic exposure quietly. Only a few months after the minimum-security camp opened in Florence, inmates organized a food strike to protest inadequate services at the new prison. In November 1993, federal prisoners in Denver rioted in protest of harsh mandatory drug sentences. Prisoners at Florence and other federal institutions warn that overcrowding, continual harassment, and ever-harsher sentencing have pushed prison populations to the brink of explosion.

Resistance to prison racism and control units has escalated on the outside as well. The Committee to End the Marion Lockdown (CEML), founded in 1985 to oppose Marion abuses, has shifted much of its focus to Florence. CEML activists visited Pueblo, Colorado and surrounding communities, networking with local human rights activists as early as 1988 to oppose the ADX construction.

In 1992, various organizations formed a statewide coalition in Colorado, to oppose control unit prisons and political imprisonment. Entitled Abolish Control Unit Torture (ACUT), the coalition publishes a bimonthly newsletter and organizes demonstrations, speaking tours, and other community events. In May 1993, ACUT, along with the American Indian Movement, the National Chicano Human Rights Council, and others, held a demonstration at the Denver Federal Building. About 200 gathered to hear Ward Churchill, Francisco "Kiko" Martinez, and others decry government counterintelligence, racism, and the new control unit in Florence.

In October 1993, ACUT and the Movimiento de Liberacion Nacional Mexicano (MLNM) invited former political prisoner Rafael Cancel Miranda to Colorado to lead a demonstration at Florence. Cancel Miranda, along with three other Puerto Rican nationalists, spent 25 years in the worst U.S. prisons, from Alcatraz to Marion, for a 1954 attack on the U.S. Congress, protesting U.S. imperialism. Student groups, such as the United Mexican American Students (UMAS), organized speaking events at universities in Boulder, Denver, and Colorado Springs.

Over 300 converged at Florence on October 23, 1993 for a mass rally and march to the prison gates. Perplexing locals and Florence police, several vans arrived from Chicago as well, bringing activists from CEML, the National Committee to Free Puerto Rican Political Prisoners and POWs, and relatives of several Marion prisoners. Ricardo Romero, MLNM leader twice imprisoned for refusing to testify before grand juries, urged activists to continue their fight for justice and national liberation.

Resistance to the Florence super-maximum prison will continue as the U.S. prison population swells, projected to soon surpass two million human beings, and anti-crime hysteria swings the political mainstream to the racist right. The Florence ADX is the quintessential embodiment of this oppression, destroying individual spirits through isolation and terror, and locking broad issues of social justice together within its gates. It represents the denial of justice to all poor people and people of color in the United States, environmental destruction and negligence, obfuscation of crime's real economic roots, and political violence against those who dare to resist. The fight against Florence, therefore, is more than a struggle for individual human rights and dignity; it is a struggle for our collective survival. As Malcolm X summarized prison politics in the United States, "Don't be surprised when I say I was in prison. We've all been in prison. That's what America means, prison."

CONCLUSION

THE REAL DRAGON

As I was putting the final touches on the first incarnation of this project in April 1993, the boilerplate of anger erupted in Lucasville, an Ohio State Prison. Prisoners held out in 11 days of siege, during which hostages were taken by both prisoners and staff, and in some cases beaten or killed. All told, nine prisoners and one officer died in the uprising. Organizers issued a list of 21 demands, which officials refused to make public.[1]

As I was working on *this* incarnation of the book, there were significant uprisings at well over 30 prisons in the federal system. The context for such widespread and pointed rebellion included several factors: first, a nationwide cell strike had been called for by New York state prisoners in September 1995 to protest against overcrowding and the attack on prisoners' rights, especially medical treatment, denial of visitation, and lack of educational opportunities. Solidarity with these prisoners and with political prisoners such as Mumia Abu-Jamal was expressed coast to coast. Secondly, the "riots" were an expression of totally justified rage at a racist decision made by Congress and President Clinton to maintain disparate criminal sentencing for possession and sales of crack cocaine.[2]

Then and now, prison uprisings set an appropriate backdrop to the messages I wish the book to convey.

In the preceding pages, a great deal of territory was covered. For me, trying to process all of this information can be truly overwhelming. There is an unbelievable amount of information available on every aspect of the whole imprisonment process. One can read 20 books, keep up-to-date on relevant periodicals, and attend prison-related events (speak-outs, forums, seminars, debates, videos, benefits) and still not have the whole picture. At a certain point in putting together this book, however, I found that having all the most up-to-date statistics is perhaps not as important as one might think. Academics and activists are constantly putting out books and studies that go deeper into this or that realm of the crisis in prisons. By the time you read this, some new study crucial to prison reform/prisoner support movement-building will undoubtedly have been released—and not accounted for here.

This book, therefore, is an evolving work in progress. It has been somewhat difficult to craft this guide in a way that would make it of immediate, yet also lasting, significance. Unlike a handbook on organizing around the Gulf War, or the Nevada Nuclear Test Site, this book had to cover many diverse agendas, and plot diverse trajectories of theory and action.

I decided to put this book together precisely because of the place penality occupies on our issues-of-the-day menu—the cruelty and social wastefulness of "our" state and federal prison systems is a cornerstone of the oppression of our time, yet in the media, popular culture, and the entire educational establishment, prisons and the whole travesty that is the criminal prosecution system roll on like some slow, unstoppable monster.

Having organized with various environmental activism groups, I am constantly amazed at the transformation that has taken place in the popular imagination with regard to "saving the environment." We have become accustomed to the idea of doing something—now—to lessen the burden on the planet. The up-to-the-moment CNN exposés and *Life* magazine special reports have seemingly legitimized a discipline once considered to be the territory of "hippies" and "freaks." Granted, the ruling line is still that radicalism, oppositional politics, and grassroots ecological struggles are extremist terrorist plots to be avoided at all costs. But the truth is, huge numbers of people are recycling, are contributing to this or that foundation, and are convinced they have been "making a difference."

The point I wish to make is that I have put this book together in an effort to make the imprisonment emergency every bit as real, as accessible, and as understandable to the public as environmentalism has become.

As the writers of the broadside *Ammunition* assert, "We are the sane ones. We are fighting to abolish human sacrifice." By using the resources provided in this book and the accompanying *Organizers' Guide* (see the last page of this book), along with others we find and create ourselves, I believe we can reach people who are now asleep. The act of keeping people behind bars, behind walls, chained and restrained against their will, is a clear violation of the human spirit. Power's unashamed denial of basic human rights, and the rape and torture that occur daily are fundamental reminders of the illness of our culture. Statistics will change, will become more and less frightening, but the interpersonal terrorism of brutalizing people and refusing their potential as human beings—especially as it has been outlined in these pages—will always be a powerful injustice against which we must continue to struggle. It has been said by many revolutionaries that a great deal of motivating, guiding energy for the overthrow of repressive structures can and will come from within prisons. This is exactly the sentiment I wish to end with. Ho Chih Minh put it this way:

> Those who fight for justice are people of true merit. When the prison doors are opened, the real dragon will fly out!

NOTES

1. See *Prison News Service*, no. 41 and following.
2. See Nkechi Taifa, American Civil Liberties Union Legislative Counsel, public memo of June 25, 1993 (updated March 14, 1994), re: Unwarranted Disparity in Sentencing Between "Crack" and Powder Cocaine, (ACLU 202.544.1681).

APPENDIX

SUGGESTIONS FOR ACTION

There are a multitude of possibilities for action that groups and individuals can take to effectively address the crisis in prisons. The following suggestions are listed in outline form, with some slightly more developed. For further inspiration, see the *Organizers' Guide* (order form last page of book); the experience of people from the organizations listed there can also be extremely helpful in planning and executing a successful project. The *Organizers' Guide* also includes copies of flyers from several recent events, to help spark our imaginations, and get a sense of what has been done thus far.

A. Events

1. Forums

Forums can be especially effective as a means of galvanizing people or communities who otherwise are not directly involved in the issues. They can be as informal as small-group report-backs from a delegation that recently visited a control unit prison, or as formal as a panel of highly respected and internationally renowned scholars and activists debating and making connections among several different issue areas. In either case, the use of literature tables, art, videos, cultural presentations, and food and drink can make a huge difference in what participants come away with.

2. Benefits

Entertainers with progressive or radical messages in their art should not be quickly written off as unapproachable. They should be prodded and coaxed and encouraged to put their politics out in the open. Even relatively simple efforts to contact them may yield surprising results. Often artists, from the struggling local poet to the world-famous rock star, will be waiting for the opportunity to aid a particular movement, and merely not know who to contact.

3. Tribunals and Mock Trials

Recently, excellent examples of such events have taken place. They were well organized and received widespread attention. The International

Tribunal of Indigenous Peoples and Oppressed Nations in the U.S.A. was held in San Francisco from October 2-4, 1992. The Special International Tribunal on the Situation of Political Prisoners and POWs Held in the United States convened in New York City from December 7-10, 1990. The International Symposium on Human Rights Violations of Political Prisoners and Prisoners of War in the United States took place in New York on April 28, 1990.

4. Prisoner Art Showings

B. Educational Organizing

1. Classes

2. Discussion Groups

Groups such as San Francisco's Open Forum, Portland, Oregon's Red Rose School, and a number of free schools starting up (such as those out of the Berkeley Long Haul Infoshop and Chicago's Autonomous Zone Infoshop) can be very effective arenas for building critical consciousness, as they attract many people with a drive to learn and act on the information they might gain.

3. House Meetings

House meetings are probably one of the best ways to bring a specific action or case to the attention of a specific community. It is out of these smaller, more social gatherings that many larger, more comprehensive campaigns have sprung.

C. Protest and Direct Action

1. Demonstrations/Pickets

2. Civil Disobedience

Business-as-usual being stopped at the doors and in the offices of prison officials can be an effective means of drawing public attention to an otherwise ignored issue or case. Groups that use such tactics include ACT-UP and CEML, which are mentioned frequently in this book.

D. Campaigning

1. Press Conferences

2. Letter Writing Campaigns

3. Phone and Fax Zaps

When calls and faxes flood an office, especially on a coordinated day having some practical or symbolic significance, the results can be surprising. Officials can be pressured very effectively, given a knowledge of their weak spots and strategically applied pressure from a variety of sources. In June 1996, PARC and prisoner advocates nationwide were quickly able to stop the retaliatory transfer of Willie Wisely, an eloquent writer and activist in California's Tehachapi State Prison.

4. Petitions

Petitions are most effective when delivered in large numbers—for instance, during a well-attended press conference.

5. Walks, Runs, and Whatever-a-thons

People like to get outside, be active, go bowling, buy stuff, eat stuff, and out-do each other in contests. We can use this to our advantage. Be creative!

E. Direct Support

1. Book Mailings

Most prisons require individuals to go through some bureaucratic process before sending books to prisoners, so if you don't know how to navigate the process, it's best to work with established groups and publishers. There are several local groups across the United States and in Canada that send books to prisoners. See the *Organizers' Guide*.

2. Fundraising for Legal Expenses and Commissary

3. Legal Assistance (Research, Administrative)

4. Writing Prisoners

Book mailings and writing prisoners are two of the most important and effective actions we can take to express and affirm our solidarity with those in struggle behind the prison walls. The strength that people in prisons can obtain from receiving supportive words from the outside is formidable. It also helps make real a phenomenon that may at times seem very unreal—we still live with the scourge of men with badges and guns putting people in cages.

CONTRIBUTORS

MUMIA ABU-JAMAL is a freedom fighter and political prisoner on Death Row in Pennsylvania. He was sentenced to death in 1982 for the shooting and killing of a police officer. During the incident, Abu-Jamal suffered a serious gunshot wound and was badly beaten. At the time, he had no police record. He was a prominent radio journalist in Philadelphia and the president of the local chapter of the Association of Black Journalists. Abu-Jamal was a member and spokesperson of the Black Panther Party in the early 1970s and has been a supporter of the MOVE organization. He has challenged his conviction and sentence on numerous grounds, including: the prosecutor's use of peremptory challenges to exclude Black jurors and the court's refusal to permit Abu-Jamal's challenge for cause of a juror who admitted uncertainty as to whether he could be open-minded; the court's permitting the prosecutor to present Abu-Jamal's political views and controversial group associations to the jury (the ACLU and the National Conference of Black Lawyers submitted an *amici curiae* brief challenging these references on First Amendment grounds); the prosecutor's closing argument asking for the death penalty in which he told the jury that Abu-Jamal would have "appeal after appeal" and that the jury "was not being asked to kill anybody."

Since his conviction, millions of activists have rallied around the effort to get Mumia off Death Row. During the summer of 1995, when the pro-death penalty governor signed Mumia's death warrant, tens of thousands of people showed up in Philadelphia to protest his action, and (apparently) won Mumia a temporary stay of execution. Millions of people have signed petitions to the governor of Pennsylvania, and other officials, urging clemency. Thousands of prominent individuals have written letters on Mumia's behalf, including French President Jacques Chirac, U.S. Representative Ron Dellums, Amnesty International Executive Director John Healey, Southern Christian Leadership Conference President Rev. Joseph Lowery, and Philadelphia Union Local 1034 President Charles Valenta.

The lower court, presided over by the same judge who supervised his travesty of a trial the first time around, refused to grant Abu-Jamal's petition for post-conviction relief. On February 9, 1996, Abu-Jamal's lawyers filed their arguments for an appeal at the Pennsylvania State Supreme Court level. At press time, Mumia was still awaiting a court date. Since his incarceration, Mumia has written articles on legal and social issues and prison life for several newspapers and periodicals, including *The Nation,* in addition to publishing, with the help of MOVE, the *Jamal Journal,* and producing radio commentaries for National Public Radio (NPR). Although NPR canceled the commentaries at the last minute without offering explanation, they *have* been aired on radio stations nationwide and internationally, and hundreds of public and community networks. He also published a collection of these commentaries, *Live from Death Row*. For more information on his case and how to join his struggle against the death penalty, contact the International Concerned Friends and Family of Mumia Abu-Jamal, PO Box 19709, Philadelphia, PA 19143, (215) 476-8812.

KANIKA AJANAKU is a self-described Pan-Africanist whose political activism began in the mid-'60s, when she was an undergraduate at Xavier University of Louisiana (New Orleans). Her work is about the achievement of self-determination by African people globally, and is inspired by the legacy of nation-building and resistance to oppression that she received from her ancestors.

AMERICAN FRIENDS SERVICE COMMITTEE (AFSC) Criminal Justice Program works with organizations across the country to create a system that is based not on prisons, jails, and executions, but on the needs of both victims of crime and victims of poverty and injustice. They want to bring about a system that recognizes drug and alcohol abuse as mainly health problems, not criminal justice problems; allows communities to help create fair and humane responses to crime; and treats offenders as individuals, not as faceless "criminals." The AFSC Criminal Justice Program publishes various materials on the criminal prosecution system, and can be reached at 1501 Cherry Street, Philadelphia, PA 19102, (215) 241-7130.

SILVIA BARALDINI is an Italian national and a political prisoner serving a 43-year sentence here in the United States. She has been imprisoned since 1982. Her excessive sentence reflects the U.S. government's attempt to punish her for her support of the Black and Puerto Rican liberation movements and also for her refusal, since her arrest, to recant her political beliefs.

Baraldini came to the United States as a teenager. In the late '60s and early '70s, she became involved in the women's movement while a student at the University of Wisconsin and became a staunch opponent of the war in Vietnam. Later in the '70s, she became more involved in building solidarity with other liberation movements that were active in those years. In 1978, Baraldini founded a material aid campaign for Zimbabwe. In recognition of that work, the Zimbabwe African National Union (ZANU) invited her to be an international observer in the independence elections there in 1980.

During this same period, Baraldini's work in support of Black human rights inside the United States focused on exposing the illegal FBI program, COINTELPRO. Through this work, Baraldini became involved in campaigns to free many Black Panther and Black Liberation Army political prisoners arrested through COINTELPRO.

Militant political activities in solidarity with these liberation movements led to her arrest in the early 1980s. She is serving a 40-year sentence for RICO conspiracy charges, and she has received unusually harsh treatment in the U.S. federal prison system. Although her disciplinary record had been exemplary through 1987, shortly after refusing to talk to FBI agents, she was transferred from a medium-security prison to the Lexington High Security Unit. After that Baraldini was sent to New York Metropolitan Correctional Center for two years, a particularly cruel move since Baraldini suffers from cancer—the New York prison has no health services because it is not a facility for long-term prisoners. In 1989, she was transferred to a women's high-security unit in Marianna Federal Penitentiary in Florida. After protesting this designation for years, Baraldini's security rating was lowered, and finally, she is in general population at FCI-Danbury. You can contact her through the Committee to Release Silvia Baraldini, 294 Atlantic Avenue, Brooklyn, NY 11201, (718) 965-9164.

HUGO ADAM BEDAU is Fletcher Professor of Philosophy at Tufts University. He has written and edited a number of books on political philosophy and on capital punishment, including *Death is Different* (1987) and *The Death Penalty in America*, 4th ed. (forthcoming 1996). He gratefully acknowledges the assistance of Henry Schwarzschild, Director Emeritus of the ACLU Capital Punishment Project.

DHORUBA BIN WAHAD is a former leader of the Black Panther Party who was the target of a racist and politically motivated frameup by the New York City Police Department and the FBI through COINTELPRO. As a result, Dhoruba spent 19 years incarcerated as a political prisoner. His March 1990 release was the culmination of an arduous and protracted legal battle. Bin Wahad presently devotes his time to writing an autobiography, working with the Campaign to Free Black and New Afrikan Political Prisoners and POWs in the United States (PO Box 339, Bronx, NY 10463-0339) and establishing a Pan-Africanist center in West Africa. Bin Wahad has been the subject of two award-winning documentaries that have enjoyed national and international exposure: *Passin' It On*, and *Framing the Panthers in Black and White*. He has traveled extensively across the United States and internationally raising public awareness about the existence of political prisoners in the United States and advocating for their release. Interviews and writings of Bin Wahad appear in *Still Black, Still Strong: Survivors of the War on Black Revolutionaries* and *Brother Man*.

B♀ (RITA D. BROWN) is an ex-political prisoner who did eight-and-a-half years in U.S. federal prisons around the country because of actions taken as a member of the George Jackson Brigade, an underground group of revolutionaries active in the Seattle, Washington area during the 1970s. She currently lives in Oakland, California and continues to do grassroots work in the Bay Area Lesbian community (and anywhere else that is Butch Friendly). Bφ works with the Norma Jean Croy Defense Committee and has produced a video about the case titled *Shasta Woman*. She also helped to found and is active with Out of Control: Lesbian Committee to Support Women Political Prisoners and Prisoners of War, which has been doing this work for nine years.

C. STONE BROWN is a writer who resides in Philadelphia. A freelance journalist, he focuses on politics and African-American issues. He can be contacted at 76716.1442@compuserve.com.

JULIE BROWNE recently graduated from the University of California, Santa Cruz, where she wrote her senior thesis on convict labor exploitation. At UCSC, Julie was instrumental in organizing demonstrations against mass incarceration and prison construction. Through this work, she helped to start Building Alliances Across Differences, a multiracial student coalition committed to anti-racist organizing that connects the issues of public education fee hikes, increased prison spending, and the economic scapegoating of immigrants. She currently lives in San Francisco, where in addition to working in the prison movement, she is actively engaged in anti-racist organizing and programs for survivors of domestic violence.

MARILYN BUCK is a North American anti-imperialist political prisoner. At 48, she has now spent nearly 15 years in U.S. prisons and has experienced different control units, segregation units, and even an early Behavior Modification Program. Despite increasing levels of repression and dehumanization, she maintains an irrepressible spirit of resistance and commitment to justice, liberation, and human dignity.

ERIC CUMMINS is a writer and lecturer at San Jose State University. His book, *The Rise and Fall of the California Radical Prison Movement*, (Stanford, CA: Stanford University Press) was published in 1993.

MIKE DAVIS is a writer and professor at Southern California Institute of Architecture. His latest book is on southern California's recent trial by riot, fire, and earthquake.

LIN ELLIOT is a gay man of Cherokee and Scotch-Irish descent. For the past several years, he has been working to promote prisoner involvement in community groups and activities—including the Lesbian/Gay/Bisexual/Transgender March on Washington. Along with John Fall, he is editing an anthology of writings by incarcerated queers entitled *Cold Iron: The Voices of Lesbian and Gay Prisoners*.

KARLENE FAITH has been a community activist for human justice since the mid-'50s and began advocacy work with women in prison in 1972. Completing her Ph.D. in History of Consciousness at the University of Santa Cruz in 1981, she became the director of the Simon Fraser University (SFU) Criminology Distance Education Program. In 1989, she joined the criminology faculty and in 1990-91 served as the J. S. Woodsworth Resident Scholar for the SFU Institute for the Humanities. Her publications include works on prison education, the "female offender," the Ras Tafarians, Michel Foucault, women's music, First Nations (indigenous) women prisoners, and media images of "criminal" women. She is the author of *Seeking Shelter: A State of Battered Women* (with Dawn Currie) and *Unruly Women: The Politics of Confinement and Resistance*.

DEBORAH GARLIN is a lawyer and president of the Center for Advocacy of Human Rights and a faculty member of the Criminal Justice Department at the University of New Mexico-Taos.

JUDY GREENSPAN is a longtime AIDS activist and prisoner advocate. She is currently the Director of the HIV/AIDS in Prison Project of Catholic Charities and a founding member of the California Coalition for Women Prisoners. She is the former AIDS Information Coordinator of the ACLU National Prison Project. In her heart and by her actions, she will always remain a member of ACT-UP Prison Issues.

BONNIE KERNESS has been an organizer since the civil rights era, when she lived in the South. After moving North in the 1970s, she was active with tenants' rights groups and Vietnam Veterans Against the War. She has worked, as a professional organizer, on gay rights and welfare rights campaigns, and obtained an MSW in community organizing. Kerness is currently Associate Director of the American Friends Service Committee Criminal Justice Program in New Jersey and National Coordinator of the National Campaign to Stop Control Unit Prisons.

MICHAEL A. KROLL is a writer who has worked with the American Friends Service Committee on various publications. (See American Friends Service Committee.)

NANCY KURSHAN is a school social worker. She has been a political activist for the past 30 years, active in the political movements of the '60s. It was through those activities that she developed an understanding of the racist nature of the prison system, as well as the important role prisons play in the containment of social change. In 1985, Kurshan became a founding member of the Committee to End the Marion Lockdown (CEML), which has been organizing to abolish control unit prisons ever since. You can contact her at CEML, PO Box 57812, Chicago, IL 60657.

ALEXANDER C. LICHTENSTEIN is a writer who has worked with the American Friends Service Committee on various publications. (See American Friends Service Committee.)

JOSÉ E. LÓPEZ was born in 1950 in San Sebastián, Puerto Rico. In 1959, his family moved to Chicago as part of the massive Puerto Rican migration to the United States. Born into a family of six brothers and sisters, José graduated from Tuley High School and received his B.A. in History from Loyola. He continued his studies at the University of Chicago, receiving his M.A. in history, and Danforth and Ford Fellowships to continue his doctoral studies. He has written extensively on the political and social reality of Puerto Ricans in the United States while serving as Executive Director of the Juan Antonio Corretjer Puerto Rican Cultural Center in Chicago, and teaching at Northeastern Illinois University and Columbia College.

In his role as educator/activist, he has been invited to speak at over 30 colleges in the United States, Mexico, and Canada, as well as in international forums such as the United Nations Decolonization Committee. He is also the editor of two publications on Puerto Rican Nationalism. For nearly a quarter of a century, he has been a leading member of the Puerto Rican independence movement and has served as spokesperson for the Movimiento de Liberación Nacional Puertorriqueño. Presently, he is active in developing new praxis/theory in community and social empowerment, as well as educational reform, in Chicago's West Town/Humboldt Park community.

JOEL OLSON is co-editor of the radical tabloid *The BLAST!* and a member of the Love and Rage Revolutionary Anarchist Federation. Currently, he is studying political science.

MARY K. O'MELVENY is an attorney in private practice in Washington, DC and New York. She represents labor unions and individuals in labor, employment law, and civil rights litigation. She was one of the attorneys whose litigation helped to close the Lexington High Security Unit. She currently represents Susan Rosenberg, one of the plaintiffs in that litigation, and provides legal assistance to other political prisoners on various issues. She has lectured and written extensively on a variety of civil rights and employment law topics, and participates as a faculty member in annual legal education projects sponsored by the DC Bar/George Washington University Continuing Legal Education program.

ROBERT PERKINSON is a longtime political activist. He is currently researching the racialization of U.S. criminal justice policy as a graduate student at Yale University.

SUSAN ROSENBERG is one of the three female political prisoners who was held in the Lexington High Security Unit, the first explicitly political prison in the United States. Her refusal to collaborate with the government and refusal to renounce her past were the reasons for her placement there. She was involved in the student, anti-war, and women's movements and has been an activist all her adult life. She is a Doctor of Acupuncture, and worked with the Black Acupuncturist Association of North America. She was targeted by the FBI for her support of the liberation of Assata Shakur from prison, and her support of the Black Liberation Army. After going underground in the 1980s, she was arrested with Tim Blunk in 1984, convicted of weapons possession and sentenced to 58 years. She spent almost 11 years in maximum-security conditions. A writer and AIDS activist, she is now at FCI-Danbury.

ELIHU ROSENBLATT has been organizing and agitating for human rights and social justice for more than 10 years, mostly in the San Francisco Bay Area. After spending several years working with Food Not Bombs and the Brazil Action Solidarity Exchange, he honed in on prison issues and began working as a freelance legal worker assisting attorneys with death penalty appeals. For many years, he has been active with the National Lawyer's Guild, the Real Dragon Prison Project, and the California Coalition for Battered Women in Prison. The original version of this book was compiled as Rosenblatt's senior project at Western Institute for Social Research, from which he earned a Bachelor's degree in 1993. Rosenblatt helped to found the Prison Activist Resource Center and the JusticeNet Prison Issues Desk, which make up his current political work. Currently also a news jockey and programmer for Free Radio Berkeley, he lives in the Bay Area with his partner Leona and numerous four-leggeds.

JAN SUSLER has been a lawyer for 20 years, working on issues such as police misconduct, civil rights, and human rights. She has done prison work for as long as she has been a lawyer, focusing on the treatment of political prisoners in the United States and on control unit prisons. She was one of the lead lawyers in the team challenging the Women's High Security Unit at Lexington, and was involved, when Marion was locked down in 1983, in coordinating lawyers and paralegals to go into the prison and write a report on the conditions. It was this report that was submitted to Congress and Amnesty International (AI), resulting in the first AI report condemning prison conditions in the United States. With the People's Law Office in Chicago since 1982,

Susler is the lawyer for the Puerto Rican Political Prisoners and Prisoners of War.

ERICA THOMPSON is a lawyer at the People's Law Office in Chicago. She is also a member of the Committee to End the Marion Lockdown and the National Lawyer's Guild.

SABINA VIRGO is a social and political analyst and activist. She was the founding president of AFSCME, Local 260, as well as the material coordinator of the Foreign Affairs Network of AFSCME. Virgo serves on the national board of directors of the Rainbow Coalition, and has traveled to El Salvador, Palestine, Cuba, and Panama with labor, and with peace and justice delegations. She is a member of the National Committee for Independent Political Action and currently spends the majority of her time with TNT+ (Thinking New Thoughts plus Re-Thinking Old Ones), a collective of presenters, writers, and facilitators who teach skills and ideas that help people empower themselves.

JOANN WALKER was an outstanding activist at the Central California Women's Facility (CCWF) in Chowchilla, CA. Among other things, she helped to establish a peer education program on HIV and AIDS there. Walker died of AIDS on July 13, 1994, just two months after winning compassionate release from CCWF due to her illness. Many on the outside are continuing her fight for justice for prisoners. For more information, contact the California Coalition for Women Prisoners at (415) 255-7036.

COREY WEINSTEIN has been working in prisoner rights advocacy for 25 years. During this time he has served as medical consultant to the Prisoner's Rights Union and Director of Prisoner Health Advocates. Presently, he serves as co-director of the Pelican Bay Information Project and co-chair of the Jail and Prison Health Committee of the American Public Health Association.

LAURA WHITEHORN is a revolutionary anti-imperialist political prisoner, serving 23 years in federal prison for armed actions in solidarity with national liberation struggles.

INDEX

Body searches: body-cavity strip searches, 168, 233, 286; pat searches, 191, 230
Bolivia, 57
Book mailings, 348
Books to Prisoners, 311
Boot camps, 35-36
Boudin, Kathy, 118, 283
Bowden, Jerome, 203
Box, Steven, 255
Boxer Rebellion, 276
Boyz 'n the Hood, 189
Brandley, Clarence, 219-20, 243-44
Break-ins, Death Threats, and the FBI (Gelbspan), 105
Brecht, Bertolt, 50
Brennan, William J., Jr., 234, 235, 236
Bright, Stephen, 201
Briley, Joe, 243
Brown, Angela, 154
Brown Berets, 51
Brown, C. Stone, 352
Brown, Debra, 326
Brown, Jerry, 74
Brown, John, 280
Brown, Kathleen, 75
brown, rita d., 352
Browne, Julie, 352
Bruck, David, 201
Brutality: "brutalization effect," 200; chain gangs, 64-65; at Lexington, 108; prison guards, 41, 85, 87, 115-16, 158-59
Buck, Marilyn, 129, 264, 267, 283, 286, 327, 352
Bureau of Alcohol, Tobacco, and Firearms, U.S., 101
Bureau of Justice Statistics (BJS), U.S., 95, 153, 254
Bureau of Labor Statistics, U.S., 23
Bureau of Prisons. *See* Federal Bureau of Prisons (BOP)
Burger, Warren, 17
Burglaries, 20, 21, 22
Burkhart, Kathryn, 156
Burnham, David, 100
Bush, George and Barbara, 52

C

California: California model and mass imprisonment, 308-10; death penalty in, 200-201, 226; Field Institute, 226; imprisonment of African-American males, 24; life-without-parole sentences, 206; prison construction program, 28; prison population and crime reduction, 40; Proposition 139, 68; Proposition 184, 75, 76; state budget, 61
California Appellate Project, 245-46
California Coalition for Battered Women in Prison, 128
California Correctional Industries Program, 66-67
California Correctional Officers Association, 316
California Correctional Peace Officers Association (CCPOA), 74, 75
California Department of Corrections (CDoC): ACT-UP and, 83; conservation camps, 67; convict labor programs, 65-66; Joint Ventures Program, 68-69; Pelican Bay SHU and, 310, 311, 312-13, 314, 318; Proposition 184 and, 76
California HIV Activist and Inmate Network, 82-83
California Institution for Women (CIW), 83, 85, 90, 133, 154-55, 174-75
California Medical Facility (Vacaville), 83, 90, 120
California State Board of Health, 90
California Teachers Association, 75
California Youth Authority, 20, 24
Calipatria State Prison, 73-74, 76
Camus, Albert, 230
Canada: death penalty and, 226-27; women's federal prison, 169-71; women's prison programs, 173
Canadian Broadcast Company, 170
Can't Jail the Spirit, 259

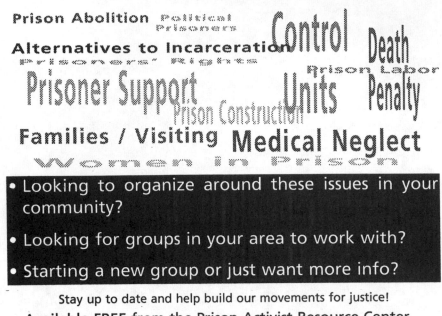

Prison Abolition Political Prisoners

Alternatives to Incarceration Control Death

Prisoners' Rights Prison Labor

Prisoner Support Units Penalty

Prison Construction

Families / Visiting Medical Neglect

Women in Prison

- Looking to organize around these issues in your community?

- Looking for groups in your area to work with?

- Starting a new group or just want more info?

Stay up to date and help build our movements for justice!
Available FREE from the Prison Activist Resource Center...

The
Organizing Guide
for Educators & Activists on the Crisis in Prisons

This volume includes a multitude of useful resources, including:

- A comprehensive directory of organizations, listed alphabetically , by state, and by subject categories.
- Examples of recent activism: flyers, brochures, campaign lit. & more.
- An annotated bibliography: books, pamphlets, videos and other resources.

If the coupon below is detached, visit our web page at www.igc.org/prisons or call 510-845-8813 for ordering information.

Send a free copy of the organizing guide to:

Name _____

Organization (if any) _____

Address _____

City/State/Zip _____

Phone &/or Fax: _____

E-mail _____

To order the Organizing Guide you can -->
visit our web page • email us • fax this coupon to us • send coupon by mail
» PLEASE donate to help cover our costs!! «
❑ **$10** ❑ **$15** ❑ **$25** ❑ **$50** ❑ **$100** ❑ other: _____ **is enclosed.**
Prison Activist Resource Center: PO Box 3201 Berkeley CA 94703
ph: 510-845-8813 **fax:** 845-8816 **email:** parcer@igc.org **web:** www.igc.org/prisons